In recent years, technological change, unemployment and industrial restructuring have highlighted training and the acquisition of skills as a policy issue. Throughout the industrialised world there is widespread concern that employees are insufficiently skilled. This deficiency can have serious economic consequences: high unemployment, deficient growth, lagging competitiveness, insufficient innovation and deficient product quality. These problems are likely to become particularly urgent over the coming years, as the dramatic increase in the share of temporary and part-time employment in the OECD leads to a decline in incentives to train in the formal sectors.

This book, from the Centre for Economic Policy Research, provides a systematic account of the causes, consequences and policy implications of failure in training provision and skills acquisition in the industrial world. Traditional human capital theory implies that the free market provides adequate incentives to train. This volume calls this conventional wisdom into question, arguing that since the markets for training are generally beset by imperfect competition and imperfect information, people generally do not receive adequate compensation for the training they acquire and provide. This book provides, for the first time, a systematic theoretical and empirical account of the causes, consequences, and policy implications of failure in training provision and skills acquisition in the industrial world.

In a world where unemployment is concentrated among the unskilled workers, where productivity growth, innovation and product quality rest critically in the hands of skilled employees, and where skill shortages can lead to inflationary pressures, the issues addressed in this volume have become increasingly urgent and important.

Acquiring skills

Centre for Economic Policy Research

The Centre for Economic Policy Research is a network of over 250 Research Fellows, based primarily in European universities. The Centre coordinates its Fellows' research activities and communicates their results to the public and private sectors. CEPR is an entrepreneur, developing research initiatives with the producers, consumers and sponsors of research. Established in 1983, CEPR is a European economics research organization with uniquely wide-ranging scope and activities.

CEPR is a registered educational charity. Institutional (core) finance for the Centre is provided by major grants from the Economic and Social Research Council, under which an ESRC Resource Centre operates within CEPR, the Esmée Fairbairn Charitable Trust, the Bank of England, 15 other central banks and 33 companies. None of these organizations gives prior review to the Centre's publications, nor do they necessarily endorse the views expressed therein.

The Centre is pluralist and non-partisan, bringing economic research to bear on the analysis of medium- and long-run policy questions. CEPR research may include views on policy, but the Executive Committee of the Centre does not give prior review to its publications, and the Centre takes no institutional policy positions. The opinions expressed in this volume are those of the authors and not those of the Centre for Economic Policy Research.

Acquiring skills
Market failures, their symptoms and policy responses

Edited by
ALISON L. BOOTH
and
DENNIS J. SNOWER

CAMBRIDGE
UNIVERSITY PRESS

Published by the Press Syndicate of the University of Cambridge
The Pitt Building, Trumpington Street, Cambridge CB2 1RP
40 West 20th Street, New York, NY 10011-4211, USA
10 Stamford Road, Oakleigh, Melbourne 3166, Australia

First published 1996

Printed in Great Britain at the University Press, Cambridge

A catalogue record for this book is available from the British Library

Library of Congress cataloguing in publication data

Acquiring skills: market failures, their symptoms and policy responses / edited
by Alison L. Booth and Dennis J. Snower.
    p.   cm.
Includes bibliographical references and index.
ISBN 0 521 47205 9 (hc). – ISBN 0 521 47957 6 (pb).
1. Occupational training – Congresses.
2. Occupational training – Government policy – Congresses.
3. Skilled labor – Congresses.
4. Technological innovations – Economic aspects – Congresses.
5. Quality of products – Congresses.
6. Competition, International – Congresses.
I. Booth, Alison L.   II. Snower, Dennis J.
HD5715.A27   1996
331.25'92–dc20   95–22781   CIP

ISBN 0 521 47205 9 hardback
ISBN 0 521 47957 6 paperback

CE

Contents

Figures

Tables

Preface

This book has three interrelated purposes.

The first, addressed in Part I, is to provide major reasons why the free market system may fail to provide adequate incentives for the acquisition of skills. For a long time mainstream economists used to believe that the Invisible Hand would invariably lead people to acquire skills as long as the resulting benefit to society exceeded the associated cost. Over the past decade, however, there has been an emerging realization that this is not so. But the new research is fragmented and the old views die hard. This book attempts to bring some of the most interesting and potentially significant market failures in providing skills – several of which have received little if any attention so far – under one cover. In doing so, it sets the stage for reasoned debate about government provision and regulation of training.

The second purpose, addressed in Part II, is to examine some salient empirical consequences of these problems using a portfolio of examples concerning the effects of different types of 'skills gaps', that is, deficiencies in the availability of trained employees. For brevity, these examples focus mainly on the UK and a limited number of other European countries. The consequences range from microeconomic problems, such as deficient productivity, insufficient innovation, and specialization in the production of goods that are of insufficient quality, to macroeconomic problems such as poor export performance, and insufficient competitiveness. They are meant to tell us what sorts of things to look for when we seek to assess whether a country's economic performance is impeded by insufficient production of skills.

And the third purpose, addressed in Part III, is to give a preliminary account of what policy initiatives are appropriate for dealing with skills gaps and their consequences. This is based not just on an analysis of market failures, but also on a recognition of important government failures in the process of policy design and implementation.

This book arose out of a conference organized by the editors under the auspices of the Centre for Economic Policy Research and funded by the UK Employment Department. The support, encouragement and generous help of both institutions in this enterprise is gratefully acknowledged. The views expressed in this volume are not necessarily those of the CEPR or the Employment Department.

Alison L. Booth and Dennis J. Snower   July 1995

Contributors

Daron Acemoglu *MIT and CEPR*
Alison L. Booth *University of Essex and CEPR*
Kenneth Burdett *University of Essex*
Alan Felstead *University of Leicester*
David Finegold *RAND Corporation, Santa Monica*
Francis Green *University of Leeds*
Jonathan Haskel *Queen Mary and Westfield College, London, and CEPR*
Ewart Keep *University of Warwick*
Stephen Machin *University College London and Centre for Economic Performance, LSE*
Christopher Martin *Queen Mary and Westfield College, London*
Geoff Mason *National Institute of Economic and Social Research, London*
Ken Mayhew *Pembroke College, Oxford*
Nicholas Oulton *National Institute of Economic and Social Research, London*
Stephen Satchell *Trinity College, Cambridge*
Eric Smith *University of Essex*
Dennis J. Snower *Birkbeck College, London, and CEPR*
Margaret Stevens *Trinity College, Oxford, and CEPR*
David Ulph *University College London, and CEPR*
Bart van Ark *University of Groningen*
Karin Wagner *Fachhochschule für Technik und Wirtschaft, Berlin*

1 Introduction: does the free market produce enough skills?

ALISON L. BOOTH and DENNIS J. SNOWER

1 Are market incentives sufficient?

Does the free market provide people with adequate incentives for acquiring skills? This question has been the subject of unremitting interest to policy makers throughout the Western world. The answers are now a matter of great urgency.

The acquisition of human capital is recognized to be absolutely central to countries' growth performance. The 'new growth theory' has put it centre-stage. And rightly so. When people acquire skills they not only make themselves more productive, able to produce more output for a given amount of time and effort, they commonly also make themselves more adaptable. When tastes and technologies are changing rapidly, necessitating a high rate of labour turnover across industries and occupations, adaptability is crucial for keeping labour and capital employed and maintaining competitiveness.

When people acquire skills, they make each other more productive. Since most work is team work, my productivity generally depends on your productivity. The more training you have – on-the-job or off-the-job – the more I can learn from you about doing the job effectively, and the more productively the two of us can interact in production, innovation, distribution, and sales.

Beyond that, people who acquire skills make capital equipment more productive. They make more effective use of the machines they work with and they enable managers to introduce more sophisticated and productive machines. Without a workforce that is continuously acquiring new skills, it would be difficult to reap most of the returns from technological progress.

For all these reasons, the acquisition of skills is a vitally important activity. This is why it is so important to address the question of whether or not the free market leads to sufficient investment in skills. If the answer is yes, government training programmes are unnecessary, even harmful, since they divert too many resources away from consumption and investment in physical capital. If governments should intervene at all, it should be with a view to making markets function more freely and efficiently. For instance, when people do not acquire skills because they face credit constraints, then the government could relax credit controls, reduce barriers to competition among financial intermediaries, or provide loan guarantees in order to make the market for loans function more smoothly. Alternatively, when people do not acquire skills because there are barriers to the entry of new firms requiring new skills, or barriers to the entry of new employees in such firms, then the government could reduce these barriers through legislation that promotes competition in the product and labour markets.

In short, if the forces of the free market provide adequate incentives for acquiring skills, then the government should concern itself solely with making markets free. This invariably involves eliminating price controls, promoting the flow of information, and encouraging competition.

If, on the other hand, it can be shown that the free market fails to induce employers to provide enough training or employees to acquire enough of it, government involvement in the finance or provision of training may be desirable. How the government should intervene must then depend on what the underlying market failure is. As a general rule of thumb, the free market promotes an efficient allocation of resources when each person's private assessment of her costs and benefits coincides with society's assessment of the social costs and benefits of the resources employed. Market failures arise when some of these private costs and benefits diverge from social costs and benefits. When the market failure prevents firms from appropriating all the gains from the on-the-job training they provide, or the off-the-job training they support, then training subsidies or training levies for firms may be called for. When the market failure prevents workers from receiving full compensation for the training costs they have incurred, then subsidies for skill acquisition may be appropriate.

Identification of market failure in skills acquisition is certainly more than an academic exercise. There is an enormous diversity of government policies towards training in market economies around the world. These policies, naturally, rest on radically different implicit assumptions about how well the market does in encouraging people to acquire skills. In the USA the implicit assumption appears to have been that free-market incentives are sufficient, but with the arrival of President Clinton came an as yet unarticulated awareness that the provision of training in some industries, particularly in high-tech sectors, may need support. This shift of opinion has also been apparent in the UK, where tax relief on vocational training costs has recently been introduced.

Australian, French, German, Japanese, and Swedish policy of course is based on an entirely different view, namely, that market incentives are grossly insufficient to generate the socially desirable amount of investment in skills. In both Germany and Japan there is a perceived need to create institutions that bond employers and employees, with a view to giving them a longer time horizon to appropriate the gains from training. In Germany the apprenticeship system serves this purpose, whereas in Japan the long career paths and controlled competition among firms do so. In Sweden, by contrast, greater emphasis is placed on the need to support retraining for the unemployed. France and Australia pursue yet another course, with their systems of training levies whereby firms that do not use a set percentage of their payroll expenditure on training must pay a penal tax.

The diversity of training policies is also apparent in the common disparity between governments' approach to vocational training versus secondary and university education. General 'training' and 'education' have a lot in common: both are designed to make people more productive and adaptable, both screen for diligent, hard-working, and ambitious people. There can be little doubt that the amount of on-the-job training firms should provide depends crucially on the quality of the educational system. Nevertheless, politicians often have radically different attitudes towards public support of training and education. In the UK, Germany, Italy and many other European countries, government finance of secondary and university education is deemed eminently appropriate, whereas government finance of training is considered far less so. Even in the USA, where both education and training are largely funded through the private sector, government loans for education appear to be far more acceptable than such loans for training.

So there is, at least implicitly, substantial disagreement among policy makers about the market's ability to produce enough skills. This issue is too important to be left entirely to the intuition of politicians, many of whom are torn between a desire to subsidize training and the need to cut budget deficits, or the demand to be seen to be doing something about unemployment. There is an urgent need to analyse systematically whether workers and firms, competing atomistically in the labour and product markets, will demand and supply sufficient skills to make themselves as well off as they can be. If they fail to do so, it is vital to identify the market failures that are responsible and to examine the conditions under which these market failures become large enough to create serious social and economic problems.

2   The case for a free market in training

The trick to finding market failures in the acquisition of skills is to identify the circumstances under which workers and firms do not get fully rewarded for the training costs they have to bear, so that the benefits from the training do not accrue fully to them. When the private benefits from training fall short of the social benefits, then people – responding solely to the private benefits – will clearly not acquire enough skills.

It is a common belief that, in a free market, people pay all the costs and get all the benefits from their training. In this view, training is no different from other goods and services, like apples or haircuts. People obviously pay the full cost and get the full benefit from the apples and haircuts they consume, and in a free market these commodities get traded until it is impossible to make anyone better off without making anyone else worse off. Thus there is no waste in the production and consumption of apples and haircuts. Why should training be any different? According to the free-market conventional wisdom, the benefits from training fall exclusively on the trainer and trainee. Thus if they share the costs of training in proportion to the benefits they each receive, then an efficient amount of training will be provided. Specifically, training will be provided as long as the associated benefits exceed the associated costs, and both the trainer and trainee will be compensated fully for the costs they each incur.

If that were the whole story, the free market would be efficient in the amount of training it provides: no one could be made better off through extra training without making others worse off (by depriving them of the resources that went into the extra training). The only problem that might remain is one of equity. There may be serious inequalities in the acquisition of skills because there are serious inequalities in income and wealth. But the appropriate way for the government to address this problem is by redistributing the income and wealth through taxes and transfers, not by intervening in the market for training.

This conventional wisdom received lavish intellectual support from Gary Becker's path-breaking and influential analysis of investment in human capital. Becker divides on-the-job training into 'general' and 'specific' components.[1] 'General training', which is useful to all employers in the economy, is to be financed exclusively by the employees. The reason is straightforward. Since all employers value this training, there is perfect competition for general skills. Thus general training raises not only workers' productivity, but their wages by the same amount. In this way, workers are able to recoup fully the benefits from their investment in training. Since employers reap none of the benefits from general training, they have no incentive to bear any of the costs; but since workers reap all the benefits, they will be prepared to accept wage reductions sufficient to cover all the cost of this training. The upshot is that workers have just the right incentives to acquire general training; there are no market failures here.

Off-the-job training (for example, education in universities and vocational training colleges) also tends to be of the 'general' variety. Thus here, too, it is appropriate for the trainees to pay for their training.

At the other end of the spectrum is 'specific training' which is useful only to a specific employer. The costs of such training are to be shared by firms and workers, so that workers internalize the cost of quitting to their firms, and the firms – in turn – internalize the cost of dismissals to their trained workers. In either case, the firms and workers get compensated for the training, and thus there are no market failures here either.

In practice, it is tacitly assumed that all training can be divided into general and specific components. And since the free market provides adequate incentives for each of these types of training, it must do so for any combination of them as well.

Our point of departure in this book is to identify a fundamental flaw in this argument and thereby achieve a position from which a variety of market failures in skill acquisition can be pinpointed. This provides the motivation of our empirical analysis concerning the consequences of skills gaps and our assessment of policies to stimulate training.

3   Market failures in training

A fundamental weakness in the argument above is identified by **Margaret Stevens** in Chapter 2 of the book. This weakness is that all training *cannot* be divided into general and specific components. Hardly any training is useful to *all* firms in the economy. Nor is there much training that is useful only to one specific firm. Most training, rather, is useful to a *limited number* of firms, and usually not to an equal degree. This point has two striking implications for market failure in the provision and acquisition of training.

The first implication is that the limited number of firms above must be imperfect competitors for labour. When firms are perfect competitors, workers' wages are equal to their marginal products; a worker who is offered less than her marginal product simply leaves her current firm and joins another that offers more. Under imperfect competition, firms have some market power, and consequently workers' wages turn out to be less than their marginal products. Thus workers cannot appropriate all the returns from their training.

The other implication is that, when workers are mobile between firms, the potential benefits from training accrue not only to the firm providing it and the worker acquiring it, but also to other firms that could make use of it. This means that the supplier and demander of the training cannot, between them, appropriate all the benefit from the training; some of it may fall on other firms. Thus, typically no arrangement whereby the costs of training are shared between the training firms and the trainee will provide sufficient incentives for training. The greater the mobility of workers among firms and the greater firms' market power in the wage setting process, the more serious this problem becomes. This is the essence of the 'poaching externality'.

But this is only the tip of the iceberg.

Another related externality lies in the 'complementarities between labour and capital', analysed in Chapter 3 by **Daron Acemoglu**. When labour and capital are Edgeworth complements, deficient investment in human capital (due to firms' or workers' market power in the wage setting process) reduces the productivity of physical capital and thereby leads to deficient investment in physical capital and insufficient economic growth.

Next, the free market may provide insufficient incentives for skill acquisition on account of 'credit constraints'. Since human capital cannot be used as collateral against loan default, the resulting credit constraints will generally prevent employees from acquiring sufficient training. This problem is also considered in Chapter 4.

In addition, there are what we may call 'matching externalities', that is, failures of the market mechanism to compensate people adequately for training due to imperfect information and imperfect competition in the job matching process. When workers who want jobs are not certain of getting job offers and when firms with vacancies are not certain of getting job applicants, the wage negotiations between them will depend on (a) the speed with which jobless workers and vacant jobs are expected to match, and (b) the wage each party expects to negotiate with other potential negotiating partners (reflecting each party's 'outside opportunities' in wage negotiations). Clearly, the greater the proportion of trained people in an economy, the faster firms can expect to attract skilled workers and the more favourable will their outside opportunities in wage negotiations be. This raises firms' market power in wage negotiations, reduces workers' returns from training, and can possibly lead to under-investment in skills. These externalities are explored in Chapter 4 by **Kenneth Burdett** and **Eric Smith**.

Furthermore, there is the market failure arising from the interaction between skills and innovative performance, examined in Chapter 5 by **David Ulph**. When successful innovation requires highly trained workers, economies can get stuck in a vicious cycle in which firms do not innovate sufficiently because the workforce is insufficiently skilled and workers do not train sufficiently because there is insufficient demand for them from the innovating firms. Moreover, a rise in labour turnover costs will increase the incentive to innovate by the successful innovators (as they seek to avoid these costs by maintaining their success) while reducing this incentive to the unsuccessful innovators (who are deterred by the higher costs of attracting new employees).

A further problem arises with the interaction between skills and skilled workers analysed in Chapter 6 by **Dennis Snower**. When firms create few skilled vacancies because there are few skilled workers available, and when few workers acquire skills because there are few skilled vacancies, sectors of the economy can get stuck in a 'low-skill, bad-job trap'.

These are the major market failures analysed in this book.

In short, once we accept that wages are usually set under imperfectly competitive conditions (with firms exerting some market power) and that most skills are imperfectly transferable (so that poaching is usually a possibility), it becomes obvious that the free market generally does not provide sufficient incentives for training. It is also clear that these failures can be amplified considerably through complementarities between labour and capital, firms' outside bargaining opportunities, credit constraints, matching externalities, the 'low-skill, bad-job trap', as well as the interaction between skills and innovative performance and between skills and product quality.

4   Empirical consequences of skills gaps

These various arguments in Part I of this book suggest that the market failures above may have an important role to play in producing 'skills gaps', that is, deficiencies in the availability of trained employees. Part II then proceeds to consider empirical consequences of these skills gaps. Since a comprehensive international study of the empirical evidence is clearly beyond our scope here, the best we can do is provide a portfolio of illuminating examples. For brevity and consistency, these examples relate to the UK and a limited number of other European countries.

As the theory in Part I implies, the free-market system cannot usually be expected to lead people to acquire sufficient skills, and this is true in general, quite independently of the cyclical conditions and historical experience of individual countries. But what makes skills gaps a subject of deep concern in the 1990s is that the composition of labour demand in the previous decade has shifted steadily in favour of skilled workers. Thus the inability of the market system to provide sufficient training has inevitably become an increasingly painful problem. This background to the current debate concerning training provision is described in Chapter 7 by **Stephen Machin**. He provides strong evidence of a large shift towards employment of skilled people at the expense of unskilled people in the UK, as is the case in the USA. Most of the shift was not the result of movement among establishments and industries, but within these sites of work. This development is shown to have been particularly strong in the relatively R&D-intensive workplaces, lending some credence to the view that labour-saving technological change has played an important role in the restructuring of employment. The presence of skill shortages in this context may pose particularly severe problems.

The chapter that follows, Chapter 8 by **Jonathan Haskel** and **Christopher Martin**, suggests that the supply of skills has not responded fully to the rising demand, leaving firms to experience significant skill shortages. The authors take their evidence of skill shortages from two panel data sets of three-digit UK manufacturing industry. They show that these shortages are higher on average and more variable over the business cycle in the UK than in comparable economies. Unskilled shortages are comparatively rare. The bulk of the evidence suggests that shortages are related to educational attainment. What effect do these skill shortages have on productivity? Haskel and Martin argue that there are two potential effects. First, skill shortages add to the cost of employing skilled workers since a firm must wait longer than usual to fill its vacancies. This may lead firms to substitute unskilled for skilled labour, thereby reducing productivity. Secondly, skill shortages improve the skilled workers' outside options, making it more difficult for firms to induce them to work hard. Both these effects reduce productivity. The authors provide evidence showing that the growth of skill shortages in the UK over the 1980s reduced productivity growth by about 0.4% per year (average productivity growth was about 5%). This problem could, in principle, also give rise to wage increases, as excess demand for skilled workers improves the outside employment opportunities of skilled workers, enabling them to negotiate higher wages. But whereas Haskel and Martin find that industry skill shortages have no effect on industry wages, they also observe that wages do appear to be affected by *aggregate* skill shortages.

A particularly interesting consequence of deficient training may lie in the composition of goods produced in the country. Specifically, a lack of skilled workers may adversely affect product quality. This incidentally sheds some light on one possibly important cause of skills gaps – the interaction between the incentives to train and the incentives to create skilled vacancies. When products of high quality require highly trained workers to produce them, economies can get stuck in a vicious cycle in which firms produce goods of low quality because there are few trained workers and workers acquire little training because few high-quality goods are produced. In Chapter 9, **Geoff Mason**, **Bart van Ark**, and **Karin Wagner** provide some evidence of a 'low-skill, bad-job trap' that could arise from the externalities generated by the creation of skills and skilled vacancies (analysed in Chapter 6), the interaction between innovative performance and skills (developed in Chapter 5), and the complementarities between labour and capital (examined in Chapter 3). The authors use biscuit processing in the UK, Germany, France, and The Netherlands as their example. They examine the relationship between workforce skill levels, product quality, and economic performance, by means of a detailed comparison of matched samples of biscuit manufacturing plants in Britain, Germany, France, and The Netherlands. The results of this comparison are contrasted with those from similar cross-country comparisons in widely differing industrial sectors such as engineering, furniture manufacturing and clothing. Value-added per employee-hour in the German sample of plants was estimated to be some 40% above that in Britain and 10–20% higher than in The Netherlands and France. This pattern of productivity performance could not be attributed to inter-country variation in the age and sophistication of capital equipment in use. But there were important differences in skill levels. These could be linked to both relative productivity performance and the predominant choice of product strategy in each country.

Mason, van Ark and Wagner argue that, broadly speaking, biscuit manufacturing exemplifies the notion of correspondence in different countries between the supply of skills (as shaped by national systems of education and training) and the demand for skills by employers (associated with their chosen product mix, capital utilization and work organization). The predominant strategic choices made by employers in any country reflect the extent to which a skilled workforce is available (or easily developed). But they also affect the supply of skills by signalling to individuals the value of investment in vocational training and education.

In Chapter 10, **Nicholas Oulton** considers the implications of skills gaps for export performance by means of a detailed comparison of the UK with Germany. He confirms earlier findings that, relative to

Germany, the UK's main deficiency is in craft and technical skills. But the extent of the skills gap varies considerably between sectors. Oulton considers the possibility that skill deficiencies lead to the UK exporting relatively poor-quality products. Perhaps surprisingly, this is not the case if quality is judged by price since, on average, UK exports sell at a similar price to German ones. Less controversially, the value per unit of quantity of German exports is shown to be typically several times larger than that of the UK. Oulton argues that skills gaps may explain Germany's superior performance. The less skilled is a country's workforce, the greater the tendency to produce non-traded commodities (such as services) rather than traded ones (such as manufactured goods), because non-traded commodities are often more shielded from competition. The result is a relatively poor export performance. The UK and German experience over the period 1978–87 is used to illustrate this thesis.

5   Government failures in training

The next step, addressed in Part III of this book, is to move from market failures towards policy formulation. The single most important point to be kept in mind in this regard is that it is naive to suppose that wherever the market fails, the government can be relied on to put it right. The government, like the market system, may fail to act in the best interests of the public. Thus policy prescription must be based not only on market failure, but also on 'government failure'. Only if the cost of market failure outweighs the cost of potential government failure can a case be made for public provision or regulation of training.

It is not hard to think of instances of government failure. First, government officials cannot always be relied on to act in the public interest. The incentives for promotion, status, and power within the civil service may lead officials to devise training programmes that are excessively bureaucratic and expensive. This is particularly likely to be a problem in the case of training services. The notorious difficulties of measuring service sector outputs give bureaucrats freedom to pursue their own objectives. And where they are free to pursue their own goals they are vulnerable to pressures from special interest groups. This 'representation failure' should not be seen as an aberration, a rare pathology. We expect everyone in the private sector to pursue their own self-interest; so when some of these people move into the public sector, it is surely unreasonable to expect their self-interest to become irrelevant to them.

Secondly, even in the absence of self-interested activity by government officials, there is no reason to expect the state always to be a more efficient provider of training than private-sector firms are. Firms' skill requirements are highly idiosyncratic; government officials cannot be expected to know the millions of needed aptitudes, let alone provide them. And the concentration of government control over a programme in a central agency may insulate decision makers from local labour market conditions and needs. The appropriate response to these problems may be state finance, without state provision, of training. But even here government activity is severely constrained. The reason, paradoxically, lies in the government's strength: the state has much greater powers of compulsion than firms and a much greater number of objectives, making it hard to assess the performance of civil servants. To avoid the gross misuses of power that these features may encourage, the state submits itself to a vast framework of regulations and procedures designed to keep the finance of training from pursuing political purposes. These regulations and procedures lead to 'bureaucracy failure', involving a lot of 'red tape', and prevent the government from responding flexibly and efficiently to new training opportunities.

Thirdly, there is also 'politician failure'. Politicians are typically concerned with their power-base and the probability of being re-elected. Frequent elections allow the electorate's preferences to be transmitted to the legislature. But they also direct politicians to short-term goals that will ensure their popularity to the majority of the electorate – less spending on training for example in an electorate where the enfranchised would not benefit from such a policy, or more spending on inappropriate programmes whose effectiveness cannot be evaluated for many years. The essence of the argument is that politicians have a higher rate of time discount than private sector firms do.

Finally, government support for training – whether in provision or finance – is expensive. Ultimately it must be financed by imposing taxes or cutting some other government expenditures. Since it is generally impossible to impose lump-sum taxes, taxing inevitably creates inefficiencies. Consequently, government intervention to correct for market failures in training generally means the creation of new market failures or the withdrawal of socially desirable public goods.

In sum, the existence of market failures does not necessarily create a presumption in favour of government intervention. It is only when the market failures outweigh the 'government failures' that a case for public provision or finance of training can be made.

This conclusion might appear too obvious for words if it were not ignored in many policy pronouncements on training. It is frequently claimed, for example, that the UK suffers from under-investment in human capital; by contrast, the German apprenticeship system and the Swedish public training programmes are often hailed as appropriate ways to overcome the market's deficiencies in providing vocational training. Such evaluations are generally based on inter-country comparisons of what governments spend on education and training, and what percentage of the population participates in these activities. Policy decisions in this area also tend to be made on this basis – both regarding aggregate government expenditures on training and the breakdown on these expenditures across different programmes.

The inter-country comparisons are clearly important and useful but, by themselves alone, they may not provide a reliable foundation for policy. This is for several reasons. First, the mere fact that government spending on education and training, per capita, is significantly lower in the UK than in Germany or Sweden obviously does not imply that the UK government spends too little; Germany and Sweden might be spending too much. Second, the mere fact that a much smaller percentage of the UK and Italian youth participates in full-time and part-time education than the German, Japanese, or US youth does not necessarily mean there is too little education in Britain and Italy. The UK and Italy produce different goods and services from Germany, Japan, and the USA; perhaps these differences are associated with different skill requirements. Third, the mere fact that expenditures on vocational training relative to further education are higher in Germany than in France does not necessarily mean that one of these countries is making a mistake. Once again, differences in outputs may require differences in training.

Of course the line of causation may run the other way as well. Countries may choose to specialize in low-quality products, for example, because highly skilled workers are not available, as Chapters 5, 6, and 9 suggest. Firms may choose particular product mixes and levels of skill in response to the *country's institutional framework*. For example, Britain has been characterized by a poor education system for all but the academically able, and a relatively confrontational industrial relations system with rigid demarcation between trades. Subject to these constraints, it may be rational for British firms to choose low-skill, highly automated production methods. Training subsidies without changes in the bargaining institutions may thus do little to raise the demand for skills in Britain. This example serves to emphasize the need for policy makers to regard training as the product of a much wider set of institutions than just the vocational training system.

It is clear that policy proposals in this area can be meaningfully formulated only once the underlying market failures and government failures have been evaluated. A medical analogy is appropriate here. Skill deficiencies are to be seen as a symptom of a variety of different 'diseases' (market failures). Only once the diseases have been identified and some attempt has been made to assess the cost of the disease relative to the cost of intervention (government failure), is it responsible to prescribe policy treatment.

Since different market economies – Germany, Japan, Sweden, the UK, the USA, and others – differ markedly in their political institutions and the size and function of their public sectors, training programmes that involve massive government failures in one country may involve little in another. Thus inter-country comparisons should be made with caution; institutions that have successfully promoted training in one country – such as the apprenticeship system in Germany – may not be easily exportable to other countries, or at least not without a careful consideration of other institutional changes that may be required.

Moreover, since countries also differ in their lines of demarcation between private-sector and government activities as well as the social norms governing competition, what is a market failure in one country may well not be one in another. For instance, one serious market failure arises when firms poach trained employees from one another; but obviously this is much more likely to be a problem in countries like the USA and the UK than in Japan, where the norms and principles governing competition among firms are far stricter. The problem is also likely to be more severe in countries with a relatively poor education system since, as recent empirical work on training has made clear, there are substantial complementarities between education and training.[2]

6   Empirical consequences of government failure and policy issues

Part III of this book considers the consequences of government failures, drawing on examples taken from Britain, and then proceeds to address a number of important policy issues.

In Chapter 11, **David Finegold** provides an overview of significant market failures and government failures that must be compared in order for policy prescriptions to be reached. Using the British education and training initiative as an example, he shows that, just as markets can fail to provide adequate training, there are also good reasons why the government has limited ability to rectify the problem.

In Chapter 12, **Alan Felstead** and **Francis Green** consider the impact of the business cycle on private-sector training, with particular attention focused on the recession of the early 1990s. They argue that training may do little to improve the skills of the British workforce where it is undertaken in response to government regulations on health and safety, or occupational requirements, or as the outcome of drives to achieve quality kitemarks. The significance of this type of training appears to have grown in the recession. For example, off-the-job training courses have become much shorter during the recession and more qualifications are now being awarded for short courses, suggesting that they may not be of a particularly high standard and certainly not of any depth. Yet these factors have helped to maintain training volumes in economic circumstances which have hitherto seen training cut back.

It would therefore be incorrect to conclude that it was unbridled market forces that held up training activity in the early 1990s, with British employers at last realizing the importance of training for their own and Britain's long-term future. On the contrary, Felstead and Green argue that the force of regulation has served to protect training from the business cycle. While the maintenance of this sort of training should be welcomed, it may well do little to upgrade the skills of the British workforce and thereby lay the grounds for a more prosperous future.

Chapter 13, by **Alison Booth** and **Stephen Satchell**, shows how the apprenticeship system functions as an institution to overcome the poaching externality analysed in Chapter 2. They use the British apprenticeship system of the 1970s as their example. The form of training provided by an apprenticeship is typically general; thus in the absence of mobility restrictions, the benefits of training will accrue not only to the provider of training and to the trained worker, but also to other firms. The apprenticeship, with its 'indenture' period acts as an institutional device to assist the firms that provide the training to appropriate the benefits in the immediate post-training period. Booth and Satchell also consider qualifications and apprenticeships. Some commentators have argued that accreditation of training is an important means of over-coming market failure where there is asymmetry of information about the value of firm-provided training. The formal qualification associated with some apprenticeships is a means of conveying to non-training firms the value of firm-provided general training. The available British evidence from the 1970s indicates that young men completing the apprenticeships were less likely to leave employment in their first jobs than were individuals with no training. Whether or not the apprentice-ship was formally accredited made no difference to this result. For British apprenticeships in the 1970, accreditation appears not to have had a significant effect on labour mobility.

While the perception of market failure in British training provision is long-lived, only since the late 1970s has there been direct government intervention in the provision of training. This policy stance is mirrored in various other OECD countries. In this context, evaluation of publicly funded training programmes is of vital importance. Are the stated objectives of a programme being met? What is the extent of bureaucratic or politician failure? How important are the deadweight loss or substitution effects associated with particular training programmes? Are training programmes simply keeping the unemployed off the streets and thereby distorting the conventional measures of unemployment? Or are trainees' job prospects and productivity being enhanced?

Chapter 14, by **Ewart Keep** and **Ken Mayhew**, discusses the assumptions underlying official training policy in the UK, as representative of a trend that has swept the USA and a good number of European countries. They argue that to a large extent these assumptions ignore the fact that Britain's vocational education and training policy is one of lack of employer demand for skills rather than one of lack of supply. They focus particular attention on the presumption that employers will require ever more highly trained workers at all levels, that training is crucial to their economic success, and that any government support for training must make use of the price system and must place primary responsibility for training decisions in the hands of the employers. The authors indicate that, in important respects, these views are out of touch with reality.

Keep and Mayhew acknowledge the potential importance of externality problems associated with training. But they argue that there is an additional problem of what might be termed 'managerial failure', a problem that is particularly prevalent in Britain. Here managers opt for a low-skilled route, relying on cost-competitiveness, which limits their demand for skilled labour. What are the reasons for this? The authors argue that managers have been brought up in a confrontational system of industrial relations, where workers are not required to think, and where initiative and talent are required of a minority. Training is a positional good, more of which may threaten existing power relationships. Moreover, the volatility of the British economy relative to other OECD economies makes returns to training harder to quantify than easily comprehended costs. Keep and Mayhew also argue that short-termism has become institutionalized in Britain through a variety of mechanisms.

The book concludes with an overview chapter that examines a wide variety of training policies against the backdrop of the major market failures in skill acquisition. It also discusses the efficiency and equity implications of alternative policy strategies, and identifies the circumstances under which various proposed measures are likely to be effective.

NOTES

1   See Becker (1964, 1975) and also Oi (1962). The idea that education and training can be treated in an analogous way to investment in physical capital has a long history, going back at least to Adam Smith (1776, ch. X). Modern theoretical analysis of investment in human capital began in the late 1950s and early 1960s with seminal work by Mincer (1958, 1962), Schultz (1961), Becker (1962) and Oi (1962).

2   See, for example, Lillard and Tan (1992), Tan *et al.* (1992), Lynch (1992), and Booth (1991).

REFERENCES

Becker, G. S. (1962), 'Investment in Human Capital: A Theoretical Analysis', *Journal of Political Economy* **70**, Supplement, 9–49

(1964, 1975), *Human Capital*, New York: Columbia University Press.

Booth, A. L. (1991), 'Job-Related Formal Training: Who Receives it and What is it Worth?' Oxford Bulletin of Economics and Statistics **53**(3), 281–94.

Lillard, L. A. and H. W. Tan (1992), 'Private Sector Training; Who Gets it and What Are its Effects?', *Research in Labor Economics* **13**, 1–62.

Lynch, L. M. (1992), 'Private Sector Training and the Earnings of Young Workers', *American Economic Review*, 299–312.

Mincer, J. (1958), 'Investment in Human Capital and Personal Income Distribution', *Journal of Political Economy* **66**(4), 281–302.

(1962), 'On-the-Job Training: Costs, Returns and Some Implications', *Journal of Political Economy* **70**(5), 50–79.

Oi, W. Y. (1962), 'Labor as a Quasi-fixed Factor', *Journal of Political Economy* **70**, 538–55.

Schultz, T. W. (1961), 'Investment in Human Capital', *American Economic Review* **51**, 1–17.

Smith, Adam (1776, 1977), *The Wealth of Nations*, Harmondsworth, England: Penguin Books.

Tan, H. W., B. Chapman, C. Peterson and A. Booth (1992), 'Youth Training in the United States, Great Britain and Australia', *Research in Labor Economics* **13**, 63–99.

Part I
Market failures: the causes of skills gaps

2 Transferable training and poaching externalities

This opening chapter on market failures has two important purposes: (i) it sets out a critique of the standard analysis skill of skills acquisition, namely, that of Gary Becker's human capital theory and, on this basis, (ii) it shows how firms' opportunities to poach trained employees generally leads to under-investment in skills.

It is argued that most training is not 'general' (useful to all firms in the economy) or 'specific' (of use only to one specific firm). Rather, most training falls between these two extremes; it is 'transferable', in that it is useful to a limited number of firms – and, among these, more useful to some firms than to others. Becker showed that the free market provides sufficient incentives for acquiring skills when all training is either general or specific. It is wrong, however, to imply that all training can simply be decomposed into general and specific components, so that the market mechanism generates sufficient skills in the intermediate cases.

This chapter concentrates on one specific flaw in this argument: when training is transferable among firms and these firms have some market power in setting wages, the potential benefits from training accrue not only to the firm providing it and the worker acquiring it, but also to the other firms that can poach the trained workers. And since some of the benefit from training falls on the poachers, there is no way for the worker demanding the training and the firm supplying it to capture all the rewards from this training. Inevitably, therefore, the free market mechanism provides insufficient incentives to acquire skills. Needless to say, the greater the mobility of workers among firms and the greater firms' market power in the wage setting process, the greater the market failure arising from the poaching externality.

Transferable training and poaching externalities

MARGARET STEVENS

1   Introduction

In *Wealth and Welfare*, published in 1912, Pigou discussed the training of employees by firms as an example of the divergence between social and private net products. He argued that 'since workpeople are liable to change employers ... socially profitable expenditure by employers in the training of their workpeople ... does not carry a corresponding private profit'. This idea, that there is a positive externality between employers which may lead to under-investment in training, became widely accepted during the first half of this century and was thought to be part of the explanation for an apparent failure in Britain to achieve sufficient skill levels in the workforce

The 1964 Industrial Training Act was a radical attempt to tackle this problem, by realigning the incentives facing employers so that they would prefer to train workers rather than 'poach' from other firms. Twenty-seven Industrial Training Boards (ITBs) were established, on the assumption that firms within an industry had similar training interests; each firm was required to pay a training levy to the ITB for its own industry, and the ITB then allocated grants to firms which were deemed to provide an acceptable quantity and quality of training to their workforce.

At the same time as the ITBs were being established, a new and alternative analysis of the economics of training emerged. In a paper published in 1962, and later expanded in his book *Human Capital* (1964, 1975) Gary Becker undertook a theoretical analysis of investment in human capital which became the basis of most subsequent theoretical and empirical work on training, and also, to some extent, influenced British government policy.

Becker began by identifying two distinct types of on-the-job training: *general* and *specific* training. General training was defined as training for skills which were potentially of use to many employers; specific training is the polar case, of training for skills which are of use only in the firm where they are acquired. The definition of general training included an implicit assumption that the market for general skills would be competitive, and, as will be seen below, this has led to some confusion in the interpretation by others of Becker's work. However, armed with this definition, Becker drew his influential conclusion that since generally-trained workers are paid their marginal product, the return to general training accrues to individual workers; firms cannot capture any of the return, and therefore have no investment incentive for providing training – they will supply training only if they do not have to pay any of the costs. But, this does not lead to under-investment in training since they can, and do, shift the cost to the trainees, who will be willing to invest by accepting low wages during training in order to obtain higher future wages. In other words, the old argument about externalities was false in the case of general training. He went on to show that specific training had no associated externality problem either.

Although Becker's refutation of the externality argument referred only to the cases of purely general and purely specific training, he was widely interpreted as having disproved the existence of a 'poaching' externality. Thus, for example, Lees and Chiplin (1970) appealed to Becker's analysis to claim that the grant–levy system of the 1964 Industrial Training Act had 'no basis in economic logic' – since it was designed to address a non-existent poaching problem. Furthermore, since investment in general training should be undertaken by individual workers, policies to counteract under-investment should be directed towards workers rather than firms. Such criticisms contributed eventually to the abolition of the grant–levy system in 1981. The focus of government policy since then has shifted towards individual investment: for example, tax relief on personal vocational training costs was introduced in 1992. The White Paper *People, Jobs and Opportunity* (Employment Department, 1992) claimed that individual incentives to train are being improved through the widening of skill differentials resulting from policies to increase wage flexibility. However, it is notable that the same White Paper placed the responsibility for improving skill levels on employers, and continues to exhort them to *invest* in training for the skills they need. It appears that firms are not regarded as the passive and myopic suppliers of general training described by Becker. There is even a hint that an externality problem is perceived: views were invited on the proposal that the law should be changed to enable an employer to enforce a training contract providing for the individual to work for a specified period after training, or to repay some of the costs.

The question to be addressed here is simply, 'Does the poaching externality exist?' Although many economists regard Becker's analysis as having settled the argument, others appear to be reluctant to accept it in full and abandon the earlier explanation for under-investment in skills. Thus, Finegold and Soskice (1988), Hart and Shipman (1991) and Greenhalgh and Mavrotas (1993) all continue to assume that such an externality exists, without reconciling the assumption with Becker's argument. Nor is empirical evidence easy to interpret in terms of general and specific training: there is considerable evidence that firms *do* invest in training which is apparently general in character (Jones, 1986; Bishop, 1991). Furthermore, it appears that poaching is a problem: in a large-scale survey carried out by the Training Agency (1989), 38% of firms who undertook some training reported that loss of trained staff to alternative employers was a serious drawback of training provision.

It will be shown in this chapter that not all types of training can be analysed using the theoretical tools of general and specific training. *Transferable* training is defined as training which is potentially of use to some (rather than many) other firms. It is then shown that an externality, of the type often referred to as a poaching externality, can exist for transferable training. The argument is very simple: a labour market in which skills are transferable but not perfectly general is likely to be imperfectly competitive, so that a skilled worker does not necessarily receive a wage equal to his marginal product. Hence some of the return to the training investment accrues to the firm which employs him – which may or may not be the firm where the training took place. The possibility that some of the return will be captured by the training firm provides it with an incentive to share in the training investment – but equally, the possibility that an alternative firm will obtain part of the return reduces the incentive of the trainee and training firm to invest, resulting in under-investment in skills of this type. Thus the empirical findings that firms appear to invest in general training, and that poaching is regarded as a problem, can be explained if, in fact, much training is transferable rather than general.

In Sections 2 and 3, the theory of general and specific training is examined in more detail; the definition of transferable training is introduced, and the conditions under which an externality exists are identified. In Section 4, the effects of the externality are considered: in addition to under-investment, it may lead to a distortion in the mix of skills for which training is undertaken. Then, in Sections 5 and 6, a simple theoretical model is developed which illustrates some of the effects.

2   Interpretations of general and specific training

General training was defined by Becker as training for skills which are valued by *many* employees: this allowed him to make the further assumption that the labour market for such skills would be competitive. It is this assumption which delivers the result that the whole of the return to general training accrues to workers, so that firms will not invest in general training and there is no externality problem. Careful reading of Becker's work suggests that he placed his refutation of the 'old argument' for a poaching problem in the context of a competitive labour market because that argument had suggested that it was precisely when the labour market was competitive that the problem would be most severe.

He also considered whether there would be an externality in the case of purely specific training. Here, he pointed out that although labour turnover would lead to external *diseconomies* associated with specific training, there were no corresponding external *economies* accruing to other firms. He argued that, to minimize the diseconomies, the wage of a specifically-trained worker would lie strictly between his marginal product and the market wage: thus the costs of, and returns to, specific training would be shared between the firm and the worker.

The next step in the argument was the claim that training which was neither perfectly general nor purely specific could be regarded as the sum of a general and a specific component. Such training would have economic characteristics intermediate between the two types. The implication (which he did not pursue) was that there was therefore no externality problem associated with intermediate types of training either. Indeed, it is not difficult to see that, *if* a training programme provides a mix of perfectly general and perfectly specific skills, competition in the external labour market will lead to an alternative wage equal to the value of the general component, so the external firms will be unable to capture any of the return to the training investment. In a sense, therefore, it is acceptance of the claim that any training programme can be decomposed into general and specific components which has led subsequent authors to believe that Becker had disproved the existence of an externality for *all* types of training. The validity of this argument will be examined in Section 2.3.

Much of the extensive discussion and criticism of Becker's theory of training in the economic and industrial relations literature centres on the interpretation of the terms *general* and *specific*. A problem with the initial definition of general training was that it involved both a statement about labour market competition, and a statement about the usefulness of skills. The potential for confusion here is illustrated by Becker's own statement that, for an employer in an isolated company town, 'all training, no matter what its nature, is specific to the firm'. Oatey (1970) attempted to clarify this point, suggesting that the classification of training should depend on the mobility potential of the trainees, rather than on the nature of the skills. A further confusion is introduced when general training is interpreted, as it commonly is, as training for skills which are of use to *some*, rather than *many* firms, without any assumptions about competition in the labour market. For example, Jones (1988), Ritzen (1991), Shackleton (1992) and Hyman (1992) all use this definition; and it is often implicit in the use of the term transferable training, which is used interchangeably with general training. So, Marsden and Ryan (1990) interpret Becker's conclusion as meaning that trainees should pay for any skills which are transferable to other firms. Becker himself was more cautious, stating that the effect on training of labour market conditions between perfect competition and pure monopsony was 'difficult to assess'.

Increasing ingenuity has been used by those who accept Becker's analysis to explain the observed investment in general training by firms. Some explanations focus on asymmetric information (for example, Katz and Ziderman, 1990): here the idea is that training which would be general if alternative employers had full information about it is effectively partially specific because the training firm has more information about its value. Others emphasize the possibility that specific and general skills are complementary: this might also lead to under-investment in general skills (Stern and Ritzen, 1991; Feuer *et al.*, 1991).

Dissatisfaction with Becker's expression of human capital theory and its policy implications, and the difficulty of reconciling his 'law' about general training with observed training practice, has led to increasing criticism in recent years. Chapman (1991) sees human capital theory as offering a narrow and over-simplified view of training, and favours an eclectic approach which incorporates efficiency wage theory, and emphasises the problems arising from imperfect information. In particular he sees the emphasis on specific training as a weakness of human capital theory, stating that it is difficult to think of examples of purely specific training. Soskice (1990) also regards a theory based on the distinction between general and specific skills as over-simplified. He describes marketable skills as 'a very complex range of products', the optimal set of marketable skills providing 'a balance between the needs of different companies'. OECD (1991) reviews other criticisms, and illustrates the difficulty that many analysts have encountered in disentangling the definitions of general and specific training from issues of labour mobility.

3   Transferable training

Specific training produces skills which are of use to a single employer, so the labour market for such skills is monopsonistic; general training (as defined by Becker) produces skills which are of use to many employers, and for which there is a perfectly competitive labour market. But, if we can hypothesise the existence of specific skills, we can also hypothesise the existence of skills which are neither general, nor specific, but are of use to a small number of employers. Such a skill cannot be regarded as a *sum* of general and specific, although its economic characteristics may be intermediate between the two. If such skills exist the corresponding labour market may be *imperfectly* competitive.

Consideration of skill acquisition in relation to modern labour markets suggests this argument is more than hypothetical. As a simple example, if the market for a product is oligopolistic, the market for skills associated with its production may be oligopsonistic. More importantly, there is an intrinsic association between training and imperfect competition, through a differentiation effect. In the course of a training programme, and more generally throughout the development of his career, a worker acquires a 'bundle' of skills, some of which may be specific, some general, and others of use to a small number of firms similar to the training firm. The particular bundle of skills which a worker accumulates can be regarded as differentiating him from other workers. Similarly, the particular set of skills valued by a firm differentiates it from other firms in the labour market. So it may happen that as a worker becomes more highly trained, the set of firms which values his skills becomes progressively smaller. Thus training may be regarded as a process which itself reduces labour market competition.

Furthermore even if a training programme produces skills which are primarily general, in that there are a large number of firms where the resultant skills are valued, it may be that the number of such firms in a particular locality is small, and if workers are not, in practice, very mobile, the relevant labour market for firms in that locality may be imperfectly competitive.

Since we have identified types of training which cannot be described as specific, or general, or a combination of the two, some new terminology is required. We will continue to use the term *general* as in Becker's definition, and define *transferable* training as training for skills which are of potential value to at least one other firm in addition to the training firm, without any assumption about the nature of labour market competition. In order to simplify the discussion, suppose that the value of an unskilled worker is zero to all potential employers. Then the characteristics of any training programme might be described by writing down the vector of outcome values – the post-training value of the worker to all his potential employers:

$$v = (v_0, \; v_1, \; v_2, \; \ldots, \; v_n)$$

where firm 0 is the training firm and v_i is his value to firm i, conditional on his working for firm i. Only firms where the post-training value is positive, and to which there is positive probability of the worker moving, are included. A slight variation on this approach would be to define v_i as the joint value of the training to the worker and firm i, which would allow the worker's moving costs to be incorporated directly. Different parameterisations of the outcome vector correspond to different types of training. For example:

Purely specific training:	$v = (s)$
Purely general training:	$v = (g, g, g, g, \ldots)$(where n is large)
Combined general and specific:	$v = (s + g, g, g, g, \ldots)$
Differentiated skill requirements:	$v = (v, \lambda v, \lambda^2 v, \lambda^3 v, \ldots)$
Skills of use in three firms (or high moving costs to other localities):	$v = (t, t, t)$

All these examples (except the first) represent transferable training. In this framework it is clear that specific and general training are special cases, but many other possibilities exist.

Having written down the outcome vector, we can then consider what kinds of assumptions should be made about competition in the labour market. For perfectly general training, if we assume that workers are very mobile, the assumption of a perfectly competitive labour market seems reasonable. For other types of training, and/or other assumptions about worker mobility, there may be less than perfect competition between employers.

Once we admit the possibility of imperfect competition, an important, and surprisingly simple, result emerges immediately: the externality associated with training, first described by Pigou but supposed to have been disproved by Becker, can exist after all. Two conditions are required. First, suppose that there is some source of uncertainty at the time when the training investment is made, which means that the training firm and trainee are uncertain about whether the trainee will remain with the firm or move to an alternative firm which values his skills. If, in addition, labour market competition is such that firms are able to pay the trained worker a wage strictly less than his marginal product, then any firm which has positive probability of employing the worker obtains a positive expected return to the training programme. As a result, the training firm has an incentive to participate in the training investment (as does the worker if his expected post-training wage is higher as a result of training). But since part of the expected return accrues to alternative employers who do not participate in the training investment, the private return is lower than the social return: that is, there is a positive externality, which may lead to under-investment.

It must be emphasised that this argument is a very general one. The source of uncertainty may lie in the trainee's behaviour or ability or it may arise from demand or productivity shocks which affect the relative value of the trained worker to different firms. Or there may be uncertainty on both sides so that the best match between workers and firms cannot be determined until after training takes place. Imperfect competition between firms in the labour market may arise (for example) from low labour mobility, or differentiation of skill requirements, or imperfect information. Whatever the reasons for these conditions, the combination of uncertainty and imperfect competition creates a potential externality problem. General and specific training can be regarded as two limiting cases, both of which have the property that the externality disappears: in general training this is because, as the wage approaches the marginal product, the expected return to alternative firms approaches zero, there is no externality associated with specific training because the training has no value for alternative firms.

Figure 2.1 shows a schematic representation of the relationship between labour market competition and the externality problem. The horizontal axis represents some measure of the degree of competition: for example, the number of firms who value the worker's skills. When training is purely specific there is no competition between firms for the resultant skills, so there is zero probability that the worker will move to a firm which values the skills but there may be a large difference between wage (w) and marginal product (mp). As the transferability of the training increases there is more competition between firms for the corresponding skills, so the divergence between wage and marginal product falls but turnover probability increases. In the limit, for general skills and a perfectly competitive labour market, the turnover probability may be high but the wage is equal to the marginal product

The magnitude of the externality problem is represented by the product of these effects: that is, the probability that the worker will move to an alternative firm which values the skills, and his net value to such a firm. If the shapes of the curves are as shown,[1] this suggests a hump-shaped relationship, with the divergence between social and private return to

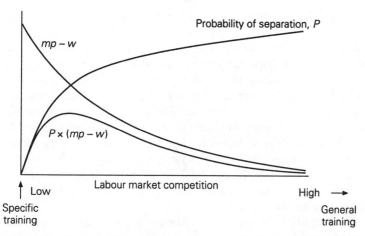

Figure 2.1 The relationship between labour market competition and the externality problem

training greatest at 'intermediate' labour market competition, and zero only in the two limiting cases of general and specific training. In terms of this picture, Pigou's analysis focused on the turnover probability, stating that the divergence between private and social net product would depend on the 'prospect . . . of employers retaining the continued service of their hands' and suggesting that this divergence would therefore be smallest for 'firms engaged in the manufacture of proprietary goods requiring a more or less specialised kind of labour'. Becker, in contrast, highlighted the non-existence of the externality under perfect competition in the labour market because of the dependence on the difference between wage and marginal product. The hump-shaped relationship in Figure 1 arises from joint consideration of the two effects.

4   Investment in transferable training

We will now consider the implications of the analysis in the previous section, and ask what factors affect the decision to invest in training which is transferable but not general. Firstly we can say that the expected return to a transferable training programme will normally be shared three ways, between the worker, the training firm, and alternative employers. It is, therefore, a particularly complex type of investment. The shares to each party will depend on their relative market power in the labour market for this particular skill, and on the mechanisms for wage determination. The costs of the investment, however, will be borne only by the worker and training firm. Even if we assume that all parties are fully informed, there are two problems which may lead to under-investment: capital market imperfections affecting the worker's ability to bear an appropriate share of the cost, and the fact that part of the expected return accrues to alternative employers not involved in the investment decision. If, in addition, there are information asymmetries between the worker and training firm (for example, about the quality of training, or its transferability, or the worker's ability or effort to learn) a joint investment *contract* may not be feasible – hindering further the achievement of optimal investment levels. This is an example of the hold-up problem (Rogerson, 1992), which occurs when parties to a future transaction must first make non-contractible specific investments.

It is the externality between firms, however, which is the focus of this chapter, and we will therefore assume that the latter problem does not arise, so the worker and training firm can undertake the training investment as a jointly optimising unit. How does the presence of this type of externality affect the investment? We can identify three categories of problems.

(1) Consider the decision to invest when the choice of training programme is exogenous. Then, if part of the total return accrues to alternative employers, we would expect *too few workers* to be trained – training will only be undertaken by firms and workers where joint costs are less than the private return. (An example of this problem is given in Section 5).

(2) Suppose that the *type* of skill to be acquired is exogenous, but the *level* of skill may be chosen by the investing parties. Then, if the marginal private benefit of increasing the skill level is less than the marginal social benefit, *too low a level of skill* will be chosen. Note, however, that this marginal condition does not necessarily hold, even when part of the total return accrues to other firms. It will depend on the precise characteristics of the training and the labour market. In the model of Section 5, this problem does not arise.

(3) Now consider the choice of type of training programme. Suppose there is a set of skills for which training might be provided, and the investing parties must choose some subset to make up the training programme. Some of these skills may be of use to many employers, others to a few firms similar to the training firm, and there may also be some purely specific skills. Then the existence of an externality associated with some of these skills may *distort the mix of skills* chosen. If there is a serious difficulty in capturing the returns to the skills which would be chosen in the absence of any externality, how will the decision

be distorted? One possibility is to choose purely general skills only – but in this case it is the trainee who must bear all the costs, and if he is unable or unwilling to do so this may not be a viable solution. Alternatively, the inclusion of very specific skills might reduce the trainee's probability of moving to another employer, and hence reduce the externality problem associated with other components of the training. An example of this type of distortion is given in Section 6. Or it may be possible to raise mobility barriers in other ways so that there is no need to distort the actual mix of skills, although they are effectively less transferable. For example, general skills (of potential use to many firms) may be provided without certification, thereby reducing their effective transferability.

5   A simple illustrative model

Consider a skill which is required by just two firms,[2] training for which is provided by the same two firms. We will model the training investment as a two-stage game. There are two periods (with no discounting between them); in the first period workers are trained, and in the second the two firms compete for the services of the skilled workers. We will suppose that the two firms have constant returns to this type of skilled labour[3] – a skilled worker is worth $v > 0$ to each firm. Unskilled workers are worth zero, as are skilled workers to alternative firms. So the outcome vector for this training programme is (v, v).

The two firms have identical cost functions for training: $C(N_i)$, where N_i is the number of workers trained by firm i. Training carries increasing marginal cost, and no fixed costs:

$$C(0) = 0, \ C'(N) > 0 \text{ and } C''(N) > 0 \text{ for } N > 0$$

So the social optimum is for N^* workers to be trained by each firm, where $C'(N^*) = v$. We will compare this with the outcome in the subgame – perfect equilibrium of the two-stage game.

Consider the second stage: the two firms compete for the services of the trained workers in the labour market. Each firm announces a wage w_i, $i = 1,2$. Suppose firstly that workers simply choose to work for the firm which has the higher wage (or choose each firm with probability 0.5 when wages are equal). Then the labour market equilibrium is the Bertrand equilibrium, $w_1 = w_2 = v$. So in this case, the labour market is effectively competitive, there is no externality, training is effectively general, and it is easy to verify that (provided

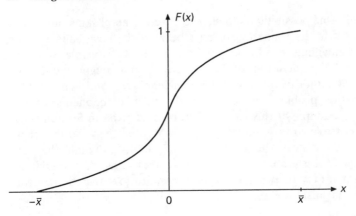

Figure 2.2   The retention probability, as a function of the wage difference

trainees are willing to pay for training) the optimum number of workers will be trained.

But now suppose that competition in the labour market is less fierce. We will model this by supposing that there is some stickiness in the movement of workers between firms, so that if one firm's wage is a little above the other, not all workers will necessarily prefer to work for the higher wage firm. The preferences of workers will not be modelled explicitly: we simply adopt a reduced form for the problem, which can capture a situation in which workers have independent and randomly distributed tastes which, in addition to wages, influence their choice of firm. So, we hypothesise the existence of a function $F(.)$ such that, when the firms announce wages w_1, w_2, $F(w_1 - w_2)$ is the probability that any individual trained worker will work for firm 1 (so with probability $1 - F(w_1 - w_2)$ he works for firm 2). Assume $F(.)$ has the following properties (see Figure 2):

$$F(0) = 0.5; \;\; F(-x) = 1 - F(x) \text{ (symmetry properties)}$$
$$F' > 0; \;\; F''(x) \leq 0 \qquad \forall x > 0$$
$$F(x) \to 1 \text{ as } x \to \bar{x} \text{ where } \bar{x} \epsilon (0, \infty) \;\; (F \text{ may have finite or}$$
infinite support)

Thus $F(.)$ is simply the distribution function corresponding to a probability density which is symmetric about zero (see Figure 2.2). The slope of this function may be interpreted as representing the sensitivity of workers to a difference in wages. The limiting case as $\bar{x} \to 0$, in which F is discontinuous at zero, represents perfect mobility or sensitivity.

We first evaluate the equilibrium at the labour market stage; then, knowing the second-stage outcome, we can examine training decisions.

5.1 The labour market

Suppose that $N = N_1 + N_2$ workers are trained. If the wages are w_1, w_2, firm 1 will obtain $F(w_1 - w_2)N$ workers. So firm 1 maximises:

$$\Pi_1 = (v - w_1)F(w_1 - w_2)N$$

with respect to w_1, and similarly firm 2's objective function is:

$$\Pi_2 = (v - w_2)(1 - F(w_1 - w_2))N$$

The first-order conditions are:

$$(v - w_1)F'(w_1 - w_2) = F(w_1 - w_2)$$
$$(v - w_2)F'(w_1 - w_2) = 1 - F(w_1 - w_2)$$

Subtracting, and putting $x = w_1 - w_2$, we obtain:

$$xF'(x) = 1 - 2F(x)$$

From the properties of $F()$ it can be seen that the only solution is $x=0$. Hence the labour market equilibrium is:

$$w_1 = w_2 \equiv w, \text{ where } w = v - F(0)/F'(0)$$

So, the 'stickiness' amongst workers gives labour market power to the firms and leads to a wage below marginal product, and hence a potential externality problem.

$$\text{Let } k \equiv F(0)/F'(0)$$

k represents the market power of the firms, and depends only on the properties of the function $F(.)$. In the limiting case of perfect sensitivity, k approaches zero.

5.2   The training market

Suppose that in the training market each firm chooses how many workers to train (Cournot competition). From the analysis of the labour market, it can be seen that workers considering training expect a post-training wage $v - k$, and each firm expects a profit $\frac{1}{2}(N_1 + N_2)k$. Suppose there is a perfectly elastic supply of identical potential trainees willing to invest in training at a price $\bar{p}$.[4] We will assume $\bar{p} \leq v - k$. If they have rational expectations and face no credit constraints, $\bar{p} = v - k$. Now consider firm i's training decision. It must choose N_i to maximise the sum of profits over the two periods:

$$\tfrac{1}{2}(N_i + N_j)k - C(N_i) + \bar{p}N_i$$

for which the first-order condition is:

$$C'(N_i) = \tfrac{1}{2}k + \bar{p} \leq v - \tfrac{1}{2}k$$

In the training market equilibrium both firms choose the number of trainees to satisfy this equation. We can deduce:

  (i) If workers are perfectly mobile (the 'competitive' limiting case of $k = 0$), and face no credit constraints, $C'(N_i) = v$ and there is optimal training with the workers bearing the full costs.
 (ii) Otherwise, the costs of training are shared and a sub-optimal number of workers receives training. The effect of the externality is to reduce the marginal benefit of training to the firm from k to $\frac{1}{2}k$.
(iii) The firms will not compensate for under-investment by workers (that is, for $\bar{p}$ less than $v - k$), but will pay for training only to the extent that they can obtain a return due to an imperfectly competitive labour market. So, for example, if $k = 0$ and $\bar{p} = 0$, no training occurs.

6   An extension of the model

In Section 5, it was demonstrated that a sub-optimal *number* of workers may be trained, but the training programme itself was taken as exogenous with outcome (v, v). An extension of the model would be to include parameters of the training programme as choice variables: we could make the outcome vector (v_1, v_2) (for each firm) endogenous. This is not difficult to do, since the two types of workers – those trained by firm 1 and those trained by firm 2 – can be regarded as being in two separate labour markets (provided the firms can offer different wages to the two types). This property of the model follows directly from the assumption of constant returns: the two types of workers are not treated as substitutes, since each firm simply wants as many of both types as it can get. Furthermore, with a perfectly elastic supply of identical trainees, the decisions of the two firms are independent at the training market stage. So, the training done by firm 1 may be analysed in a three-stage game (and an identical but separate game determines the training done by firm 2).

  I Firm 1 chooses how many workers to train
 II Firm 1 and its trainees choose the characteristics of the training programme
III The two firms compete for the services of workers trained by firm 1

A full analysis of this game would require specification of a cost function $C(N, v_1, v_2)$. But without doing this, a distortion in the choice of characteristics for training can be demonstrated. Suppose we re-parameterise the problem as follows: $v_1 - v_2 = s$, the specific component, assumed positive, and $v_2 = v$, the transferable component.

6.1   Stage III: the labour market

The first-order conditions can be derived exactly as before:

$$(v + s - w_1)F'(w_1 - w_2) = F(w_1 - w_2)$$
$$(v - w_2)F'(w_1 - w_2) = (1 - F(w_1 - w_2))$$

Subtracting, and putting $x = w_1 - w_2$:

$$s - x = (2F(x) - 1)/F'(x)$$

From this equation it is immediately clear that (provided F' is finite and $s > 0$) $0 < x < s$: firm 1 pays a wage premium for the specific element in the training. This follows since if $x \leq 0$, the left-hand side is strictly positive and the right-hand side is negative. So $x > 0$, but then the right-hand side is positive, so $x < s$. This is an instance of *sharing* the return to specific training (Becker, 1964, 1975; Hashimoto, 1981): firm 1 pays a wage that lies strictly between the value of the worker to firm 1, and his value elsewhere. Differentiating this equation with respect to s, we also find that

$$\frac{dx}{dx} > 0$$

so the premium increases with the level of the specific component. Having solved for the wage premium x, in terms of s, we obtain the actual wages:

$$(w_1) = v + s - F(x)/F'(x)$$
$$(w_2) = v - (1 - F(x))/F'(x)$$

6.2   Stage II: choice of training programme

From the expressions above we can derive expected returns to all parties for a single worker undertaking a training programme $(v + s, v)$;

Worker: $R_w = F(x)w_1 + (1 - F(x))w_2$
Firm 1: $R_1 = (v + s - w_1)F(x)$
Total private return:

$$R_p = R_w + R_1 = (v + s)F(x) + (1 - F(x))w_2$$
$$= v + sF(x) - (1 - F(x))^2/F'(x)$$

Firm 2: $R_2 = (v - w_2)(1 - F(x)) = (1 - F(x))^2/ = F'(x)$
Social return: $R = (v + sF(x))$

The worker and training firm choose v and s to maximise their joint return, which can be written as $R_p = R - R_2$. Differentiating with respect to v we obtain:

$$\frac{\partial R_p}{\partial v} = \frac{\partial R}{\partial v}$$

So the marginal private benefit of the transferable component is the same as the marginal social benefit: there is no distortion in the choice of the *level* of the transferable component. However:

$$\frac{\partial R_p}{\partial s} = \frac{\partial R}{\partial s} - \frac{\partial R_2}{\partial s}$$
$$= \frac{\partial R}{\partial s} - \frac{d R_2}{dx}\frac{dx}{ds}$$

Since the second term is non-zero, there will in general, be a distortion in the choice of level of specific component. In which direction will this be? We know that $dx/ds > 0$. But:

$$\frac{dR_2}{dx} \overset{sgn}{=} -\{(1 - F(x))F''(x) + 2F'(x)\}$$

Here, the first term inside the curly brackets is negative and the second is positive, so the sign depends on the precise properties of the function $F(.)$. Since the slope of F represents the sensitivity of workers to the wage (and therefore the fierceness of competition), we can interpret this ambiguity as follows. Increasing the wage premium has two effects: it reduces the probability that workers will move to firm 2, but also (if $F'' < 0$) reduces labour market competition. Hence:

(i) If the sensitivity of workers to relative wage does not decline much with the wage premium x, (that is, the term in F' dominates the term in F''), then the return to firm 2 falls as x increases because it can obtain fewer workers. In this case

$$\frac{\partial R_p}{\partial s} = \frac{\partial R}{\partial s}$$

so there is an incentive to over-invest in specific training.

(ii) If increasing the wage premium x reduces the sensitivity of workers to relative wages very quickly (that is, the term in F'' dominates), then R_2 may increase with the wage premium since although firm 2 obtains fewer workers, it can pay them a lower wage. In this case

$$\frac{\partial R_p}{\partial s} < \frac{\partial R}{\partial s}$$

so the incentive is to under-invest in specific training.

The first of these conditions seems intuitively more likely: it can be shown to hold for all log-concave distribution functions – a wide class which includes the Normal distribution.[5] But whichever of the conditions holds, it is clear that a specific component in training can be used to reduce the share of the return to training which goes to an external firm, and hence a socially suboptimal mix of skills may be chosen.

7   Conclusion

In this chapter it has been demonstrated that there can be a positive externality between firms which would lead to under-investment in training as claimed by Pigou – if there is imperfect competition between firms in the labour market for the resultant skills. Further, it has been argued that there is good reason to suppose that the labour market associated with many types of on-the-job training will be imperfectly competitive – skills and skill requirements have the effect of differentiating both workers and firms.

It is widely believed that Becker disproved the existence of this type of externality. In fact, he showed that it did not exist either for purely general or purely specific training, and then claimed that intermediate types of training could be represented as the sum of general and specific components. If this claim were true, then there would be no training externality. But it has been shown here that there are intermediate types of training which cannot be so represented, and for which an externality does exist. These are types of training associated with intermediate levels of competition in the labour market. Indeed, it is natural to consider the theoretical characteristics of training under intermediate levels of competition, since specific and general training represent the limiting cases of zero and infinite competition respectively.

Three possible consequences have been identified: there may be too few workers trained, or too low a level of transferable skills, or a distortion in the mix of skills. A simple two-firm model was used to demonstrate how the first and third of these problems can arise. It should be noted that a variety of models can generate similar results. In Stevens (1994) the same effects are demonstrated using a model in which firms are affected by independent demand or productivity shocks, so there is uncertainty about their future values for the trained worker and training is described by a random vector. This also generates ex-post heterogeneity of firms, and hence imperfect competition in the labour market.

It has been pointed out that the investment in transferable on-the-job training has complex characteristics, in that costs may be shared between two parties, and the return between three or more. A simple model such as the one used in this chapter cannot hope to capture all the complexities of the problem. However, it does demonstrate the implications of the nature of labour market competition for training investments.

Having identified a theoretical problem in the training market, it remains to be demonstrated that markets for skilled labour do have the characteristics which would give rise to this problem in practice. However, we may note that two observed phenomena – investment by firms in apparently general training, and concern about poaching – can be explained if training is transferable but not perfectly general.

A result of the type of under-investment identified in this chapter is that firms will not be able to obtain as much skilled labour as they would like to employ. A variety of responses by firms can be predicted. The firm might choose a different (and more costly) method of production which relies on automation and unskilled labour, if its preferred method would involve training which is subject to an externality problem. Or firms may choose only those products which can be produced without the requirement for highly skilled workers. Finegold and Soskice (1988) have argued that British firms tend to produce low-quality goods and services, and that under-investment in training is part of the explanation for this. Mason, van Ark and Wagner, Chapter 9 in this volume, demonstrate how British firms in the biscuit industry employ workers of lower skill and produce lower-quality products than their European counterparts. Although we cannot necessarily regard this as evidence that a lack of skills is damaging to the British economy (if there is a demand for cheap, low-quality biscuits) we can say that *if* Britain has a less skilled labour force as a result of failing to solve an externality problem, then British firms face restricted choices which may also restrict their ability to compete in world markets.

NOTES

1 Stevens (1994) gives a longer and more formal presentation of some of the ideas discussed in this chapter, and includes a model which generates curves of the shape shown in Figure 2.1.
2 Alternatively, consider two firms which are isolated from others in the labour market for this skill.
3 This simplifying assumption is very important – without it the model would be far less tractable.
4 In reality, workers may not pay directly for on-the-job training, but may do so indirectly by accepting a wage less than marginal product during training.
5 See Caplin and Nalebuff (1991) for the properties of log-concave distributions.

REFERENCES

Becker, G. (1962), 'Investment in Human Capital: A Theoretical Analysis', *Journal of Political Economy* **70**(5, part 2), 9–49.
  (1964, 1975), *Human Capital*, New York: Columbia University Press.
Bishop, J. H. (1991), 'On-the-job Training of New Hires', in D. Stern and J. M. M. Ritzen (eds.), *Market Failure in Training?*, Berlin: Springer-Verlag.
Caplin, A. and B. Nalebuff (1991), 'Aggregation and Social Choice: A Mean Voter Theorem', *Econometrica* **59**(1), 1–23.
Chapman, P. G. (1991), 'Institutional Aspects of Youth Employment and Training Policy in Britain: A Comment', *British Journal of Industrial Relations* **29**(3), 491–5.
Employment Department, Scottish Office and Welsh Office (1992), *People, Jobs and Opportunity*, Command Paper 1810, London: HMSO.

Feuer, M. J., H. A. Glick and A. Desai (1991), 'Firm Financed Education and Specific Human Capital', in D. Stern and J. M. M. Ritzen (eds.), *Market Failure in Training?*, Berlin: Springer-Verlag.

Finegold, D. and D. Soskice (1988), 'The Failure of Training in Britain: Analysis and Prescription', *Oxford Review of Economic Policy* **4**(3), 21–53.

Greenhalgh, C. and G. Mavrotas (1993), 'Workforce Training in the Thatcher Era – Market Forces and Market Failures', *International Journal of Manpower*, **14**(2).

Hart, P. E. and A. Shipman (1991), 'Financing Training in Britain', *National Institute Economic Review*, **136**(May), 77–85.

Hashimoto, M. (1981), 'Firm-specific Human Capital as a Shared Investment', *American Economic Review* **71**(3), 475–82.

Hyman, J. (1992), *Training at Work*, London: Routledge.

Jones, I. (1986), 'Apprentice Training Costs in British Manufacturing Establishments: Some New Evidence', *British Journal of Industrial Relations* **24**(3), 336–62.

——— (1988), 'An Evaluation of YTS', *Oxford Review of Economic Policy*, **4**(3), 54–71.

Katz, E. and A. Ziderman (1990), 'Investment in General Training: the Role of Information and Labour Mobility', *Economic Journal* **100**, 1147–58.

Lees, D. and B. Chiplin (1970), 'The Economics of Industrial Training', *Lloyds Bank Review*, **96**, 29–41

Marsden, D. and P. Ryan (1990), 'Institutional Aspects of Youth Employment and Training Policy in Britain', *British Journal of Industrial Relations*, **28**(3), 351–69.

Oatey, M. (1970), 'The Economics of Training with the Firm', *British Journal of Industrial Relations* **8**(1), 1–21.

OECD (1991), 'Enterprise-related Training', *OECD Employment Outlook*, July, Paris: OECD.

Pigou, A. C. (1912), *Wealth and Welfare*, London: Macmillan.

Ritzen, J. M. M. (1991), 'Market Failure for General Training, and Remedies', in D. Stern and J. M. M. Ritzen (eds.), *Market Failure in Training?* Berlin: Springer-Verlag.

Rogerson, W. P. (1992), 'Contractual Solutions to the Hold-up Problem', *Review of Economic Studies* **59**, 777–94

Shackleton, J. R. (1992), 'Training Too Much? A Sceptical Look at the Economics of Skill Provision in the U.K.', Hobart Paper 118, London: Institute of Economic Affairs.

Soskice, D. (1990), 'Reinterpreting Corporatism and Explaining Unemployment: Co-ordinated and Non-co-ordinated Market Economies', in R. Brunetta and C. Dell'Aringa (eds.), *Labour Relations and Economic Performance*, Basingstoke: Macmillan.

Stern, D. and J. M. M. Ritzen (1991), 'Introduction and Overview', in D. Stern and J. M. M. Ritzen (eds.), *Market Failure in Training?*, Berlin: Springer-Verlag.

Stevens, M. (1994), 'A Theoretical Model of On-the job Training with Imperfect Competition', *Oxford Economic Papers*, Vol. 46, pp. 537–62.

Training Agency (1989), *Training in Britain*, London: HMSO.

3 Credit constraints, investment externalities and growth

This chapter focuses on market failures in skill acquisition arising from (i) credit constraints and (ii) imperfectly competitive wage determination combined with complementarities between labour and capital.

The chapter begins by demonstrating how, in the absence of market imperfections, workers acquire efficient levels of skill in the context of a standard growth model. Here Gary Becker's conclusions, regarding the adequacy of the free market in generating sufficient training, are correct.

Next, the chapter shows that when workers face borrowing constraints, workers will not invest sufficiently in skills. Nevertheless, it is shown that this market failure, on its own, will not lead to a deficient long-run growth rate of the economy.

The situation is very different, however, when the labour market is imperfectly competitive, so that workers are paid less than their marginal product. Under these conditions workers have sub-optimally low incentives to acquire general skills. When labour and capital are complementary in production, this will reduce the profitability of investment and lead to a sub-optimally low capital stock. In short, deficient training may lead to deficient investment, leading to even more deficient training, and so on. In this way, an economy can get stuck in a low-skill/low-investment trap.

The chapter also considers institutional arrangements to stimulate training and discusses some empirical evidence that seems to fit the presence of labour market imperfections particularly well.

Credit constraints, investment externalities and growth

DARON ACEMOGLU

1   Introduction

The successful post-war growth performances of countries such as Japan or Germany are often attributed to the high skill levels of their workforce while stagnation in the UK is being blamed on the inadequate levels of training and skill in this country. Economic historians also point out the high levels of crafting skills and human capital just before the Industrial Revolution as an important factor in the British take-off and subsequent sustained growth in Britain and continental Europe (e.g. Mokyr (1990)). It is probably no coincidence that among the newly industrialized countries of South-East Asia, the most successful productivity growth was by Hong Kong which had the best quality of human capital. In view of these observations we need to ask a number of questions:

(i) In what way does the skill and human capital level of the workforce impact on economic performance? In particular do differences in skill between countries translate into differences in long-run growth (as argued to be the case by Lucas (1988)) or only temporary differences?
(ii) What factors determine the incentives to acquire skills and invest in human capital?
(iii) Can we rely on the market to provide the right incentives for skill acquisition and if there are failures in this market, how can we correct these?
(iv) Relatedly, does an individual's decision to acquire skills confer positive benefits on other agents? In particular, will an individual be better off when the workforce of which he is part is more skilled?

We will start by discussing the standard growth model where the human capital of the workforce is factor of production alongside the

43

capital stock of the economy. In the most simple version of this model, the skill level (human capital) of the workforce will influence the current level of output in the economy but not the long-run growth potential of the economy. In this setting, incentives to acquire skills are simple to determine and without other market imperfections (such as credit or labour), Becker's (1962) analysis holds and the efficient amount of skill is acquired by the workers. Also in this setting workers only care about the wages they receive and thus the skill level of the workforce is irrelevant for individual returns given the wage rate per efficiency unit of labour.

We next move to consider the case of borrowing constraints on workers. As is well known in this case, underinvestment in skill can arise since workers will not be able to finance as much investment as they desire. However, we will argue that in this case too there are no obvious grounds for expecting the long-run performance of the economy to be affected by the initial skill level of the workforce and again, given the wage rate per efficiency unit of labour, workers do not care about the skill level of the workforce.

In Section 4, we will consider the case of labour market imperfections. This will be a simplified version of the models analysed in Acemoglu (1993a, 1993b). We will show that in this case there are natural reasons to expect long-run growth performance to be affected by skill differences, as we seem to observe in practice. Moreover, a worker in an economy with a highly skilled workforce will be better off and will in general have incentives to acquire further skills. The basic idea underlying this result is quite intuitive. When labour market imperfections are important, workers will be paid less than their marginal products; thus the more skilled workers are, the more profits the firms will make and also the more investment they will be willing to undertake. In turn the higher capital stock of the economy will benefit the workers who will want to invest more. This is an effect sometimes referred to by economists as strategic complementarities (e.g. Cooper and John (1988)): each agent would like to invest more when others do so. The implication of such strategic complementarities is that a multiplicity of equilibria may exist; the economy can have an equilibrium in which investment and skill levels are high while a low-activity 'trap' with low investment, low skills and low productivity is also possible.

Section 5 of the paper discusses how institutional arrangements become important in the presence of imperfections in the capital and labour markets. Section 6 concludes with a heuristic evaluation of the models presented in Sections 2, 3 and 4.

2   Investment in skills with complete markets

2.1   A static model

We would like to construct a simple model which includes investment in skills on the part of workers and investment in physical capital on the part of firms. Such a model will first be used to illustrate how these decisions are taken in the absence of any missing markets and will later enable us to introduce some imperfections and study their impact. We will try to emphasize as much as possible the following questions raised in the introduction:

(i) whether the model at hand can explain the cross-country correlation between growth and human capital variables, as found by Barro (1991), and others that countries with higher school enrolment rates grow faster;

(ii) whether initial skill differences introduce growth effects, in other words whether skill gaps matter;

(iii) whether externalities are important in the human capital accumulation process;

(iv) if such externalities exist, how they interact with the investment decisions of firms.

Let us consider the following simple economy that lasts for two periods $(t=0,1)$. This economy consists of a large number of competitive firms and workers. For convenience we will think of a continuum of firms and workers normalized to 1.[1] In period $t=0$, each worker chooses the level of his human capital, h, and incurs costs $c(h)$ in date $t=1$ money where $c(.)$ is a non-negative increasing and convex function. Also each firm chooses the level of its capital stock, k, and each unit of capital is assumed to cost, r, again in date $t=1$ money. At $t=1$, firms and workers come together and produce the final consumption good of this economy according to the constant returns to scale production function, $F(H,k)$, where H is the sum of the human capital of the workers employed by the firm in question. Thus H (or h) should be thought of as efficiency units of capital and is also referred to as the skill level of the workforce.

As human capital investment decisions are made before workers are employed it can best be thought of as education. We are also assuming that the education that workers obtain is perfectly general, in other words, it can be used with the same degree of efficiency in all firms. This is an assumption that we will maintain throughout the chapter because the interaction of firm-specific and general human capital investments introduces more difficult (albeit also very interesting) issues that are not central to this chapter (see Chapter 2 in this volume).

Returning to our analysis, physical and human capital investments will obviously be guided by the maximizing motives of the firms and the workers. Firms will invest so as to maximize their expected profit at $t = 1$ and workers will choose a level of human capital that will maximize their income. Wages in the $t = 1$ labour market will determine the income of the workers and the profits of the firms. Hence investment decisions of these agents will crucially depend on the expected wages and thus on the organization of the labour market at $t = 1$ and the constraints that firms and workers face at $t = 0$.

We start by assuming that all agents in this economy have access to perfect borrowing opportunities so that workers and firms face no constraints at $t = 0$. We also assume that the labour market is competitive at $t = 1$ implying that a wage rate per efficiency unit of capital will be determined as a result of competition among firms and workers.

Competitive labour market clearing obviously requires the marginal product of labour to be equal to the (real) wage rate. Therefore

$$F_1(H^e, k^e) = w \tag{1}$$

where subscripts denote derivative with respect to the first argument and superscript e is used to emphasize that we are referring to an equilibrium value. Knowing this, in the period $t = 0$ each firm will maximize its profit, i.e. the value of output minus labour and capital costs. Thus

$$F(H^e, k) - rk - wH^e \tag{2}$$

will be maximized with respect to k. This maximization problem will yield the following first-order condition

$$F_2(H^e, k^e) = r \tag{3}$$

which tells us that investment will be carried out up to the point where the marginal productivity of capital is equal to the cost of capital.

Finally workers will maximize the difference between their period 1 income and period 0 cost.

$$\max_{h} \ wh - c(h) \tag{4}$$

which yields, $w = c'(h^e)$, i.e the marginal return from human capital investment is equal to marginal cost. As the measure of workers is normalized to 1, we also obtain

$$w = c'(H^e). \tag{5}$$

This equilibrium outcome can easily be seen to coincide with the social optimum. Informally, workers invest in human capital up to the point where the marginal benefit from doing so, $F_1(H^*,k^*)$, is equal to the cost, $c'(H^*)$, and firms set the cost of capital equal to the marginal productivity of investment. Formally we can set a social maximization problem where the planner maximizes the net surplus of the economy,

$$F(H,k) - rk - c(H) \tag{6}$$

with respect to the two-choice variables, H and k. This maximization problem yields the following first-order conditions:

$$F_2(H^*,k^*) = r \tag{7}$$
$$F_1(H^*,k^*) = c'(H^*) \tag{8}$$

which coincide with the marginal conditions of the competitive equilibrium and hence the social optimum (H^*,k^*) coincides with (H^e,k^e). This result is hardly surprising since in the presence of complete markets, no externalities exist and the competitive outcome is Pareto-optimal. Since no externalities exist in this economy, we would also expect the profitability of investments and the growth rate to be independent of the skill level of the workforce and the human capital accumulation decision of agents to be independent of each other. Both of these conjectures are correct. As firms are paying the marginal product for each efficiency unit of labour, variations skill level of the workforce around (H^e,k^e) have zero impact on profits. To see this, consider the profits of a representative firm and differentiate it with respect to H. However, as $F_1(H^e,k^e) = w$, an increase in H around H^e will have no effect on profits. This illustrates a more general phenomenon that when firms pay the marginal valuation for the human capital of workers, they will be indifferent to the skill level of the workforce. Only when they are receiving rents from hiring skilled workers that an increase in the skill-level of the workforce will have a first-order effect on the profits of these firms.

Similarly also note that each worker is a wage taker and thus does not care about the human capital accumulation decisions of other workers. Thus given the wage rate, his welfare and investment decisions are independent of the behaviour of other agents in the economy. Therefore strategic complementarities do not exist in the sense of Cooper and John and a multiplicity of Pareto-ranked equilibria is not possible. To explain this argument we give a heuristic definition of strategic complementarity. We say that strategic complementarities exist, if each agent wishes to increase his investment when the investment level of other agents is increased. The presence of this type of interaction implies that each agent may be happy to choose a low level of investment when the aggregate level of investment in the economy is low, thus giving us a 'low-activity equilibrium'. However, when aggregate investment is high, he too would like to invest more. As the same incentives would be true for all other agents, there may also exist an equilibrium in which all agents choose a higher level of investment. As positive externalities are key to this type of interaction, all these equilibria will in general entail under-investment and the high investment equilibrium will Pareto-dominate the low-activity one. In contrast when strategic complementarities are not present, a multiplicity of Pareto-ranked equilibria is not possible since, when aggregate investment is increased, each agent still would like to choose the same (or lower) investment level and a second equilibrium with everyone choosing a higher level of investment cannot exist. Therefore, since there exist no externalities in this model, agents do not care about others' human capital investments and Pareto-ranked multiple equilibria are not possible.

Returning to the questions we wished to answer, we have not touched upon whether the competitive model is consistent with our 'stylized fact', the cross-country relationship between the stock of human capital and growth performance. We can intuitively answer this question by noting that an exogenous increase in F_1 will lead to higher wages and thus to higher stock of human capital and also to higher output. Thus the cross-country correlation between human capital variables and growth may be due to variations in the productivity of human capital in different countries. In the next section we present the complete markets endogenous growth model of Rebelo (1991), to show how differences in the marginal productivity of and the cost of acquiring human capital get translated into growth effects and can thus account for our 'stylized fact'.

2.2   A glance at a linear endogenous growth model with human and physical capital

In this section we briefly summarize the results of Rebelo (1991) which can be viewed as a closed-dynamic version of the above model. This model will serve two purposes; first, it will demonstrate that the competitive economy can account for the importance of human capital in cross-country growth regressions and second it will act as a benchmark to show how capital and labour market distortions can lead to sub-optimal growth rates.

Instead of one-off production, Rebelo's economy continues infinitely in continuous time. It may be useful to think of each instant still consisting of two parts; first investment decisions and then production. An important difference between the two models is that, in order to have a simple exposition of the main ideas, we assumed the investment costs of human and physical capital to be exogenous. More generally we expect the cost of investment to be the opportunity cost of not putting resources to an alternative use, most commonly consumption. Thus Rebelo's model starts with a utility function for the representative agent of this economy defined over final consumption (no labour supply decisions are considered):

$$Utility = \int\limits_{0}^{\infty} e^{\rho t} \frac{C(t)^{1-\sigma}}{1-\sigma} \, dt \qquad (9)$$

Thus the representative agent of this economy obtains utility from the flow of consumption and future consumptions are discounted at the rate ρ. The aggregate production function exhibits constant returns to scale and is given by

$$Y(t) = A_1(\phi(t)K(t))^{1-\gamma}(n(t)H(t))^{\gamma} \qquad (10)$$

where $\phi(t)$ is the share of capital and $n(t)$ is the proportion of efficiency units of labour (or of the total skill of the workforce) allocated to the production of the consumption good at time t. Note that instead of labour as in standard static production functions, $H(t)$, the efficiency units of labour which depends on the skill level of the workforce enters the utility function. All the final good that is produced in this economy has to be consumed or invested thus $Y(t) = I(t) + C(t)$ and capital depreciates at the rate δ, hence $K'(t) = I(t) - \delta K(t)$, where a prime denotes a time derivative.

Human capital production takes place according to a constant returns Cobb–Douglas production function and depreciates at the rate δ. Hence

$$H'(t) = A_2[K(t)(1 - \phi(t))]^{1-\psi}[(1 - n(t))H(t)]^{\psi} - \delta H(t) \qquad (11)$$

This equation implies that if the economy now forgoes the production of consumption good, it can increase its skill level (i.e. invest in skill), thus produce more in the future.

The steady-state equilibrium of this economy can be found by referring to the 'social planning' problem, since, as we saw in the previous section, there are no externalities and both workers and firms receive their marginal products. As the derivation of the dynamic equilibrium of this economy is long, we refer the reader to Rebelo and just write the final result that, along the balanced growth path, output grows at the rate

$$g_y = \frac{\Gamma A_1^{\nu} A_2^{1-\nu} - \delta - \rho}{\sigma} \qquad (12)$$

where Γ is a strictly positive parameter and $\nu = (1 - \psi)/(1 - \psi + \gamma)$. Thus this economy, that exhibits neither any increasing returns nor externalities, experiences sustained endogenous growth. It can also be seen that the growth rate of this economy is a function of the productivity of both human and physical capital. Now returning to our stylized fact, does the observation that countries with higher human capital stock grow faster imply that an intertemporal externality exists? The answer is, not necessarily. Suppose countries differ in the productivity of their human capital accumulation, i.e. let each country have a different A_2. Those countries with higher A_2 will accumulate more human capital and grow faster. However there is no causal link from the high stock of human capital to faster growth. Similarly differences in A_1 will also be translated into differences in human and physical capital accumulation decisions and long-run growth rates. Further, Barro's (1991) results and others in the literature find the school enrolment rate as the most significant human capital variable. This variable can be interpreted as human capital investment and even when all countries have the same technology but are away from their steady-state income levels, they will have different levels of human capital investment and growth rates which can potentially explain the cross-country evidence.[2] Finally, Rebelo also shows that differences in taxation policy will also have an impact on long-run growth rates and different growth performances can also be explained by differences in policy across countries (though there is little support for such a hypothesis, see Levine and Zervos (1993)). Yet we have to bear in mind that although this model can account for the cross-sectional correlation between the stock of human capital variables and long-run growth rates, it does not generate growth effects from differences in the stock of human capital. In the light of this feature of the model, it may be argued not to account well for micro-econometric evidence, as in Haskel and Martin (1993; and Chapter 8 of this volume) who show that skill shortages lead to slower productivity growth. The presence of skill shortages and their impact on productivity growth are both inconsistent with a simple reading of the competitive model. A further empirical result that is difficult to explain with a complete market model is that of Borjas (1992) who investigates the determinants of human capital for individuals and finds that a measure of the past levels of human capital of the ethnic group to which the individual belongs correlates with higher levels of human capital investment for individuals. This suggests that the return to skills increases if other agents are more skilled. Also a number of studies show how the stock of knowledge in different dimensions is a determinant of investment in physical capital (and also growth), for instance Scherer (1982), Lach and Schankerman (1989), Benhabib and Jovanovic (1991). Although these results can be interpreted in different ways, they are suggestive of the presence of certain externalities.

3   Investment in skills with capital market constraints

Capital market imperfections are often suggested to be at the root of market failures in human capital accumulation. This obviously related to the famous result due to Becker (1962) that workers should bear the full cost of their investments in general human capital. However, if these workers cannot borrow in order to carry out their desired investment, under-investment and inefficiencies will arise.

Consider the static model of the last section but assume that at $t=0$ workers are unable to borrow. As a result, each worker can only spend his initial endowment.[3] This is a very crude form of borrowing constraint which we adopt to avoid complications. However, for support we can draw upon a large literature that analyses how asymmetric information and moral hazard can lead to equilibrium credit rationing in static and dynamic contexts (for instance Leland and Pyle (1977), Stiglitz and Weiss

(1981) and Banerjee and Newman (1991), to name a few). Let us denote the initial endowment of worker i by y_i and let the distribution of y_i be given by $g(y)$. Each worker would ideally like to purchase h^* such that $c'(h^*) = w$, i.e. set the marginal return of an additional unit of human capital equal to the marginal cost as in the last section. If $y \geq c(h^*)$, then the worker's endowment is larger than the cost of education and he can choose $h_i = h^*$. But otherwise, the worker will be liquidity constrained and can only spend his wealth to purchase human capital, thus $c(h_i) = y_i$ or equivalently $h_i = c^{-1}(y_i)$. Provided that some of the workers are liquidity constrained (i.e. are not wealthy enough), we will get a distribution of human capital levels across workers. This distribution will obviously depend on the distribution of wealth, $g(.)$, but it will also vary as we change the wage per efficiency unit of labour. Let us denote this distribution of human capital levels across workers by $g^h(h,w)$.

Labour market clearing at $t = 1$ again requires that the marginal product of labour at $t = 1$ equals the wage rate. However, the marginal product of labour needs to be evaluated at the total stock of human capital inherited from $t = 0$, which we denote by H_0. Thus H_0 is defined as

$$H_0 = \int h_i g^h(h_i, w) \, di \tag{13}$$

In words, H_0 is the sum of the human capital of all the workers. As the labour market is competitive, we once again require the marginal product of labour to be equal to the wage rate, thus

$$F_1(H_0, k^e) = w \tag{14}$$

Investment decisions are once again chosen to maximize profits, yielding

$$F_2(H_0, k^e) = r \tag{15}$$

Equilibrium will be given by a distribution function g^h, a wage rate and an investment level for each firm. As all firms are identical they will all choose the same investment level but this is obviously not true for workers who are constrained by their different levels of wealth at $t = 0$. We can immediately see that this economy will generically under-invest in human capital because of the missing credit markets. Also as human and physical capital are complements in production, i.e. $F_{12} > 0$, the lower stock of human capital (compared to the first-best) will imply a lower marginal productivity of capital and thus lead to lower investment in physical capital than would have been the case without the capital market imperfection. This same mechanism also implies that economies with low skill levels will invest less and thus tend to have a lower growth rate. Thus the skills gap may matter if capital market imperfections are important. This result is, of course, not surprising; liquidity constraints lead to under-investment in skills and the greater is the extent of this under-investment, the worse is the impact on economic performance. Also, as a result, this simple model is capable of explaining the correlation between the long-run growth rates and human capital variables through a different route; economies with less severe capital constraints or more favourable wealth distributions will invest more in human capital and thus possess a more skilled workforce (i.e. higher H_0). This will increase product per worker and also increase the marginal productivity of capital, thus leading to higher investment. Additionally, a dynamic version of this model will include important long-run interactions between income levels and distribution on the one hand and investment in human capital on the other. An increase in the skill level will not only lead to higher investment in the present but to higher skill and investment levels in the future too. This is because, when skill levels are higher, output will be higher and the wealth of the workers will rise, thus making capital constraints less binding.[4]

However, note that, although these imperfections may lead to slower growth, they do not distort the physical capital investments since firms are not credit constrained and thus investment is carried out up to the point where the marginal benefit is equal to the marginal cost. Further, under-investment in skill by workers has no first-order welfare impact on other workers and firms in the economy. To see this, consider the profit of a representative firm given by

$$F(H_0, k^e) - wH_0 - rk^e \tag{16}$$

A change in H_0 has no effect on this expression, as can be seen by differentiating it with respect to H_0. This is because wages are still set equal to the marginal product of labour. Also given the wage rate, workers do not care about others' human capital. Thus, although there is under-investment and the economy may be growing too slowly, agents do not care about each other's actions; there are no strategic complementarities and a multiplicity of equilibria is not possible in this model.

4   Human capital accumulation with ex post bargaining over wages

In this section we investigate another possible market imperfection that may affect human capital accumulation: non-competitive wage determination. We assume that the capital market is perfect at $t=0$ but the labour market at $t=1$ is no longer competitive. Instead, workers are matched with firms and bargain over the distribution of the ex post surplus (see Diamond (1982) and Pissarides (1985)). Let us assume for simplicity that the number of firms and workers is equal and each firm is always matched with one worker.[5] This assumption implies that there is no risk of unemployment for workers and of unfilled vacancies for firms. We will look for a 'symmetric equilibrium' of this economy; thus all workers will have the same skill level and wages across firms will be equal.

We take the simplest form of wage determination in which both the firm and the worker are supposed to have zero outside options and thus share the ex post surplus. The ex post surplus is what the firm and the worker can produce together and is therefore equal to the total output, $F(h,k)$. We also denote the workers' share by β and hence that of the firm is $1 - \beta$. At $t=0$ each worker will maximize

$$\beta F(h, k^{e}) - c(h) \tag{17}$$

which yields

$$\beta F_{1}(h^{e}, k^{e} = c'(h^{e}) \tag{18}$$

Compared to the competitive economy (and the first-best, see equation (8)), there are insufficient incentives to accumulate human capital. Similarly, the first-order condition for accumulation of physical capital now becomes

$$(1 - \beta)F_{2}(h^{e}, k^{e}) = r \tag{19}$$

and there is also under-investment in physical capital driven by the same labour market imperfections (compare this equation with (3)). Further note that changes in β improve the investment incentives of one side while deteriorating that of the other.

Again if this example is closed in a dynamic equilibrium framework, there will be sub-optimally low growth because of under-investment in both physical and human capital. Returning to the inter- and intra-temporal externalities, we can see that both of these externalities are now present. Firstly, the profit a representative firm is given by

$$(1 - \beta)F(h,k) - rk \tag{20}$$

An increase in h has a first-order effect on profits. Also as F_{12} is positive, a higher stock of human capital increases the marginal product of capital and leads to higher investment and to higher growth. Thus our stylized fact can be explained by the presence of bargaining instead of competitive wage determination in the labour market.

Secondly, intra-temporal externalities are present in this case: when H is higher, firms make more profits but also invest more, as argued in the previous paragraph. This higher investment increases $\beta F(h, k^e)$ and as a result, workers are better off too. Moreover, this externality does not only affect the welfare of workers but also their optimal investment decisions. As k^e increases, the marginal product of human capital, $F_1(h, k^e)$ increases, owing to the positivity of F_{12}. Hence in the terminology that we have used so far, there exist strategic complementarities. In turn higher human capital investment by workers leads to an increase in the marginal product of capital and hence firms invest more. A multiplicity of equilibria is therefore possible. This possibility also suggests another explanation for the cross-country correlation between growth and human capital. Even if different countries have similar technologies and institutions but have ended up in different equilibria because of historical reasons,[6] those in the favourable (Pareto-superior) equilibrium will have invested more in human capital and will also be growing faster.

5   The importance of institutions in human capital investments

The models presented in Sections 3 and 4 involve substantial imperfections compared to the first-best world and hence the role of institutions, which govern exchanges among agents, becomes a key issue. Consequently these models enable us to talk about the importance of institutions, such as the organization of the credit and the labour market ownership structure, in the determination of investment in skills and growth. Most of the growth literature ignores institutional considerations, both because of the difficulty of obtaining any measure of their quantitative importance and because of the highly aggregative nature of the models often used. However, the related literature of economic development lays special emphasis on the importance of institutions.

Ideally we would like to understand how different institutions affect growth performance and also how they endogenously evolve over time. This is a very challenging task to which this chapter has little to contribute. However, the analysis of the past sections gives a simple example of how different institutions may affect incentives to accumulate human capital and thus form a link between the institutional setting and growth. The issue emphasized by the model in Section 2 is the importance of the credit market. A more developed credit market that leads to less severe borrowing constraints will ensure better investment in skills and higher growth. Similarly, in an economy with higher wealth or more equal wealth distribution, workers will require less from the credit market and will also have higher collateral values, leading to more investment and growth.

Two institutional issues are also raised by the model of the previous section. The first is the importance of allocation of property rights and the second is the organization of the labour market. Rather than analyse these issues fully, we will simply suggest some interesting avenues suggested by our model. Starting with the first of these points, we know from Grossman and Hart (1986) and Hart and Moore (1989), that the allocation of property rights and residual rights of control can be very important in determining effort and investment decisions in the presence of contractual incompleteness and how this can in turn endogenize property rights. The general principle is that agents will have better investment incentives when they are the residual claimants of the returns generated by their actions. Thus the allocation of property rights over human and physical assets will have an important role to play in determining investment incentives. Similar principles can be applied in this context. Firstly, suppose that the entrepreneur of the firm has no specific know-how that is essential for the firm; in this case we can transfer the ownership of the firm to the worker.[7] The worker, knowing that he will be the residual claimant, makes the human and physical investment decisions. This would obviously restore the first-best in this model. However, we can seldom plausibly assume that both types of investments can be carried out by the same party. Firms are separate entities and each has its entrepreneur, managers and organizational forms. Managers need to study the market and choose the correct investment areas and strategies. In the case where human and physical capital investments have to be carried out by two different parties, first-best cannot be achieved, although welfare can still be improved by some reallocation of property rights. For instance, suppose that β is very close to zero so that workers choose a very low level of human capital. A regulation that gives the worker a share of the profits of the firm will increase β, and therefore, investments in human capital and welfare will rise. The criticism that the market should be able to achieve such beneficial organizational change without intervention is not as strong in this case since at date $t = 0$, it is not known which workers will be matched with which firms and hence such a reallocation of residual claims cannot easily be accomplished without government intervention.[8]

Now let us return to the organization of the labour market. First note that we have previously assumed the outside options of both sides to be equal to zero. In general, breaking a match and looking for a partner is costly but still provides a positive outside option. In the presence of outside options, equations (18) and (19) of the previous section can be written as

$$\beta F_1(h^e, k^e) + (1 - \beta) R_W = c'(h^e) \tag{21}$$
$$(1 - \beta) F_2(h^e, k^e) + \beta R_F = r \tag{22}$$

where R_W denotes the marginal outside option of the worker as he changes the level of his human capital and R_F is the marginal outside option of the firm as the capital stock of the firm varies.[9] Recall now the benchmark competitive labour market without mobility costs in which workers and firms can get their marginal product from other partners in the market and therefore their marginal outside options are equal to their marginal products. However, if the labour market is not competitive, a worker who disagrees with his firm will not be able obtain his full marginal product and R_W will be less than $F_1(h, k^e)$. Thus as the outside options increase towards the relevant marginal product, the market becomes more competitive and investment incentives approach their first-best values. This implies that measures that increase mobility and reduce hiring/firing costs will lead to better investment incentives. This observation may at first sight appear at odds with some facts. Germany and Japan have more regulated labour markets than the UK and the USA but seem to provide better skills. To think about this question, consider the case of training where a worker obtains skills while he is employed. If the worker is likely to quit his job soon and be employed by a new firm, our analysis above will apply and there will be under-investment in skills. However, if the employment relation between the worker and his employer is long-term as in Japan and Germany, the above problem will not arise and the right level of skills will be provided (see Acemoglu (1993a) for details) which nicely fits the effects emphasized in this chapter.

Finally, β which is a measure of the bargaining power of the workers, plays a crucial role. If the level of human capital investment is too low, welfare may improve when workers' bargaining power increases. Therefore, measures that alter the relative bargaining strength of firms and workers need to be carefully evaluated, taking into account their impact on ex ante investment incentives. In particular the trade-off, that a reallocation of bargaining power from one party to the other will increase the ex ante incentives of one party while reducing the investment of the other side, should be borne in mind. Further, although it may sometimes be beneficial to increase the bargaining power of the workers, it does not follow from this analysis that the introduction of unions is beneficial, even when β is close to zero. This is because, in general, unions do not only change the bargaining power of the workers but also reduce mobility, which we know is detrimental for investment incentives.

6   Comparison of different models and policy implications

In Section 2 we presented a benchmark model with complete markets and no externalities. Two assumptions that underpinned this model were perfect capital and labour markets. Sections 3 and 4 respectively relaxed each of these assumptions and Section 5 discussed how institutional considerations could become important when we allow for such imperfections. We have also shown that all three models are capable of explaining Barro's (1991) finding that countries with higher stock of human capital tend to grow faster. However, these three models have radically different policy implications. The competitive model obviously implies that decentralized choices are optimal and that there should be no policy intervention. On the other hand the models of Sections 3 and 4 suggest under-investment in skills is an important problem and that the government could be able to intervene and correct this market failure. However, the exact policy implications of the two models are quite different.

The best government policy in the model with capital constraints would be to provide finance for those who want to invest further in their skills. This can be in the form of education and training vouchers or a loan scheme administered by the government. The model also implies that the government should not subsidize firms' investment (as they are choosing the optimal level of investment)[10] and should not intervene with the labour market. Subsidizing investment in skills is not a good idea either. Although such a subsidy will improve the investment levels of those workers who are constrained, it would also make those who are not liquidity constrained over-invest in skills.

In contrast, the policy conclusions are rather different if we believe that the main imperfection lies in the labour market. Firstly, intervention in the labour market that reduces the wedge between the real wage rate and the marginal product of labour would often be beneficial. Secondly, as there is under-investment both in human and physical capital, both types of investment need to be subsidized. Moreover, the economy may get stuck in a 'low-activity' equilibrium which would constitute a challenging problem for the government. In a dynamic setting switches from one equilibrium will seldom be possible; so the government needs to choose policy so as to gradually improve the dynamic path of such an economy. Finally, policies such as vouchers and loan schemes, that were promising in the presence of capital market imperfections only, will obviously have no effect here unless they reduce the cost of investment.

This discussion suggests that it is important to determine whether a market failure exists in human capital investment and if so what its main source is. Here we will just make some suggestive observations that favour a model with a non-competitive labour market. First, all three models can explain the cross-country correlation between human capital variables and growth performance. However, the complete markets model can do this by assuming that technology is different across countries. This is not a thoroughly satisfactory explanation because we then need to investigate why technologies have such marked differences. Presumably technology is a convenient way of summarizing the know-how of the society. If a country has more favourable technology, we should expect other countries to imitate this more successful know-how, at least in the long-run. In contrast the second model can explain our 'stylized fact' by appealing to different degrees of borrowing constraints in different countries or different initial wealth distributions. Those countries that have severe capital constraints will be unable to invest much in human capital and will have low human capital combined with low growth. Alternatively, in economies that are richer and have more equal wealth distribution, there will be less need to borrow, thus enabling higher human capital accumulation and growth. Although this explanation is theoretically quite satisfactory, it predicts that richer economies and those with lower lending interest rates should grow faster. In Barro's regressions we see that richer countries on the whole tend to grow more slowly and interest rate variables do not seem to affect growth.[11]

Finally the third model can explain our 'stylized fact' in a variety of ways. Firstly, economies have different institutional structures and in

Section 5 we saw how these institutional differences can be translated into differences in growth performance. For instance a more rigid labour market will lead to worse investment incentives for both firms and workers. Also, property rights are distributed differently and this can impact upon the growth performance of these economies. The second explanation, on the other hand, draws upon the possibility of multiplicity. Economies with similar technologies and institutions may still exhibit radically different activity levels. In a dynamic model this can be due to some historical accidents that puts two similar economies onto different dynamic growth paths or due to the differences in initial stock of human and physical capital (see Matsuyama (1991) and Krugman (1991); this also provides an additional and perhaps more potent link between initial skill levels and long-run growth).

The next test for these models may be to investigate whether they are consistent with other empirical evidence bearing on this topic. We have already noted Haskel and Martin's finding (1993; and Chapter 8 of this volume (see also references therein)) that skill shortages have an important negative influence on productivity growth. However, only the third story is consistent with this finding because the first two models, by virtue of assuming labour market clearing, are not at ease with the presence and importance of skill shortages; there can only be a shortage if the wage rate is not equal to the marginal product of labour. The micro-econometric evidence due to Borjas (1992), which was mentioned above, also suggests that externalities can be important. As there is a statistically significant relationship between the aggregate human capital level of a group and its members' investment decisions, strategic complementarities are likely to be present. Again, strategic complementarities are only consistent with the third story since with complete markets no externalities exist, and with only capital market imperfections there is under-investment but no strategic complementarities.

Therefore our heuristic evaluation suggests that externalities are important and mostly related to labour market imperfections. This does not, of course, imply that capital market imperfections do not matter. Rather it suggests that capital market imperfections alone are unlikely to be the whole story. We can therefore tentatively conclude that there exist substantial market failures related to labour market imperfections (and probably, to capital market imperfections) and there will generally be under-investment both in human and physical capital. This implies that government policy on training, education and labour markets should take into account the possible effects it may have on investment in skill and physical capital.

NOTES

Paper prepared for the 'Skills Gap and Economic Activity' organized by CEPR, London 19–20 April 1993. I am grateful to Alison Booth, Andrew Scott and Dennis Snower for helpful comments.

1 This is not a restrictive assumption as it only entails a simple re-scaling and enables us to ignore aggregation across firms and workers which is straightforward owing to the constant returns to scale assumption we make.
2 However, recent work by Barro indicates that better measures of the stock of human capital are also important in these regressions.
3 We are setting period 0 consumption equal to zero.
4 See, for example, Galor and Zeira (1993) who also show that multiplicity of steady-state equilibria is possible when credit market imperfections are combined with a non-convex aggregate technology. In general, endogeneity of wage and interest rates can also lead to multiplicity as in Banerjee and Newman (1993).
5 If we allow for the possibility of unemployment we can get interesting interactions between unemployment and growth as in Acemoglu (1993a, 1993b).
6 The possibility of multiple equilibria in a dynamic context does not necessarily imply indeterminacy of equilibrium paths. In other words, an economy that ends up with the unfavourable equilibrium may be unable to jump back onto a favourable equilibrium even if the expectations of agents change significantly (see Matsuyama (1991) and Krugman (1991)).
7 Naturally it should also be asked why the market does not accomplish this without intervention and why therefore we do not observe labour hiring capital. The answer is most likely to be that entrepreneurs do have skills that are essential to the firm.
8 Also we observe profit-sharing in the real world which may be viewed as a way of achieving such a reallocation of residual claim rights.
9 In other words, R_W is the derivative of the worker's outside option with respect to h and R_F is similarly defined. We have also assumed the cross derivatives to be negligible.
10 However, second-best policy may require such intervention.
11 It should, however, be borne in mind that the degree of borrowing constraints may not be reflected by the interest rate; Zilibotti (1994) finds the wedge between the lending and the borrowing rate to be a significant determinant of growth rates. Also the evidence of Persson and Tabellini (1994) that equity is positively correlated with growth rates is also consistent with this model.

REFERENCES

Acemoglu, D. (1993a), 'Training and Innovation in an Imperfect Labour Market', MIT Working Paper.
    (1993b), 'Search in the Labour Market, Incomplete Contracts and Growth', MIT mimeo.
Banerjee, A. and A. Newman (1991), 'Risk-Bearing and the Theory of Income Distribution', *Review of Economic Studies* **58**, 211–35.

(1993), 'Occupational Choice and the Process of Development', *Journal of Political Economy* **101**, 274–98.

Barro, R. J. (1991), 'Economic Growth in a Cross Section of Countries', *Quarterly Journal of Economics* **106**, 407–44.

Becker, G. (1962), *Human Capital*, New York: Columbia University Press.

Benhabib, J. and B. Jovanovic (1991), 'Externalities and Growth Accounting', *American Economic Review* **81**, 82–113.

Borjas, G. (1992), 'Ethnic Capital and Intergenerational Mobility', *Quarterly Journal of Economics* **108**, 123–50.

Cooper, R. and A. John (1988), 'Coordinating Coordination Failures in Keynesian Models', *Quarterly Journal of Economics* **102**, 703–35.

Diamond, P. (1982), 'Wage Determination and Efficiency in Search Equilibrium', *Review of Economic Studies* **49**, 217–27.

Galor, O. and J. Zeira (1993), 'Income Distribution and Macroeconomics', *Review of Economic Studies* **60**, 35–52.

Grossman, S. and O. Hart (1986), 'The Costs and Benefits of Ownership: A Theory of Vertical and Lateral Integration', *Journal of Political Economy* **94**, 691–719.

Hart, O. and J. Moore (1989), 'Property Rights and the Theory of the Firm', *Journal of Political Economy* **96**, 205–76.

Haskel, J. and C. Martin (1993), 'Do Skill Shortages Reduce Productivity? Theory and Evidence from UK', *Economic Journal* **103**, 386–94.

Krugman, P. (1991), 'History versus Expectations', *Quarterly Journal of Economics* **106**, 617–51.

Lach, S. and M. Schankerman (1989), 'Dynamics of R&D and Investment in Scientific Sector', *Journal of Political Economy* **97**, 880–904.

Leland, D. and D. Pyle (1977), 'Informational Asymmetries, Financial Structure and Financial Intermediation', *Journal of Finance* **32**, 371–88.

Levine, R. and S. Zervos (1993), 'What Have We Learned about Policy and Growth from Cross-country Regressions', *American Economic Review, Papers and Proceedings* **83**, 426–30.

Lucas, R. E. (1988), 'On the Mechanics of Economic Development', *Journal of Monetary Economics* **22**, 3–42.

Matsuyama, K. (1991), 'Increasing Returns, Industrialization, and Indeterminacy of Equilibrium', *Quarterly Journal of Economics* **106**, 651–67.

Mokyr, J. (1990), *The Levers of the Riches: Technological Creativity and Economics Progress*, Oxford: Oxford University Press.

Persson, T. and G. Tabellini (1994), 'Is Inequality Harmful to Growth', *American Economic Review* **84**, 600–21.

Pissarides, C. (1985), 'Short Run Equilibrium Dynamics of Unemployment, Vacancies and Real Wages', *American Economic Review* **75**, 676–90.

Rebelo, S. (1991), 'Long Run Policy Analysis and Long Run Growth', *Journal of Political Economy* **99**, 500–21.

Scherer, F. M. (1982), 'Inter-industry Technology Flows and Productivity Growth', *Review of Economics and Statistics* **64**, 627–34.

Stiglitz, J. and A. Weiss (1981), 'Credit Rationing in Markets with Imperfect Information', *American Economic Review* **71**, 393–410.

Zilibotti, F. (1994), 'Economic Growth and Intermediation in an "Archipelago" Economy', *Economic Journal* **104**, 462–73.

4 Education and matching externalities

As noted in the Introduction (Chapter 1), the free market fails to provide adequate incentives for training when the people who pay for the training cannot appropriate all the resulting benefits. This chapter shows that when workers who want jobs are not certain of getting job offers and when firms with vacancies are not certain of getting job applicants, a person who acquires training confers benefits on those who do not have to bear the training expenses. In particular, the more workers acquire training, the faster firms can expect to attract skilled workers and the more favourable will their outside opportunities in wage negotiations be (specifically, the lower the wage the firm can expect to achieve with potential substitutes for the skilled workers they are currently negotiating with). This raises firms' market power in wage negotiations and reduces workers' returns from training. The resulting 'matching externality' can lead to under-investment in skills.

Education and matching externalities

KENNETH BURDETT and ERIC SMITH

1   Introduction

Human capital theory provides a theory of the demand for education. This approach sets out a standard investment problem in which individuals acquire education until the expected returns from an additional year equal the expected costs; that is, investment in training depends upon the benefits from higher lifetime earnings arising from increased skill levels. Moreover, this approach allows us to calculate simple comparative statics. For example, if a subsidy reduces the cost of education, then holding all other prices constant, it is a well-known result that workers will want to become more educated.

Yet, while it is useful to understand the optimization problem of a single agent, it is also necessary to consider the subsequent interaction with the labour market. As well as considering how changes in costs of education affect demand, we must also analyse how the resulting change in the supply of educated or skilled workers affects the labour market equilibrium. Specifically, while it is straightforward that an increase in the education subsidy will lead to an increase in the number of skilled workers, we must also take into account the change in market wages and the associated returns to education.

This interdependence becomes more complicated when we recognize that the labour market is characterized by features not accounted for in the neoclassical paradigm. We live in a world where information is imperfect and costly; workers do not know the location of jobs and firms do not know the location of workers. Both parties must search for respective partners. Matching models address precisely these difficulties and provide a coherent framework for analysing their consequences.

However, these models raise additional questions about the operation of labour markets. Unlike the perfectly competitive framework in which workers and firms take the wage as given, matching models must consider the actual process of income determination. That is, given a firm and a worker contact each other and decide to form a match, they must then establish the income to be paid to the worker. The income negotiated will, of course, typically reflect not only the firm and the worker's outside options but also the worker's skill level. These skills levels are typically exogenous so that the worker's training decision is neglected.

This chapter bridges this gap incorporating both human capital decisions and the bargaining process in a search theoretic framework. We consider a matching model of the labour market where workers and firms bargain over the wage. We specify an exact set of bargaining rules and consider the equilibrium returns to education in such a market. In so doing, we present a coherent treatment of the simultaneous education, labour supply, and income determination processes. We further demonstrate how it can be used to illustrate the equilibrium consequences of policy changes.

2   An overview of the bargaining process and the education decision

Consider a market for (say) electricians in a particular town. Initially all the electricians are equally productive, but by going to night-school any electrician can take a course (at a cost) that makes him or her more productive. Suppose that a given percentage of electricians take this course. Call these electricians skilled workers, the others unskilled. Skilled workers perform the same tasks for firms as unskilled workers, but they produce a greater output per unit of time.

In this labour market for electricians, workers and firms have difficulty contacting each other. While it takes time to find employees and employers, the contact frequencies that each face are known to all. Hence firms face a certain arrival rate of skilled workers and an arrival rate of unskilled workers. Similarly, unskilled workers face a particular arrival rate of firms as do skilled workers.

When an unemployed electrician meets an employer they bargain over the wage to be paid (it is a non-union market). The wage they bargain will reflect in some way the outside opportunities faced by both parties which suggests that certain factors will clearly affect the negotiations. We identify seven such factors:

(1) The arrival rate of skilled workers faced by the firm.
(2) The wage the firm expects to bargain with another skilled worker, if one is contacted.

(3) The arrival rate of unskilled workers faced by the firm.
(4) The wage the firm expects to bargain with another unskilled worker, if one is contacted.
(5) The arrival rate of firms faced by the skilled worker.
(6) The wage the skilled worker expects to negotiate with another firm, if one is contacted.
(7) The difference in skill between skilled and unskilled workers.

Similar factors will influence bargaining between an unskilled worker and a firm.[1]

Given that the above factors play a role in the bargaining process, we now need to formally specify their precise roles. To do this, one has to clearly set out the rules of the bargaining process since different rules yield different results. We employ a particular set of bargaining rules which although not entirely realistic, provide a base from which to analyse the consequences of using a more complicated framework. Given this, we demonstrate how the expected wage bargained by a skilled worker (unskilled worker) depends upon the seven factors specified above. In this situation, the expected wages paid to the two types of workers depends in a very precise way, upon the arrival rates faced by all agents in the market as well as the productivities of the skilled and unskilled workers.

Moreover, although firms and workers take these arrival rates as parameters, they will depend on the number of workers relative to the number of firms participating in the market as well as the proportion of skilled workers. As pointed out in the introduction, the decision to acquire training and the decision to participate depends on the wages negotiated. Thus, while the individual bargainers take the negotiation environment as fixed, this environment is determined by the demand for education and the supply of labour.

Workers will take the course, become skilled and enter the labour market as long as the expected return to being a skilled worker equals the cost of enrolling in night-school. Unskilled workers will continue to enter or leave the labour market until the expected return to doing so is equal to the expected return they can obtain elsewhere. Thus, the supplies of skilled and unskilled labour adjust the relevant arrival rates until the wage differential equals the cost of becoming skilled. In *equilibrium* the proportions of skilled and unskilled workers adjust until the reservation wage determines the unskilled wage and the cost of training determines the skilled wage differential.

3   The model

Assume that when an employer hires a skilled worker the total expected discounted revenue from the match equals X. Hiring an unskilled worker, on the other hand, yields an expected discounted revenue equal to Y $(X > Y)$.

Given that the agents searching for an unemployed worker will, from time to time, contact a firm looking to hire a worker. Let α_w denote the arrival rate of such firms faced by an unemployed worker.[2] Therefore, $\alpha_w \, dt$ is the probability an unemployed worker contacts a firm in a small time interval dt. Similarly let α_f denote the arrival rate of unemployed workers faced by a firm that wishes to hire a worker.

For now let the number of firms, skilled workers (N_s) and unskilled (N_u) workers be fixed. The number of firms is normalized to one. Hence, we are envisaging a steady state such that when a worker and firm make a match and leave the market they are instantly replaced by an identical pair. Initially, the new firm and worker will be without a partner and will have to search for one.

Let the proportion of unemployed workers who are skilled be given by

$$\beta = N_s/(N_s + N_u) \tag{1}$$

Assuming that contacts are random, $\beta \alpha_f dt$ and $(1 - \beta)\alpha_f dt$ equal the respective probabilities that a firm contacts a skilled and unskilled worker during the interval dt. Once a firm employs a worker, both parties leave the market forever; there are no layoffs, or on-the-job search.

When an unemployed worker contacts a searching firm, the firm recognizes instantly whether the worker is skilled or not. They then bargain over the worker's income if they intend to form a match, or separate and continue to search for partners. Suppose for now they choose to bargain. How will they do it? Below the bargaining rules, which form the basis for much that follows, are specified in detail.

Bargaining rules

  (i) With probability one half of the firm makes a wage offer.
 (ii) The party receiving the offer can either accept or reject. If the offer is accepted, the worker immediately starts working for the firm.
(iii) If the offer is rejected, they must wait time interval dt for a new offer to be made according to (i).

(iv) During the time interval between offers, another unemployed worker may contact the firm, or another hiring firm may contact the worker.

(v) If the firm bargaining with a skilled worker contacts another skilled worker, it stops the ongoing negotiations and begins to bargain with the newly contacted worker.

(vi) If a skilled or unskilled worker bargaining with a firm contacts another firm, the ongoing negotiations are stopped and the worker begins to bargain with the newly contacted firm.

(vii) If the firm bargaining with a skilled worker contacts an unskilled worker, it continues to bargain with the skilled worker.

(viii) If the firm bargaining with an unskilled worker contacts another worker, then it stops ongoing negotiations and begins to bargain with the newly contacted worker, regardless of skill level.

Rule (i) appears at least as good as any other as we have little knowledge about who makes the offers in actual bargaining situations.[3] Rules (ii) and (iii) reflect the essential restriction that bargaining takes time. As all skilled workers, unskilled workers, and firms are essentially the same, restrictions (v) and (vi) appear harmless. It will be shown that in equilibrium (v) and (vi) are indeed compatible with optimal behaviour. Restrictions (vii) and (viii) are only reasonable if a firm's expected return to hiring a skilled worker is at least as great as that from hiring an unskilled worker. In the appendix, we show that this restriction holds in equilibrium.

The agents face a stationary environment, and so the expected outcome of the negotiations between a firm and a skilled worker (unskilled worker) remains constant through time. Let EW_s (EW_u) denote a skilled (unskilled) worker's maximum expected discounted lifetime income when bargaining begins. This implies a firm's expected return when bargaining begins with a skilled worker is $X - EW_s$ and $Y - EW_u$ with an unskilled worker. Let r be the instantaneous discount rate.

Consider first a firm that wants to contact an unemployed worker. Then, the firm's maximum discounted expected profit when looking for a worker is

$$U_f = [1/(1 + r\,dt)]\{\alpha_f\,dt[\beta E_{max}\{U_f, X - EW_s\} \\ + (1 - \beta)E_{max}\{U_f, Y - EW_u\}] + (1 - \alpha_f\,dt)U_f\} \qquad (2)$$

where $E_{max}\{a,b\}$ is the expected value of the maximum of a, b.

If the firm chooses to continue searching, then the expected benefits next period are discounted by $1/(1 + r\,dt)$. With probability $\beta\alpha_f\,dt$, the firm enters bargaining with a skilled worker which results in U_f if the match is rejected, and $X - EW_s$ if accepted. With probability $(1 - \beta)\alpha_f dt$, the firm contacts an unskilled worker where the payoffs are U_f and $Y - EW_u$ respectively. The alternative that the firm does not meet a worker but must continue searching occurs with probability $(1 - \alpha_f dt)$, in which case the worker receives U_f. Simplifying yields

$$U_f = [\alpha_f/(r + \alpha_f)][\beta E_{\max}\{U_f, X - EW_s\} + (1 - \beta)E_{\max}\{U_f, Y - EW_u\}] \quad (3)$$

Similarly, it is possible to specify the expected discounted lifetime income of an unemployed skilled worker, U_s, and unskilled worker, U_u. Using the same techniques, it follows that

$$U_s = [\alpha_w/(r + \alpha_w)]E_{\max}\{U_s, EW_s\} \quad (4a)$$
$$U_u = [\alpha_w/(r + \alpha_w)]E_{\max}\{U_u, EW_u\} \quad (4b)$$

We assume for now that the bargained wages are such that both types of workers are acceptable to a firm and workers accept the bargained wage, i.e.

$$U_f = [\alpha_f/(r + \alpha_f)][\beta(X - EW_s) + (1 - \beta)(Y - EW_u)] \quad (5a)$$
$$U_s = [\alpha_w/(r + \alpha_w)]EW_s \quad (5b)$$
$$U_u = [\alpha_w/(r + \alpha_w)]EW_u \quad (5c)$$

Equations (5) represent the expected returns to the agents as functions of the outcome of the bargaining process. Later, in the appendix, we will check that the equilibrium expect returns satisfy these conditions.

4 Bargaining

Suppose a firm and an unskilled worker begin to bargain. Let W_{fu} be the income offer that maximizes the firm's expected discounted net revenue. This offer makes the worker indifferent between accepting or rejecting and hence is described by

$$W_{fu} = [1/(1 + r\Delta)][\alpha_w \Delta EW_u + (1 - \alpha_w \Delta) \\ [\alpha_f \Delta U_u + (1 - \alpha_f \Delta)EW_u]] \quad (6)$$

The left-hand side represents the worker's benefit from accepting the wage offer. The right-hand side captures the expected returns from rejecting. All terms on the right-hand side are discounted by $1/(1 + r\Delta)$, reflecting the idea that the worker must wait time interval Δ if the offer is rejected.[4] With probability $\alpha_w\Delta$, the worker will be contacted by another firm during this interval. According to bargaining rule (vi), the worker will break off ongoing negotiations and begin to bargain with the newly contacted firm. This event generates the expected return EW_u. The probability the worker does not contact a firm but the firm contacts another worker in time interval Δ is $(1 - \alpha_w\Delta)\alpha_f\Delta$. Under the bargaining rules, the firm begins to negotiate with the newly contacted worker, whereas the unskilled worker is left to look for a new firm and thus expects U_u discounted lifetime income. The probability that neither the firm nor worker contact another agent is $(1 - \alpha_w\Delta)(1 - \alpha_f\Delta)$. In this case the worker receives EW_u.

On the other hand, suppose the unskilled worker makes an offer. The worker maximizes expected discounted income but must also make the firm indifferent between accepting and rejecting. As such

$$Y - EW_u = [1/(1 + r\Delta)][\alpha_f\Delta[\beta(X - EW_s) + (1 - \beta)$$
$$(Y - EW_u)] + (1 - \alpha_f\Delta)[\alpha_w\Delta U_f + (1 - \alpha_w\Delta)(Y - EW_u)]] \quad (7)$$

describes this indifference. Again the left-hand side is the benefit to the firm from accepting while the right-hand side sums the discounted benefits from rejecting – the probabilities about what can happen to the firm and worker multiplied by the expected return to the firm given each possible event occurs.

Substituting equations (5) into the above and letting Δ go to zero gives, after much manipulation (see appendix),

$$EW_u = [\Omega_1/\Omega_2]Y - [\beta\alpha_f(r + \alpha_w)/\Omega_2](X - EW_s) \quad (8)$$

where

$$\Omega_1 = (r + \alpha_w)(r + \beta\alpha_f)$$
$$\Omega_2 = \Omega_1 + r(r + \alpha_f)$$

Note that EW_u is a positive function of Y but decreasing in the expected net profit from hiring a skilled worker, $X - EW_s$.

Now suppose a firm and a skilled worker begin to bargain. Let W_{fs} denote the income offer made by the firm to a skilled worker. As before, the firm will make an offer that makes the skilled worker indifferent between accepting and rejecting. The expected costs and benefits are calculated as in the unskilled worker case which leads to the following equality:

$$W_{fs} = [1/(1+r\Delta)]\{\alpha_w \Delta EW_s + (1-\alpha_w\Delta)(\alpha_f\Delta\beta U_s$$
$$+ \alpha_f\Delta(1-\beta)EW_s + (1-\alpha_f\Delta)EW_s)\} \qquad (9)$$

Likewise a skilled worker maximizes his or her expected discounted income W_s such that the firm's indifference is described by

$$X - EW_s = [1/(1+r\Delta)]\{\beta\alpha_f\Delta(X - EW_s) + (1-\beta)\alpha_f\Delta$$
$$[\alpha_w\Delta(Y - EW_u) + (1-\alpha_w\Delta)(X - EW_s)] + (1-\alpha_f\Delta)$$
$$[\alpha_w\Delta U_f + (1-\alpha_w\Delta)(X - EW_s)]\} \qquad (10)$$

With probability $\beta\alpha_f\Delta$ the firm meets another skilled worker receiving $X - EW_s$. With probability $(1-\beta)\alpha_f\Delta\alpha_w\Delta$ the firm meets an unskilled worker and the skilled worker meets another firm. The worker departs for the other firm leaving the original firm to bargain with the unskilled worker where the payoff is $Y - EW_u$. When the firm meets an unskilled worker and the worker does not find an alternative firm (with probability $(1-\beta)\alpha_f\Delta(1-\alpha_w\Delta)$), the firm continues to bargain with the skilled worker with payoff $X - EW_s$. When the firm does not meet another worker, which occurs with probability $(1-\alpha_f\Delta)$ two events can occur. Either the worker meets another firm with probability $\alpha_w\Delta$ in which case the firm returns to search with payoff U_f or the worker does not meet another firm with probability $1(-\alpha_w\Delta)$ and continues to bargain yielding payoff $X - EW_s$.

Subtracting (10) from (9) letting Δ go to zero, and manipulating yields:

$$EW_s = [\Pi_1/\Pi_2]X - [\alpha_f(1-\beta)(r+\alpha_w)\alpha_w/\Pi_2](Y - EW_u) \qquad (11)$$

where

$$\Pi_1 = (r+\alpha_w)[(r+\alpha_w)(r+\alpha_f) - \beta\alpha_w\alpha_f] > 0$$
$$\Pi_2 = \Pi_1 + r(r+\alpha_f)(r+\alpha_w + \beta\alpha_f) > 0$$

(see appendix) Since $0 < \Pi_1/\Pi_2 < 1$, the bargained income paid to skilled workers is a positive function of the revenue generated by skilled workers, X, and a negative function of the firm's net revenue from hiring an unskilled worker.

From these equations we observe that wages bargained by both types of worker depend upon

(a)   their respective productivities, X and Y
(b)   the arrival rates faced by workers and firms, α_w and α_f
(c)   the proportion of workers who are skilled, β
(d)   the discount rate, r

The wage bargained by unskilled (skilled) workers also depends upon the firm's profit if it hires a skilled (unskilled) worker, $X - EW_s$ ($Y - EW_u$). These parameters correspond to the previously suggested factors but they are now explicitly specified for a well-formulated bargaining situation.

5   Equilibrium

If skilled workers believe EW_u is the wage bargained by unskilled workers, then EW_u must satisfy (8) given the common parameters. Likewise, EW_s must satisfy (11). Hence in an equilibrium these equations hold. After some tedious algebra, the two wage equations reduce to

$$EW_s = \frac{(r + \alpha_w)}{\Sigma}\{[(r + \alpha_w)(2r + \alpha_w + \alpha_f) + r\beta\alpha_f]X - [(1 - \beta)\alpha_w\alpha_f]Y\} \quad (12)$$

$$EW_u = \frac{(r + \alpha_w)(r + \alpha_w + \beta\alpha_f)}{\Sigma}[-\beta\alpha_f X + (2r + \alpha_w + \beta\alpha_f)Y] \quad (13)$$

where $\qquad \Sigma = (2r + \alpha_w + \alpha_f + \beta\alpha_f)[r(2r + \alpha_w + \beta\alpha_f) + \alpha_w(2r + \alpha_w)]$
$\qquad\qquad\qquad + \beta^2\alpha_f^2\alpha_w$

In what follows the parameters X, Y and r are treated as exogenous. In this case, the expected wage paid to unskilled and skilled workers can be written as functions of α_w, α_f and β. Furthermore, although both workers and firms treat these three parameters as given, they depend upon the actions of the workers, specifically the education and participation decisions. We now focus on the determinants of N_s and N_u.

To do this, we treat the wage or bargaining outcome as given and turn attention to the market structure. First note that the total number of worker–firm contacts equals the probability that a firm meets a worker multiplied by the total number of firms. Because the total number of firms is fixed and normalized to one, the number of contacts is simply $\alpha_f \cdot 1 = \alpha_f$. Moreover, the probability that a worker meets a firm is simply the total number of contacts divided by the number of unemployed skilled and unskilled workers, $N_s + N_u$. This implies

$$\alpha_w = \alpha_f/(N_s + N_u) \tag{14}$$

The above relates the probabilities of meeting partners to the total number of matches but we still need to describe the determinants of the total number of matches. It is reasonable to assume that the total number of matches is somehow related to the total number of searchers. Specifically, since there are a fixed number of firms, we can write the number of contacts in terms of N_s and N_u alone:

$$\alpha_f = \hat{\alpha}_f(1, \ N_s + N_u) = \alpha_f(M) \tag{15}$$

where $M = N_s + N_u$. We assume that $\alpha_f' > 0$, $\alpha_f'' < 0$: as the total number of workers increases, the total number of contacts also increases but at a decreasing rate. The decreasing returns, analogous to those assumed for the production function, capture the 'congestion effects' that searchers cause for each other when looking for work.

This matching technology and its relationship to α_w and α_f imply that the wages as given in (12) and (13) can be written as functions of the endogenous variables, N_s and N_u, and the parameters X, Y and r. These wages in turn allow us to determine the equilibrium number of skilled and unskilled workers.

Assume that there is an unlimited number of potential workers who obtain expected utility U if they do not participate. Without loss of generality, normalize this non-participation utility to zero, $U=0$. These workers can either (a) acquire skills at cost c and then enter the market as skilled workers; (b) enter the market as unskilled workers; (c) or decide not to enter the labour market at all.

Workers will continue to enter the market without skills as long as there is a positive return. Similarly, workers will be willing to pay c to become skilled as long as it is worthwhile. This implies that in equilibrium we must have

$$U_s - c = U_u = U = 0 \tag{16}$$

Using this relationship, we can now construct an equilibrium defined by a pair (N_s^*, N_u^*).[5] First note that if unskilled workers are indifferent between non-participation and market entry, their expected wage must equal zero (see equation (5c)). Setting $EW_u = 0$ gives

$$X/Y = [2rM + \alpha_f(M) + N_s\alpha_f(M))/(N_s\alpha_f(M))] \tag{17}$$

$$EW_s = X - [(rM + N_s\alpha_f(M))/(N_s\alpha_f(M))]Y \tag{18}$$

Equation (17) implies that at any equilibrium there is a precise relationship between X and Y which depends on N_s and N_u.

Substituting (17) into (18) and recognizing that

$$U_s = [\alpha_f(M)/(rM + \alpha_f(M))]EW_s \tag{19}$$

implies $U_s = Y/N_s$. Hence at any equilibrium the number of participating skilled workers is simply determined by

$$N_s = Y/C \tag{20}$$

This plus (17) determines whether an interior market equilibrium exists. Let the right-hand side of (17) be written as

$$\Psi(N_s, M) = [2rM + \alpha_f(M) + N_s\alpha_f(M)]/(N_s\alpha_f(M)) \tag{21}$$

Since $M = N_s + N_u$ and in equilibrium $N_s = Y/c$, we can focus on $\Psi(Y/c, Y/c + N_u)$. This is an increasing function in the number of unskilled workers. Provided the productivity difference is sufficiently large, that is $X/Y > \Psi(Y/c, Y/c)$, there will be both skilled and unskilled workers in the market. This interior equilibrium case is illustrated in Figure 4.1.

6   Comparative statics

Consider now the consequences of a change in one of the market parameters. Suppose there is an increase in the productivity of skilled workers. For example, the course that educates workers may become more effective. Since $N_s = Y/c$, an increase in X will not affect the equilibrium number of skilled workers. Moreover Ψ does not depend on X, so an increase in X will simply shift up X/Y and correspondingly increase the number of unskilled workers.[6] This is shown in Figure 4.2.

Secondly consider a decrease in the cost of training. As $Y/c = N_s$, the number of skilled workers increases. In addition, $\Psi(Y/c, Y/c + N_u)$ shifts to the right and becomes flatter, so that the number of unskilled also increases $N_s + N_u$. It can be shown that this latter effect outweighs the first which causes a fall in the proportion of unskilled workers as Figure 4.3 demonstrates. To equilibriate market wages, the increased number of skilled workers must be balanced by a greater increase in the number of unskilled workers.

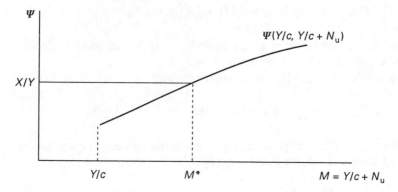

Figure 4.1

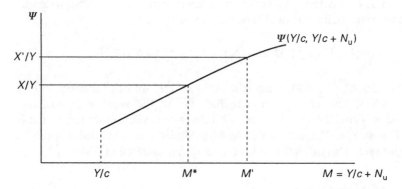

Figure 4.2

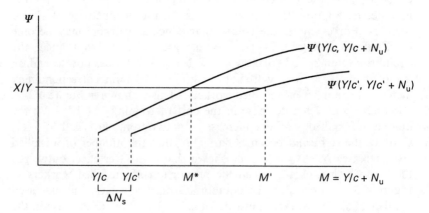

Figure 4.3

7   Conclusions

It is (almost) universally recognized that workers and firms face considerable problems contacting each other and that these difficulties have profound consequences on the equilibrium characteristics of the labour market. This chapter has demonstrated that these difficulties can also cause peculiar effects on the education levels of workers.

We have presented a labour market with two types of workers who bargain over wages. Accounting for the outside opportunities and productivity differences, we derived the outcome of a particular bargaining process. Embedding the bargaining outcome in a search model with worker entry, we described equilibrium wages, unemployment and skill levels. Moreover, the comparative statics suggest that, owing to the complex interactions among search, bargaining and labour substitution, public policy may be ineffective or counter-productive.

While it is generally understood that there are inefficiencies in search and bargaining models which lead to under-investment in training and government intervention (see Pissarides (1990) and Tirole (1990)), the comparative statics exercises above show that in equilibrium substitution among more than one type of worker can significantly alter the policy choices. These consequences cannot flow from an analysis of a simple labour supply and demand model. It is the interaction of solutions to individual optimizing decisions put in an equilibrium setting which generates the results.

Appendix

Derivation of equation (8)

Rewriting (6) and (7) we have

$$w_{fu} = [1/(1+r\Delta)]\{\alpha_w\Delta EW_u + (1-\alpha_w\Delta)[\alpha_f\Delta U_u + (1-\alpha_f\Delta)EW_u]\} \quad (22)$$

$$Y - w_u = [1/(1+r\Delta)]\{\alpha_f\Delta[\beta(X-EW_s) + (1-\beta)(Y-EW_u)]$$
$$+ (1-\alpha_f\Delta)[\alpha_w\Delta U_f + (1-\alpha_w\Delta)(Y-EW_u)]\} \quad (23)$$

Subtracting (23) from (22) yields

$$[1/(1+r\Delta)][w_{fu} + w_u - Y] = \Delta[\alpha_w + r + \alpha_f - \alpha_w\alpha_f][U_u - U_f]$$
$$+ [2EW_u - Y](1 - \alpha_w\Delta - \alpha_f\Delta + \alpha_w\alpha_f\Delta^2) \quad (24)$$

But $2EW_u = w_{fu} + w_u$ and therefore (24) implies

$$2EW_u = U_u + Y - U_f \tag{25}$$

Substituting into (25) the equations of (5) and manipulating yields the desired result in (8).

Derivation of equation (11)

Rewriting (9) and (10) yields

$$V_s = [1/(1 + r\Delta)]\{(r + \alpha_w)\Delta U_s + (1 - \alpha_w)[\beta\alpha_f\Delta U_s \\ + (1 - \beta)\alpha_f\Delta EW_s + (1 - \alpha_f\Delta)EW_s]\} \tag{26}$$

$$V_{fs} = [1/(1 + r\Delta)]\{r + \alpha_f)\Delta U_f - (1 - \beta)\alpha_f\Delta(Y - EW_u) + (1 - \beta) \\ \alpha_w\Delta\alpha_f\Delta(Y - EW_u)(1 - \beta)\alpha_f\Delta(1 - \alpha_w\Delta)(X - EW_s) + (1 - \alpha_f\Delta) \\ [\alpha_w\Delta U_f + (1 - \alpha_w\Delta)EW_s]\} \tag{27}$$

Further,

$$EW_s = (w_s + w_{fs})/2 \tag{28}$$

Subtracting (27) from (26) and substituting in (28) for EW_s yields

$$[r + \alpha_w + \beta\alpha_f - \beta\alpha_f\alpha_w\Delta]2EW_s = (1 - \beta)\alpha_f(1 - \alpha_w\Delta)(Y - EW_u) \\ + [r + \alpha_w + \beta\alpha_f - \beta\alpha_f\alpha_w\Delta]U_s[r + \alpha_w + \alpha_f - \alpha_f\alpha_w\Delta]U_f \\ + [r + \alpha_w + \beta\alpha_f - \beta\alpha_f\alpha_w\Delta]X \tag{29}$$

Letting Δ become arbitrarily small yields

$$2EW_s = X + U_s + [\alpha_f(1 - \beta)/(r + \alpha_w + \beta\alpha_f)](Y - EW_u) \\ - [(r + \alpha_w + \alpha_f)/(r + \alpha_w + \beta\alpha_f)]U_f \tag{30}$$

Substituting the equations of (5) into (30) yields (11)

Search and bargaining restrictions

The bargaining rules require that $X - EW_s > Y - EW_u$. Plugging in the equilibrium wages and using $\alpha_w = \alpha_f/M$ implies

$$c < [\alpha_f/(rM + \alpha_f)](X - Y) \tag{31}$$

But combining equations (17) and (20) yields the equilibrium equation:

$$c = [\alpha_f/(2rM + \alpha_f)](X - Y) \tag{32}$$

which satisfies (31). For search we required that the worker and firms prefer the bargaining to continued search, that is $EW_s \geq U_s$, $EW_u \geq U_u$, $X - EW_s \geq U_f$ and $Y - EW_u \geq U_f$. The first two are satisfied trivially. Since $X - EW_s \geq Y - EW_u$ by (31) above, we need only $Y \geq U_f$. This implies

$$(r + \alpha_f)Y \geq \alpha_f[\beta(X - EW_s) + (1 - \beta)Y] \tag{33}$$

Plugging in for EW_s and for the equilibrium value of c and manipulating gives

$$X \leq [(2rM + \alpha_f + \beta\alpha_f M)/\beta\alpha_f M]Y \tag{34}$$

NOTES

We would like to thank the Department of Employment for their financial support. They are, of course, not responsible for any errors made or views expressed in the paper. We would like to thank T. J. Webb for research assistance.
1 While one would expect these factors to play a role in the bargaining process, traditional economic theory has very little to say about this process. With perfect information, the arrival rate of any type of agent is either infinite or zero, depending on whether there are agents searching.
2 More formally, all arrival rates are parameters of Poisson processes.
3 Indeed, it is not obvious that making the offer is an advantage. In any case, it is relatively straightforward to modify this restriction and therefore modify the results.
4 Note that the bargaining interval Δ differs from the search interval dt. They are both small intervals of time but should be distinguished.
5 We shall consider only interior equilibria where N_s and N_u are both strictly positive. It is a relatively simple task to extend the analysis where there is only one type of worker.
6 On the other hand, it can be shown that as unskilled workers become more productive, the number of skilled workers increases while the number of unskilled decreases. Mathematically, these results are given by

$$dN_s/dX = 0 \quad \text{and} \quad d(N_s + N_u)/dX = \frac{N_s\alpha_f}{2rY(\alpha_f - \alpha_f'(N_s + N_u))} > 0$$

$$dN_s = 1/c > 0 \quad \text{and} \quad d(N_s + N_u)/dY = \frac{-\alpha_f^2}{2rc(\alpha_f - \alpha_f'M)}$$

REFERENCES

Becker, G. (1975), *Human Capital*, 2nd edn, Chicago: University of Chicago Press.

Binmore, K. and P. Dasgupta (1987), *The Economics of Bargaining*, Oxford: Basil Blackwell.

Burdett, K. and R. Wright (1993), 'Two-Sided Search', University of Pennsylvania Working Paper.

Freeman, R. (1986), 'Demand of Education', in *The Handbook of Labor Economics*, O. Ashenfelter and R. Layard (eds.), Amsterdam: North-Holland.

Pissarides, C. (1990), *Equilibrium Unemployment Theory*, Oxford: Basil Blackwell.

Rubinstein, A. (1982), 'Perfect Equilibrium in a Bargaining Model', *Econometrica* **50**, 97–109.

Shaked, A. and J. Sutton (1984), 'Involuntary Unemployment as a Perfect Equilibrium in a Bargaining Model', *Econometrica* **52**, 135–64.

Tirole, J. (1990), *The Theory of Industrial Organization*, Cambridge, MA: MIT Press.

5 Dynamic competition for market share and the failure of the market for skilled labour

This chapter examines the market failures in skill acquisition arising from the interaction between skills and innovative success.

The chapter considers a process of dynamic competition in which firms view innovation as a way of competing for market share. In this context, the chapter focuses on an important characteristic of skilled workers: their adaptability. Skilled workers are regarded as being more flexible than unskilled workers, in the sense that the skilled workers can adapt to new technologies at lower cost than can the unskilled workers.

Thus the more skilled workers a firm employs, the cheaper will that firm's process of innovation be; consequently the more R&D it will undertake, the more profitable it will be, and the larger will be its market share. This, in turn, means that the higher will be the workers' return on acquiring skill. Moreover, the greater the return on skill acquisition, the greater will be the number of skilled workers available to the firm.

In such an economy, the marginal social product of a skilled worker comprises two terms. The first is the present value of all training costs that will be saved by using a skilled worker rather than an unskilled worker in production. The second is the increased value of profits in the economy, because, with the reduced cost of innovation brought about by this extra worker, the economy will end up with more successful firms and fewer unsuccessful firms. This latter term seems to capture formally what much of the informal discussion of skills gaps perceives as one of the benefits from having more skilled workers.

Now this gain could only be captured by a firm if skilled workers were employed on infinitely long contracts, because then the firm would perceive not just the benefit from the reduced training costs, but the fact that it would be more successful on average in the future.

However, typically firms cannot hire skilled workers on long-term contracts. This chapter shows that, when workers are hired on a series of short-term contracts whereby they are paid a bonus every time the firm innovates and they agree to adopt new working practices, workers receive too low a return on their skills. Moreover, since skilled workers incur no costs in adapting to the new technology, this bonus represents an over-payment that raises the cost of innovation. These features of the model capture an important aspect of the skills gap problem: workers see too low a rate of return to acquiring skills, while simultaneously firms perceive skilled workers and hence innovation as too expensive.

Dynamic competition for market share and the failure of the market for skilled labour

DAVID ULPH

1   Introduction

In this chapter I want to consider a model in which firms are engaged in an ongoing process of dynamic competition for market share by spending resources on R&D to improve product quality. In this model there is an endogenously determined market structure in which some firms have larger market share and greater profits than others because of their previous R&D success. I distinguish between skilled and unskilled workers: skilled workers are *flexible* and can costlessly adapt to new technologies; unskilled workers have to undergo costly retraining. I show that such a model captures what I think are the essential features of the skill gap problem.

Thus I calculate the marginal social product of a skilled worker, and show that since having more skilled workers lowers the cost of innovation and causes firms to do more R&D, the marginal social product contains a term that reflects the gain to society from having more successful firms. I identify reasons why firms might not be able to write the appropriate long-term contracts with skilled workers that would sustain a social optimum. I examine a market equilibrium in short-term contracts, and show that in this equilibrium skilled workers are regarded as being too expensive by firms who demand too few of them and, as a consequence, undertake too little R&D, while it is *simultaneously* true that skilled workers receive too low a return on acquiring skill. Another feature of this equilibrium is that successful firms hire skilled workers more cheaply than unsuccessful firms, and this generates the phenomenon of having some firms being in a virtuous circle of high market share, high profitability and high R&D, while other firms are in a vicious circle of low profitability, low market share and low R&D.

Now there have been a number of recent papers that have looked at the link between skill gaps and economic growth. Thus Aghion and Howitt

(1994) have examined the links between growth and unemployment in a model where new technologies require new skills and innovating firms have to search to acquire workers with these skills. They note that if growth is generated endogenously through expenditure on R&D then factors that make search more costly will reduce the return to R&D and so lower the rate of investment and hence the rate of growth. However, in this model all firms are essentially identical, and so it is hard to capture the skill gap features referred to above.

Acemoglu (1992) examines the nature of the labour market in more detail, and focuses on potential externalities between firms through their labour training decisions. This could lead some firms to delay innovation in order to benefit from the trained workers made available by others. This is another example of the familiar problem caused when firms may not be able to fully appropriate the returns to non-specific training.

As indicated above, in this chapter I want to focus on a very different facet of the link between skill gaps and economic growth, by exploring the issues that arise when one takes seriously the idea that firms are engaged in an ongoing process of R&D competition simply as a means of competing for market share. The crucial point here is that the market does not expand through the process of innovation, but firms simply view innovation as a way of getting or maintaining (a possibly temporary) market advantage. What I have in mind is a case where firms are continuously improving the quality of the product they produce, but, over time, a competitive sector is able to incorporate the improvements of some years previously and produce a continuously improved product at a constant cost. Thus despite the continuous improvement in quality by innovating firms they are forced to keep prices in line with costs in the competitive sector and so are unable to get ever greater price–cost margins. As an example think of the car market where the most recent models are competing with low-priced models produced in places like Eastern Europe which incorporate the features which were at the forefront of design a decade or so ago.

What I want to stress is that when firms use R&D as a means of competing for market share, then innovative success and failure at any one time is generally going to affect different firms in different ways, depending on their past history of innovative success and failure. For firms that have been successful in the recent past and currently have high profits, output and market share, innovative success will simply be a way of maintaining their current position while innovative failure will lead to a reduction in profit, output and market share. Their incentive to innovate is that of trying to avoid the reduction in profits that comes from being an unsuccessful innovator. The popular way of describing this is to say that these firms are having to run just to stand still. On the other hand, firms that have failed to innovate in the recent past and so currently have low profits and output and a small share of the market will find that innovative success leads to an expansion in profit, output and market share, while failure just maintains the status quo. Their incentive to innovate is to try to get the higher level of profits that comes from innovative success.

Because the nature of the incentive to innovate varies across these different types of firm, so too, in general, will be the actual amount of R&D they undertake, and a central question in the theory of R&D competition is whether firms that are already successful have a higher or lower incentive to innovate than those that have previously been unsuccessful.

In a model of such R&D competition it is possible to determine the equilibrium amount of R&D done by each type of firm (that is by firms of differing histories of R&D success) and hence, in a steady-state equilibrium, both the distribution of firms of different type and the rate of growth of real income arising through the steady rate of growth of product quality.

There are several important points to notice about such a steady-state equilibrium. The first is that even though the number of successful and unsuccessful firms remains constant, any one firm will oscillate back and forward between R&D success and failure just because of the inherently random nature of the innovative process whereby the expenditure of considerable sums on R&D does not guarantee success while conversely a firm that spends a small amount can make a lucky discovery.

The second point to notice is that *if* it turns out that in equilibrium previously successful firms tend to spend considerably more on R&D than previously unsuccessful firms then the equilibrium will be characterised by a high degree of *persistence*. Thus firms that become successful are on average more likely to be successful in the future, and so will on average stay successful for quite a while. On the other hand once firms become unsuccessful they will spend little on R&D and hence tend to remain unsuccessful in the future. Thus the equilibrium will be characterised by some firms displaying *virtuous circles* of high R&D spending, high profits and high innovative success, while others display *vicious circles* of low profits, low R&D and low innovative success. Notice that this can happen in a world where all firms are operating in the same economic environment and are essentially identical.

The conventional industrial organisation literature on R&D competition – see, for example, Beath *et al.* (1994) for a survey – assumes that the process of innovation is frictionless and in particular that firms face no costs in acquiring any new skills they need once they have innovated.

In this chapter I want to explore what happens to the outcome of R&D competition and hence to economic growth when we drop this assumption.

There are two ways in which firms can incur costs of acquiring labour with the appropriate skills once they have innovated. The first – which I will call *horizontal costs* of skill acquisition – arises purely because of the process of expansion and contraction in output (and hence employment) that firms would face as they go through the cycle of success and failure at innovation. Thus, even if the introduction of an innovation does not *per se* require new skills – as might be the case with product innovation leading to the introduction of a better-designed product where all the improvement is in the components and which requires essentially the same construction skills as the old product – then successful innovation will still create a need for *some* firms (those that have been unsuccessful in the past) to acquire new workers. These workers will have to come from outside the firm, and will typically require to be trained in the skills required by the particular product being produced by the firm. In a companion paper (Ulph, 1994), I explore the implications of these training costs.

The second way in which innovation could face firms with costs of acquiring labour with appropriate skills arises through what I will call *vertical training costs*. These arise if the introduction of a new product requires new techniques of production which workers have to master. These new techniques need not increase the physical productivity of labour in the sense that, once mastered, the amount of output produced per unit of labour is the same as with the old product. However, workers have to master the new technology before they can be used in production. It is the implications of these kinds of training costs on which I want to focus in this chapter.

In considering the implication of this for innovation, I distinguish between skilled and unskilled workers. I take it that whereas unskilled workers always have to be re-trained at some cost to the firm in order to be able to use the new technology, skilled workers have the attribute of being able to adapt costlessly to the new technology. Thus for a firm that has just innovated training costs will be lower to the extent that it employs skilled rather than unskilled workers. The use of skilled workers by firms that have just succeeded in discovering a new technology will therefore lower the costs of innovation and increase the return to R&D.

A number of implications follow from this characterisation of skilled workers. The first is that in an optimum allocation of resources a firm that has just succeeded in innovation should see the use of a skilled worker to operate the new technology as being costless – thus correctly perceiving that there is a genuine cost-saving to using skilled rather than unskilled workers to introduce a new technology.

The second is that if a firm fails to innovate it should still retain some of its skilled workers – simply in order to avoid having to hire unskilled workers and train them in a technology the skilled workers have already learned. To give a firm an incentive to retain its workers it should see no effective cost to re-employing a skilled worker.

The third is that the marginal social product of a skilled worker exceeds the present value of the training costs that are saved. This is because an additional skilled worker lowers the true costs of innovation, which in turn encourages firms to do more R&D. This means that in steady state there are more successful firms and fewer unsuccessful firms, and, since successful firms are more profitable than unsuccessful firms this is a genuine gain to the economy that would not be perceived by any individual firm in making its R&D decision. Notice that this is a gain that can only arise when we recognise that in any equilibrium there will be different kinds of firms and that the distribution of these firms is endogenously determined through the process of R&D competition. This is precisely what I think many people have in mind when they worry about the economic consequences of having too few skilled workers.

The fourth implication is that markets may not be able to achieve this optimum. What would be required would be that some employment agency recruits skilled workers at a lifetime income that reflects their true value to the economy. It then writes long-term contracts with individual firms whereby, in return for a fixed fee, these firms get the option of employing a specified number of skilled workers in the future whenever they need them. It is only by some such arrangement that we could guarantee that skilled workers were continuously re-assigned between firms, but that firms perceived no extra cost from their decision to employ or retain a skilled worker.

We don't typically observe such arrangements. I then consider what happens if firms are unable to write long-term contracts with skilled workers, but can contract only period by period. I examine what I call a 'bonus equilibrium'. Here firms employ skilled workers on a contract that guarantees them a bonus payment every time a firm innovates, but no additional payment if the firm fails to innovate.

An interesting feature of this equilibrium is that unsuccessful firms have to pay a bonus equal to the training costs of an unskilled worker, whereas successful firms, because they are paying the bonus more frequently can still attract skilled workers by paying a bonus less than the training costs of an unskilled worker.

The equilibrium also has the feature that it is costless for firms to retain skilled workers once hired – which is one of the desirable properties of the optimal allocation. Nevertheless, compared to the optimum the 'bonus equilibrium' results in two forms of market failure.

The first is that, because firms have to pay a bonus to skilled workers every time they innovate, they therefore see the costs of innovation as being above their true costs (in which skilled workers would be costless to employ when innovating). This results in under-investment in R&D.

The second is that skilled workers get paid less than their true social marginal product. In part this is because the bonus they get paid by successful firms is less than the training cost of an unskilled worker, but also because they do not receive a payment which reflects the gain to society from having more successful firms around. So there is under-investment in skill acquisition.

Thus we have the interesting phenomenon that skilled workers are *simultaneously* regarded as too expensive by firms yet get too low a return on their skills. This seems to me to be the fundamental market failure associated with the idea of a skill gap.

Notice that this market failure has nothing to do with the conventional market failures discussed in the skills literature and in the work by Acemoglu (1992) which arise from externalities and the consequent inability of firms to fully capture the returns to training.

A final feature of the 'bonus equilibrium' is that it replicates a feature of the *horizontal training costs* model considered in Ulph (1994) – namely that successful firms find R&D cheaper than unsuccessful firms and so tendencies to *persistence* are reinforced.

In Section 2 I set out the basic model. Section 3 sets out the analysis of *vertical training costs*, introduces the idea of skilled workers as being more flexible than unskilled workers and demonstrates how markets might fail.

2   The model with no skill differences

The basic model of the product market and of R&D is based on that given in Ulph (1991). I will start by explaining how competition takes place in the product market.

2.1   *The product market*

A lot of the discussion of skill shortages takes it that the advantage of having skilled labour is that it enables firms to engage in product innovation. A firm with a new higher quality good has a competitive advantage (albeit temporary) which it can exploit to set a price above the marginal cost of production. By contrast, firms that fail to innovate will be forced to produce highly standardised goods where competition will drive the price down to lowest costs and so eliminate any markups. The following model is designed to capture this idea.

The model assumes that we have a market in which goods are differentiated both horizontally and vertically. Thus goods have different *horizontal* characteristics: for example, if we are thinking of cars, they have features like speed, fuel efficiency, safety, comfort etc. Consumers care about these features, but different consumers place different weights on these various characteristics. Producers compete to produce products which embody higher and higher levels of these characteristics. However, each producer is better at improving one characteristic than others, and so, if they successfully innovate, they produce a good that is better than others in one respect, but no better than others in other respects. This improved product will certainly appeal to consumers who value that characteristic and guarantees that innovation does not allow firms to produce a product that totally dominates.

To start, suppose that we have an industry in which goods are produced which comprise n different characteristics. There are at least n different firms producing these goods. At any given time there is some basic level for characteristic i, a_i^0 which every firm has the technical know-how to incorporate in their product. Thus every firm is capable of producing the *basic good* described by the characteristic vector $a^0 = (a_1^0, \ldots, a_n^0)$. I will assume that there are many firms that are capable of producing this basic good, so competition will always drive its price down to unit costs.

However, associated with each characteristic is one, *and only one*, *specialist* firm. The specialist firm associated with characteristic i produces a good which has a level $a_i > a_i^0$ of characteristic i, but just the basic level a_j^0 of all the other characteristics. That is, the ith *specialist good* has a characteristic vector $a^i = (a_1^0, \ldots, a_{i-1}^0, a_i, a_{i+1}^0, \ldots, a_n^0)$. Let $a_j = a_j - a_j^0 > 0$ be the *quality gap* in the jth characteristic. Notice that there are therefore $n + 1$ goods in the market: the basic good (good 0) and n specialist goods, goods $1, \ldots, n$.

Following the specification of individual preferences given in Ulph (1991) it can be shown that the demand for the ith specialist good is given by

$$D_i = \frac{S}{P_i}\left(\frac{P_0}{P_i}\right)^{1/\alpha_i}\left\{1 - \frac{1}{n-1}\sum_{\substack{j=1 \\ j \neq i}}^{n}\frac{\alpha_j}{\alpha_i + \alpha_j}\left(\frac{p_0}{p_j}\right)^{1/\alpha_j}\right\} \qquad (1)$$

where, for $i = 0, \ldots, n$, p_i is the price of the good i, and S is a parameter reflecting the size of the market which will depend on aggregate consumer income.

Notice that the own-price elasticity of demand for good i is just the constant $1 + 1/\alpha_i$, so if the ith specialist firm can increase its quality gap α_i, then, other things equal, the effect on this on the demand for good i will be

(i)   it will *reduce* the elasticity of demand;
(ii) by lowering all the terms $\alpha_j/(\alpha_i + \alpha_j)$, it will *increase* the share of the market taken by good i.

In what follows I will assume that

(1)   all firms have the same marginal costs of production, which I will normalise to be 1;
(2)   competition in the product market takes the form of Bertrand competition.

It therefore follows that

$$p_0 = 1 \qquad p_i = 1 + \alpha_i \qquad i = 1, \ldots, n \qquad (2)$$

Thus, precisely because higher-quality goods have a lower elasticity of demand, in equilibrium they will have a higher markup of price over cost.

I now want to move to a continuum of firms by letting $n \to \infty$. However, for reasons that will emerge shortly, I want to assume that there are only three sizes of characteristic gap that specialist firms can ever have: α_0, α_i and α_2, where $0 \leq \alpha_0 < \alpha_1 < \alpha_2$. If the fraction of specialist firms with quality gap α_k is $f_k \geq 0$, $\sum_{k=0}^{2} f_k = 1$, then the *equilibrium output* of a product with characteristic gap α_k is

$$D_k = \frac{S}{1 + \alpha_k} \phi(\alpha_k) \left\{ 1 - \sum_{\substack{j=0 \\ j \neq k}}^{2} \frac{\alpha_j}{\alpha_k + \alpha_j} f_j \phi(\alpha_j) - \frac{f_k}{2} \phi(\alpha_k) \right\} \qquad (3)$$

where $\phi(z) = (1/(1+z))^{1/z}$, if $z > 0$, and $\phi(0) = 1/e$.

Moreover, because of the pricing formulae given by (2), the equilibrium profits from production by a product of type k are

$$\pi_k = \alpha_k D_k \qquad (4)$$

There are three important points to make about this.

(a) The equilibrium output and hence profits of a firm will depend on not just how successful it is (as reflected in its own quality gap) but on how successful all the other firms in the market are – as reflected in the vector $f = (f_0, f_1, f_2)$ giving the fractions of firms with different sizes of quality gap – because this will determine the amount of competitive pressure there is on firms of different types. So, for example, a firm producing a top-quality good with gap α_2 will find its output and profits falling if there is an increase in f_2 with an offsetting reduction in f_1 and/or f_0. The vector f reflects the market structure that prevails in the market, and is completely endogenous, being determined through the R&D competition between firms.

(b) Taking f as given, it is not always going to be the case that firms with higher quality gaps always have higher equilibrium levels of output. There are two forces at work. As I indicated above, *taking prices as given*, the larger a firm's quality gap, the larger will be its share of the market, and hence output. However, as we have seen, firms producing higher-quality goods will set higher equilibrium prices and this will tend to lower their equilibrium output. So output can be increasing or decreasing in quality, and which way this goes will depend crucially on the vector f. This is important, because it is often said that firms/countries face a choice between producing in the high-volume/low-quality/low-markup end of the market, or the low-volume/high-quality/high-markup end of the market. But, within this model, for a wide range of vectors f successful firms can end up gaining not only higher markups but higher equilibrium output levels as well.

(c) Whichever way output varies with quality, it is straightforward to show that firms producing higher-quality goods always make greater profits than firms producing lower-quality goods.

To complete the description of the product market, it will be useful to anticipate a little the description of the R&D competition given in Section 2.3 below. In the specification of the R&D part of the model I will be assuming that specialist firms can improve the level of the characteristic in which they specialise by investing in R&D. However, R&D is an inherently random activity, so the amount spent on R&D in any period will simply determine the *probability* of making an improvement in the level of the characteristic within that particular period. I assume that if a specialist firm succeeds in making an improvement then the level of its characteristic will increase by $g > 0$ which is independent of the characteristic being improved, of the existing level of that characteristic, and of the amount spent on R&D.

A successful discovery brings patent protection, but a crucial assumption I make is that this lasts for only two periods, after which *any* other firm can incorporate the newly discovered level of the characteristic in its product. This is crucial to the model because it captures in a very sharp way the idea that even though a firm is continuously successful in innovating it cannot open up an ever-increasing quality gap in the market, because other non-innovating firms are always relentlessly catching up and producing what was at the forefront of the market just a short while ago. So successful firms have the much-reported impression that they have to keep on running just to stand still. More formally, the maximum gap that a firm can open up in its characteristic is $\alpha_2 = 2g$, and to do this, it needs to be successful in innovating, two periods in a row. If a firm is successful and unsuccessful in successive periods, it will have a characteristic gap $\alpha_1 = g$. Finally if a specialist firm fails to innovate two periods in a row then its gap, and so its profits, will have shrunk to zero, i.e. $\alpha_0 = 0$.

With the values of the quality gaps thus determined, then, once we know f, we can use (3) and (4) to determine the equilibrium output and profits of each type of firm.

For expositional purposes only, I am going to assume in all that follows that

$$D_2 > D_1 > D_0$$

so that firms that are more successful at innovating always end up with higher levels of output and hence market share, as well as higher levels of profit.

2.2   The labour market

I assume that labour is the only input and that all products require a constant number of manhours per unit of output, irrespective of the level of output or of the characteristics of the product produced. Each worker can provide up to a fixed number of manhours per period.

In this section I assume that all workers are identical. In particular workers have exactly the same level of physical productivity, and are all paid the same fixed wage per hour of work. These assumptions ensure the constant and identical marginal cost assumption employed in Section 2.1.

Suppose that the common physical productivity of all workers is such that when the demand facing a firm is D_i, $i = 0, 1, 2$, then its total demand for labour is $x_i > 0$.

I assume that labour contracts with workers last one period, and that there are no costs associated with the formal process of hiring and firing workers.

However, I assume that whenever a firm innovates it has to incur *vertical training costs*, of $c > 0$ per worker in order to train the workers in how to operate the technology for producing the new product. However, to repeat, this training does not change the physical productivity of workers, it simply acquaints them with a new technology for producing a higher-quality product. The analogy I have in mind is that of a secretary who learns a new word-processing package, but retains the same typing speed on the keyboard.

2.3   The R&D decisions of firms

At the start of each period each specialist firm chooses and sinks its R&D expenditure. This determines the probability with which the firm succeeds in improving its specialist characteristic. The firm's innovative success or failure is also determined right at the outset of the period. If a firm is successful, it gets a patent which covers its discovery for the remainder of the current period and for the next period.

At the start of period t there are two types of firm: those who were successful at innovating in period $t-1$ (type 1 firms) and those who failed to innovate in $t-1$ (type 0 firms). Table 5.1 shows the outputs of each type of firm in t conditional on their innovative success in t.

Let $h^t = (h_1^t, h_0^t)$ be the history of the economy at the start of period t, where $h_i^t \geq 0$, $\sum_{i=0}^{1} h_i^t = 1$ is the fraction of firms of type i at the start of t.

Each different type of firm will potentially choose a different level of R&D expenditure and hence have a different probability of innovative success. Let p_i^t, $0 \leq p_i^t \leq 1$, be the probability with which a firm of type i succeeds in innovating in t. Given the large numbers assumption it is also the fraction of these firms that actually will innovate in t. Let $p^t = (p_1^t, p_0^t)$.

Notice that, given h^t, then, once we know p^t, the distribution of firms with different sizes of gaps in t, f^t is given by

$$f_2^t = h_1^t \, p_1^t \tag{5}$$

$$f_1^t = h_1^t (1 - p_1^t) + h_0^t \, p_0^t \tag{6}$$

$$f_0^t = h_0^t \, (1 - p_0^t) \tag{7}$$

Table 5.1 Outputs conditional on innovative success

Innovative success in	Output in t if innovative	Success in period t is
1	D_2	D_1
0	D_1	D_0

Also, given h^t and p^t, then we can calculate what the history of the economy will be at the start of $t+1$ through the equations

$$h_1^{t+1} = h_1^t\, p_1^t + h_0^t\, p_0^t \tag{8}$$
$$h_0^{t+1} = h_1^t(1 - p_1^t) + h_0^t(1 - p_0^t) \tag{9}$$

In all that follows, I am going to focus on calculating steady-state growth paths in which p, f and h are constant over time. In this case, once we have determined p, then equations (8) and (9) determine the steady-state distribution of firms of different histories of R&D success, while (5)–(7) determine the distribution of firms of different levels of output, profit and markets share.

In order to determine the R&D choices of each type of firm, we need to introduce the terms V_i which give the expected present value of profits in the steady state of being a firm that is of type i at the start of any given period. If we let A_i be the payoff to a firm of type i if it succeeds in innovating in any period, and B_i be its payoff if it fails to innovate, then we get the table of payoffs shown in Table 5.2. Here δ, $0 < \delta < 1$, is the common discount factor.

Recall that all the profits and demands depend on the steady-state distribution of firm types f which in turn depends on the vector of innovation probabilities that we still have to determine.

Suppose now that each firm takes as given the R&D choices of all other firms. This means that each effectively takes p, h and f and hence A and B as given. A typical firm of type i will therefore choose its probability of success so as to maximise the expected present value of profits.

$$A_i p_i + B_i(1 - p_i) - \gamma(p_i)$$

Here $\gamma(p)$ is the cost function determining the R&D expenditure necessary to obtain the probability p of success. I assume

$$\gamma(0) = 0 \quad \text{and} \quad \forall p,\ 0 \leq p \leq 1,\ \gamma'(p) > 0 \quad \gamma''(p) > 0 \quad \gamma'(p) \to \infty \text{ as } p \to 1$$

Table 5.2 Payoffs conditional on innovative success and past history

Firm type	A	B
1	$\pi_2 + \delta V_1 - cx_2$	$\pi_1 + \delta V_0$
0	$\pi_1 + \delta V_1 - cx_1$	$\pi_0 + \delta V_0$

The latter part of the condition ensures that no firm ever innovates with complete certainty.

The first-order conditions for the optimum choice of innovation probability are:

$$A_i - B_i \leq \gamma'(p_i) \qquad p_i \leq 0 \qquad (10)$$

Conditions (10) define the equilibrium p.

To complete the model we have to determine the steady-state values V_i. These are defined through the recursive equations

$$V_i = p_i A_i + (1 - p_i)B_i - \gamma(p_i) \qquad (11)$$

To determine the steady-state equilibrium requires finding vectors $\hat{h}$, $\hat{p}$, $\hat{f}$ and $\hat{V}$ which satisfy (5)–(11).

Now in this steady state we can determine not just the rate of innovative success for each individual type of firm, the vector $\hat{p}$, but also the average rate of success of the economy as a whole

$$\bar{p} = \hat{p}\,\hat{h} \qquad (12)$$

and hence the equilibrium steady-state growth rate

$$\bar{g} = g\bar{p} \qquad (13)$$

As discussed in Ulph (1991), even though all income, profits and prices remain constant over time, commodities are being steadily improved in quality and $\bar{g}$ is an exact measure of the growth in real incomes that consumers are obtaining from this improved product quality. In that paper I also show that there is a one-to-one link between the steady-state rate of growth and the average price–cost margin – so that faster growth is inevitably accompanied by a greater degree of monopoly power as reflected in this average price–cost margin. This relationship remains true in this model here.

This completes the discussion of the basic model in which there are *vertical training costs*, but no differences in skills. The next section introduces these and explores the implications for market failure and hence for skill gaps.

3   Skill gaps

I assume now that there are two types of worker – skilled and unskilled. The distinguishing feature is that whereas unskilled workers have to be trained to learn a new technology, skilled workers are assumed to be *flexible* and can costlessly adapt to any new technology. While this is not supposed to capture all the differences between skilled and unskilled workers, it does capture, albeit in a stark way, what is often regarded as an important type of higher skill.

I am also going to assume, somewhat more controversially, that this property of being skilled comes from something like higher education which teaches fundamental principles rather than specific knowledge and so enables individuals to more easily work out for themselves how to approach new situations. The important point is that then the property of being skilled is a general rather than a firm-specific skill, and so we would not typically expect firms to train their workers in this skill, leaving it to individuals to acquire it through appropriate education. A key question will be whether individuals perceive the right incentives to acquire skill.

In line with what I assumed above, I am going to continue to assume that once they have mastered the new technology, all workers have exactly the same level of productivity.[1] I also assume that there is a fixed pool, L, of infinitely-lived skilled workers, and that these workers are only ever employed in the particular sector of the economy we are looking at where the innovation is taking place. Call this the high-tech sector.

To understand what kinds of market failures might arise in this economy, I need to compare how a market equilibrium corresponds to the social optimum. Now a full specification of the social optimum would start with some historically given distribution of successful and unsuccessful firms and work out the optimum allocation of skilled workers to each type of firm in every subsequent period, leading, presumably to some steady-state allocation. Similarly for the market equilibrium. There are considerable technical difficulties in undertaking such an exercise, so, just as in the previous section, I am going to focus on steady states and compare the optimum steady-state allocation with the steady state that arises in the market equilibrium. While not providing a complete analysis, this offers considerable insights into the underlying issues.

3.1 Optimum steady-state allocation

Before setting out the details, it is important to consider certain features of the resource allocation problem.

One important feature that any efficient allocation should satisfy is that of the *non-replacement of workers*. To see this, suppose a firm has just innovated. All its workforce will have acquired the new skill – the skilled costlessly, the unskilled at a cost $c > 0$. If, next period, it innovates again, then the firm will either expand or stay the same size. In either event its workforce will have to acquire a new skill. If, however, it fails to innovate next period, then the firm will either remain the same size as it currently is, or else contract. If it remains the same size, and hence requires the same size of workforce, it would not make sense to replace any unskilled worker with either a skilled or unskilled worker – the fixed cost $c > 0$ has been sunk and it might as well be spread as long as possible. Nor is there any point in replacing a skilled worker with an unskilled worker since that unskilled worker will incur a training cost $c > 0$ to learn a skill that has already been learned by the skilled worker. Equally there is no point in replacing a skilled worker with another skilled worker. Suppose, however, the firm contracts as a result of the failure to innovate. Then it can cut back both its skilled and its unskilled workforce. However, it would not make sense to cut back its use of skilled workers so much that it had to take on new unskilled workers who had to be taught the skills the existing skilled workers have at the cost $c > 0$.

With this in mind let me turn to the specification of the optimal allocation. Suppose once again that the common physical productivity of all workers is such that when the demand facing a firm is D_i, $i = 0, 1, 2$, then its total demand for labour is $x_i > 0$.

To simplify the exposition in this section, in all that follows I am going to treat the numbers D_i, x_i and π_i as constants and ignore their dependence on the endogenous distribution f. This dependence just complicates the analysis in a way that is inessential to the points I am making.

An *allocation of skilled labour* is a vector $s = (s_2, s_1, s_0)$, where s_i, $0 \leq s_i \leq x_i$, $i = 0, 1, 2$ is the amount of skilled labour that a firm uses when its quality gap is i.

To satisfy the *principle of non-replacement* this allocation has to satisfy

$$x_1 - s_1 \leq x_2 - s_2 \tag{14}$$

and

$$x_0 - s_0 \leq x_1 - s_1 \tag{15}$$

Thus provided we specify an allocation as above and require it to satisfy (14) and (15) firms will incur training costs only when they innovate.

Now any remuneration paid to skilled workers is just a pure transfer between firms and skilled workers, so it ought to be the case in the optimum that the only costs that firms perceive to innovating are the true training costs of unskilled workers that they have to undertake whenever they innovate. Hence the optimal R&D decisions of the two types of firm are then given by

$$\gamma'(p_1) \geq \{\pi_2 + \delta V_1 - c[x_2 - s_2]\} - \{\pi_1 + \delta V_0\} \qquad p_1 \geq 0 \tag{16}$$

and

$$\gamma'(p_0) \geq \{\pi_1 + \delta V_1 - c[x_1 - s_1]\} - \{\pi_0 + \delta V_0\} \qquad p_0 \geq 0 \tag{17}$$

These are just exactly the same as the expressions that appeared in (10) in the previous section, except that there, because there were no skilled workers, the s_i were zero.

Moreover, in steady state, the expected present values of profits of the two types of firm would satisfy the recursive equations

$$V_1 = p_1\{\pi_2 + \delta V_1 - c[x_2 - s_2]\} + (1 - p_1)\{\pi_1 + \delta V_0\} - \gamma(p_1) \tag{18}$$

and

$$V_0 = p_0\{\pi_1 + \delta V_1 - c[x_1 - s_1]\} + (1 - p_0)\{\pi_0 + \delta V_0\} - \gamma(p_0) \tag{19}$$

(16–19) define the steady-state innovative probabilities and values for both kinds of firm given any particular allocation of skilled workers. Notice that these equations incorporate the feature of an allocation that training costs are incurred only when a firm innovates.

In steady state, the fraction of firms that would then start any period being of type 1, h_1, must satisfy the recursive equation

$$h_1 = h_1 p_1 + (1 - h_1) p_0$$

and so

$$h_1 = \frac{p_0}{p_0 + (1 - p_1)}$$

Finally any feasible allocation has to satisfy the resource constraint

$$h_1 p_1 s_2 + h_1 (1 - p_1) s_1 + h_0 p_0 s_1 + h_0 (1 - p_0) s_0 \leq L$$

or, using the definition of h_i

$$\frac{p_1 p_0 s_2 + 2 p_0 (1 - p_1) s_1 + (1 - p_1)(1 - p_0) s_0}{p_0 + (1 - p_1)} \leq L \tag{20}$$

Now notice that, in steady state, the expected value of profits earned by all firms is

$$\Pi = h_1 V_1 + (1 - h_1) V_0 = \frac{p_0 V_1 + (1 - p_1) V_0}{p_0 + (1 - p_1)} \tag{21}$$

Recalling that any remuneration to skilled workers is just a pure transfer between workers and firms, this also represents the true social value of production in the high-tech sector. However, since the probabilities and values that appear in this expression are endogenous, to determine the *optimal steady-state allocation of skilled workers* we have to choose $s_2, s_1, s_0, p_1, p_0, V_1, V_0$ so as to maximise Π as determined by (21) subject to (14)–(20).

One of the key questions I am interested in is how the social marginal product of skilled workers compares to the income that would be received by skilled workers in a market equilibrium. Once again, it is important to note that the social marginal product would be calculated by working out what increase in welfare would come about along the full transition path between the original steady state and the new one. For the reasons indicated above, what I am going to examine is the *social marginal steady-state product* $\lambda \equiv \partial \Pi / \partial L$. This is the increase in steady-state profits that would come about if we compared two economies, one with 1 additional unit of skilled labour than the other, and is just the Lagrange multiplier associated with the skilled worker resource constraint (20).

There are various inequalities which may or may not hold in the optimum, and the precise expression for λ will depend on precisely which combination is satisfied. Since I am not trying to be exhaustive here, let me just focus on one case – that in which s_2, s_1 and s_0 are all positive in the social optimum. It is easy to see that in this case (15) must definitely hold as an equality, since the aim will be to make s_0 as small as possible in order to divert skilled labour to innovating firms where they can be more useful. It is straightforward to show that in this case λ satisfies the equation

$$\lambda = \frac{c}{1-\delta} h_1 + (V_1 - V_0) \left[\frac{\frac{c(1-p_1)}{\gamma''(p_0)} + \frac{cp_0}{\gamma''(p_1)}}{[p_0 + (1-p_1)]^2} \right] -$$

$$\lambda \left[\frac{\frac{c[p_1(1-p_1)s_2+2(1-p_1)^2 s_1-(2-p_1)(1-p_1)s_0]}{\gamma''(p_0)} + \frac{c[p_0(1+p_0)s_2-2p_0^2 s_1-p_0(1-p_0)s_0]}{\gamma''(p_1)}}{[p_0 + (1-p_1)]^2} \right]$$

Though it looks complex, the interpretation of this expression is straightforward. The first term on the right-hand side is just the present value of the stream of training costs that will be saved by having an additional skilled worker. $c/(1-\delta)$ is just the present value of the stream of training costs. If, in steady-state, all firms were innovating for sure (and so $h_1 = 1$), or if we could continuously re-allocate skilled workers to innovating firms, then this would be the training costs we would save by having an extra skilled worker. However, since firms need to retain skilled workers even in periods when they do not innovate, and since, at any time a fraction h_1 of firms are innovating, then this first term gives precisely the value of the training costs saved with an extra skilled worker. This is precisely what one would expect to appear in the marginal social product of a skilled worker.

The second term on the right-hand side of the expression for λ captures another effect of having an additional skilled worker, which is that this allows both types of firm to increase their use of skilled workers when they are innovating, which in turn lowers the costs of innovation. This encourages both types of firm to do more R&D, raising the equilibrium values of p_1 and p_0. Both of these increases raise the equilibrium value of h_1, and the term in square brackets (which is positive) measures by how much h_1 increases. So, in equilibrium, we will have more successful firms, and since $V_1 > V_0$, this is beneficial.

There are several points to notice about this effect. The first is that the fact that individual firms are doing more R&D does not, *per se*, cause any effect on welfare. Firms are making the right R&D decisions, and so, to first-order, encouraging them to do a bit more or less has no effect on welfare. The second is that the effect arises only because there is a change in the equilibrium distribution of firms, and so would not be present in a model which assumed all firms were identical, or which took the distribution of firm types as exogenous. It is only in a model such as this which allows there to be an equilibrium distribution of firms of different kinds, but which generates this distribution endogenously as the outcome of the dynamic process of R&D competition, that this effect will be picked up. Taken together these two points indicate that this effect arises not through making any single firm more successful, but through making the economy as a whole more successful. I think that it is precisely this effect that people have in mind when they make inter-country comparisons and talk about one of the benefits of having a more skilled workforce being that the economy as a whole is more successful.

The third term on the right-hand side of the expression for λ captures the final effect of having an additional skilled worker, which works once again through the effect that this has of increasing the equilibrium values of p_i and p_0. This has complex effects on the demand for skilled workers: it will unambiguously increase the number of firms who need s_2 skilled workers, while lowering the number of firms who need s_0 skilled workers. Since firms who need s_1 skilled workers comprise previously successful firms who fail to innovate and previously successful firms who succeed in innovating the effect on the demand from these firms of encouraging more R&D can go either way. In any event the expression in square brackets in this third term measures the overall increase in the demand for skilled workers that arises when we encourage firms to do more R&D. Since skilled workers carry a price of λ this final effect measures the cost of intensifying the use of skilled workers.

An important point to notice about this effect is that if L is small then so too will be s_2, s_1 and s_0. Hence in economies with a small number of skilled workers this third effect can be ignored.

The important point then is that in a wide class of cases the social marginal steady-state product of a skilled worker exceeds the present value of the stream of training costs that are saved.

Having characterised the social optimum, let me now turn to a comparison with the market equilibrium.

3.2   Market equilibrium

The first question I want to address is what kind of market equilibrium might support the optimum steady-state allocation.

Three features of the optimum allocation are important:

(i) in making their R&D decision, firms perceive unskilled workers as incurring a training cost in the period in which they innovate, but no further training costs when they do not innovate, while they perceive skilled workers as incurring no training costs in any period;

(ii) while some skilled workers are retained by firms even when they are not innovating, firms do expand and contract their use of skilled workers as they go through periods of success and failure at innovation, so skilled workers are being continuously re-assigned to firms;

(iii) skilled workers perceive the 'right' return to acquiring skill (say through the acquisition of higher education).

Without going into detail, what this would seem to require is something like an employment agency for skilled workers which hires them on lifetime contracts guaranteeing continuous employment and at a price that reflects their 'true' value. This agency then signs contracts with individual firms which, in return for a fixed initial payment, gives the firm the option of using a specified number of skilled workers whenever it subsequently needs them. In this way firms perceive no costs of using skilled workers when they are needed and so their R&D decisions reflect the true costs to society of using a skilled worker to innovate.

In the absence of such institutions, or of alternative institutions that might mimic such behaviour, markets will perform differently from the social optimum. To see this, consider what would happen in an economy in which it was costless to hire and fire labour, but in which it was also impossible to write any long-term contracts to hire skilled labour – either by an agency or by individual firms.

Suppose instead that skilled workers are hired on one-period contracts. The contract has to be signed at the start of each period before the firm knows the outcome of any R&D decision it makes.

There may be a number of different equilibria depending on the kinds of contracts written between firms and workers. Again I am not going to be exhaustive but just focus on one kind of equilibrium – what I will call the *bonus equilibrium*. To describe this, notice that the first term in the expression for λ, was a term that indicated that a skilled worker should get paid an amount equal to receiving c every time a firm innovated, but nothing in periods when the firm failed to innovate. This looks like a bonus payment, but the crucial point about the social optimum is that this should get paid in advance, and not every time the firm innovates.

Suppose, however, that in the absence of long-term contracts firms also offer their skilled workers a contract in which they are paid a fixed wage every period which reflects their marginal physical productivity, but in periods when the firm innovates they get a bonus payment, but nothing extra at other times. This contract is not a long-term contract, so workers would be free to leave any firm at any period. What would a bonus equilibrium look like?

Suppose first of all that all firms paid a bonus c every time they innovated. There are two consequences of this: all firms are indifferent about hiring skilled workers rather than unskilled workers; a skilled worker joining a firm that innovated last period anticipates getting c with probability p_1, while it anticipates getting c with probability p_0 if it joins a firm that failed to innovate last period. If, as we have seen to be the case, successful firms do more R&D than unsuccessful firms, then skilled workers would always quit firms as soon as they had failed to innovate. But this means that firms are failing to retain their skilled workers and are being forced to face additional training costs. So one feature we want for equilibrium is that skilled workers should be indifferent to where they get employed.

So suppose then that a firm of type i offers to pay a bonus of b_i to its workers when it innovates, but now, recognise that in equilibrium we need to keep workers indifferent to where they work, and so impose the equilibrium condition

$$p_1 b_1 = p_0 b_0 \tag{22}$$

As long as skilled workers are indifferent as to where they work, firms can retain them for as long as they like, and so do not need to face the possibility of incurring re-training costs if their skilled workers all quit.

Notice that an important implication of (22) is that firms that are more successful at innovating can hire skilled workers more cheaply than less successful firms. This means that successful firms will face lower cost of innovating than unsuccessful firms which will reinforce their tendency to be successful. So just as with *horizontal training costs*, we see that *vertical training costs* tend to produce virtuous and vicious cycles of firms.

In what follows I am going to take it that all our previous results hold and that firms that have been more successful in the past are going to have greater incentives to innovate than unsuccessful firms, which in turn gets reinforced through the effects on bonus payments just discussed. Thus I will take it that $p_1 > p_0$ and so $b_0 > b_1$.

Now notice the following.

(i) The fact that a firm has to sign contracts before they know their R&D success means that firms have to decide how many skilled workers to hire solely on the basis of last period's R&D success. Suppose firms of type 1 hire s_i skilled workers.

(ii) If $b_0 > c$ then firms of type 0 will prefer to hire no skilled workers.

(iii) If $b_1 < c$ then firms of type 1 would prefer skilled to unskilled workers. However, there are two limitations on the number of skilled workers they can hire. The first is that it has to choose $s_1 \leq x_1$ since there is always a chance it will fail to innovate – in which case it certainly has to train $(x_2 - s_1) > 0$ unskilled workers if it succeeds in innovating. If it does fail to innovate this period then it goes into next period with a workforce of x_1 workers, s_1 of whom are skilled and all of whom know the technology learned in the previous period. In making the choice of how many skilled workers to now hire it has to obey the analogue of the constraint (14) since otherwise it will have to re-train unskilled workers in a technology that has already been learned.

In what follows I am going to take it that having $s_0 = 0$ so constrains the value of s_1 that the resource constraint on skilled labour is not satisfied. This implies that we wish to have firms of type 0 choosing to hire skilled workers, and for this we need them to be indifferent to skilled and unskilled workers.

So two other conditions that have to be satisfied in equilibrium are

$$b_0 = c \tag{23}$$

$$s_1(x_1 - x_0) + s_0 \tag{24}$$

With these conditions then the optimal R&D decisions and values of the two types of firm are given by

$$\gamma'(p_1) \geq \{\pi_2 + \delta V_1 - c[x_2 - s_1] - b_1 s_1\} - \{\pi_1 + \delta V_0\} \qquad p_1 \geq 0 \tag{25}$$

$$\gamma'(p_0) \geq \{\pi_1 + \delta V_1 - c x_1\} - \{\pi_0 + \delta V_0\} \qquad p_0 \geq 0 \tag{26}$$

$$V_1 = p_1\{\pi_2 + \delta V_1 - c[x_2 - s_1] - b_1 s_1\} + (1 - p_1)\{\pi_1 \delta V_0\} - \gamma(p_1) \tag{27}$$

$$V_0 = p_0\{\pi_1 + \delta V_1 - c x_1\} + (1 - p_0)\{\pi_0 + \delta V_0\} = \gamma(p_0) \tag{28}$$

Finally we need to ensure that the market for skilled workers clears. This requires

$$\frac{p_0}{p_0 + 1 - p_1} s_1 + \frac{(1 - p_1)}{p_0 + 1 - p_1} s_0 = L \tag{29}$$

(22)–(29) are eight equations determining the eight variables p_0, p_1, s_0, s_1, b_0, b_1, V_0, V_1 that constitute a *bonus equilibrium with short-term contracts*.

There are two features of this equilibrium that are worth contrasting with the optimum:

(i) Firms see themselves as having to pay a positive amount for skilled workers every time they innovate, which makes skilled workers appear more expensive than they ought to be when the firm is contemplating its R&D decision. Thus firms see the cost of innovation as being excessively high and will do too little R&D.

(ii) Skilled workers typically receive too little pay. Their expected pay every period is p_0c and the present value of this is

$$\frac{p_0 c}{1 - \delta} < \frac{c}{1 - \delta} h_1$$

Moreover, since firms are doing too little R&D, the equilibrium value of h_1 is less than the optimum value. Over and above this, workers are not receiving anything that reflects the gain to society from having a higher proportion of skilled workers in equilibrium.

Thus the model shows how th● ●ability of firms to write long-term contracts with skilled workers ●●● a market failure in which skilled workers see too little incentive to acquire training and firms see skilled workers as being too expensive and so do too little R&D.

An additional feature of the model that is interesting is that successful firms will see R&D as being cheaper (per worker) than unsuccesful firms. Thus *vertical training costs* introduce a factor that tends to reinforce *persistence* and its associated phenomenon of *virtuous and vicious circles*.

4   Conclusions

In this chapter I have tried to explore a number of issues about how skill gaps might arise in the context of an explicit model of *dynamic R&D competition*. This is a model in which firms are engaged in a process of *ongoing* R&D competition in which they use R&D as a strategic weapon in the competition for market share. The critical feature of such a model is that the structure of industry (the distribution of more and less successful firms) is fully endogenous and both determines and is determined by the outcome of the R&D competition.

A number of key conclusions have emerged.

(1) The analysis of *vertical training costs* allows us to introduce the interesting idea of characterising skilled workers as being more flexible than unskilled workers while being no more physically productive.

(2) The social marginal product of a skilled worker exceeds the expected present value of the training costs that are saved on unskilled workers, by a factor that reflects the gain to society from having more successful firms around. This is a factor that only arises in a model such as this where there is an endogenous equilibrium distribution of firms. This makes precise the worries many people have about the importance of having a more skilled workforce.

(3) Markets typically fail to reward flexibility adequately since it is hard to write the long-term contracts that ensure that firms perceive no cost to actually using or retaining a skilled worker as the consequence of its R&D decisions.

(4) In the absence of long-term contracts, firms do too little R&D as they perceive skilled workers as being too expensive, while at the same time skilled workers receive too low a return to their education. This, I would argue, is the essential feature of the notion of a skill gap.

(5) In the market equilibrium with *vertical training costs* we find once again the phenomenon of persistence: successful firms hire skilled workers more cheaply than unsuccessful ones and this helps perpetuate their tendency to be more successful than unsuccessful firms.

The market failures identified in (4) are precisely those often referred to in informal discussion. While I think that the model presented here is a useful start to getting a complete analysis of the phenomenon of skill gaps there are clearly many areas where more work needs to be done.

I have only really sketched some of the ideas in the analysis of both the market equilibrium and social optimum in the presence of flexible skilled workers. This requires a much more systematic analysis. All the various possible equilibria and optima need to be explored and related to the model parameters. I have focused on only one type of short-term contractual arrangement – the *bonus equilibrium*. There may be many others that have enhanced efficiency properties.

NOTES

This is a substantially extended version of the paper presented at the conference 'The Skill Gaps and Economic Activity', organized by CEPR, London, 19–20

April 1993. I am grateful to Alison Booth, Dennis Snower and the other participants at the conference for suggestions which led to the extensions.
1 This is not essential. I could alternatively assume that in production skilled workers and unskilled workers were perfect substitutes with each receiving the same *efficiency* wage. If skilled workers were more productive than unskilled workers they would receive a correspondingly higher *nominal* wage.

REFERENCES

Acemoglu, D. (1992), 'Labour Market Imperfections, Innovation Incentives and the Dynamics of Innovation Activity', Massachusetts Institute of Technology, mimeo.

Aghion, P. and P. Howitt (1994), 'Growth and Unemployment', *Review of Economic Studies* **61**, 477–94.

Beath, J., Y. Katsoulacos and D. Ulph (1994), 'Strategic R&D & Innovation', in J. Cable (ed.), *Current Issues in Industrial Economics*, Basingstoke: Macmillan.

Ulph, D. (1991), 'Endogenous Growth and Industrial Structure', University of Bristol, mimeo.

  (1994), 'Training Costs, Differential Firm Performance, and Economic Growth', University College London, mimeo.

6 The low-skill, bad-job trap

This chapter analyses how a sector of an economy can fall into a 'low-skill, bad-job trap', characterized by a vicious cycle of low productivity, deficient training, and deficient skilled jobs, preventing the sector from competing effectively in the markets for skill-intensive products.

'Bad-jobs' are associated with low wages and little opportunity to accumulate human capital. They are the lot of the working poor. 'Good jobs' command higher wages and higher skills. The chapter argues that in sectors with a small proportion of skilled workers, firms have little incentive to provide good jobs, since such positions would be difficult to fill; but if few good jobs are available, workers have little incentive to acquire skills, since such skills would be likely to remain underutilized and consequently insufficiently remunerated.

The chapter examines the interaction between two mutually reinforcing externalities: a 'vacancy supply externality' and a 'training supply externality'. The former arises when an increase in the number of skilled vacancies raises the probability that skilled workers find good jobs and thereby raises the expected return from training. Thus when a firm creates new vacancies, its private return falls short of the social return, since the latter also includes the rise in the workers' expected return from training. The 'training supply externality' arises when an increase in the number of skilled workers raises the probability that firms with good jobs find skilled workers and thereby raises the expected return from supplying vacancies. Thus when a worker acquires education, his private return falls short of the social return, which also includes the increase in the firms' expected gain from supplying vacancies.

Each of these externalities in isolation would lead the market mechanism to provide insufficient training. When both externalities are present simultaneously, as in the model above, the market failure is considerably amplified. Consequently, unless there are major government failures in this area, there is a case for the government to stimulate the acquisition of skills.

The chapter provides a possible explanation for why Western countries, experiencing a broadly common shift in labour demand from unskilled to skilled labour, should have responded so differently since the 1980s – with earnings differentials across skill groups rising in some market economies, but remaining constant or even falling in others. The analysis here suggests that countries' different responses may be due to differences in opportunities for skilled employment, which may have arisen for historical and policy reasons: in countries that offer little support for education and training, that contain a large proportion of unskilled workers, the market mechanism may reinforce the existing lack of skills by providing little incentive to acquire more; whereas in countries with well-functioning educational and training institutions and large bodies of skilled labour, the free market may do much more to induce people to become skilled.

Finally, the chapter contributes to the current debate about the reasons for the rising dispersion of wages and/or employment opportunities that many OECD countries have witnessed over the past decade and a half. Most economists have come to see these problems as the outcome of (i) skill-biased international trade flows, (ii) skill-biased technological change, or (iii) deficient education and training. This chapter suggests another source, complementary to those above: namely, that the increasing dispersion is due to the interaction between the vacancy supply externality and the training supply externality. Whereas some sectors are able to respond to the observed rise in the demand for skilled labour, others are unable to do so, either because the initial supply of skilled workers was insufficient to leave firms a significant incentive to create skilled vacancies, or because the initial supply of skilled vacancies was insufficient to leave workers a significant incentive to acquire skills. The upshot of these divergent experiences is the increasing dispersion of wages and employment opportunities.

The low-skill, bad-job trap

DENNIS J. SNOWER

1   Introduction

The secular rise in the demand for skilled labour represents an important opportunity for people to become more productive, earn higher wages, and find jobs with longer-term career prospects. Over the past decade policy makers in several advanced market economies have expressed increasing concern that certain sectors and population groups are failing to grasp this opportunity. It is often argued, for example, that some sectors of the UK and US economies have been less successful than their German and Japanese counterparts in taking advantage of the swing from unskilled to skilled work. Some segments of employers and employees, it is alleged, are caught in a vicious cycle of low productivity, deficient training, and insufficient skilled jobs, that prevents them from competing effectively in the markets for skill-intensive products.

This chapter provides a formal basis for this argument. It analyzes how a sector or population group can fall into what I shall call a 'low-skill, bad-job trap'. 'Bad jobs' are ones associated with low wages and little opportunity to accumulate human capital. They are the lot of the working poor. 'Good jobs' command higher wages and higher skills. The chapter argues that, in sectors with a small proportion of skilled workers, firms have little incentive to provide good jobs, since such positions would be difficult to fill; but if few good jobs are available, workers have little incentive to acquire skills, since such skills would be likely to remain underutilized and consequently insufficiently remunerated.

A growing body of empirical evidence is consonant with this view. For example, in his analysis of the export performance of the UK and Germany, Oulton (chapter 10 in this volume) argues that since Britain has a less skilled workforce than Germany, the UK has a greater incentive to produce non-traded services, that are comparatively protected from foreign competition, and this specialization creates a

111

comparatively large demand for less skilled labour. Mason, van Ark, and Wagner (Chapter 9 in this volume), in their study of biscuit manufacturing plants in Britain, Germany, France, and The Netherlands, show that British value-added per employee-hour is significantly below that of the other three countries and that these productivity differences correspond to differences in workforce skills rather than differences in the age and quality of capital equipment. They argue that employers' decisions about what type of products to produce depends on the degree to which skilled labour is available.

Politicians and journalists often suggest that the relatively low levels of education and training acquired by American blacks and Hispanics make the proliferation of low-grade, dead-end jobs profitable which, in turn, weakens these people's incentives to accumulate skills. The persistence of the 'urban underclass' is sometimes attributed to this phenomenon. Broadly similar arguments have been used to help explain the difficulties of some developing countries – such as India, Pakistan, and many African states – in building up the human capital necessary to produce sophisticated manufactured products.

In addition to providing a possible explanation for such phenomena, the paper also suggests a reason why Western countries, experiencing a broadly common shift in labour demand from unskilled to skilled labour, should have responded so differently since the 1980s – with earnings differentials across skill groups rising in some market economies, but remaining constant or even falling in others. The analysis here suggests that countries' different responses may be due to differences in opportunities for skilled employment, which may have arisen for historical and policy reasons: in countries that offer little support for education and training and that contain a large proportion of unskilled workers, the market mechanism may reinforce the existing lack of skills by providing little incentive to acquire more; whereas in countries with well-functioning educational and training institutions and large bodies of skilled labour, the free market may do much more to induce people to become skilled.

Finally the chapter contributes to the current debate about the reasons for the rising dispersion of wages and/or employment opportunities that many OECD countries have witnessed since the 1980s. Whereas the currently dominant explanations of this phenomenon rest on skill-biased technological change, skill-biased international trade flows, and education and training deficiencies, this chapter suggests another, complementary explanation: the increasing dispersion may arise because different sectors differ in terms of their stocks of skilled job searchers and skilled vacancies. Where these stocks are high, sectors can respond to the observed rise in the demand for skilled labour. But where the stock of skilled job searchers is low, firms have little incentive to post skilled vacancies; and where the stock of skilled vacancies is low, workers have little incentive to become trained.

The policy implications of this analysis are strikingly at variance with those underlying the standard human capital theory, where workers and firms appropriate the entire return from training, regardless of whether this training is 'general' or 'specific'. In this setting, good and bad jobs are allocated efficiently. Employers and employees are fully compensated for the good jobs that are filled, and the bad jobs go to workers whom it would not be in society's interests to train.

The analysis here suggests that this conclusion is untenable when firms are imperfectly informed about the availability of skilled workers and the workers, in turn, are imperfectly informed about the availability of good jobs. Under these conditions, training that is potentially useful to all firms is nevertheless not 'general', since the imperfect information prevents all firms from having access to all the available skilled workers. Nor is this training 'specific', since the information is generally available to more than one firm.

The critical issue is that in this intermediate range between the two extremes of 'general' and 'specific' skills, firms and workers are no longer able to appropriate all the benefits from training, and thus free market activity may provide insufficient training incentives.[1] A firm that creates vacancies for good jobs thereby raises workers' returns to education and vocational training (by increasing the probability that skilled workers find good jobs), but the firm clearly cannot make these workers pay for this privilege.[2] A worker who acquires further education or vocational training raises firms' returns from creating good job vacancies, but the worker cannot make these firms pay for his education or training.[3]

It is this market failure that is responsible for the low-skill, bad-job trap. There are two externalities at work here. The first is a 'vacancy supply externality', whereby an increase in the number of skilled vacancies raises the skilled workers' chances of finding good jobs and thereby raises the expected return from training and education. The second is a 'training supply externality', whereby an increase in the number of skilled workers raises firms' chances of filling their good jobs and thereby raises the expected return from opening skilled vacancies.

The first externality implies that when there are few good jobs, workers are under-compensated for acquiring skills. The second externality means that when a sizeable proportion of the workforce is unskilled, firms are under-compensated for the creation of good jobs. These two market failures, clearly, reinforce one another.

The chapter is organized as follows. Section 2 outlines the empirical background that motivates the analysis and examines alternative explanations for the diverse responses to the growth in demand for skilled labour. Section 3 presents a model of the low-skill, bad-job trap. Section 4 spells out the policy implications.

2   The background

One of the most remarkable labour market developments in advanced market economies over the 1980s has been the rise in the demand for skilled work relative to unskilled work. This relentless shift is usually attributed to the skill bias of technological progress and of international trade, as well as to changes and in the product demand mix toward sophisticated services. Specifically, (a) the 'computer revolution' has raised the demand for highly educated labour; (b) the increasing volume of imports, relatively intensive in unskilled labour, from the Far East and Central Europe, and elsewhere, together with the relocation of production-line jobs to these countries, has reduced the demand for unskilled labour in the West; and (c) the rise in the demand for professional, managerial, medical, and technical services has raised the demand for skilled labour.

These developments were general, affecting all the advanced market economies in much the same way. Nevertheless, there has been a wide diversity of responses over the 1980s. Earnings differentials – by education, occupation, and skill – all widened dramatically in the United States and the United Kingdom over this period. By comparison, there was only a very modest rise in earnings differentials in Austria, Australia, Belgium, Canada, France, Japan, The Netherlands, Portugal, Spain, and Sweden. In Denmark, Finland, Italy, and Norway, earnings dispersion (in terms of the ratios of the upper and lower deciles to the median) remained roughly unchanged over the 1980s; while in Germany there was a small reduction in dispersion over that period.[4]

The usual way of explaining these diverse responses to the broad-based labour demand shift is through inter-country differences in (i) *labour supply* movements and (ii) labour market *institutions*. Let us consider each in turn.

There is ample evidence in the USA and many European countries of a large influx of young people (in the 15 to 24 age range), and since youth earnings tend to be low, this depressed wages at the lower end of the wage distribution.[5] There is also evidence in some countries of a fall in the growth of the supply of college-educated people, relative to the demand, which may have raised wages at the upper end of the distribution.[6]

As an explanation of why countries responded differently to a common rise in the demand for skilled labour, however, the labour supply story is not wholly satisfactory: the accelerated entry of young participants into the labour force, and the slow-down in the entry of well-educated people are developments that many Western countries had in common over the 1980s, and thus they cannot provide a full account of why those countries had such diverse wage-employment experiences.[7]

The other account rests on institutional differences: differences in minimum wage laws, wage bargaining structures, and social insurance institutions may help explain why the increased demand for skilled labour generated greater earnings disparities in the USA and the UK than in the advanced market economies of continental Europe. Though plausible, this view has not yet been formulated with the precision necessary to provide a firm theoretical and empirical foundation. Empirically, the difficulty with this account is that it does not tell us why the large earnings differentials in the USA and the UK have lasted for so long in the 1980s. For those who (like myself) do not believe that the existing unskilled workforces in these countries are essentially untrainable, it is puzzling why more unskilled workers did not become skilled, thereby reducing the degree of earnings inequality.

Another problem with the labour supply and institutional explanations above is that they are not really explanations at all. To say that a country fails to take full advantage of the rising demand for skilled labour because the supply of skilled labour has not grown sufficiently, is not terribly informative; it does not tell us *why* the skilled labour supply has been so unresponsive. To say that institutional rigidities – such as minimum wages and wage-compression agreements – rob people of the incentive to become educated and trained, does not explain *why* voters keep these rigidities in operation.

This chapter, as noted, takes a different approach. It explains how a sector of an economy could fall into a low-skill, bad-job trap, while another – facing similar labour demand and labour supply conditions – may have a high proportion of skilled workers and good jobs.[8] The analysis also suggests an answer to the question why the large earnings differential between skilled and unskilled labour has lasted so long in the USA and the UK: the degree to which a given earnings differential induces workers to acquire skills depends on the availability of good jobs. When people are caught in the low-skill, bad-job trap, relatively few good jobs exist, and thus even a large earnings differential may provide little incentive for the unskilled to become skilled. In that event, the earnings differential may persist.

In this respect the analysis also provides an underpinning for the institutional and labour supply accounts of earnings disparities. It suggests that in countries with a large proportion of unskilled labour and insufficient provision of education and training, voters will have relatively little incentive to dismantle institutional rigidities, since that would hurt a relatively large group of unskilled workers and help a relatively small group of skilled ones. Similarly, the skilled labour supply may not be very responsive to earnings differentials in such countries, since there are relatively few job skilled opportunities for skilled workers – and the dearth of job opportunities, of course, is due to the dearth of skilled labour.

The following sections analyze the low-skill, bad-job trap in terms of a particularly simple model.

3　The interaction between training and good jobs

Consider a sector with the following straightforward structure. There is a fixed number of workers, who are either 'unskilled' or 'skilled'. The unskilled workers are only able to work at 'bad jobs', at which their marginal product is a_u (a positive constant). The skilled workers are also able to work at 'good jobs', where their marginal product is a_s (also a positive constant), with $a_s > a_u$.

All workers live for two periods. At the beginning of the first, each worker decides whether to acquire the education or training ('education', for short) necessary to become skilled. The unskilled workers acquire no education and are available for work in both periods. The others acquire education in the first period and are then able to provide skilled labour services in the second.

The training is useful to all firms, in the sense that it raises the workers' potential productivities at all firms equally. Nevertheless, the training is not perfectly 'general' since firms have imperfect information about the availability of skilled workers. Ex post (after the skilled worker has found a skilled job), the costs of the training are shared between the employer and employee, since the wage for skilled labour exceeds that for unskilled labour. However, ex ante (when the decision to train is made), the explicit training cost falls on the worker.[9]

When workers make their training decisions and firms decide on how many skilled vacancies to create, they take account of (a) the number of trained workers, (b) the number of skilled vacancies, and (c) the wages for skilled and unskilled labour – all of which are exogenous to each individual training and vacancy decision. The wages will be shown to depend on the productivities of skilled and unskilled workers. Since we will assume constant returns to labour, these productivities do not depend on the levels of skilled and unskilled employment. Consequently, it makes no difference to this model whether wages are determined before or after the training and vacancy decisions are made.

Plausibly, the market for 'bad jobs' is assumed to be perfectly competitive, whereas the market for 'good jobs' is taken to be imperfectly competitive, subject to the entry barriers that give employers and employees market power in the wage determination process. On account of perfect competition, the real wage in the unskilled sector is equal to the marginal product:

$$w_u = a_u \tag{1}$$

For simplicity, assume that this wage exceeds the workers' reservation wage, so that there is no unemployment.

The skilled wage is the outcome of a Nash bargain between the firm and each of its skilled employees. Under bargaining agreement, the skilled worker receives the real wage w_s and the employer receives $a_s - w_s$. Under disagreement, the skilled worker's fall-back position is w_u (from employment in the perfectly competitive unskilled sector) and the employer's fall-back position is zero. The Nash bargaining problem is thus to maximize the Nash product $(w_s - w_u)^\mu (a_s - w_s)^{1-\mu}$ with respect to w_s. The negotiated wage, that solves this problem, is

$$w_s = \mu a_s + (1 - \mu) a_u \tag{2}$$

Given these wages w_u and w_s, we now turn to the workers' training decision and the firms' skilled vacancy decision.

3.1 The training decision

Workers are assumed to be heterogeneous in terms of their ability to acquire education, so that the marginal skilled worker's cost of education rises with the aggregate number of workers being educated (N_s). In particular, let this cost be eN_s^ϵ, where e and ϵ are positive constants. Once a worker has acquired education, he has a probability ρ of finding a good job and receiving the wage w_s, and a probability $(1 - \rho)$ of not finding it and thus having to take a bad job with wage w_u. Thus, assuming a zero rate of time discount, the marginal skilled worker's net return from education is $\rho w_s + (1 - \rho)w_u - eN_s^\epsilon$. This must be compared with an unskilled worker's income over the two periods: $2w_u$. In equilibrium, the marginal worker is indifferent between becoming skilled and remaining unskilled: $\rho w_s + (1 - \rho)w_u - eN_s^\epsilon = 2w_u$, or equivalently,

$$\rho w_s - (1 + \rho)w_u = eN_s^\epsilon \tag{3}$$

Letting V_s be the aggregate number of skilled vacancies, N_s be the aggregate number of skilled job searchers, and X_s be the aggregate number of matches, the matching technology is given in the following simple terms:

$$X_s = A \min(V_s, N_s) \tag{4}$$

where A is a positive constant, and $A<1$ since skilled workers have imperfect information about the availability of skilled vacancies.[10] Consequently the probability ρ of finding a good job is

$$\rho = \frac{X_s}{N_s} = A \min\left(\frac{V_s}{N_s}, 1\right) \tag{4a}$$

Substituting the wage equations (1) and (2), together with the probability function (4a), into the marginal condition (3), yields the 'training function':

$$A\mu(a_s - a_u)\frac{V_s}{N_s} - a_u = eN_s^\epsilon \qquad \text{for } V_s < N_s \tag{5a}$$

$$A\mu(a_s - a)_u - a_u = eN_s^\epsilon \qquad \text{for } V_s \geq N_s \tag{5b}$$

This training function is depicted by the TF curve in Figure 6.1.[11]

3.2   The skilled vacancy decision

For simplicity, we assume that there is free entry of firms to the sector, so that the aggregate number of skilled vacancies may be determined by a zero-profit constraint. Firms are heterogeneous in terms of their costs of supplying vacancies. The total cost of vacancy supply for the entire sector is given by $\kappa_1 + \kappa_2 V_s^\delta$, where κ_1, κ_2 and δ are positive constants and $\delta > 1$. (The underlying intuition is standard: the fixed cost κ_1 arises from the institutional infrastructure necessary for publicizing vacancies and the rising variable cost $\kappa_2 V_s^\delta$ is due to diminishing returns to factor inputs.) Suppose that potential entrants know only that they are

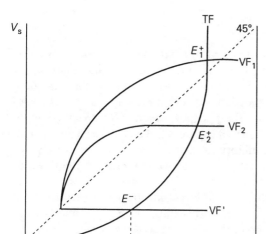

Figure 6.1   The low-skill, bad-job trap and the high-skill, good-job equilibrium

uniformly distributed along this total cost curve. Then the average expected cost of each newly entering firm is $(\kappa_1/V_s) + \kappa_2 V_s^{\delta-1}$.

Each firm has the same average return from creating a skilled vacancy, namely, $\theta(a_s - w_s)$, where θ is the firm's probability of finding a skilled worker. Thus the zero profit (free entry) condition is

$$\theta(a_s - w_s) = \frac{\kappa_1}{V_s} + \kappa_2 V_s^{\delta-1} \qquad (6)$$

The firm's probability of finding a skilled worker is

$$\theta = \frac{x_s}{V_s} = B \min\left(\frac{N_s}{V_s}, 1\right) \qquad (4b)$$

where $0 < B < 1$. Substituting (4b) into (6), we obtain the 'skilled vacancy function':

$$\kappa_1 + \kappa_2 V_s^{\delta} = BN_s(1-\mu)(a_s - a_u) \qquad \text{for } V_s > N_s \qquad (7a)$$
$$\kappa_1 + \kappa_2 V_s^{\delta} = BV_s(1-\mu)(a_s - a_u) \qquad \text{for } V_s \leq N_s \qquad (7b)$$

This vacancy function is depicted by the VF curve in Figure 6.1.[12]

3.3   *The labour market equilibria*

The labour market equilibria lie at the intersections of the training function and the vacancy function. Observe that a rising marginal cost of training makes the lower portion of the training function (corresponding to equation (5a)) convex, and that a rising marginal cost of vacancies makes the upper portion of the vacancy function (corresponding to equation (8a)) concave, as shown in Figure 6.1. Thus it is easy to see that, provided a labour market equilibrium exists,[13] there must be exactly two equilibria. One equilibrium lies at the intersection between the upward-sloping portion of the TF curve and the lower horizontal branch of the VF curve (VF').[14] This is the 'low-skill, bad-job trap', denoted by point E^-. The other equilibrium lies above this trap, either at the intersection of the upward-sloping portion of the VF curve and the vertical portion of the TF curve[15] (the intersection of VF_1 and TF in Figure 6.1) or at the intersection of the upper horizontal portion of the VF curve and the upward-sloping portion of the TF curve (the intersection of the VF_2 curve and the TF curve in the figure). This is the 'high-skill, good-job equilibrium' denoted by point E^+.

Observe that the greater is the number of skilled workers and skilled vacancies in our model, the greater is the income that workers receive (since skilled workers receive higher wages than unskilled ones) and the greater is the total profit earned by firms (since profits are earned only from the imperfectly competitive, skilled jobs). As skilled workers are more productive than unskilled ones, a greater number of skilled workers means that more is being produced in the sector. In this sense, therefore, assuming quite plausibly that skilled work is not more onerous than unskilled work, it is in the public interest to attain the high-skill, good-job equilibrium and to avoid the low-skill, bad-job trap.

From the marginal training condition (3) we infer that for all points lying above the training function TF in the figure, the expected marginal gain from training ($\rho w_s - (1 + \rho)w_u$) exceeds the associated marginal cost (eN_s^ϵ) and thus the supply of skilled workers will increase; conversely, for all points lying below TF, the supply of skilled workers falls. Moreover, from the free entry condition (6) we infer that for all points lying below the vacancy function VF in the figure, the expected average gain ($\theta(a_s - w_s)$) from supplying vacancies exceeds the associated average cost ($\kappa_1/V_s + \kappa_2 V_s^{\delta-1}$) and thus the supply of vacancies will increase; and conversely, for all points lying above VF, the supply of vacancies rises. For these reasons, the two equilibria in Figure 6.1 are stable.

At the low-skill, bad-job trap, few workers acquire education since there are few skilled vacancies, and firms supply few skilled vacancies because there are few educated workers. Thus skilled employment is N_s^- and, given that the labour force is constant at L, unskilled employment is $N_u^- = L - N_s^-$. At the high-skill, good-job equilibrium, skilled vacancies are plentiful and so many workers acquire education, and since many workers are educated, firms offer many skilled vacancies.

4   Policy implications

Regarding policy formulation, it is important to recall that there are two reinforcing externalities in the model above, a 'vacancy supply externality' and a 'training supply externality'.[16] The vacancy supply externality is implicit in the training decision described by equation (3). The greater is the aggregate number of skilled vacancies, the greater will be the probability that a skilled worker finds a good job (provided that $\rho < 1$) and thus the greater will be the expected return from training. Thus when a firm creates new vacancies, its private return falls short of the social return, since the latter also includes the rise in the workers' expected return from training.

The training supply externality is implicit in the vacancy decision described by equation (6). The greater is the aggregate number of skilled workers, the greater will be the probability that a firm with a good job finds a skilled worker to fill it (provided that $\theta < 1$) and thus the greater will be the expected return from supplying vacancies. Thus when a worker acquires education, his private return falls short of the social return, which also includes the increase in the firms' expected gain from supplying vacancies.

Each of these externalities in isolation would lead the market mechanism to provide insufficient training. When both externalities are present simultaneously, as in the model above, the market failure is considerably amplified. This is the case not only for the low-skill, bad-job trap, but also for the high-skill, good-job equilibrium. Consequently, unless there are major government failures in this area, there is a case for the government to stimulate the acquisition of skills.

In the context of the model, there are two straightforward ways of doing this: either through an education subsidy to the workers or a skilled employment subsidy to the firms. The former shifts the training function rightwards (as when a proportional education subsidy reduces the parameter e of the training cost in equation (3)); the latter shifts the vacancy function upwards (as when a proportional employment subsidy reduces the parameter κ_2 of the vacancy supply cost in equation (6)).

Both subsidies induce workers to acquire more skills when the sector is in the low-skill, bad-job trap. However – and this is the important point

– the analysis above indicates that the two approaches are not equally effective in creating skilled employment. Given that the proximate effect of the education subsidy is to increase the number of workers receiving training, the low-skill, bad-job equilibrium will merely shift horizontally rightward in the figure. Thus the workforce becomes more skilled but no extra jobs are generated.[17] On the other hand, the skilled employment subsidy creates jobs by stimulating both the supply of vacancies *and* the supply of skilled workers.

Furthermore, the skilled employment subsidy – by shifting the VF curve upwards along the 45° line – brings the low-skill, bad-job trap into progressively closer proximity to the high-skill, good-job equilibrium. The education subsidy does not have this effect: the distance between the two equilibria either increases (as at the intersection between the VF_1 and TF curves) or remains unchanged (as at the intersection between the VF_2 and TF curves).

Finally, since both equilibria are stable, 'small' subsidies are not sufficient to overcome the low-skill, bad-job trap. A 'big push' – in the form of sufficiently large skilled employment subsidies – is required before the sector can be propelled toward the high-skill, good-job equilibrium.

NOTES

I am very grateful to Alison Booth, David Coe, Melvin Coles, Jeff Frank and Jose de Gregorio, and to Jonathan Haskel for his insightful comments. The paper was written while I was at the Research Department of the International Monetary Fund. The views expressed in this paper do not necessarily represent those of the IMF or its member countries.

1 Stevens (Chapter 2 of this volume) analyses this problem with respect to the poaching externality. This chapter, by contrast, examines the externality from the creation of skilled vacancies on the returns from skill acquisition and the externality from education and vocational training on the returns from skilled vacancies.

2 The firm is compensated not for opening vacancies, but for filling them. On account of the firm's imperfect information about the availability of skilled workers, existing vacancies are not automatically filled.

3 The worker is not compensated for his education, but for using his education to perform a skilled job. Owing to his imperfect information about the availability of skilled jobs, an educated worker is not certain to find a skilled job. Even if he does, he cannot appropriate the entire gain from his education, because of his employer's market power in the wage formation process (described in Section 3).

4 See Freeman and Katz (1993) and the OECD *Employment Outlook* (1993, pp. 158–65) for inter-country comparisons. Widening earnings differentials in

the USA have been documented by Bound and Johnson (1992), Katz and Murphy (1992), Levy and Murname (1992), and Murphy and Welch (1992).

5 See Davis (1992) and the OECD *Employment Outlook* (1993, pp. 169–70) for inter-country comparisons, Ermish (1988) for the UK, and Katz and Revenga (1989) for the US versus Japan.

6 See Davis (1992) and the OECD *Employment Outlook* (1993, pp. 170–3) for inter-country comparisons, Katz and Murphy (1992), and Murphy and Welch (1992) for the USA, Katz and Revenga (1989) for the US and Japan, and Erickson and Ichino (1993) for Italy. However, there is no evidence that the 'college premium' widened in Germany, France, and The Netherlands over the 1980s. Moreover, the literature on the college premium does not distinguish between the demand for vocational skills and the demand for more general skills, such as those achieved in college. This may be important, since it is not clear that an increased supply of college-educated people is wholly appropriate for satisfying the increased demand for skills.

7 Although the earnings of the young fell relative to prime-age earnings in Canada, France, Japan, the UK, and the USA, these trends clearly offer no consistent explanation of why these countries have experienced such diverse changes in earnings differentials.

8 The formal analysis of Sections 3 and 4 focuses on the low-skill, bad-job trap as a sector-wide phenomenon. In practice some sectors may be subject to this trap while others are not since different types of skilled labour may not be substitutable for one another.

9 Allowing firms to pay part of this explicit cost would not change the qualitative conclusions of the model.

10 Observe that since workers are assumed to live for only two periods and it takes one period to acquire education, each skilled worker works for only one period. Thus the aggregate number of skilled searchers is equal to the aggregate number of skilled workers and the aggregate number of skilled vacancies is equal to the aggregate number of good jobs.

11 Equation (5b) pertains to the vertical part of the TF curve, lying above the 45° line, whereas equation (5a) pertains to the portion of the curve lying below the 45° line. The latter portion is convex since, along the TF curve,

$$\frac{\mathrm{d}V_s}{\mathrm{d}N_s} = \frac{a_u + e(1 + \epsilon)N_s^\epsilon}{A\mu(a_s - a_u)}$$

since $(\mathrm{d}V_s/\mathrm{d}N_s)$, $(\mathrm{d}^2V_s/\mathrm{d}N_s^2) > 0$, the curve is convex.

12 Equation (7b) depicts the horizontal portion of the VF curve, lying beneath the 45° line, while equation (7a) depicts the portion lying above the 45° line. The latter portion is concave.

13 An equilibrium exists whenever the VF curve intersects the 45° line below the point at which the TF curve intersects the 45° line.

14 Recall that, beneath the 45° line, the TF curve *must* slope upwards while the VF curve *must* be horizontal.

15 Recall that, above the 45° line, the VF curve *must* slope upwards while the TF curve *must* be vertical.

16 For completeness, note that there are two further externalities as well: (i) when a firm creates a new vacancy, it reduces other firms' returns from creating new vacancies (since it thereby reduces the other firms' probability of

finding skilled workers) and (ii) when a worker acquires training, he reduces other workers' returns from training (since he thereby reduces the other workers' probability of finding skilled vacancies). It is easy to see, however, that these two externalities are dominated by the vacancy supply externality and the training supply externality. The reason is that the multiplier effects from the two externalities are less than unity (viz. when a firm creates a new vacancy, the other firms have an incentive to reduce their supply of vacancies by less than unity; when a worker acquires training, the other workers have an incentive to reduce their training by less than that), but the multiplier effects from the vacancy supply externality and the training supply externality are greater than or equal to unity (as is clear from the figure).

17 Given the matching function (4), the number of matches remains unchanged since the number of vacancies remains unchanged.

REFERENCES

Becker, Gary S. (1962), 'Investment in Human Capital: A Theoretical Analysis', *Journal of Political Economy* **70**, Supplement, 9–49.

(1964), *Human Capital*, New York: Columbia University Press.

Bound, John and George Johnson (1992), 'Changes in the Structure of Wages in the 1980s: An Evaluation of Alternative Explanations', *American Economic Review* **82**, 371–92.

Davis, S. J. (1992), 'Cross-Country Patterns of Change in Relative Wages', in O. Blanchard and S. Fischer (eds.), *NBER Macroeconomics Annual*, Cambridge, MA: MIT Press.

Erickson, C. L. and A. C. Ichino (1993), 'Wage Differentials in Italy: Market Forces, Institutions and Inflation', in R. B. Freeman and L. F. Katz (1993).

Ermish, John (1988), 'Fortunes of Birth: The Impact of Generation Size on the Relative Earnings of Young Men', *Scottish Journal of Political Economy* **35**(3), 266–82.

Freeman, Richard B. and Lawrence F. Katz (1993), *Differences and Changes in Wage Structures*, Chicago: University of Chicago Press and NBER.

Katz, Lawrence and Kevin M. Murphy (1992), 'Changes in Relative Wages, 1963–1987: Supply and Demand Factors', *Quarterly Journal of Economics* **107**, 35–78.

Katz, Lawrence and A. L. Revenga (1989), 'Changes in the Structure of Wages: The United States vs Japan', *Journal of the Japanese and International Economies* **3**, 522–53.

Levy, Frank and Richard Murname (1992), 'US Earnings Levels and Earnings Inequality: A Review of Recent Trends and Proposed Explanations', *Journal of Economic Literature* September.

Murphy, Kevin M. and Finis Welch (1992), 'The Structure of Wages', *Quarterly Journal of Economics* **107**, 285–326.

OECD (1993), *Employment Outlook*, July, Paris: OECD Publications.

Part II
Empirical consequences of skills gaps

7   Changes in the relative demand for skills

A crucial argument of the theory in Part I is that the free market system typically cannot be expected to lead people to acquire sufficient skills. But the problem of skills gaps in the 1990s is exacerbated by the fact that the composition of labour demand in previous decades has shifted steadily in favour of skilled workers. In short, the inability of the market system to provide sufficient training is becoming an increasingly painful problem. Chapter 7 assesses the background to the current debate on training provision, with the UK economy as focus of interest.

The chapter describes changes in the patterns of employment and wages in the UK. In UK manufacturing, the percentage share of non-manual employment in total employment rose from 16.1% in 1948 to 32.7% by 1990; the percentage share of non-manual wage costs in the total wage bill rose from 23.1% in 1948 to 42.0% in 1990. In addition, the gap between the lowest-paid and highest-paid workers widened dramatically over the 1980s. Not only did the relative employment share of non-manual workers rise dramatically, but the pay of non-manuals relative to manuals increased sharply in the 1980s as well. In conventional economic terms, it appears that the relative demand curve shifted outwards.

This chapter focuses on possible explanations of this shift. One explanation is that increased international competition has dampened the wages of manual workers across industries producing traded goods. An alternative hypothesis is that technological developments (such as the introduction of computers) increase employers' demand for skilled workers within particular industries. The chapter computes the percentage of the variation in the share of non-manual employment attributable to these factors. Within-industry changes are found to be of overwhelming importance in UK manufacturing between 1979 and 1990.

A similar pattern of employment change is also found using workplace-level *data from the panel element of the 1984 and 1990 Workplace Industrial Relations Surveys. Over the period 1984 to 1990, there was a rise of about 0.4 percentage points per annum in the share of non-manuals in total employment. The majority of this increase is due to within-establishment shifts. Most of the observed shift towards non-manual labour occurred at the top end of the occupational range, with large within-establishment rises in the employment shares of middle managers and senior professionals.*

The move to non-manual employment was more marked in more R&D-intensive industries, in more innovative industries, and in establishments introducing microcomputers over the period 1984–90. These findings are consonant with the hypothesis that the introduction of manual-saving technical change bears significant responsibility for the shift towards non-manual employment and the increased remuneration of non-manual workers.

Changes in the relative demand for skills

STEPHEN MACHIN

1   Introduction

The importance of skills in shaping economic outcomes has long been a preoccupation of economists and other social science researchers. In recent years, much emphasis has been placed on the UK being a 'low skill' economy, faced by skill shortages, and that its economic performance has suffered as a consequence. In this chapter I consider what has happened to the distribution of skills (defined in terms of relatively broad employment classes) through the 1980s. I use two longitudinal data sources, an industry-level panel data set between 1979 and 1990 and the panel component of the 1984 and 1990 establishment-level Workplace Industrial Relations Surveys. There is evidence of a considerable shift towards the use of what may be termed more skilled labour (i.e. towards non-manual work, away from manual work and towards more highly educated labour). The majority of such relative increases are seen to be within-industry or establishment changes. Further, they are seen to be stronger in more R&D-intensive and innovative workplaces or industries, hence suggesting some support for the idea that manual-labour-saving technological changes were behind some of the observed employment shifts that occurred during the decade.

This finding is important when one considers what has happened to patterns of wages and employment in the UK labour market through the 1980s. As has been documented elsewhere (Gregg and Machin, 1994; Schmitt, 1995) the 1980s saw a very big widening out of the pay distribution with the best-paid workers doing much better than those at the lower end of the distribution. In international terms, several countries saw increases in earnings and income inequality in the 1980s, but the biggest increase seems to have occurred in the UK (with the USA not far behind and at a much higher level with a longer-term trend increase dating back to the 1960s: see Davis (1992) or Freeman

and Katz (1993)). It is therefore extremely important to evaluate
whether changes in the employment structure can account for part of
such changes.

As in the United States it appears that both wages and employment
have moved in favour of more 'skilled' workers in the UK in the 1980s:
that is, their share in total employment and wage costs has increased.
The empirical work presented in the remainder of this chapter attempts
to draw out the main trends and offer potential explanations of these
observed shifts in the structure of employment.

2   Changes in the structure of manufacturing industry employment

2.1   Aggregate changes in relative employment shares

Table 7.1 reports long-term aggregate changes in the relative shares of
manual and non-manual labour in manufacturing employment drawing
on Census of Production data in the post-war period between 1948
and 1990. Two sets of share statistics are reported, the share of non-
manual employment in total employment and the share of the non-
manual wage bill in the total wage bill. These are also plotted in
Figure 7.1.

Figure 7.1 and Table 7.1 make it clear that, over the post-war period,
the nature of employment shifted considerably in UK manufacturing,
away from manual to non-manual labour. The magnitude of the shift
is large, with the non-manual employment share rising from 16% in
1948 to 33% in 1990. A similar pattern emerges for the share of non-
manual wages in total wages which rose from 23% in 1948 to 42% by
1990. However, the non-manual/manual relative wage, reported in the
third column of the table and plotted in Figure 7.2, points to an
interesting pattern. Up to 1980, as price-theoretic mechanisms (i.e.
wage employment combinations lying on a downward-sloping labour
demand curve) would suggest, the increased (relative) number of non-
manuals went hand-in-hand with a reduced relative wage advantage.
This was not true of the 1980s. After 1980 both the non-manual/
manual relative wage differential and the share of non-manual labour
in total employment increased. This seems to suggest that the relative
demand curve for non-manual (*vis-à-vis* manual) labour shifted out in
the 1980s.

The remainder of this section focuses on the 1980s changes in the
employment structure in some detail using UK industry-level data
sources.

Table 7.1. Shares of non-manual labour and wage costs and relative wages in UK manufacturing, 1948–90

Year	Share of non-manual employment in total employment	Share of non-manual wage bill in total wage bill	Non-manual/ manual relative wages
1948	0.161	0.231	1.567
1955	0.189	0.249	1.400
1963	0.235	0.301	1.399
1970	0.259	0.320	1.349
1975	0.272	0.330	1.315
1980	0.299	0.358	1.306
1985	0.319	0.390	1.365
1990	0.327	0.420	1.499

1. Sources for data: *Historical Record of the Census of Production 1907–1970* for data up to 1970 and various of the annual Census Summary Tables after 1970.
2. Non-manual employment and wages correspond to the Census category Administrative, technical and clerical employees: this is defined as including managing and other directors in receipt of a definite wage, salary or commission; managers, superintendents and work foremen; research experimental, development, technical and design employees; draughtsmen and tracers; editorial staff, staff reporters, canvassers, competition and advertising staff; and office (including works office) employees (*Historical Record of the Census of Production 1907–1970*, page xiii; the definition is almost identical in subsequent Census Summary Tables PA1002).
3. Manual employment and wages correspond to the Census category operatives which is defined, broadly speaking, as all manual wage earners. This includes all those employed in and about the factory or works; operatives employed in power houses and transport work; stores, warehouses, shops and canteens; inspectors, viewers and similar workers; maintenance workers; cleaners; operatives engaged in outside work of erecting, fitting etc. (*Historical Record of the Census of Production 1907–1970*, page xiii; the definition is almost identical in subsequent Census Summary Tables PA1002).

2.2 Industry-level changes in the manual/non-manual employment structure, 1979–90

In this section I document changes in the nature of manufacturing employment between 1979 and 1990 in 100 three-digit industries. The reason for limiting the analysis to this time period is the change in the Standard Industrial Classification in 1980 which makes it impossible to accurately consider disaggregated data in comparable industries prior to the 1980 change (with the exception of 1979 data which is published in the 1980 Summary Tables).

Table 7.2 reports annualised aggregate changes in the shares of

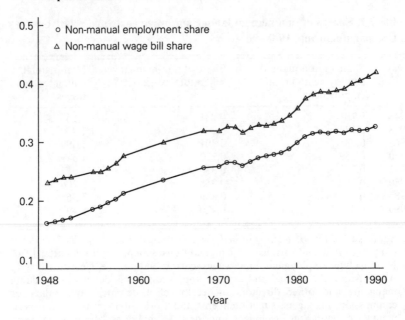

Figure 7.1   Shares of non-manual labour and wage costs in UK manufacturing, 1948–90

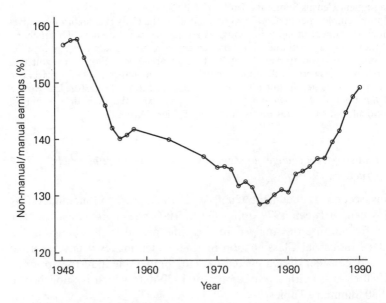

Figure 7.2   Non-manual/manual relative wages in UK manufacturing, 1948–90

non-manual employment and wage costs between 1979 and 1990. As Figure 7.1 and Table 7.1 make clear, this time period saw a move away from manual to non-manual labour, the average change being some 0.37 percentage points per annum. Compared to the 1979 share of 28.7% this corresponds to a cumulative rise of four percentage points (or 14% of the 1979 share) over the sample period. This is a big shift and, perhaps not surprisingly, is concentrated for the most part (but not entirely) in the recessionary period between 1980 and 1982. Having said that, there is an important trend shift towards non-manual labour throughout the whole of the time period under consideration.

These patterns are entirely in line with recent US work on this issue. For instance, Berman *et al.* (1993) present similar evidence for relative shifts in the demand for skilled (non-manual) labour in US manufacturing. Their results point to a long-term shift away from manual labour with the share of non-manual labour rising from about 0.26 in 1959 to 0.31 in 1981 and reaching 0.35 by 1987.

The second row of Table 7.2 documents that the share of the non-manual wage bill in the total wage bill rose by about 0.67 percentage points per annum between 1979 and 1990. This corresponds to a cumulative increase of some 7.3 percentage points (or 22% of the 1979 share). The greater magnitude of this rise, compared to the employment share increase, further emphasises that the 1980s saw a coincident rise in the relative non-manual/manual wage differential. It is evident that, to rationalise such shifts in a supply–demand framework as advocated by much of the US work, there needs to have been a shift in the relative demand for non-manuals. What may have been behind this demand shift is considered in more detail below in Section 4.

One might argue that these definitions of manual and non-manual employment are too broad to view the observed changes in shares as skill upgrading. I have therefore considered an alternative definition of employment structure based on the relative shares of educated and non-educated labour in total employment by three-digit industry from the annual Labour Force Survey (LFS).[1] The three share variables I have considered are shares based on individuals with a degree, an intermediate educational qualification (less than a degree, but with some educational qualification) and those with no qualifications. These education-based shares are strongly correlated with the non-manual share. For example, the correlation coefficient between the industry-based share of non-manual labour and the share of workers with a degree is 0.631. The correlation with the share of workers with no educational qualifications is −0.531. Moreover, the pattern of changes over time is similar, with a small rise (about 0.3 percentage

Table 7.2. Changes in the structure of employment in UK manufacturing in the 1980s and between and within industry decompositions

Variable	Number of three-digit industries and sample period	Total change (annualised) for whole of manufacturing in percentage points	Between-industry component	Within-industry component	Percentage contribution of within-industry component to total change
Share of non-manual employment in total employment	100 (1979–90)	0.367	0.066	0.301	82
Share of non-manual wage bill in total wage bill	100 (1979–90)	0.668	0.114	0.554	83

1. The decomposition is described in the text.
2. Based on Census of Production data at the three-digit industrial level.

points a year) in the relative share of graduates in the 1980s and a very large decrease in the share of uneducated workers (over two percentage points a year).[2] This is in line with the notion that there was a shift in relative employment demand in the 1980s, especially if one takes these rises in educated employment shares in conjunction with Schmitt's (1995) evidence that the rate of return to education rose in the 1980s. It is also reassuring that education-based definitions of employment structure trace out the pattern that more 'skilled' workers did considerably better in the UK labour market in the 1980s than their less 'skilled' counterparts.

2.3   Decompositions of changes in industrial employment shares

The 1980s increases in the shares of non-manual and educated workers in total employment, together with improvements in the relative wages of both groups, strongly suggest that the 1980s did see an increase in the relative demand for skilled workers. These patterns very much mirror the changing employment structure in US manufacturing (see Berman *et al.* (1993)). In the US literature several possible explanations have been proposed to explain shifts in relative demand. Two schools of thought currently dominate. One asserts that it is essentially due to product demand shifts that affect industries with a greater share of manuals by more. (The strongest case is the rise of import competition which has hit traditionally manual-using industries like the car industry by more.) The second is that skill upgrading has occurred due to skill-biased manual labour saving technical changes. (The most common example is the increased use of computer technologies: see Krueger, 1993, for empirical evidence that computer use has significantly altered the US wage structure.)

The key distinction between these two arguments is that the first concerns across-industry changes whilst the second refers to within-industry changes. Hence, an examination of whether the variation in changing employment shares is down to changes in the reallocation of labour between industries or whether it is due to shifts within industries can shed some light on the relevance of these two views.

To examine this one can decompose aggregate changes in the structure of employment into within-industry and between-industry components of the total change (as in Berman *et al.* (1993)). For N manufacturing industries one can decompose the aggregate change in employment shares, say ΔE, as follows:

$$\Delta E = \sum_{i=1}^{N} \Delta S_i \bar{E}_i + \sum_{i=1}^{N} \Delta E_i \bar{S}_i \tag{1}$$

where $E_i = X_i / N_i$ is the share of employment category X in total employment (N) for industry i. $S_i = N_i / N$ is industry i's share of employment in total manufacturing industry employment. The first expression in (1) gives changes in ΔE due to changes in the share of employment between industries; the second is the within-industry component due to changes in the share of type X labour within industries. This decomposition is also reported in Table 7.2. For both share variables the within-industry component is far and away the most important. It seems that much of the shift away from relatively unskilled labour occurred within given industries.

Hence, it appears that much of the change in employment and the average skill upgrading of workers is a within-industry phenomenon. This is similar to the US work on this issue. Berman *et al.* (1993) report that 70% (0.387 of the overall 0.552 percentage points per year) of the increase in the relative share of non-manual labour between 1979 and 1987 can be attributed to within-industry factors. The UK experience suggests a comparable figure of 81% (or 0.30 of the 0.37 percentage points per year rise) between 1979 and 1990.

3   Establishment-level changes in the employment structure, 1984–90

There are clearly some potentially important limitations associated with the industry data used in the previous section. Probably the three most important are: (i) the three-digit industrial classifications are quite highly aggregated; (ii) the only employment categories they contain are broadly defined manual/non-manual and (after matching in LFS data) education related groups; (iii) only manufacturing industries are covered. In this section I use a data source that, at least partially, circumvents these problems. I draw on establishment-level data from the panel element of the 1984 and 1990 Workplace Industrial Relations Surveys (WIRS) to consider changes in the composition of the relative demand for labour. The WIRS data give quite detailed classifications of the workforce within each plant in the survey and, since it has a panel element (albeit for two years only), this makes it possible to carry out an analysis similar to that undertaken above for the industry data.

In the Workplace Industrial Relations Surveys, total employment in each establishment is broken down into manual and non-manual components which are then split into fairly detailed skill/occupational groupings: (a) manual employment composed of skilled, semi-skilled and unskilled employment; (b) non-manual employment comprising clerical, secretarial and administrative staff, supervisors and foremen, junior professionals, senior professionals and middle management.

Table 7.3 reports the mean proportions of each group in a matched sample of 402 establishments in 1984 and 1990.[3] It is clear that the establishment-level data also paints a picture of an increased demand for non-manual workers. The 1984 to 1990 increase in the share of non-manuals in total employment is about 2.5 percentage points, or just over 0.4 percentage points a year.

The principal advantage of the WIRS data is that it enables a more detailed examination of the nature of the shift towards increased usage of non-manual workers.[4] It is very clear from Table 7.3 that the biggest increases are concentrated at the upper end of the non-manual hierarchy. The bulk (about three-quarters) of the increase in the non-manual share is down to an increased use of middle/senior managers and senior technical/professional staff.

One does need to be somewhat careful in generalising from these trends. The WIRS panel does cover a specific set of establishments: for instance, the panel is limited to trading establishments alone and the sample size is quite modest. However, it is very reassuring that the WIRS casebook (Millward et al., 1993, p. 18) also notes these trends in the larger samples of the 1984 and 1990 cross-sections. The clear advantage of using the

Table 7.3. Changes in the structure of employment in 402 establishments, 1984–90

Employment category	1984 share	1990 share	1984–90 annualised change in percentage points	Between-establishment component	Within-establishment component
Non-manual	0.467	0.492	0.41	0.07	0.34
Middle/senior managers	0.062	0.070	0.14	0.02	0.12
Senior technical/ professional	0.067	0.078	0.19	0.01	0.18
Junior technical/ professional	0.094	0.093	−0.01	−0.09	0.08
Foremen/ supervisors	0.051	0.051	−0.01	−0.03	0.02
Clerical/ administrative/ secretarial	0.194	0.200	0.10	0.15	−0.05

1. These are aggregate proportions based on weighted data in 402 establishments from the panel component of the 1984 and 1990 Workplace Industrial Relations Surveys. Weights used are those given in the survey to allow for the deliberate oversampling of larger establishments and to make them nationally representative in terms of the Census of Employment three years prior to each survey.

panel is that one can consider within-establishment changes over time and it is this that I consider next.

The decomposition described in equation (1) can easily be translated over to establishment data and changes in the aggregate share of a given labour type can be decomposed into within- and between-establishment changes. The results of carrying out this exercise are also reported in Table 7.3. An interesting pattern emerges. At the higher end of the non-manual occupational structure (middle managers and senior technical and professional staff) the majority of the positive changes are within establishments; at the bottom end (clerical workers) most of the observed changes are between establishments. This lends some support to the notions raised in the US work that much of the upgrading is down to manual labour saving changes that occur within given workplaces. I explore the association with an observable establishment-level indicator of technological change, increased computer usage, later in the chapter.

4   Explaining the 1980s shift in demand

The raw data descriptions of the preceding two sections seem to suggest that, as in the US work, much of the observed shift towards non-manual employment is linked to specific changes that occur within certain workplaces or industries. Some of the US work attributes this to some kind of technology-based demand shock which favours non-manual workers. Probably the most commonly cited example is the massive increase in computer usage that occurred in the 1980s (Berman *et al.*, 1993; Krueger, 1993). Other potential causes of manual labour saving technological change are hypothesised to be innovation and high R&D intensity.

It is somewhat difficult to present concrete evidence that technological changes are the principal factor driving the demand shifts since such changes are hard to measure. Unfortunately, this measurement problem is very much true of existing UK data sources. Nevertheless, in this section of the chapter I use what data exist to present several simple regression models that attempt to uncover any potential inter-linkages with observable measures of technological change. The three measures I consider are R&D intensity, an innovation measure (both at industry-level), and an establishment-based measure of computer usage. As will become clear below, these indices are observed to have some power in explaining the shift towards an increased share of non-production workers.

The econometric specifications I estimate can be easily derived from a simple cost function for production unit i in year t, say $C[(W_{nm})_{it}, (W_m)_{it}, K_{it}, Y_{it}]$ where $C[.]$ is variable costs defined as a function of the variable input prices (here the non-manual and manual wages, W_{nm} and W_m), output (Y) and quantities of the fixed factor inputs (here K, the capital stock). Assuming $C[.]$ has a translog functional form, it is easy to derive the following equation for the share of non-manual wage costs in total wage costs (see, for example, Berndt (1990, ch. 9)):

$$SHARE_{it} = \beta_0 + \beta_1 t + \beta_2 \ln(W_{nm}/W_m)_{it} + \beta_3 \ln K_{it} + \beta_4 \ln Y_{it} \quad (2)$$

where $SHARE$ is the share of non-manual wages in total wages and t is a time trend to allow for changes in $SHARE$ over time. First differencing (2) and appending an error term u gives a change in the share equation as

$$\Delta SHARE_{it} = \beta_1 + \beta_2 \Delta \ln(W_{nm}/W_m)_{it} + \beta_3 \Delta \ln K_{it} + \beta_4 \Delta \ln Y_{it} + u_{it} \quad (3)$$

Equation (3) is a useful device for empirically analysing changes in factor cost shares over time. Estimates of β_3 give an indication of whether non-manual labour and capital are complementary inputs (where $\beta_3 > 0$) or substitutes ($\beta_3 < 0$) in the production process. Estimates of β_4 give an indication of whether or not faster growing industries have differential changing employment shares.

Before estimating this model, however, one should note that, whilst K and Y may reasonably be assumed exogenous, the relative wage term cannot. In their US work using the above methodology, Berman *et al.* (1993) argue that variation in the relative wage confounds price changes with quality changes. On these grounds, and owing to the division bias problems $\ln(W_{nm}/W_m)_{it}$ creates by being on the right-hand side of a relative wage share equation, I follow their approach and exclude the relative wage from the model. I do, however, report estimates of wage cost share and employment share equations to see if there is any marked difference.

The final amendment that I make to the estimating model is to allow an assessment of the empirical importance of observable measures of technical change in explaining increases in the shares of non-manual wages and employment. Hence, the estimating equation I consider becomes

$$\Delta SHARE_{it} = \beta_1 + \beta_3 \Delta \ln K_{it} + \beta_4 \Delta \ln Y_{it} + \beta_5 TECH_{it} + u_{it} \quad (4)$$

where *TECH* denotes the various indicators of technical change/innovation that I consider in the following three sections of the paper.

4.1   The impact of industry R&D intensity

Table 7.4 presents some annual industry-level regressions of the growth in the share of non-manual labour in terms of wage bill and employment between 1982 and 1989. The index of technical progress that I consider is industry-level research and development intensity defined as R&D expenditure divided by sales. The R&D data is available on a consistent basis at two-digit industry level from the *Business Monitor* surveys undertaken in 1981, 1983, and 1985–89 inclusive. This defines the sample of industries used in the regressions in Table 7.4. The table reports regressions of the share of non-manuals in total wages and employment on the ratio of R&D expenditure to sales in 16 two-digit industries between 1982 and 1989.

The regressions in Table 7.4 are weighted by the share of a given industry's employment in total manufacturing employment in the year. This means the variable aggregates to the within-industry measure described in the decompositions of the previous section of the chapter.

Table 7.4. Changes in employment and wage bill shares and R&D intensity in 16 two-digit manufacturing industries, 1982–89

Change in share of:	Non-manual wage bill	Non-manual wage bill	Non-manual employment	Non-manual employment
Δ log (capital stock)	0.075	0.053	0.050	0.034
(t)	(0.030)	(0.032)	(0.025)	(0.026)
Δ log (real sales)	−0.023	−0.024	−0.019	−0.020
(t)	(0.015)	(0.013)	(0.011)	(0.011)
R&D expenditure/		0.065		0.047
sales $(t-1)$		(0.026)		(0.021)
One-digit industry dummies	Yes	Yes	Yes	Yes
Year dummies	Yes	Yes	Yes	Yes
R-squared	0.140	0.175	0.227	0.256
Sample size	128	128	128	128

1. Weighted least squares estimates (weights are the annual employment share of the industry in total manufacturing industry employment).
2. Heteroscedastic consistent standard errors in parentheses.

Four specifications are reported, two explaining changes in the non-manual employment share and the other two considering changes in the non-manual wage bill share. The specifications for each dependent variable differ in whether or not they include the R&D intensity variable. The R&D variable is dated at $(t-1)$ so as to include a previously dated variable in the current t dated growth model (the precise dating is not important: use of t-dated or $t-2$-dated R&D intensity or instrumenting t or $t-1$ dated R&D intensity using previous values as instruments produced very similar results).

Considering first the equations that exclude the R&D intensity variable, there is some evidence of capital–skill complementarity since the estimated coefficient on the capital stock variable is estimated to be positive and significant for both dependent variables. The negative coefficient on the output proxy real sales variable[5] is consistent with the hypothesis that declining industries tend to lay off production workers (this is also found by Berman et al., 1993).

The other two specifications in Table 7.4 include the ratio of R&D expenditure to sales and produce some evidence in line with the hypothesis that high R&D industries are more likely to have increased their non-manual share through the 1980s. Effects on both the employment and wage bill share are significantly positive. For example, the specification in column (2) suggests that a one percentage point rise in R&D expenditure relative to sales increases the annual non-manual wage bill share by about 0.0007 or 0.07 percentage points; the analogous impact on the non-manual employment share is approximately 0.05 percentage points.

Hence, the evidence discussed in this section is in line with the hypothesis that more technologically advanced industries are more likely to have increased their shares of non-production workers. The four two-digit SIC industries with the highest R&D intensities are Office Machinery and Data Processing Equipment (SIC 33), Manufacture of Transport Equipment (SIC 36), Electrical and Electronic Engineering (SIC 34) and Chemicals (SIC 25). These are clearly more 'high-tech' industries and are those which have experienced more marked within-industry moves to the increased share of non-manuals.

4.2   The impact of innovation

A second measure of industry technological change, an innovation count at two-digit industry, is considered in Table 7.5. The measures of innovation I use are two-digit industry-level stocks of major innovations produced and used between 1970 and 1979 in the relevant industry. This is drawn from the Science Policy Research Unit (SPRU) database on commercially significant innovations introduced between 1945 and 1983. I constructed a count of the innovations produced and used by each two-digit SIC industry in the 1970s.[6] The reason for matching by two-digit industry is that the SPRU data is coded to the pre-1980 industrial classification and it is not possible to match three-digit level data accurately pre- and post-1980. I utilise the 1970–79 stock as it pre-dates the period under consideration and examine its relation with the evolution of employment shares in the 1980s (results are not sensitive to the precise dating used here: counts from 1975–80 or 1970–83 produced qualitatively similar results).

In Table 7.5 I report a set of regressions explaining changing wage bill and employment shares between 1980 and 1985. They are analogous to the specifications in Table 7.4 except I utilise the innovation variables as measures of technical progress. The estimated coefficients on the two variables are significant at a 10% level of significance or better in all four models. Hence, it also appears that innovative industries are more likely to have altered their employment mix in favour of non-manuals. The other strong feature of the empirical models in Table 7.4, the positive capital accumulation effects, are still present, though the evidence of

Table 7.5. Changes in employment shares and innovation in 16 two-digit manufacturing industries, 1980–85

Change in share of:	Non-manual wage bill	Non-manual wage bill	Non-manual employment	Non-manual employment
Δ log (capital stock)	0.115	0.127	0.048	0.060
(t)	(0.042)	(0.042)	(0.035)	(0.034)
Δ log (real sales)	-0.018	-0.021	0.001	-0.002
(t)	(0.017)	(0.017)	(0.013)	(0.010)
Count of innovations	0.092[†]		0.091[†]	
produced, 1970–79	(0.053)		(0.043)	
Count of innovations		0.235[†]		0.198[†]
used, 1970–79		(0.155)		(0.116)
Year dummies	Yes	Yes	Yes	Yes
R-squared	0.414	0.416	0.367	0.382
Sample size	96	96	96	96

1. As for Table 7.4.
2. A † superscript denotes that a coefficient estimates and associated standard error have been multiplied by 10 000.

negative real sales effects is not. It should also be noted that the reported effects are for 1980–85 and that the results with respect to the innovation variables do become weaker (but remain positive) if the sample is extended up to 1989. Nevertheless, the results do provide some support for the importance of technical change shocks in changing the distribution of employment within industries.

4.3   The impact of increased computer usage

Despite some other limitations (especially on wages in the panel), the WIRS data are extremely useful in the context of this chapter in that, unlike other microdata sources, they contain direct measures of establishment-level computer usage. This enables a direct test of the hypothesis that the observed upgrading of labour is linked to the increased use of computers within establishments.

To consider these hypotheses I estimated some simple regressions of 1984–90 changes in the share of a given labour type in total employment. The lack of good economic data on capital stock or output in WIRS means that I cannot follow the model described above precisely but I do try to control for various other demand shifts in the reported models. I estimate changing employment share equations which include the following variables: (i) a dummy variable indicating whether microcomputers were introduced into the establishment between 1984 and 1990 (i.e. I constructed a variable equal to one for establishments in which managers stated they had microcomputers in 1990 but not in 1984); (ii) a dummy variable indicating whether the establishment was declining between 1984 and 1990 (equal to one if employment in 1984 exceeded that in 1990); (iii) a set of industry dummies to allow for common industry effects.

The results are reported in Table 7.6. The results are entirely in line with those from the industry-level regressions above and suggest that technical changes are an important determinant of the changing skill structure. The regression in column (1) of the table is a regression of the change in the non-manual employment share on the variables defined above. The coefficients on both the computer usage and the variable indicating employment decline are estimated to be significantly positive suggesting that these establishments are more likely to have increased non-manual employment shares. The latter is interesting for it suggests one should be wary of referring to increased shares as upgrading in the sense that, in some cases, it is more a case of non-manual shares increasing due to reductions in the number of manual workers.

The remaining specifications in Table 7.6 correspond to the shares of the non-manual subgroups. Again an interesting pattern emerges. Whilst the increased use of computers seems to explain more of the changes at the top end of the occupational structure, there is no evidence of such an effect for lower-grade non-manuals (clerical and supervisory workers). Furthermore, the effects actually become negative for unskilled manuals. This provides evidence for the importance of increased computer usage as a means of upgrading the workforce. If one wishes to compare within-establishment rises in the relative importance of upper grade non-manuals as compared with unskilled manuals, in a specification like those in Table 7.6, the estimated regression coefficient (standard error) on the increased computer usage variable is 0.085 (0.033) which is strongly positive. Hence, increased computer usage is associated with reduced employment shares at the lower end of the occupational employment spectrum. This suggests that direct indicators of technical change, such as computer use, can explain at least some of the observed changes in the employment structure that occurred in the 1980s.

5   Concluding remarks

In this chapter I have tried to document and offer some explanations of recent changes in the employment structure of the UK economy. The

Table 7.6. Changes in employment shares and introduction of computers, 1984–90

1984–90 change in share of:	Non-manuals	Middle managers, senior and junior professional and technical staff	Supervisory staff and foremen	Clerical	Skilled manuals	Semi-skilled manuals	Unskilled manuals
Micro-computers introduced to establishment, 1984–90	0.031 (0.017)	0.044 (0.022)	−0.001 (0.009)	−0.012 (0.021)	−0.004 (0.022)	0.014 (0.025)	−0.041 (0.022)
Establishment employment declining, 1984–90	0.048 (0.020)	0.012 (0.022)	0.013 (0.011)	0.023 (0.022)	−0.027 (0.020)	−0.011 (0.026)	−0.010 (0.025)
One-digit industry dummies	Yes	Yes	Yes	Yes	Yes	Yes	Yes
R-squared	0.064	0.053	0.017	0.027	0.083	0.057	0.032
Number of establishments	398	398	398	398	398	398	398

1. Weighted least squares estimates (weights are WIRS weights).
2. Heteroscedastic consistent standard errors in parentheses.

1980s saw big changes in the structure of pay and employment in the UK labour market. There was a clear shift (as in earlier decades) towards the increased use of non-manual labour but in the 1980s this also went hand-in-hand with rises in the relative pay of non-manuals (the earlier decades saw relative pay falls in conjunction with increased non-manual shares). This pattern has also been observed in the USA in the 1980s and has been rationalised by many commentators in terms of an outward shift in the relative demand for labour curve, probably due to manual labour saving technical changes. The principal suspect there has been identified as the increased use of computer technology.

This chapter suggests that this is probably also at least a partially reasonable explanation of what has happened in the UK, where the majority of the observed shifts towards non-manual labour have been within-establishment and within-industry shifts. There is some evidence that one can explain some of these within-sector shifts in terms of technological change indicators, such as R&D or innovative activity and the introduction of computers. The latter effect appears to be particularly marked at the upper end of the occupational spectrum. However, as recent considerations of the rise in pay inequality have noted, the UK labour market underwent many important transformations in the 1980s. Most of these involved a shift in the balance of power between management and workers and these shifts are likely to favour non-manual workers (e.g. weakened trade unions; big rises in unemployment; tax and benefit system changes). It would be interesting and important to consider also the effects of these potentially important determinants of employment structure in future work. Extension of the analysis to cover other within-establishment or industry shifts (e.g. male/female, full-time/part-time) is also desirable, but beyond the scope of this current piece of work.

NOTES

Stephen Machin is extremely grateful to Amanda Gosling, Paul Gregg and John Van Reenen for useful discussions, Steve Woodland for excellent research assistance, Amanda Gosling for setting up the Workplace Industrial Relations Survey data, Richard Dickens and Jonathan Wadsworth for supplying the New Earnings Survey and Labour Force Survey data and to Martin Conyon and Ian Small for providing some of the other industry-level data used in this paper.

1   These cover a smaller sample of industries owing to small cell sizes in some LFS industries (those with fewer than fifty workers in the LFS, comprising about 20% of all manufacturing industries, were excluded). Also, only the period from 1981 onwards could be considered.
2   In terms of defining consistent education groups over time, the definition of a 'no educational qualifications' category is an issue. For example, a large portion of the observed increase in intermediate education categories (less than a degree, but with some kind of qualification) in the 1980s is due to increases in the number of individuals with some kind of vocational qualification. This is clear from the tables in Schmitt (1993) who reports very big falls in the proportion of manufacturing workers with no qualifications: from 0.483 in 1978–80 to 0.324 by 1986–88 corresponding to a 16 percentage point fall (or one-third of the 1978–80 level). The LFS numbers matched in here point to falls of a similar magnitude.
3   The WIRS panel covers 537 trading sector establishments. The sample of 402 establishments used here is arrived at after deleting those establishments with missing data on any of the employment categories used and after selecting out those establishments identified as having problems of comparability across the two years.
4   The main deficiency of the panel is the lack of comparable wage data across the two years (since the pay question in 1990 is limited to establishments with at least five workers in the appropriate skill group). The other limitation with respect to pay data is that pay is not available in either year for upper grade

non-manuals (i.e. junior and senior technical/professional staff and senior/ middle managers).
5   Real sales, rather than real output, is used since the published price deflators correspond to sales.
6   The firm-level data contained in SPRU are used in an empirical analysis of the relationship between innovation and profitability in Geroski *et al.* (1993) and the data are described in depth in Van Reenen (1992).

REFERENCES

Berman, Eli, John Bound and Zvi Griliches (1993), 'Changes in the Demand for Skilled Labour within US Manufacturing Industries: Evidence from the Annual Survey of Manufacturing', National Bureau of Economic Research Discussion Paper No. 4255.

Berndt, Ernst (1990), *The Practice of Econometrics*, Reading, MA, Addison-Wesley.

Davis, Steven (1992), 'Cross-country Patterns of Change in Relative Wages', *NBER Macroeconomics Annual* 1992, 239–300.

Freeman, Richard and Lawrence Katz (1993), 'Rising Wage Inequality: The United States vs. Other Advanced Countries', National Bureau of Economic Research, mimeo.

Geroski, Paul, Stephen Machin and John Van Reenen (1993), 'The Profitability of Innovating Firms', *RAND Journal of Economics* **24**, 198–211.

Gregg, Paul and Stephen Machin (1994), 'Is the UK rise in inequality different?', in Ray Barrell (ed.), *The British Labour Market*, Cambridge: Cambridge University Press.

Krueger, Alan (1993), 'How Have Computers Changed the Wage Structure? Evidence from Microdata', *Quarterly Journal of Economics* **108**, 33–60.

Millward, Neil, Mark Stevens, David Smart and W. R. Hawes (1993), *Workplace Industrial Relations in Transition: The ED/ESRC/PSI/ACAS Surveys*, Aldershot: Dartmouth Publishing Co.

Schmitt, John (1995), 'The Changing Structure of Male Earnings in Britain, 1974–88', in Richard Freeman and Lawrence Katz (eds.), *Changes and Differences in Wage Structures*, Chicago: University of Chicago Press.

Van Reenen, John (1992), 'Innovation, Market Structure and Bargaining: An Investigation into the Creation and Capture of Economic Rents', unpublished Ph.D. thesis, University of London.

8   Skill shortages, productivity growth and wage inflation

This chapter argues that the supply of skills is widely believed to be a problem in the UK and other advanced market economies; thus firms experience significant skill shortages.

Evidence of skill shortages is obtained from two panel data sets of three-digit UK manufacturing industry. It is shown that skill shortages are higher on average and more variable over the business cycle in the UK than in comparable economies. Unskilled shortages are comparatively rare. The bulk of the evidence suggests that shortages are related to educational attainment rather than the failure of firms to adjust wages.

Skill shortages may have two effects on productivity. First, skill shortages add to the cost of employing skilled workers, since a firm must wait longer than usual to fill its vacancies. This leads firms to substitute unskilled for skilled labour, thereby reducing productivity. Secondly, skill shortages improve the skilled workers' outside options, making it more difficult for firms to induce them to work hard. Both these effects reduce productivity.

The chapter provides evidence showing that the growth of skill shortages in the UK over the 1980s reduced productivity growth by about 0.4% per year (average productivity growth was about 5%). This problem could also give rise to inflation, as excess demand for skilled workers improves the outside employment opportunities of skilled workers, enabling them to negotiate higher wages. Haskel and Martin find that although industry skill shortages have no effect on industry wages, wages do appear to be affected by aggregate skill shortages.

Skill shortages, productivity growth and wage inflation

JONATHAN HASKEL and
CHRISTOPHER MARTIN

1   Introduction and summary

This chapter will provide empirical evidence on the effects of the skills gap on two key economic variables: productivity growth and wage inflation. Following seismic changes in the UK labour market, which are widely believed to have reduced overmanning and restrictive practices, the rate of productivity growth rose in the 1980s. Despite this, concern continues to be expressed about the alleged shortage of human capital. Studies that compare technologically similar establishments in Germany and other EC countries with the UK, consistently find that productivity is lower in the UK.[1] This appears to support the view that the UK suffers from a 'skills gap', whereby workers are disadvantaged by low levels of human capital, caused by inadequacies in the education and training systems. The skills gap is also thought to lead to 'excessive' wage inflation. If the supply of skilled workers is insufficient, then firms are more likely to concede larger wage rises in order to preserve their base of skilled labour. This occurs despite high levels of unemployment since the unemployed are largely unskilled.

This chapter is concerned with one aspect of the skills gap: skill shortages. Our skill shortages data comes from firms who report difficulty in recruiting as many skilled workers as they desire.[2] We assume that this corresponds to vacancies with a long duration, so our interpretation of skill shortages is that they are skilled vacancies that take some time to fill. The effect of the skills gap is therefore to increase the duration of skilled vacancies. What are the consequences of this? Since jobs remain unfilled longer, the amount of lost production rises; firms also need to devote more resources to recruitment. As a result the cost of hiring a skilled worker is increased.

Skill shortages are an enduring feature of the British labour market. They have been the subject of investigation and discussion for many years (see, for example, CBI (1989), MSC (1983), Hart and Shipman (1990) and Haskel and Martin (1993a, 1993c).

To test for the impact of skill shortages we use two panel data sets of UK manufacturing industry, 1980–89. The first is a panel of 81 industries covering almost all of manufacturing.[3] The second consists of 33 industries from engineering. Skill shortages in engineering are much discussed and we have been able to collect quite detailed information on the skill composition of this sector.

We examine three ways by which skill shortages might reduce productivity:

(1) Since skill shortages increase the cost of employing skilled workers, they lead the firm to substitute unskilled for skilled workers.
(2) A shortage of skills puts the skilled workers into a strong bargaining position when negotiating about working conditions at the firm. They may therefore be more able to demand an easier pace of work.
(3) A shortage of skilled workers might inhibit learning and the development and implementation of new technology.

In order to gauge the impact of shortages we estimate equations that relate the growth in productivity to the growth in skill shortages. We control for other factors that might affect productivity such as inputs of capital and raw materials, union and firm market power, and utilisation. Results for both our data sets suggest that the growth of skill shortages over the 1980s reduced productivity growth by about 0.4% p.a. (average productivity growth was 5% p.a.).

Turning to the effects of skill shortages on wages, we examine two ways in which skill shortages might raise wages:

(1) Skill shortages lead to a smaller number of skilled workers, therefore firms may bid up wages in order to recruit and retain skilled labour.
(2) Skill shortages put skilled workers into a stronger bargaining position when bargaining over wages.

We estimate equations that relate wage inflation to the growth in skill shortages, controlling for factors such as productivity, unemployment and union and firm market power. Results on both our data sets suggest that skill shortages raised nominal wage growth over the period by about 1% p.a. (average nominal wage growth was 7%). However, our results show that wages are affected by skill shortages at the national level rather than at the firm level. Variations in skill shortages across industries have little effect on wages, rather wage inflation is higher when average levels of shortage are higher.

This completes a summary of our results.[4] The rest of this chapter is in two parts. The remaining sections are a non-technical description of our methodology and findings. For those more interested in the technical aspect of our work, the Technical Appendix details the models and econometric techniques used. The non-technical part begins in Section 2 where we set out the facts about skill shortages and our framework to understand them. Sections 3 and 4 describe the effect of skill shortages on productivity and wages respectively. Section 5 concludes.

2   The skills gap and skill shortages

We begin with a brief review of the facts about UK skill shortages. Figure 8.1 sets out information about both the level and cyclical pattern of shortages. Shortages are highly procyclical, affecting as few as 2% of firms in the recession of the early 1980s yet over 20% of firms in the later upturn. Unskilled shortages are also cyclical but lower on average. In a longer version of this chapter, Haskel and Martin (1993b), we examine the distribution of skill shortages across industries and between regions. We find that some industries, such as chemicals and food, never face significant problems. Others, particularly the engineering sectors, consistently face severe shortages. Since conditions in engineering appear to be particularly acute, we address engineering separately in our regressions. Turning to regional differences, East Anglia, the South-East and the South-West are regions with worse shortages while the North, Yorkshire and the North-West generally face fewer problems.

It might be argued that skill shortages simply reflect a failure, on the part of firms, to adjust their wages up to the level necessary to attract sufficient workers. We believe that this is a misconceived view of skill shortages. The chemical and food industries suffer similar levels of shortage although wages have always been higher in chemicals. In addition, survey evidence on responses of firms to shortages (Training Agency, 1990), found firms only ranked wage increases as only sixth in importance out of eleven possible responses. Finally, if firms adjusted wages to remedy skill shortages, then, since shortages are procyclical, we would observe a greater differential between skilled and unskilled wages in upturns than in slumps. In fact, the differential is relatively constant and does not follow the business cycle (Elliot and Murphy, 1990).

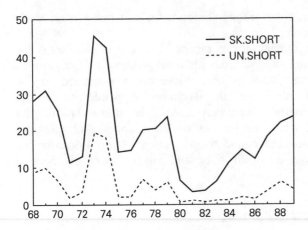

Definition: SK.SHORT are shortages of skilled labour,
UN.SHORT are shortages of unskilled labour.
See Data Appendix for definitions and source.

Figure 8.1   Shortages of skilled and unskilled labour

At a theoretical level, the view that skill shortages are only the result of misaligned wages relies on a frictionless labour market. This seems an inappropriate description of a typical labour market. In practice there are a host of frictions that impede supply responses to an increase in wages. Workers may be unable to move areas, they may have imperfect information about the wage offers available and so forth. A rise in the number of skilled workers would reduce the delay in filling vacancies but would not, because of frictions, eliminate it. While adjustments to the wage structure may well affect shortages in the longer term, the response from the supply of skilled labour would take time to show through. To support our interpretation of skill shortages as a measure of the duration of vacancies for skilled workers, we calculated the correlation between reported skill shortages and vacancy duration. This was 0.90, which suggests that our interpretation is reasonable. Econometric evidence on the causes of skill shortages is presented in Haskel and Martin (1993c) who estimate a model of the probability of facing a skill shortage using establishment level data. They consider the effect of factors such as wages, the internal organisation of the firm and local labour market conditions. They find that higher wages paid by individual firms have no effect on shortages, although shortages are reduced by higher wages in the industry and region, which increase the amount of skilled labour available to the firm. The most important determinant of shortage is the local skills base, so that firms whose locality is well endowed with skilled labour are less likely to suffer shortages.

This discussion indicates how we might explain the facts outlined above (see the Technical Appendix for more detail). A vacancy for a skilled worker will take longer to fill the greater the overall level of demand for skilled labour. In a cyclical upturn, there will be fewer suitable skilled workers available. Therefore skill shortages will be procyclical, as shown in Figure 8.1. Since the occupational mobility of labour is low, we find persistent differences in shortages between industries. Regional differences in shortages can be explained by local differences in the supply of skilled labour. This is reinforced by low rates of migration and the stability of the regional wage structure.

3   The effect of skill shortages on productivity

3.1   Theory

There are three main mechanisms by which skill shortages reduce productivity. First, when skill shortages rise, skilled vacancies take longer to fill. As a result, the cost of lost production is greater, while more resources need to be devoted to recruitment. Since the marginal cost of a skilled worker is the wage plus the hiring cost, a rise in skill shortages will increase the marginal cost of skilled labour relative to the marginal cost of unskilled labour.[5] Therefore firms hire fewer skilled workers. In the Technical Appendix we show that skill shortages will reduce productivity when the cost of an additional skilled worker is greater than that of the unskilled. While this is ultimately an empirical matter, the observation that wages for skilled workers exceed those for the unskilled suggest that skill shortages will generally reduce productivity.

The second mechanism operates through the level of effort. It seems reasonable to suppose that the quantity of output produced by workers depends on the amount of 'effort' they devote to production. Evidence from UK establishments (Millward and Stevens, 1986) suggests that 'effort' is to some extent a subject of negotiation between firms and workers. Thus if there are frequent rest periods during shifts, or if the number of workers operating a particular process is higher than is strictly technically necessary, working conditions are easy and a relatively low amount of effort is put in by workers. If labour shortages rise, firms are less able to extract greater levels of effort since workers have improved outside options when bargaining.

A third view is that productivity growth depends on the introduction of new technology, on-the-job learning and experience. Firms may not proceed with innovations and install new technology if they do not have the skilled workers to operate the new machines. In addition, skilled workers may be particularly adept at learning and translating their experience into more productive activities; a shortage of skilled workers inhibits this process.

3.2   Data, estimating equation and results

To estimate the effect of skill shortages on productivity, we use two panel data sets. The first is a panel of 81 three-digit industries 1980–89, with data drawn principally from the Census of Production. The basic source of the data is the UK Census of Production which gives information on output, employment, wages, employment composition and product market power. To this we have matched information on skill shortages taken from the CBI Quarterly Industrial Trends Survey as well as information on capital, unemployment, unionisation and hours. This wealth of data enables us to carry out a more comprehensive study than has previously been possible.

The first and second hypotheses imply that productivity growth depends on the growth of skill shortages. We estimate empirical equations that relate these two variables, controlling for other relevant factors. Increased inputs of capital, materials, hours worked and improved worker composition will raise productivity. Increased union power might lower productivity growth if unions insist on easier conditions or work. Monopolistic firms might be expected to have lower productivity since they do not face the competitive imperative to raise efficiency.

The equation that we estimate is

$$\Delta(y - l) = a_1 \Delta(k - l) + a_2 \Delta SKSHORT + a_3 \Delta$$
$$UNSKSHORT + a_4 \Delta UNEMP + a_5 \Delta CR + a_6 \Delta UNION \quad (1)$$
$$+ a_7 \Delta h + a_8 \Delta ADMIN + a_9 \Delta(p_\mathrm{m} - p) + \text{time dummies}$$

where lower-case letters are logs, output is denoted by y, capital by k, employment by l, skill shortages by $SKSHORT$, unskilled shortages by $UNSKSHORT$ and hours by h, and Δ denotes the change in the subsequent variable. Union power is measured by union density ($UNION$) while $UNEMP$ is unemployment. Monopoly power is measured by the proportion of industry sales accounted for by the top five firms (the five-firm concentration ratio, CR) and worker mix by the proportion of administrative, technical and clerical workers ($ADMIN$).

Finally, we include the relative price of raw materials $(p_m - p)$, to correct for any double deflation bias (Stoneman, 1992; Oulton, 1991).

The results of estimating (1) are set out in Table 8.1. Looking at the first column, the capital/labour ratio is correctly signed, and on the margins of significance. Hours are significant.[6] The skilled labour shortage term is also correctly signed and significant; we had the most success with a one-year lag which is not implausible. Unskilled shortages are insignificant, as are the other terms.[7] Column 2 reports the result of successively dropping the insignificant variables from (1). Our preferred specification has significant effects from capital, shortages and hours. The diagnostics are satisfied. Our results therefore suggest that increases in skill shortages reduce productivity growth.[8]

To examine the idea that shortages might inhibit learning and the implementation of new technology, in column 3 we included the level of shortages in the growth regression. The effect is negative, as would be expected, but just insignificant. However, we would not want to put too much weight on what is a rather crude test. Since shortages differ systematically between industries, if the level of shortages affected the growth of productivity we would expect to observe divergence between sectors; this does not appear to be the case. We probably require a longer data set than we have available to pin this effect down. A complex hypothesis such as this may be better suited to examination via case studies.

To examine the robustness of our results we may compare them with previous regressions for the same industries but for the shorter period 1980–86, reported in Haskel and Martin (1993a). As Figure 8.1 shows, 1987–89 showed a marked rise in shortages and so this comparison represents a check of some weight. The regressions on the shorter panel also found no significant effects from unskilled shortages, but a significant negative effect from skilled shortages. The latter coefficient was somewhat larger than found here, 0.27 ($t = 2.02$), but the coefficient reported in Table 8.1 is within a standard error of this. Furthermore using aggregate manufacturing time series data, 1966:1–88:4, Haskel and Martin (1992) found a coefficient of -0.12 ($t = 3.21$), very similar to that of Table 8.1. So overall the negative effect of skill shortages on productivity seems quite robust.

Our second data set is a smaller panel of 33 industries from the engineering sector. Much of the concern over the effect of skill shortages has tended to focus on engineering. Using the data collected by the Engineering Industries Training Board we have constructed data on the proportion of managerial and technical workers (PMAN), foreman (PFOR), and craftsmen (PCRA).

Table 8.1. Productivity regressions: estimates of equation (1) for 81 industries (dependent variable, $\Delta(y\text{-}1)$)

	(1)	(2)	(3)
$\Delta(k-1)^*$	0.39	0.33	0.45
	(1.77)	(2.37)	(2.58)
Δh^*	0.63	0.58	0.78
	(2.22)	(1.92)	(2.90)
$\Delta SKSHORT_{t-1}$	−0.15	−0.16	
	(2.20)	(2.18)	
$\Delta UNSKSHORT_{t-1}$	0.13		
	(0.78)		
$\Delta UNEMP$	0.01		
	(0.31)		
$\Delta(\Delta UNEMP)$	−0.03		
	(0.52)		
ΔCR^*	−0.03		
	(0.05)		
$\Delta ADMIN^*$	0.36		
	(0.38)		
$\Delta UNION^*$	0.02		
	(0.11)		
$\Delta(p_m - p)$	−0.91		
	(0.84)		
$SKSHORT_{t-1}$			−0.15
			(1.93)
$m_1, [N(0,1)]$	1.31	1.07	1.61
$m_2, [N(0,1)]$	0.75	0.93	−0.65
Sargan, χ^2	14.24 (15)	14.95 (18)	14.40 (19)

Notes:
1. Absolute t-statistics in brackets. Those reported are robust, one-step estimates from DPD package. See Arellano and Bond (1988).
2. For all equations there are 81 industries 1983–89 = 567 observations. All equations include constant and time dummies.
3. m_2 is the Arellano–Bond (1988) one-step heteroscedastic robust test against second-order serial correlation, and Sargan is their instruments validity test. m_2 checks there is no correlation between the differenced errors and their second lag (necessary condition for undifferenced errors to be white noise); Sargan is valid if this is not rejected.
4. Asterisked variables are treated as endogenous. Additional instruments are all lags on $\Delta(k/l)$ and ΔCR from $t-2$ back, asterisked variables dated $t-2$, import share t and $t-1$, and lagged Δ two-digit $SKSHORT$ and UN-$SKSHORT$.

To estimate the impact of shortages we adopt a similar approach to above and estimate

$$\Delta(y - l) = a_1\Delta(k - l) + a_2\Delta SKSHORT + a_3\Delta$$
$$UNSKSHORT + a_4\Delta UNEMP + a_5\Delta CR + a_6\Delta UNION \qquad (2)$$
$$+a_7\Delta h + a_8\Delta ADMIN + a_9\Delta(p_m - p) + a_{10}\Delta PMAN$$
$$+a_{11}\Delta PFOR + a_{12}\Delta PCRA + \text{time dummies}$$

for our panel of 33 engineering industries. The results of estimating (2) are set out in Table 8.2. As column 1 shows the most significant effects are from capital and hours. The effect of shortages is negative but insignificant. The human capital measures are all insignificant. Eliminating the insignificant variables yields column 2 where we have retained SKSHORT for comparison with previous results. The coefficients on capital and hours are similar to the full panel. The coefficient on SKSHORT is somewhat less well determined than in the whole panel. The best determined effect is from the current change in shortages; the lagged effect had a coefficient of -0.04 ($t = 0.60$). Lastly, in column 3 we tried the level of shortages for the reasons set out above. This is negative and significant, suggesting that the learning/new technology effect may be stronger in the engineering industry.

One explanation of why these results are not very precisely determined may be that there is very little variation in the skill composition measures. For example, the proportion of craftsmen in the mechanical engineering industry was 28.9% in 1982 and 29.0% in 1989 (Haskel and Martin, 1993b). One possibility is that this lack of movement actually hides compositional changes. Faced with a skill shortage for foremen for example, firms might hire a slightly less well-qualified worker. So, while the percentage of workers who are foremen does not change over the cycle, the human capital embodied in these workers will. To examine this hypothesis, in column 4 of Table 8.2 we report the effects of interacting skill with the proportion of craftsmen and foremen. This is correctly signed but only significant at the 15% level.

3.3   Quantifying the effects of shortages on productivity growth

So how much have skill shortages restrained productivity growth? To evaluate the relative contributions of the significant variables in column 2 of Tables 8.1 and 8.2 we multiplied their coefficients by their average changes over the period.[9] The results of this are set out in Table 8.3. For the whole panel the growth in the capital/labour ratio added 2.1% to

Table 8.2. Productivity regressions: estimates of equation (2) for subpanel (dependent variable, $\Delta(y\text{-}1)$)

	(1)	(2)	(3)	(4)
$\Delta(k-1)^*$	0.50	0.49	0.39	0.48
	(1.83)	(2.30)	(1.80)	(2.27)
Δh^*	0.49	0.90	0.75	1.00
	(1.81)	(2.79)	(2.46)	(3.25)
$\Delta SKSHORT$	−0.05	−0.06		
	(0.80)	(1.13)		
$\Delta UNSKSHORT$	−0.10			
	(0.80)			
$\Delta UNEMP$	0.13			
	(0.47)			
$\Delta(\Delta UNEMP)$	−0.06			
	(0.17)			
ΔCR^*	−0.01			
	(1.00)			
$\Delta UNION^*$	−0.03			
	(0.10)			
$\Delta(p_m - p)$	−1.67			
	(0.88)			
$\Delta PMAN$	0.34			
	(0.47)			
$\Delta PFOR$	1.77			
	(1.33)			
$\Delta PCRA$	−0.36			
	(0.34)			
$SKSHORT$			−0.24	
			(2.66)	
$\Delta(SHORT \times (PFOR + CRA))$				−0.48
				(1.43)
$m_1, [N(0,1)]$		1.38	1.64	1.28
$m_2, [N(0,1)]$		0.21	0.59	0.59

Notes:
1. See notes 1, 3 and 4 of Table 8.1.
2. For all equations there are 33 industries 1983–89 = 231 observations. All equations include constant and three time dummies.
3. $(PFOR + CRA)$ is the proportion of the workforce who are either foremen or craftsmen.

Table 8.3. *Decomposition of productivity growth, 1983–89 (percentage growth per annum)*

Variable	Panel	Subpanel
$\Delta(y-1)$	4.5	5.6
$\Delta(k-1)$	2.1	3.7
Cyclical	2.8	2.2
$\Delta SKSHORT$	−0.4	−0.3

Note: Figures under the dotted line calculated on basis of averages in endnote 9 and the coefficients in Tables 8.1 and 8.2, column 2. Cyclical factors comprise hours and the effects of the time dummies.

productivity, leaving 2.4% to other factors. Cyclical factors added 2.8% to productivity growth. But, the growth in shortages served to reduce growth by 0.4%. A similar decomposition can be performed for the results from the subpanel, the results of which are set out in the next column. This shows that skill shortages reduced productivity growth by 0.3%, which is very similar to the full panel results.

4   The effect of skill shortages on wages

4.1   Theory

We consider two possible effects of skill shortages on wages. One obvious route that is often discussed is that wages are bid upwards as firms compete with each other to hire an increasingly diminishing skilled employment pool. We doubt this effect is very strong since there is little evidence that firms adjust wages to reduce skill shortages. This conclusion is supported by survey evidence (Thomas and Deaton, 1977; MSC, 1977, 1983; Hart, 1990; Hart and Shipman, 1990) which finds that firms are much more likely to respond to a skill shortage by searching harder, putting unskilled workers to skilled jobs, adjusting working practices or using subcontracting than they are by increasing wages. One reason that firms do not raise wages in upturns when shortages appear is that they feel unable to cut them in downturns when shortages are not so severe.

Turning to the second possible effect, as we saw above, skill shortages put workers in a better position to bargain for easy conditions at the workplace. A similar logic might apply for wage bargaining. If firms are having difficulty in recruiting skilled workers then any given skilled worker is in an improved position when negotiating with the firm, and so can demand higher wages.

4.2   Data, estimating equation and results

To estimate the effect of shortages on wages, we use the same data sets as described above, namely the panel of 81 industries and subpanel of 33 industries. As before we attempt to control for a number of other possible effects on wages. The controls required are those affecting the warranted wage and those causing the actual wage to deviate from it. The former is determined by productivity, hours worked and employment mix, and the latter by unemployment and other outside options of the workers, union bargaining power and firm product market power. This leads to an estimating equation

$$\Delta w = b_1 \Delta (p + y - n) + b_2 \Delta ADMIN + b_3 \Delta SKSHORT$$
$$+ b_4, \Delta UNSKSHORT - b_5 \Delta UNEMP + b_6 \Delta UNION \qquad (3)$$
$$+ b_7 \Delta CR + b_8 \Delta HOURS + \text{time dummies}$$

where w is the log nominal wage consisting of wages, salaries and employers' national insurance contributions per worker, $(p + y - n)$ is log prices plus log real net output less the cost of non-industrial services received less log employment.

The results of estimating (3) are set out in Table 8.4. In column 1 we include all the measures that we have available. The most significant variables are output per head and *ADMIN*. *SKSHORT* is positive, but insignificant. Dropping the insignificant variables, but retaining *SKSHORT* for illustration yields column 2, where *SKSHORT* has a very small coefficient and is not well determined.

The subpanel estimates are set out in Table 8.5, where the estimating equation is (3) plus the *PMAN*, *PFOR*, and *PCRA*. These are similar to the other panel estimates, where the strongest effects come from the proportion of administrative staff and productivity. None of the other human capital variables are significant. Column 2 reports estimates with the most significant variables included. Again the coefficient on skill shortages is less well determined than in the case of the 81 industries.

It is likely that these estimates are poorly determined because the inter-industry wage structure is very stable, so that the variance of wages changes across industries is small. Most factors that lead to changes in the wages are aggregate in nature and so are captured by the time dummies. This suggests that the effect of skill shortages might be obscured by the time dummies if wages are affected by the aggregate level of skill shortages. To examine this we replaced the time dummies by aggregate skill shortages, unemployment, the proportion long-term

Table 8.4. Wage regressions: panel data estimates of equation (3) for 81 industries (dependent variable, Δw)

	(1)	(2)	(3)
$\Delta(p+y-1)^*$	0.08	0.08	0.07
	(2.71)	(2.20)	(2.14)
$\Delta ADMIN^*$	0.27	0.28	0.14
	(4.08)	(4.60)	(1.90)
$\Delta SKSHORT^*$	0.003	0.02	−0.01
	(0.07)	(1.20)	(0.43)
$\Delta UNSKSHORT^*$	0.002		
	(0.17)		
$\Delta UNEMP$	−0.02		
	(1.46)		
$\Delta(\Delta UNEMP)$	0.01		
	(0.49)		
$\Delta UNION^*$	−0.001		
	(0.62)		
ΔCR^*	−0.001		
	(0.56)		
Δh^*	0.71		
	(1.11)		
$\Delta AggSKSHORT$			0.24
			(5.04)
$m_1, [N(0,1)]$	−3.66	−3.52	−3.77
$m_2, [N(0,1)]$	−0.71	−0.48	−0.74
Sargan, χ^2	25.1 (16)	28.7 (19)	

Notes:
1. See notes 1–3 to Table 8.1.
2. Asterisked variables are treated as endogenous. Additional instruments are all lags on $(p+y-n)$ from $t-2$ back, starred variables dated $t-2$, import share t and $t-1$ and lagged Δ two-digit $SKSHORT$ and $UNSKSHORT$.
3. Column 3 has a constant but no time dummies.
4. All variables are industry specific, except for $AggSKSHORT$, which are aggregate skill shortages.

Table 8.5. Wage regressions: estimates of equation (3) for 33 industries (dependent variable, Δw)

	(1)	(2)	(3)
$\Delta(p+y-n)^*$	0.05	0.05	0.05
	(1.13)	(1.68)	(1.80)
$\Delta ADMIN^*$	0.25	0.26	0.26
	(3.90)	(3.87)	(3.66)
$\Delta SKSHORT^*$	0.03	0.04	0.03
	(0.80)	(1.09)	(1.00)
$\Delta UNSKSHORT^*$	-0.07		
	(0.75)		
$\Delta UNEMP$	-0.04		
	(2.05)		
$\Delta(\Delta UNEMP)$	0.02		
	(1.86)		
$\Delta UNION^*$	-0.00		
	(0.10)		
ΔCR^*	-0.33		
	(1.57)		
Δh^*	-0.31		
	(0.79)		
$\Delta PMAN$	0.04		
	(0.15)		
$\Delta PFOR$	0.47		
	(1.05)		
$\Delta PCRA$	0.15		
	(0.47)		
$\Delta AggSKSHORT$			0.27
			(4.19)
$m_1, [N(0,1)]$	-2.22	-2.37	-2.42
$m_2, [N(0,1)]$	-2.09	-2.37	-2.57

Notes:
1. See notes 1, 3 and 4 to Table 8.4.
2. Asterisked variables are treated as endogenous. Additional instruments are all lags on $(p+y-n)$ from $t-2$ back, starred variables dated $t-2$, and import share t and $t-1$.

unemployed and benefits and reran the equations in column 3 of Tables 8.4 and 8.5. None of the latter three aggregate variables were significant, but in both cases aggregate skill shortages were strongly significant, see column 2 of Tables 8.4 and 8.5. In addition the coefficient on aggregate skill shortages was ten times that of the industry level. In conclusion, we have found no evidence that industry wages are affected by skill shortages at the industry level. However, we have found evidence that industry wages are affected by skill shortages at the aggregate level, although we would not wish to put too much stress on this result.

4.3   The effects of shortages on wages

In Table 8.6 we provide a decomposition for wages along the same lines as productivity. Using the panel and subpanel estimates from Tables 8.4 and 8.5, in columns 1 and 2 we see that of the 7% average annual growth in wages, skill shortages contributed about 0.1% and 0.2% points in each case. The bulk of the effect comes from aggregate and cyclical factors picked up by the time dummies. Industry-level skill shortages therefore do not appear to have raised wage pressure by a large amount.

However in columns 3 and 4 we perform a decomposition using column 3 of Tables 8.4 and 8.5, which dropped the time dummies and replaced them with skill shortages. As the table shows the contribution of skill shortages is about 1% per annum.

5   Conclusion

We have estimated the effect of skill shortages using two panel data sets of three-digit UK manufacturing industry, 1980–89, comprising 81 industries across all manufacturing and 33 engineering industries. We found that the increase in skill shortages over the 1980s reduced productivity growth by about 0.4% per year (average productivity growth was about 5%). Unskilled shortages had no effect. Turning to the effect of skill shortages on wages, shortages might cause wages to be bid up as firms compete with each other to hire an increasingly diminishing skilled employment pool, or they may put workers in a stronger bargaining position in wage negotiations. We tested these effects on the two industry panels. Here we find that the increase in skill shortages over the 1980s increased wage growth by about 1% per year (average wage growth was about 7%). However, wages are affected by skill shortages at the aggregate level rather than the industry level. Again, unskilled shortages had no effect.

Table 8.6. Decomposition of wage growth, 1983–89 (percentage growth per annum)

Variable	(1) Panel	(2) Subpanel	(3) Panel	(4) Subpanel
Δw	7.2	7.4	7.2	7.4
$\Delta(p + y - 1)$	0.7	0.4	0.6	0.4
$\Delta SHORT$	0.1	0.2	0.0	0.2
$\Delta ADMIN$	0.0	0.0	0.0	0.0
Aggregate and cyclical factors	6.5	6.8	5.7	5.7
Aggregate $\Delta SHORT$			1.0	1.0

Notes:
1. Figures in columns 1 and 2 under the dotted line calculated on basis of coefficients in column 3 of Tables 8.4 and 8.5. Aggregate and cyclical refer to the joint effects of the constant and time dummies.
2. In columns 3 and 4 aggregate and cyclical factors are the constant. Aggregate $\Delta SHORT$ is the effect of whole economy shortages.

What of policy? The appropriate policy measures depend on the form (if any) of the market failure that leads to the skills gap. This issue is taken up in other contributions to this volume. However, we hope that our estimates will enable the effects on productivity growth and wage inflation of any policy-induced reduction in skill shortages to be calculated.

6   Data appendix

The main sources for the data are the Census of Production, Annual Report and the corresponding Quarterly Report.

6.1   Data definitions and sources for 81-industry panel

Skilled and unskilled shortages (SKSHORT and UNSKSHORT)
Question 14 of the CBI Industrial Trends survey asks firms to indicate which of a list of factors is expected to limit output over the coming four months (the survey is quarterly, conducted at the beginning of each quarter). The factors are 'orders and sales', 'skilled labour', and 'other labour', 'plant capacity', 'credit or finance', 'materials or components' and 'other'. Firms are encouraged to indicate more than one factor where appropriate. *SKSHORT* is the percentage of firms listing that skill shortages as a factor, similarly for *UNSKSHORT*. The CBI publish their data in a series of tables which are between two- and three-digit SIC categories. We match the CBI data to the appropriate SIC code. Source: authors' calculations from the CBI Quarterly Industrial Trends Survey.

Growth in output per head (y − 1)
Output (*y*) is measured by the 'index of volume of output', from the Quarterly Returns. This is essentially a gross output measure. Heads are employment, from Annual Report.

Import share
Imports divided by sales plus imports less exports. From Annual Report and Quarterly returns.

Five-firm concentration ratio (CR)
Measured on the basis of employment. From Annual Report.

Capital stock (k)
Capital stock data was obtained on the 1968 SIC from R. Allard. It was then converted to the 1980 SIC by a translation matrix devised by A. Vlassopoulos of London Business School that is based on overlapping Census reports for that year. Data for 1980–89 was generated using net capital expenditure data (from Annual Report), an assumed depreciation rate of 4% and capital goods deflators from the Blue Book.

Union density (UNION)
Union density estimates were obtained on a three-digit basis from Kevin Denny for 1980 and 1984 (the WIRS years). Intervening years were generated by linear interpolation, and 1985 to 1989 generated on the basis of aggregate figures.

Unemployment (UNEMP)
Two-digit unemployment rates were generated by the LFS, from Mark Walsh of the LSE.

Hours (h)
Average hours worked, full time males on adult rates. Source: *Department of Employment Gazette*, various issues. Data for 1980–82 interpolated from aggregate figures.

Ratio administrative (ADMIN)
Ratio of administrative, technical and clerical employees to total employment, from Annual Report.

Real price of raw materials (in logs, $p_m - p$)
p_m is the 'producer price index of materials and fuel purchased' from the *Annual Abstract of Statistics*, table 18.2, unfortunately only available in two-digit form. *p* is calculated as gross output divided by *y*.

Aggregate data (used in wage equations)
Aggregate data on UK unemployment rate, proportion long-term unemployed and benefits from LBS macro databank. We thank Tony Garrett for kindly providing these data.

Wages (w)
Wages, salaries and NI contributions for all employees, from Annual Report.

6.2   Additional definitions and sources for 33-industry panel

This data covers the engineering sector.

Ratio managerial (PMAN)
Ratio of managerial, administrative, technical and clerical employees to total employment, from Engineering Industries Training Board survey published in *Annual Abstract of Statistics*, various years.

Ratio foremen (PFOR)
Ratio of foremen to total employment. Source as above.

Ratio craftsmen (PCRA)
Ratio of craftsmen (production and maintenance) to total employment. Source as above.

6.3   Details of industries used

The 81 industries:
The industries are (by SIC) 224, 243, 244, 246, 247, 248, 251, 255, 256, 257, 258, 259, 260, 312, 313, 314, 316, 320, 321, 322, 323, 324, 325, 326, 327, 328, 329, 330, 341, 342, 343, 344, 345, 346, 347, 351, 352, 361, 362, 363, 364, 365, 371, 372, 373, 411, 412, 414, 415, 419, 421, 423, 424, 426, 428, 431, 432, 434, 436, 437, 438, 439, 441, 442, 451, 453, 455, 461, 463, 464, 465, 466, 467, 471, 472, 475, 481, 483, 491, 494, 495.

The 33 industries,
224, 312, 313, 314, 316, 320, 321, 322, 323, 324, 325, 326, 327, 328, 329, 330, 341, 342, 343, 344, 345, 346, 347, 351, 352, 361, 362, 363, 364, 365, 371, 372, 373.

7   Technical appendix

7.1   Matching approach to skill shortages

Following Pissarides (1990), we assume that X, the number of job matches in a given time period in the search area of the firm, is described by the following relationship (the constant returns assumption is unimportant in what follows)

$$X = (cJ)^{\alpha}(dV)^{1-\alpha} \tag{4}$$

where J workers are searching for V vacancies. The parameters c and d measure the average effectiveness of workers and firms in the search process. The average probability of filling a vacancy in the local market, q, is given by $q = X/V$, so that

$$q = \left(\frac{cJ}{V}\right)^{\alpha} d^{1-\alpha} \tag{5}$$

The average completed duration of a vacancy is given by $1/q$. We assume that a firm reports a skill shortage when there is an increased average duration of its skilled vacancy, an assumption supported by the correlations reported in the text. Equation (5) allows us to explain the facts documented in Tables 8.1–8.3. First, V will be high relative to J in an upswing, so q will be anticyclical. Thus skill shortages, measured by $1/q$ will be procyclical; this is consistent with Table 8.1. Industries or regions with a greater endowment of skilled labour have higher values of c or J and hence lower levels of skill shortages. This observation explains Tables 8.2 and 8.3.

7.2 The effect of skill shortages on productivity

(a) Theory

We suppose that a proportion δ_s and δ_u of the skilled and unskilled workforce quit in each period. Writing q_s and q_u for the probabilities that skilled and unskilled vacancies are filled in any period, the change in employment equals $q_i V_i - \delta_i N_i$, $i = s,u$. In the steady-state the firm must therefore post $V_i = \delta_i L_i/q_i$, $i = s,u$, vacancies per period. If we suppose that vacancies cost γ_i per period then profits to the firm can be written $\pi = PY - w_s L_s - w_u L_u - \gamma_s V_s - \gamma_u V_u$. Using the steady-state relationship between employment and vacancies, we write profits as

$$\pi = PY - w_s' L_s - w_u' L_u \tag{6}$$

where $w_i' = w_i + \gamma_i \delta_i/q_i$. So, w_s' is the marginal cost of each skilled labour which is the sum of the wage and marginal hiring costs. The effect of a rise in skill shortages on the firm is then to reduce the probability of filling a skilled vacancy; this increases hiring costs and hence increases the marginal cost of skilled labour. Likewise for unskilled shortages.

Firms choose skilled and unskilled employment to maximise (6). These first-order conditions give

$$\frac{MPL_s}{MPL_u} = \frac{w_s'}{w_s'} \tag{7}$$

where MPL_s, and MPL_u are the marginal products of skilled and unskilled labour. A rise in skill shortages will raise w_s' relative to w_u'. To preserve (7), MPL_s will rise relative to MPL_u. If there are diminishing returns to labour, then employment of the skilled must fall relative to employment of the unskilled. Therefore a rise in skill shortages will reduce the proportion of the employed who are skilled.

How will this affect productivity? Suppose that we exchange one skilled worker for one unskilled worker. If output falls, then productivity must fall since employment is constant. If we use the general production function $Y = F(L_s, L_u)$, then it is easy to show that productivity will fall if

$$MPL_s > MPL_u \tag{8}$$

so that productivity will fall if the marginal product of skilled workers is greater than the marginal product of the unskilled. In some circumstances this condition will be satisfied automatically. Suppose that the production function is

$$Y = A(L_s + \theta L_u)^\alpha K^\beta \tag{9}$$

where $\theta < 1$. This states that an unskilled hour leads to as much output as a proportion θ of a skilled hour. The relationship between the marginal products is then $MPL_u = \theta MPL_s$. In this case a rise in the proportion of unskilled workers will reduce output per head; therefore a rise in skill shortages will unambiguously reduce productivity.

While this conclusion will hold for any production function in which the marginal product is independent of the factor shares and where $MPL_s > MPL_u$, in general (8) will not hold automatically. Suppose that we use the Cobb–Douglas production function

$$Y = AL_s^\alpha L_u^\theta K^\beta \tag{10}$$

then the relationship between the marginal products is $MPL_u = (\theta L_s / \alpha L_u) MPL_s$. Since this depends on the factor shares, it is possible for the marginal product of the unskilled to exceed that of the skilled (this is likely to occur when most workers are skilled). However, we note from (7) that (8) is satisfied when $w_s' > w_u'$, that is, when the marginal cost of skilled labour is greater than the marginal cost of the unskilled. Since skilled wages exceed unskilled wages, our general presumption is therefore that skill shortages will reduce productivity.

Our estimating equation is derived from the Cobb–Douglas production function (10). If we define $L = L_s + L_u$, where L is total employment, we can express output per worker in log linear terms as

$$(y - l) = a + (1 - \alpha)(k - l) + \alpha\theta \log \sigma + \alpha(1 - \theta) \log(1 - \sigma) \tag{11}$$

where $\sigma = L_s/L$ is the employment share of skilled workers and lower-case Latin letters denote logarithms.

We now consider the effect of skill shortages on effort. We augment the production function to be

$$Y = AH^\kappa L_s^\alpha L_u^\theta K^\beta E^\gamma \tag{12}$$

where E is effort per worker-hour[10] and H is hours. Following Nickell et al. (1992), and Rosen (1990), we take E to be determined through bargaining between the firm and its workforce. Thus the bargained level of effort is that which maximises the Nash product $\Omega = (U - U^*)^\lambda (\pi - \pi^*)$ subject to the employment relationships from the first-order conditions for skilled and unskilled workers, where U is union utility and asterisks denote payoffs in the event that the bargain is not successfully concluded. λ is the relative bargaining power of the workers.

Assuming for the moment that skilled and unskilled workers negotiate together and that union preferences can be represented simply in Stone–Geary form as

$$U = (L - L^*)^{\phi_1} \left(\frac{w}{p_e} - \frac{w^*}{p_e} \right)^{\phi_2} (E^* - E)^{\phi_3} \tag{13}$$

where, L^*, w^*, and E^* are reservation levels of employment, wages and effort and p_e are economy-wide prices. We can then show that the level of effort will be bargained as

$$E = \frac{\gamma E^*}{\gamma + \lambda \phi_3 m} \tag{14}$$

where $1/1 - m$ is the markup of price over marginal costs. Equation (14) reveals that effort and so productivity fall as union bargaining power rises. If monopoly power rises, productivity falls, since a firm with more market power has a greater level of surplus to share in the form of low effort with their workers. Finally, as fallback effort E^* falls, effort falls. E^* is the expected level of effort disutility workers could get if no bargain is struck. If this happens, they must look for work elsewhere and the availability of other jobs depends on the state of the labour market. In particular, the higher is the level of shortages the better are outside prospects so the E^* falls. Therefore a rise in shortages will result in a lower level of effort and thus a lower level of productivity.

The same conclusions arise if we assume separate bargaining by skilled and unskilled workers. Suppose they both have utility functions of the form (13) where each argument refers to skilled and unskilled respectively. Then effort for the two groups is given by a pair of equations of the form (14).

(b) Estimating equation

To obtain our estimating equation we proceed as follows. From (14), E is a function of E^*, λ and m. We shall assume that E^* is measured by skilled and unskilled shortages, which reduces them, and time dummies.

For all 81 industries we do not have data on σ. From (12) we obtain $MPL_s/MPL_u = \alpha L_u/\theta L_s$. Substituting this into (7) gives $\sigma = [1 - (w_s'/w_u')]^{-1}$, where w_s', and w_u' are defined below equation (6). We measure $1/q_i$ by data on skilled and unskilled shortages. However, there is no data on wages by skill at such a disaggregated level.[11] Since the inter-industry wage structure is very stable, while the structure of relative wages at the one-digit industry level is also quite stable (Elliot and Murphy, 1990, table 3.4), we use an industry-specific fixed effect and time dummies to measure relative wages. We also use the fixed effects to pick up vacancy costs and turnover rates. We have also added the ratio of administrative, technical and clerical staff to total employment as a measure of labour heterogeneity. Finally, since our measure of Y is gross output we add the log of the relative price of raw materials, see Bruno and Sachs (1985) for a discussion. Making the appropriate substitutions into (11), adding hours and effort, and first differencing we have our estimating equation (1), where first-differencing has removed the fixed effects.

(c) Estimation method

Estimation is carried out by the generalised method of moments technique using the DPD programme; see Arellano and Bond (1989). We report heteroscedastic-robust test statistics for instrument validity and serial correlation, and hetero-scedastic- robust one-step t-statistics.

7.3   The effect of skill shortages on wages

(a) Theory

We suppose that skilled and unskilled workers are bargaining separately with the firm. Their utility function is as above in equation (14). Maximising with respect to W_s and W_u gives

$$\frac{\lambda}{W_s - W_s^*} = \frac{N_s}{\pi} \tag{15}$$

and

$$\frac{\lambda}{W_u - W_u^*} = \frac{N_u}{\pi} \tag{16}$$

Adding the two first-order conditions together gives

$$W = W^* + 2\lambda \frac{\pi}{N} \tag{17}$$

where $W = (W_s N_s + W_u N_u)/N$ and $W^* = (W_s^* N_s + W_u^* N_u)/N$. This has the plausible intuition that firm average wages are the outside option plus a share of the firm's profits. Skill shortages come in via W^*, the alternative expected income in the event of no settlement at the level of the firm. With a tighter labour market outside opportunities are better for skilled workers and so we might immediately write it as a positive function of shortages. Of course W^* is affected by other factors such as unemployment, benefits, mismatch and skill composition, and so all this suggests that

$$W^* = W^*(SKSHORT, UNSKSHORT, UNEMP, b, MM, \sigma) \tag{18}$$

Recalling that $\pi = PY - W_s'N_s - W_u'N_u$, we have that from (12), (6) and (7) $\pi = PYm$. Substituting this and (17) into (18) gives

$$W = W(SKSHORT, UNSKSHORT, UNEMP, b, MM, \frac{PY}{N}, m, \lambda, \sigma) \tag{19}$$

which says that skill shortages raise wages for a given productivity.

(b) Estimating equation

To estimate (19) we measure m by CR and λ by $UNION$. Adding the ratio of administrative staff as our only measure of σ for all 81 industries, and hours, and log linearising and first differencing gives our estimating equation (3) in the text.

NOTES

This chapter was originally prepared as a paper for the Centre for Economic Policy Research Conference on 'The Skills Gap and Economic Activity', 19–20 April 1993, London. The work has been supported by the Department of Employment, under their Labour Market Imperfections programme, to whom we are very grateful. The views expressed are those of the authors. We thank conference participants and Alison Booth, Dennis Snower and David Ulph for comments on an earlier draft. Errors are our own.

1 See Daly *et al.* (1985), Steedman and Wagner (1987, 1989) and Prais *et al.* (1989).
2 We take our data from responses to the Industrial Trends Survey of the Confederation of British Industry (CBI), see the Data Appendix for details.
3 Out of a possible 105 (three-digit) industries we lose 24 due to incomplete data. We are prevented from using a longer data set by a substantial change in industry definition in 1980.
4 Haskel and Martin (1993a) estimate the effects of skill shortages on productivity using the panel of 81 industries for 1980–86. We go beyond our earlier paper by (a) estimating equations for wages as well as productivity; (b) using the panel of engineering industries; and (c) extending the panel of 81 industries to cover 1980–89.
5 In surveys, firms commonly cite skill shortages as raising recruitment costs (Training Agency, 1990; Hart, 1990).
6 We have no overtime data to construct a more sophisticated measure of utilisation as in Muellbauer's (1988) aggregate study. Changes in utilisation here are picked up by changes in hours and the time dummies.
7 We find no significant effect from unions, in contrast with micro studies such as Nickell *et al.* (1992) and Gregg *et al.* (1993). This is probably due to the fact that our union data are not as good as we would wish because we have been forced to interpolate data from WIRS 1980 and 1984.
8 We found that shortages of unskilled workers had no effect on productivity growth, although Figure 8.1 shows that movements in skilled and unskilled shortages at the aggregate level are quite similar. Our panel data use cross-section variation which enable us to discriminate between the effects of the two series in a way that a study using aggregate data would be unlikely to do. Replacing $\Delta SKSHORT$ in Table 8.1, column 2, by $\Delta UNSKSHORT$ gives a coefficient of -0.02, $t = 0.16$.
9 So, for example, the change in the log of the capital/labour ratio was 0.0063. From Table 8.4, column 2 the contribution of this to productivity growth is 0.0063 times 0.33. This gives the figure of 2.1% in Table 8.3. Other changes over the period are 0.0075 for $(k-1)$ for the subpanel, 2.5 and 4.1 for $\Delta SKSHORT$ of the panel and subpanel respectively and 0.002 and 0.005 for Δh.

10 By effort we mean that if workers work harder every hour or production is reorganised then effort and hence output will rise.
11 The cells in the New Earnings Survey are too small to construct relative wages at the three-digit level.

REFERENCES

Arellano, M. and S. Bond (1988), 'Dynamic Panel Data Estimation Using DPD – A Guide for Users', Institute for Fiscal Studies, Working Paper, September.
    (1989), 'Some Tests of Specification for Panel Data: Monte Carlo Evidence and an Application to Employment Equations', Oxford Institute for Economics and Statistics, Discussion Paper, revised August.
Bruno, M. and J. Sachs (1985), *The Economics of Worldwide Stagflation*, Oxford: Basil Blackwell.
CBI (1989), *The TA/CBI Special Survey on Skills*, Confederation of British Industry, London.
Daly, A., D. Hitchens and K. Wagner (1985), 'Productivity, Machinery and Skills in a Sample of British and German Manufacturing Plants', *National Institute of Economic and Social Research Review* February, 48–61.
EEC (1990), *Results of the Business Survey Carried out among Management in the Community*, EEC Commission, Directorate-General for Economic and Financial Affairs.
Elliot, R. and P. Murphy (1990), 'Manual Skill Differentials', in *A Portrait of Pay, 1970–92*, M. Gregory and A. Thompson (eds.), Oxford: Clarendon Press.
Gregg, P., S. Machin and D. Metcalf (1993), 'Signals and Cycles: Productivity Growth and Changes in Union Status in British Companies, 1984–89', *Economic Journal* **103** (419), 894–907.
Hart, P. (1990), 'Skill Shortages in the UK', National Institute, mimeo.
Hart, P. and E. Shipman (1990), 'Skill shortages in the UK: Evidence from Surveys', National Institute, mimeo.
Haskel, J. and C. Martin (1992), 'The Economic Consequences of Skill Shortages', Department of Economics, Queen Mary and Westfield College, Discussion Paper 250.
    (1993a), 'Do Skill Shortages Reduce Productivity? Theory and Evidence from the UK', *Economic Journal* **103**, 386–94.
    (1993b), 'Skill Shortages, Productivity Growth and Wage Inflation in UK Manufacturing', CEPR Discussion Paper 859.
    (1993c), 'The Causes of Skill Shortages in Britain', *Oxford Economic Papers*, 45, pp. 573–86.
Jackman, R., R. Layard and C. Pissarides (1984), 'On Vacancies', London School of Economics, Centre for Labour Economics, Discussion Paper 165 (revised).
MSC (1977), *Survey of Hard-to-fill Vacancies*, Sheffield: Manpower Services Commission.
    (1983), *Engineering Labour Shortages in the North-West: A Case Study Approach*, Sheffield: Manpower Services Commission.
Millward, N. and M. Stevens (1986), *British Workplace Industrial Relations, 1980–84*, Aldershot: Gower.

Muellbauer, J. (1988), 'The Assessment: Productivity and Competitiveness in UK Manufacturing', *Oxford Review of Economic Policy* **2**, 1–25.

NEDO (1984), *Competence and Competition*, London: National Economic Development Office.

Nickell, S., S. Wadhwani and M. Wall (1992), 'Productivity Growth in UK Companies 1975–1986', *European Economic Review*, **36**, 1055–91.

OECD (1990), *Labour Market Policies for the 1990s*, Paris: OECD.

Oulton, N. (1991), 'Did Raw Material Prices Cause the Productivity Slowdown? Evidence from the US and the UK', National Institute of Economic and Social Research, Discussion Paper No. 198.

Pissarides, C. (1990), *Equilibrium Unemployment Theory*, Oxford: Basil Blackwell.

Prais, S., V. Jarvis and K. Wagner (1989), 'Productivity and Vocational Skills in Services in Britain and Germany: Hotels', *National Institute of Economic and Social Research Review* November, 52–74.

Rosen, A. (1990), 'Bargaining over Effort', Centre for Labour Economics, London School of Economics, Discussion Paper 351.

Steedman, H. and K. Wagner (1987), 'A Second Look at Productivity, Machinery and Skills in Britain and Germany', *National Institute of Economic and Social Research Review* November, 84–95.

(1989), 'Productivity, Machinery and Skills: Clothing Manufacturing in Britain and Germany', *National Institute of Economic and Social Research Review* May, 40–57.

Stoneman, P. (1992), 'Productivity in UK Manufacturing: Double Deflation and a Real Cost Index', Warwick Business School, mimeo.

Thomas, E and D. Deaton (1977), *Labour Shortages and Economic Analysis*, Oxford: Basil Blackwell.

Training Agency (1990), 'Skill Supply and Demand', *Labour Market Quarterly Report* August.

9　Workforce skills, product quality and economic performance

In many different sectors of the economy there are particularly interesting links between workforce skill levels and the type of goods produced. For example, if few skilled workers are available in a sector, firms there may have an incentive to produce low-quality products. This finding sheds some light on one possibly important cause of skills gaps. When products of high quality require highly trained workers to produce them, sectors can get stuck in a vicious cycle in which firms produce goods of low quality because there are few trained workers and workers acquire little training because few high-quality goods are produced. This chapter provides evidence of such interaction between skills and product quality that could arise from market failures generated by the 'low-skill, bad-job trap' (analysed in Chapter 6), the interaction between innovative performance and skills (developed in Chapter 5), or the complementarities between labour and capital (examined in Chapter 3).

The chapter examines the relationship between workforce skill levels, product quality and economic performance, by means of a detailed comparison of matched samples of biscuit manufacturing plants in Britain, Germany, France and The Netherlands. These findings are compared with those from similar cross-country comparisons in widely differing industrial sectors such as engineering, furniture manufacturing and clothing. Value-added per employee-hour in the German sample of plants was estimated to be some 40% above that in Britain and between 10% and 20% higher than in The Netherlands and France. This pattern of productivity performance could not be attributed to inter-country variation in the age and sophistication of capital equipment in use. But there were important differences in skill levels. These could be linked to both relative productivity performance and the predominant choice of product strategy in each country.

The authors argue that, broadly speaking, biscuit manufacturing exemplifies the notion of correspondence in different countries between the supply of skills (as shaped by national systems of education and training) and the demand for skills by employers (associated with their chosen product mix, capital utilization and work organization). The predominant strategic choices made by employers in any country reflect the extent to which a skilled workforce is available or achievable. But they also affect the supply of skills by signalling to individuals the value of investment in vocational training and education.

Workforce skills, product quality and economic performance

GEOFF MASON, BART VAN ARK and
KARIN WAGNER

1   Introduction

Concern about British manufacturers' ability to compete effectively in
international product markets is now frequently couched in terms of a
'low skills/low quality equilibrium'. It is argued, firstly, that a large
proportion of British manufacturing output is concentrated towards the
'lower' (more standardised, less complicated) end of the quality spectrum
for which skill requirements are relatively low; and, secondly, that the
relatively low demand for and supply of skills in Britain derive from
rational decisions made by both enterprises and individuals in the
context of the particular legal and institutional framework within which
they operate (Finegold and Soskice, 1988; Finegold, 1991).[1]

Why should it matter if British manufacturing industry is in some way
'trapped' in a low skills/low quality equilibrium? For many industries it
may be argued that, so long as market demand for low- or basic-quality
goods produced by relatively low-skilled British workers remains strong,
then the enterprises concerned should continue to thrive. However, in
other cases such confidence may not be justified: British producers could
find themselves unable to compete in the production of standardised
goods against firms based in lower-wage, newly industrialising countries,
and yet could also be poorly equipped to respond to such problems by
shifting output into higher value-added product areas. For industries of
this kind, the implications of a low skills/low quality trap for future
output, employment and trade performance would clearly be disturbing.

One way of exploring the issues raised in this debate is through
international comparisons at industry level of the relationship between
workforce skill levels, product quality and economic performance.
Accordingly, in this chapter we report on a detailed comparison of
matched samples of food processing plants in Britain, Germany, France
and The Netherlands. The results of this comparison are then contrasted

177

with those deriving from other similar, cross-country comparisons in widely differing industrial sectors such as engineering, furniture manufacturing and clothing (Daly *et al.*, 1985; Steedman and Wagner, 1987, 1989; Mason and van Ark, 1993).

Some of these earlier studies directly contributed to concerns about British manufacturers' apparent tendency to specialise in standardised and relatively low value-added product areas. For example, in the clothing industry comparison, typical batch sizes in the British industry were found to be roughly a hundred times greater than in Germany, and British products were generally made to lower quality standards in the sense of using plainer materials and fewer constituent pieces (thus making for less 'tailored' garments) (Steedman and Wagner, 1989).

It is widely recognised that 'quality' of output is difficult to measure. In consequence, for the investigation reported here, a relatively simple branch of the food industry, namely biscuits, was chosen for examination in order to facilitate productivity comparisons which took explicit account of inter-country differences in the mix of product-qualities produced.

The ordering of this chapter is as follows: Section 2 describes recent trends in biscuit output, employment and trade performance in the four countries; Section 3 reports on a detailed comparison of real productivity levels in the four national samples of plants; Sections 4 and 5 examine how inter-country differences in the quality and utilisation of physical and human capital inputs are related to differences in product strategy and productivity performance; Section 6 draws the findings of the biscuit study together with the results of earlier comparisons based on other industries.

The main conclusions of the chapter can be summarised as follows: there is indeed a close correspondence between the structure of workforce skills delivered by Britain's education and training system over recent decades and the orientation of large numbers of British manufacturers towards relatively low-skill, low-quality product areas. The impact of this pattern of specialisation on future economic performance will vary between industries depending on product market characteristics such as the composition of home demand. However, even in an industry such as biscuits where production of low value-added goods is strongly supported by domestic consumers' tastes and preferences, the efficiency with which this strategy is implemented may still be weakened by skill deficiencies relative to other countries.

2   Output, employment and trade performance

The present structure of biscuit manufacturing in Western Europe reflects the impact of competitive pressures over many decades, which have inspired amalgamations of producers (through mergers and takeovers) and concentration of output in a relatively small number of highly mechanised – in some cases highly automated – plants designed to take advantage of scale-economies in production, marketing and distribution.[2]

This restructuring of biscuit production has taken place in all four of the countries examined here. However, the process began earlier and has developed most fully in the British industry where the average plant size is substantially larger than in the other three countries.[3] Continued rationalisation involving plant closures and reductions in employment has also dominated the British biscuit industry's performance in the last decade: between 1980 and 1990 output rose in Britain by only 16% but with employment contracting by some 37% over the same period, there was a very sharp increase in labour productivity of 84%, higher than in any of the other three countries.

As Table 9.1 shows, output grew much more rapidly in (West) Germany (up 73%) and in The Netherlands (up 43%) than in Britain and (in spite of fluctuations during the decade) employment levels in 1990 were only about 4% down on 1980 levels in each of those two countries. The German performance in part reflects a remarkable 25% growth of output in a single year (1990) when the domestic market was suddenly expanded by reunification; in the same year German employment rose by some 11% over 1989. In the case of the French industry, output and productivity growth over the decade was the slowest of the four countries but there were signs of improvement in the late 1980s; the percentage decline in French biscuit employment was about half that in Britain.

The faster rates of output growth in the German and Dutch industries during the 1980s partly reflect rapid growth in export volumes in both countries. The relatively high export share of production in The Netherlands (43% of output in volume terms in 1990; see Table 9.2) is typical of a small open economy; the 38% export share in Germany is markedly higher than in Britain or France which are of similar population size. The British market is characterised by a small (6%) but rising import share of consumption, in particular of higher-priced varieties. The French industry is the only one of the four to run a trade deficit with imports accounting for 27% of consumption while its export ratio is much the same as Britain's.

3   Productivity and product quality

In the course of this study some 29 biscuit manufacturing plants were visited – ten in Britain, eight in Germany, six in France and five in The

Table 9.1. Estimated percentage changes in output (volume), employment and labour productivity in national biscuit industries, 1980–90

	Britain	The Netherlands	Germany	France
Output (volume)	+ 16	+ 43	+ 73	+ 14
Employment	− 37	− 4	− 4	− 18
Output per employee	+ 84	+ 49	+ 80	+ 39

Sources: National production censuses and trade associations.

Table 9.2. Biscuit export and import (volume) shares, 1980 and 1990 (percentages)

	Exports/production		Imports/consumption	
	1980	1990	1980	1990
Britain	12	14	2	6
The Netherlands	31	43	12	22
Germany	17	38	29	29
France	10	15	15	27

Source: International Office of Cocoa, Chocolate and Confectionery (IOCCC), *Statistical Bulletin*, Brussels, 1991.

Netherlands. Details of sample selection and methodology are provided in Appendix A. During these visits we gathered detailed information on biscuit output and associated employment – both direct and indirect – over a recent 12-month period (a sufficient length of time for our calculations not to be distorted by seasonal fluctuations). As a first step in the comparison of labour productivity levels, a simple measure of output (tonnage) per employee-hour was calculated which took no account of quality-differences. By this measure the highest (weighted) average level of productivity was found in our Dutch sample of plants, about 15% ahead of Britain. The average output per unit of labour input in the British plants was only 5% lower than in the French sample and was some 25% *higher* than in the German plants (even in spite of the above average levels of capacity utilisation prevailing in Germany at the time of our visits).[4]

The relatively good performance of the British biscuit industry primarily reflected the contributions made by its very largest plants which produced in excess of 1000 tons per week and achieved higher levels of labour productivity in terms of (crude) output per person-hour than any of the Continental plants visited. In smaller and medium-sized British plants producing similar tonnages to the great majority of their

Continental rivals (between 100 and 500 tons per week), productivity levels in Britain were considerably lower than in the other three countries.

However, in the course of our visits we noted marked differences in the mix of biscuit-qualities produced by each national industry, which suggested that an output measure based solely on tonnages was hardly adequate for comparisons of real productivity performance. For example, the more basic (undecorated) varieties of biscuits accounted for a larger proportion of total output in the British sample than in the other three countries and this was particularly the case in relation to the German sample. As well as requiring less secondary processing and packaging, basic-quality biscuits are typically produced in large batches and are thus more amenable to automation of production than are the higher-quality grades of biscuit.

A standard approach to the measurement of product quality differences is to define such differences in terms of technical characteristics.[5] For the present study, the detailed information we had gathered enabled us to classify the outputs of all plants visited into three different grades of product defined in terms of the number of processes involved in their production and the types of ingredients and packaging materials used. Sales price data for the different grades of product were then used along with Production Census information to derive a rough index of value-added per ton in each national sample (see Appendix C for details of these calculations).

As shown in the middle row of Table 9.3, the results of this exercise suggest that average value added per ton of biscuits in Britain is (in real terms) about 40% lower than in Germany and some 10–15% lower than in France and The Netherlands. When this value-added index is combined with our earlier measures of (crude) output per employee-hour in each national industry, 'quality-adjusted' productivity levels in Britain are found to be some 25% below those in Germany, 20% below The Netherlands and 15% below France.

The approximate nature of our measure of 'value added' will be apparent; nonetheless, the orders of magnitude conveyed by these estimates suggest that inter-country variation in the mix of product-qualities makes a significant contribution to international differences in real productivity levels in biscuit manufacturing. In relation to the British industry, the German productivity advantage derives from the higher average quality of its products which is more than sufficient to offset its lower physical quantity produced per employee-hour.[6] Quality differences are also the predominant element in the productivity gap between Britain and France. The exception in this regard is the Dutch industry

Table 9.3. 'Quality-adjusted' measures of labour productivity levels in biscuit manufacturing in Britain, The Netherlands, Germany and France (index numbers: Britain = 100; rounded to nearest five)

	Britain	The Netherlands	Germany	France
Output (tons) per person-hour	100	115	80	105
Value added per ton	100	110	175	115
'Quality-adjusted' output per person-hour	100	125	140	120

which succeeds in out-performing Britain primarily through its more efficient production of medium-quality biscuits.

The estimated differences in 'quality-adjusted' labour productivity levels between Britain and the three Continental countries are broadly mirrored in the pattern of inter-country variation in hourly labour costs: in 1989–91 average labour costs per employee-hour in the food processing and related industries were some 15% to 35% lower in Britain than in the other three countries.[7] The implications of such labour cost differentials for relative price competitiveness are discussed below in Section 6. In the next two sections we explore the ways in which relative productivity performance is affected by inter-country differences in the quality and utilisation of production inputs.

4   Machinery selection and utilisation

Modern biscuit manufacturing typically employs continuous-flow methods of production, with primary ingredients being bulk-fed to mixing machines from where the dough passes through rolling and biscuit-shaping ('forming') machinery before entering conveyor-fed 'travelling' line ovens. In the subsequent post-baking stages of production the biscuits are conveyed by moving belts through secondary processing machines if required (for example, for creaming, chocolate-coating or jam-filling) and then to the final stages of wrapping and packing.

The extent to which this production process is automated is closely related to the product strategy adopted. In a few plants with exceptionally long production runs of standardised biscuits, the entire mixing process is run on an automated continuous basis; however, the great majority of plants visited in all four countries engaged in batch mixing on all their production lines with regular 'changeovers' of dough-forming, wrapping and other equipment further down the line.

Regardless of the product mix, the wrapping process was invariably automated, but there was considerable variation in the methods adopted to handle the biscuits before and after they passed through the wrapping machines. In some cases collating and positioning of the biscuits was carried out by hand as was the subsequent packing of the biscuit packets in cartons ready for transportation to the warehouse. The labour-intensive nature of packing work reached a peak in those factories, most commonly observed in Germany but also important in France, which specialised in preparing tins of assorted biscuits.

In plants where changes of product varieties and packet sizes were relatively infrequent, vibratory systems or other equipment had been installed to stack the biscuits gently in lanes and feed them into automatic collating machines prior to the wrapping stage. Machinery of this kind was seen most often in Britain and to a lesser extent in The Netherlands and France, reflecting their respective output shares of basic- and medium-grade biscuits. In a very few cases post-wrapping activities such as cartoning and palletisation had also been automated.

In the British, German and French plants visited, the average age of ingredient-handling, mixing and baking machinery ranged between 12 and 16 years compared to just under 20 years in the Dutch industry (see Table 9.4). All four industries had renewed much of their wrapping machinery in the last ten years, reflecting both the heavy wear and tear to which such equipment is subjected and the need to keep up with the rapid pace of technical change. Differences in the age and sophistication of capital equipment in the four industries therefore showed little relation to the inter-country differences in productivity performance outlined in Section 3.

The most intensive use of machinery occurred in the British biscuit industry with nearly all plants visited engaging in full or partial 24-hour working, albeit usually for five rather than seven days per week. In France half the plants had 24-hour operations and half had two shifts per day. In Germany most plants operated only two shifts per day, in part because of legal restrictions on the employment of women (packing workers) during night shifts. In The Netherlands spare capacity limited production to a single shift per day in the majority of plants visited (with some evening work in the high season).

These inter-country differences in machine utilisation affected labour productivity performance in several ways. Where production lines were largely dedicated to single products – with few changes in packet sizes – there were clear benefits in continuous multi-shift working; examples of this type of production were observed in all four countries but were most common in Britain. However, most producers were under pressure to

Table 9.4. Estimated average age (in years) of machinery in biscuit plant samples

	Britain	The Netherlands	Germany	France
Preparation and mixing equipment	12	19	14	15
Ovens	16	19	13	14
Wrapping equipment	9	10	7	7

Calculations based on detailed age-distributions in Appendix Table 9B.1: mid-points taken for two closed intervals; top (open) interval assumed to have mid-point of 15 years in the case of wrapping equipment and 20 years in the case of preparation and mixing equipment and ovens.

respond quickly to diverse and rapidly changing customer requirements, with even ostensibly similar products having different specifications in terms of ingredients, dimensions, packaging and so on. In this context plants making less intensive use of equipment were better placed to schedule major changeovers of machinery for times when production lines were not fully manned (e.g. overnight); conversely, plants working a 24-hour day were less able to avoid inefficient use of labour while changeovers were being made.

Relative productivity levels were also affected by different rates of machine breakdown and malfunctioning which, in a continuous-flow production process, have serious consequences in terms of product wastage and the additional labour required to sort out problems. During our plant visits we observed some examples in all four countries of production lines which had been halted in mid-production or were not working smoothly; however, the incidence of equipment failure was highest in the British sample, with the most common problems arising from hard-worked conveyor belts and wrapping and carton-sealing machines and, in some cases, from long-standing difficulties in getting complex new ingredient-handling and -mixing systems to perform to requirements.

These observations were born out by records of 'emergency downtime' rates in the four samples: British plants reported an average 10% of planned machine-working time lost due to breakdowns and other unexpected stoppages compared to only about 3–4% downtime in the other three countries. This disparity was associated with different priorities in respect of preventative maintenance: only a fifth of the British plants visited reported serious efforts to carry out routine maintenance; by contrast, four-fifths of the Dutch and German plants had implemented full planned maintenance programmes as had two-thirds of the French plants.

As in other international comparisons carried out by the National Institute, the majority of British plants appeared to be trapped in a vicious circle with high levels of emergency maintenance militating against the introduction of preventative maintenance procedures which might help reduce the incidence of breakdowns. This dilemma partly reflected the pressure on British managers to work machinery harder and longer than on the Continent in order to ensure a rapid 'payback' on new investments. At the same time, as described below, high levels of emergency downtime in Britain were also associated with relative deficiencies in production management, supervisory and other workforce skills.

5   Workforce skills and product quality

5.1   Vocational qualifications and training

Direct labour accounted for between 70% and 80% of total employment in all four national samples, with the great majority of shopfloor workers employed in post-baking (secondary processing, wrapping and packing) areas of production. In all four countries wrapping and packing work was carried out by a largely unqualified workforce. The main differences arose in the more technically demanding occupational areas – production process, engineering and technical support departments and senior management – where the proportions of staff qualified to craft level or above were some 85% in Germany, 65% in The Netherlands, 45% in France and 25% in Britain.

Broadly speaking, the pattern of formal qualifications in each sample of plants reflected the institutional structure of vocational education and training provision in each country. Thus the majority of vocationally qualified German employees had passed through the well-known 'Dual System' which combines employment-based training with obligatory part-time attendance at vocational schools. By contrast, in the Dutch and French plants most vocational qualifications had been acquired in the course of full-time vocational schooling which, for many employees, had begun in the latter stages of compulsory education. In addition, the Dutch sample had relatively high proportions of employees in key occupations with technician-level qualifications, reflecting the widespread provision of full-time vocational education at age 16-plus in The Netherlands. In the British case there was a mix of qualifications gained through employment-based apprenticeships and full-time vocational courses but, in common with most other branches of manufacturing, the proportions of employees with either type of qualification were relatively low by Continental standards.[8]

As a consequence of competitive pressures in domestic and export markets and the need to keep up with new technological developments, the majority of plants visited in all four countries had recently increased their expenditure on both initial and continuing training for certain groups of employees. However, with the possible exception of France – where spending on adult training is encouraged by specific legislation – the nature and volume of such training hardly began to bridge the inter-country skill gaps indicated by differences in formal qualification levels.[9] As will now be shown, these differences in skill levels were closely related to the predominant choice of product strategy in each country, and also had important consequences for the relative efficiency with which each chosen strategy was implemented.

5.2   Process skills and product quality

The employees involved in the ingredient-handling, dough-mixing, forming and baking stages of biscuit production are defined here as 'process workers'; they include mixermen/women (and/or computer operators in a mixing control room), machine operators and ovensmen/women.

In German plants some 90% of process workers were craft-trained bakers who had been recruited on the open market, a process facilitated by a surplus of apprentices in the craft-baking industry.[10] In addition three-quarters of German production supervisors had undertaken further training to *Meister* standard in a range of technical and management areas, which had equipped them well to liaise with technical support services such as maintenance and (as discussed further below) to advise on incremental improvements to production processes.

By contrast, in the British plants visited there were no process workers and very few supervisors with vocational qualifications, and some managers went so far as to say that they would not give priority to craft-skilled bakers or other qualified persons for production jobs even if such employees were readily available to them. These differences in perceived skill requirements directly reflected the predominant product strategies in each of the two countries.

Process work in biscuit manufacturing largely centres around the achievement and maintenance of detailed product specifications in the face of considerable variability in raw material qualities (texture, moisture and so on) and differences in weather conditions (affecting ambient temperatures). In the course of production, variables such as the temperature and consistency of the dough mix and the diameter, thickness, weight, shape, moisture content and colour of the biscuits need to be repeatedly monitored. As conditions change from day to day (or batch to batch) it may be necessary to make a series of alterations to the dough-mixes initially specified by standard recipes and to adjust forming machine-settings, conveyor belt speeds and oven temperatures (Manley, 1991).

The skills and knowledge required for this work rise sharply as the number and complexity of products made is increased. At the same time small batch sizes and the use of expensive ingredients reduce the scope for protracted 'trial runs' with individual varieties before full production begins. In consequence, the several German plants specialising in small- and medium-batch production of high-quality multi-textured biscuits greatly depended on the 'know-how' and experience of the craft-trained bakers in their process departments.

By contrast, in the British industry the designation of process work as 'semi-skilled' reflected its primary orientation towards longer runs of relatively simple types of biscuit. In this type of production, the need for judgement and skill on the part of process workers is much reduced. This is particularly the case in factories where manual monitoring and adjustment activity has been supplemented or replaced by computerised control systems, although even in these circumstances there is a recurrent need for some manual intervention to maintain a consistent product, and wastage may occur if operators do not fully understand the consequences of their actions or inaction (Buchanan and Boddy, 1983, ch. 11).

In relation to these German and British extremes of product strategy and process skill requirements, the Dutch and French samples both occupied intermediate positions. As outlined in Section 3 above, the average value added per ton of output in The Netherlands and France was higher than in Britain but was still substantially below the average level of value added in Germany. Both the Dutch and French samples had significant proportions of vocationally qualified process workers and supervisors but few of them were apprentice-trained bakers as in Germany; this deficiency had been partially offset by longer average periods of on-the-job training than occurred in Germany.

5.3   Work organisation and manning levels

In the three Continental industries, initial on-the-job training for process workers equipped them to switch flexibly as required between all main areas of operation (mixing, biscuit-forming and oven control). In the German plants this training averaged only four months in length, reflecting the prior experience of trainees in the craft-baking sector. In The Netherlands, newly recruited process workers received on average seven months initial training and in France approximately 12 months.

In the British plants, initial on-the-job training for process workers averaged only two months and typically covered only a single task area (e.g. mixing). At later stages of their careers some British process workers received further training for other jobs (e.g. oven-operator) but – in contrast to their counterparts on the Continent – they were rarely expected to take responsibility for more than one task area at a time.

As a result, in the British plants visited each individual oven-line usually needed a three-person team to cover the mixing and baking stages of production. By contrast in all three Continental industries similar teams of process workers typically had responsibility for at least two oven-lines at a time.

In post-baking areas, manning levels were naturally highest in plants engaged in small- and medium-batch production of biscuits requiring multiple secondary processes (chocolate-coating, cream-filling, etc.) and subsequent packing in assortments. As noted, this type of product strategy was most commonly observed in Germany and (to a lesser extent) France; the associated high labour inputs were reflected in the higher average value added per unit of output in those two national samples.

In British plants geared to basic- or medium-quality product strategies, manning levels in wrapping and packing areas were frequently higher than in comparable Continental plants but did not contribute positively to value added: additional personnel in these British plants were typically required to sort out problems caused by higher rates of machine breakdown and malfunctioning, for example, to stack biscuits temporarily while machines were being repaired, to unwrap packets which had not passed properly through wrapping machines or had been rejected by check-weighing machines and to sweep up biscuits which had spilled onto the floor.

5.4   Engineering skills and production flow

In all four countries maintenance staff were generally required to hold at least a craft-level engineering qualification, reflecting their responsibility for setting and re-setting of complex wrapping and packing equipment as well as dealing with repairs and servicing of machinery. However, this minimum standard had only been fully met in Germany (through the well-established apprentice training system) and in The Netherlands; indeed, in Dutch plants, roughly half the maintenance personnel had gained technician-level qualifications at intermediate technical (MTS) schools. In both Britain and France about a fifth of engineering workers were vocationally unqualified; in France this deficiency was partially offset by recent recruitment of engineering staff with technician-level qualifications and by the relatively large size of maintenance departments.[11]

As noted earlier, in most Continental plants there was a clear link between relatively low rates of emergency downtime and the implementation of planned maintenance programmes. Concerted efforts to maintain a smooth production flow were most evident in German plants, many of which had an essentially 'pro-active' engineering policy: apart from undertaking preventative maintenance, engineering staff worked in close collaboration with production supervisors on machinery development and adaptation with a view to speeding up production and eliminating bottlenecks and delays.

The Dutch and French plants were able to match their German rivals in minimising emergency downtime through preventative maintenance; the majority of Dutch plants benefited from the diagnostic skills of their technician-qualified engineering staff and several French plants had tackled production flow problems by deploying groups of skilled engineering workers to work full-time in shopfloor wrapping and packing departments. However, the majority of Dutch and French supervisors were much less well-qualified than German *Meister* to collaborate systematically with engineering specialists on process innovations.

In the British industry, as already noted, the great majority of production supervisors lacked any form of technical or other vocational training and engineering departments were largely absorbed in dealing with emergency repairs. In some cases these problems required the regular attention of highly qualified managers and project engineers, who were thus diverted from their primary tasks of making long-term improvements in processes and products.

6   Summary and assessment

The branch of food manufacturing examined in this chapter exemplifies the notion of a correspondence in different economies between the supply of skills (as shaped by national systems of education and training) and the demand for skills by employers (associated with their chosen product mix and methods of machinery utilisation and work organisation).

For the biscuit industry, our estimates suggested that international differences in average value added per ton were at least as important as differences in crude productivity measured by tons produced per employee-hour. Taking differences in quantity and value added together to obtain a 'quality-adjusted' measure of labour productivity, we found that real output per employee-hour was highest in the German sample, about 40% higher on average than in Britain; in The Netherlands and France real productivity levels were some 20–25% higher than in Britain.

Although the relatively low demand for skills in the British industry is consistent with the predominant mix of basic- and medium-quality products, these comparisons of real productivity levels suggest that skill deficiencies can seriously undermine the efficiency with which even a relatively low value added product strategy is carried out. In this case the weaker productivity performance of the British sample of plants can be linked not just to specific shortfalls in skill areas such as shopfloor supervision and engineering but also to the relatively low expectations of workforce 'trainability' held by many British managers.

Thus, even in highly automated British factories specialising in bulk production of basic-quality biscuits, manning levels were comparatively high because of the perceived need for process workers to 'stick to their own jobs' on particular production lines in order to cope with possible problems that might arise even with ostensibly uncomplicated products. Similarly, the comparatively narrow training received by British shop-floor workers restricted their ability to anticipate problems such as machine malfunctioning and take appropriate action which might limit product wastage (for instance, by making minor adjustments themselves or calling in specialist help immediately).

However, in spite of these problems, biscuit manufacturing continues to be a relatively successful industry in British terms. In respect of price competitiveness, its relatively low labour costs help to offset the labour productivity shortcomings identified in this study. In recent years the largest British-based biscuit producers have made substantial investments in new equipment and new product development and some now play a significant role in the wider European industry.

The prospects for the British biscuit industry thus differ from those of other industries investigated by National Institute researchers. In the furniture and clothing industries, for instance, British firms which have pursued a relatively 'low quality/low skill' product strategy are poorly equipped to withstand foreign competition in the production of standardised goods or to respond quickly to rapid changes in consumer demand in favour of higher value-added products (Steedman and Wagner, 1987, 1989). By contrast, given the highly specific nature of domestic tastes and preferences associated with biscuits, British biscuit producers face a very limited threat of import penetration and, through wide-scale advertising expenditure by the larger companies, the industry is well-placed to try to shape, rather than simply react to, future changes in consumer demand.

Substantially different points of contrast arise in connection with the precision engineering industry, which has been the subject of two detailed studies, one comparing Britain and Germany (Daly *et al.*, 1985) and the other Britain and The Netherlands (Mason and van Ark, 1993). This industry – making products such as pumps, valves and springs – faces intense competition from mass producers of standardised goods in lower-wage countries. As a result the majority of surviving producers in Britain have had no choice but to seek to emulate their Continental rivals in re-focusing production towards skill-intensive small- and medium-batch production of higher value-added products. However, in spite of a notably strong commitment to workforce training by many British engineering firms in recent years, average skill levels in the British industry still fall short of those found in Germany and The Netherlands, where vocational education and training systems are better-established and have long catered for a significant proportion of new entrants to the manufacturing workforce.

Taken together, the various cross-country comparisons suggest that there is a close correspondence between the structure of workforce skills delivered by Britain's vocational education and training system over recent decades – polarised between a large majority of low-skilled workers and a small minority of highly qualified personnel – and the continued specialisation of large numbers of British manufacturers in highly automated, low value-added production activities of the kind which predominate in the biscuit, clothing and furniture industries. The implications for output, employment and trade performance of this kind of specialisation will vary from industry to industry depending on product market characteristics such as the rate (and direction) of change in consumer demand and the scope for import penetration from newly industrialising countries.

To the extent that British producers are unable to match real ('quality-adjusted') productivity levels achieved by their rivals in other advanced industrial nations, their competitiveness will continue to depend heavily on factors such as relatively low labour costs and favourable exchange rates. This is especially true of industries such as precision engineering where employers have to 'swim against the tide' of the national education and training system simply to preserve the core skills base needed to survive in international markets. However, as we have shown in this chapter, even in a much less vulnerable industry such as biscuits which appears well suited to a high-automation, low-skill production strategy, productivity performance may still be weakened by the associated choices regarding machinery utilisation and maintenance, shopfloor organisation and training.

Appendix A: Selection of national samples of plants

In all four countries the plants visited were initially identified through trade directories; further information about employment and product lines was sought by telephone before formal requests for visits were made. Response rates in each country were fairly similar with approximately two-thirds of plants who were approached about a visit agreeing to participate. All the visits were carried out between October 1989 and December 1991. During the visits semi-structured interviews were held with production and/or personnel managers and, where possible, with shopfloor supervisors as well. Each visit included direct observation of production processes and work organisation on the shopfloor. At least two researchers from different countries were present on 90% of visits. To economise on travelling costs the plants were geographically clustered in all the countries except for The Netherlands (where distances are small).

Table 9A.1 shows the distribution of plant sizes in the national samples. There were several problems to be overcome in drawing up four samples of plants which could be usefully compared with each other and at the same time be regarded as adequately representative of each national industry. In broad terms our sampling strategy was to cover a spread of plants in the inter-quartile employment-size range in each country (defined in terms of the industry's total employment, not in terms of numbers of plants). As noted in note 3 to the main text, the median plant size in the British industry is substantially larger than in the other three countries; in order to obtain a substantial overlap of plant-sizes in the four samples, additional visits were made to British plants in smaller size groups and to two important German plants above the upper quartile plant size. However, for purposes of data analysis the sample plants were weighted in such a way that our estimates remained broadly representative of the inter-quartile employment size range in each national population. (See Mason *et al.*, 1993, sections 1 and 3 for details of this weighting procedure and a comparison of the productivity estimates derived using weighted data with alternative estimates based on unweighted data.)

Table 9A.1. Distribution of plant sizes in national samples of biscuit manufacturers

No. of employees	Number of plants			
	Britain	The Netherlands	Germany	France
Under 200	2	2	} 4	4
200–499	2	} 3		
500–999	2		2	2
1000-plus	4	0	2	0
Total	10	5	8	6

Appendix B: Age of machinery in national samples

Table 9B.1. Distribution of ages of machinery in biscuit plant samples (employment-weighted percentage shares, rounded to nearest 5%)

Age (years)	Preparation and mixing equipment			Ovens			Wrapping/packing equipment		
	< 5	5–10	> 10	< 5	5–10	> 10	< 5	5–10	> 10
Britain	30	20	50	15	15	70	25	35	40
The Netherlands	5	5	90	5	5	90	20	40	40
Germany	20	20	60	15	35	50	40	40	20
France	20	10	70	30	10	60	50	25	25

Appendix C: Estimates of 'quality-adjusted' productivity levels

As noted in Section 3 of the main text, the detailed information we had gathered during plant visits enabled us to classify each plant's output into three different grades of product, defined in terms of the number of processes involved in their production and the types of ingredients and packaging materials used. The outcome of this classification of output by quality-grade is shown in Table 9C.1. The 35% share of basic-quality biscuits in British output is well above the 15–25% shares found in Germany, France and The Netherlands. Some 35% of German sample output is classified to the high-quality grade, a much higher proportion than in the other three countries. A very large share of production in all four countries (ranging from 50% in Germany to 70% in France) falls into the medium-quality grade.

As a first step towards the calculation of a 'quality-adjusted' measure of output in each industry, an index of average retail prices in each country was compiled using price data (net of VAT) for the different grades of biscuit in each country, based on products observed in the plants visited. As described in detail in Mason *et al.* (1993), we were able to rely on closely matched products in the 'basic-quality' grade in each country to act as a *numéraire* in these cross-country price comparisons.

Subsequently, in order to obtain estimates of inter-country differences in the average *value added* per ton of output, this index of average retail prices was converted to an index of average ex-factory prices on the basis of estimated average retail gross margins (exclusive of VAT) in each country, and a rough index of value-added per ton was then derived by recalculating the index of average ex-factory prices on a 'net of raw materials' basis using Production Census data on inter-country differences in the shares of production costs relating to intermediate inputs such as ingredients, fuel and packaging materials. (For further details of these calculations, see Mason *et al.*, 1993, section 3.)

As shown in the middle row of Table 9.4 in the main text, the results of this exercise suggest that average value added per ton of biscuits in Britain is (in real terms) about 40% lower than in Germany and some 10–15% lower than in France and The Netherlands. When this value-added index is combined with our

Table 9C.1. Distribution of output (tonnage) by quality-grade in national samples of biscuit manufacturers (all numbers rounded to nearest five)

	Percentage shares of output			
	Britain	The Netherlands	Germany	France
Basic-quality	35	25	15	20
Medium-quality	60	60	50	70
High-quality	5	15	35	10

The three grades of biscuit quality were defined as follows:

(1) Basic-quality: 'dry' undecorated biscuits made from relatively cheap ingredients (e.g. vegetable or animal fats), stacked in cylinder-form and wrapped in a single layer of plastic film.
(2) Medium-quality: biscuits requiring at least one secondary production process after baking such as chocolate-coating or sandwich-filling with cream or jam; usually sold with at least two layers of packaging. Undecorated biscuits made with more expensive ingredients such as butter are also included in this category.
(3) High-quality: elaborate, multi-textured biscuits requiring two or more secondary (post-baking) production processes, usually stacked in successive small piles, multi-wrapped and boxed; includes assortments of biscuits made from expensive ingredients.

earlier measures of (crude) output per employee-hour in each national industry, 'quality-adjusted' productivity levels in Britain are found to be some 25% below those in Germany, 20% below The Netherlands and 15% below France.

NOTES

We are glad to acknowledge financial support for this project provided by the Economic and Social Research Council; however, the Council is not responsible in any way for the views expressed in the paper.

Particular thanks are due to Sig Prais (NIESR) for his generous advice and encouragement throughout the project and to Sylvie Célerier (Centre d'Etudes et de Recherches sur les Qualifications, Paris) who arranged and participated in French plant visits. We are also grateful to Mary O'Mahony (NIESR) for the use of data from her recent comparison of Anglo-German manufacturing productivity levels. Useful comments on earlier drafts were made by Jim Burns, Valerie Jarvis, Duncan Manley, Paul Ryan, Hilary Steedman, Alan Swinbank and participants at the CEPR conference on 'The Skills Gap and Economic Activity' and a joint NIESR/London Business School seminar. Responsibility for any errors in the chapter is of course ours alone.

We are grateful to the many companies in the four countries who agreed to receive visits in connection with this study and who were generous with both time and information. In addition we would like to thank the following industry and educational experts for their helpful advice and comments:

In Britain: A. Benns, L. Frew (Glasgow College of Food Technology); M. Foy (Blackpool and the Fylde College); D. Manley, I. Wheal (food industry consultants); M. Webber, W. Newman (Biscuit, Cake, Chocolate and Confectionery Alliance, London); T. MacNeary (County NatWest); S. Burt, L. Sparks (Institute for Retail Studies, University of Stirling).

In The Netherlands: J. Gravemaker (LSBL, Apeldoorn); J. van Hoof (SISWO, University of Amsterdam); S. Kelder, J. Fledderus, H. Spronkers (LBO De Nieuwe Vaart, Zaandam); A. Timmers (Damland College, Sector Techniek, Zaandam); P. van Vliet (Stichting Studiecentrum Zoetwaren, Zeist).

In Germany: A. Bertram (Zentralfachschule der Deutschen Süsswarenwirtschaft); Herr Kruit (Berufsbildene Schule, Varel); staff members of the Staatliche Fachschule der Lebensmitteltechnik, Berlin, and the Bundesverband der Deutschen Süsswarenindustrie.

In France: Mme R. Desgrez (Alliance 7, Paris); O. Bertrand (CEREQ, Paris).

1 The term 'equilibrium' is used by Finegold and Soskice 'to connote a self-reinforcing network of societal and state institutions' which in Britain interact to restrict both the demand for and supply of workforce skills (1988, p. 22).

2 More recently the concentration of ownership in biscuits, as in several other branches of food processing, has been further reinforced by commercial pressures resulting from the bulk-purchasing power of major retail chains (Burns, 1983; Balasubramanyam and Nguyen, 1991).

3 The median size of biscuit-making plant in Britain is estimated at some 1200 employees compared to roughly 330 in France, 300 in Germany and 150–200 in The Netherlands (Mason *et al.*, 1993, table 2).

4 As mentioned in the main text, the German domestic market experienced very rapid growth in demand immediately following reunification; if German productivity in 1990 had grown only at the average annual rate experienced between 1980 and 1989 (5.5%), then average tonnage per employee-hour in our German sample would have been closer to 75% of the average British level instead of 80%.

5 For example, 'hedonic' regression techniques are often used to estimate 'shadow prices' for goods with a specified list of technical characteristics (such as, in the case of motor cars, length, width and engine capacity); for a recent assessment, see Griliches (1990).

6 This result applies even if an appropriate downward adjustment is made to the estimated crude productivity level in the German industry to eliminate the effects of above average levels of capacity utilisation at the time of our visits; such an adjustment would reduce the average tonnage per person-hour in the German sample from 80% to 75% of the British level (see note 4) but average 'quality-adjusted' output per person-hour in Germany would still be an estimated 30% higher than in Britain.

7 In more detail, total labour costs per employee-hour (including social charges) in food, drink and tobacco manufacturing in 1989–91 were on average: (index numbers: Britain = 100; converted at current exchange rates) Britain 100, France 120, Germany 147, The Netherlands 150. (Source: Swedish Employers Confederation, *Wages and Total Labour Costs for Workers: International Survey 1981–1991*, 1993.)

8 Analysis of Labour Force Surveys carried out in the four countries shows the following proportions of the total workforce holding intermediate vocational

qualifications in 1987–89: Britain 27%, France 40%, The Netherlands 57%, Germany 63% (Mason et al., 1992, table 2).

9 In France since 1971 all companies have been obliged to spend a minimum proportion of their total wage and salary bill on continuing training. During our visits to French plants we encountered several examples of innovative adult training programmes which had few, if any, parallels in the other three countries. For further details see Mason et al., (1993, section 5.7).

10 'Over-production' of craft-skilled workers is common in many *Handwerk* (artisan) sectors of German industry where the productive contribution made by apprentices appears to more than offset the cost of training them (Casey, 1986).

11 In terms of hours worked the ratio of maintenance to direct employment was approximately 1:8 in the French sample, 1:10 in Britain and The Netherlands and 1:12 in Germany.

REFERENCES

Balasubramanyam, V. and D. Nguyen (1991), 'Structure and Performance of the UK Food and Drink Industries', *Journal of Agricultural Economics* **42**, 1.

Buchanan, D. and D. Boddy (1983), *Organisations in the Computer Age: Technological Imperatives and Strategic Choice*, Aldershot: Gower.

Burns, J. A. (1983), 'The UK Food Chain with Particular Reference to the Inter-relations Between Manufacturers and Distributors', *Journal of Agricultural Economics* **34**, 4.

Casey, B. (1986), 'The Dual Apprenticeship System and the Recruitment and Retention of Young Persons in West Germany', *British Journal of Industrial Relations* **24**, 1.

Daly, A., D. Hitchens and K. Wagner (1985), 'Productivity, Machinery and Skills in a Sample of British and German Manufacturing Plants', *National Institute Economic Review* February.

Finegold, D. (1991), 'Institutional Incentives and Skill Creation: Preconditions for a High-skill Equilibrium', in P. Ryan (ed.), *International Comparisons of Vocational Education and Training for Intermediate Skills*, London: Falmer.

Finegold, D. and D. Soskice (1988), 'The Failure of Training in Britain: Analysis and Prescription', *Oxford Review of Economic Policy* **4**, No. 3.

Griliches, Z. (1990), 'Hedonic Price Indexes and the Measurement of Capital and Productivity: Some Historical Reflections', in *Fifty Years of Economic Measurement*, E. R. Berndt and J. E. Triplett (eds.), Chicago: University of Chicago Press.

Manley, D. (1991), *Technology of Biscuits, Crackers and Cookies*, 2nd edition, Chichester: Ellis Horwood.

Mason, G. and B. van Ark (1993), 'Productivity, Machinery and Skills in Engineering: An Anglo-Dutch Comparison', NIESR Discussion Paper (New Series), No. 36.

Mason, G., S. Prais and B. van Ark (1992), 'Vocational Education and Productivity in the Netherlands and Britain', *National Institute Economic Review* May.

Mason, G., B. van Ark and K. Wagner (1993), 'Productivity, Product Quality and Workforce Skills: Food Processing in Four European Countries', NIESR Discussion Paper (New Series), No. 34.

Steedman, H. and K. Wagner (1987), 'A Second Look at Productivity, Machinery and Skills in Britain and Germany', *National Institute Economic Review* November.

(1989), 'Productivity, Machinery and Skills: Clothing Manufacturing in Britain and Germany', *National Institute Economic Review* May.

10 Workforce skills and export competitiveness

This chapter considers the implications of skills gaps for export performance by means of a detailed comparison of the UK with Germany. The results of analysis reported in the chapter confirm earlier findings that, relative to Germany, the UK's main deficiency is in craft and technician skills. But the extent of the skills gap varies considerably between sectors. Contrary to a common view, the quality of UK exports does not appear to be on average inferior to that of German ones, at least if quality is judged by price.

The chapter argues that the UK and Germany have comparative advantage in the same type of sophisticated manufactured goods. The UK's skill deficiencies tend therefore to show up as a lower volume *of exports: the bigger the skills gap in any sector, the worse the UK's export performance relative to Germany's. UK and German exports to five major markets over the period 1978–87 are used to test this hypothesis.*

199

Workforce skills and export competitiveness

NICHOLAS OULTON

1   Introduction[1]

German exports of manufactured goods are two to four times the volume of UK ones, depending on the market. Can the UK's poor performance in manufactured trade by comparison with Germany's be explained by her well-known and well-documented skill deficiencies? It is the purpose of this chapter to cast light on this issue. I attempt first to see whether it is in fact the case that (as frequently claimed) UK exports are of comparatively low quality. Second, and irrespective of the answer to this first question, I compare skill levels at the sectoral level in both countries and investigate whether differences in skill levels explain differences in export performance.

The debate on the causes of the UK's longstanding weakness in manufacturing has been placed on a new footing by work in recent years at the National Institute. These studies have established that the skill levels of the UK workforce are deficient in comparison to those of our major competitors such as France, Germany and Japan across a wide range of industries (Prais (1981); more recent work includes: Jarvis and Prais (1989), Prais and Steedman (1986), Prais and Wagner (1988) and Steedman (1987, 1988)). Some of these studies have gone further and demonstrated that low skills translate directly into low productivity (Daly et al. (1985), on metal-working; Steedman and Wagner (1987), on kitchen furniture and (1988), on clothing manufacture; Mason et al. (1993), on biscuits)). These studies, however, do not address the possibility of a link between skills and trade performance.

One way in which skill deficiencies might cause poor performance in export markets is if they led to British firms specialising in 'low value added' products, for which demand in large industrial markets is limited. Perhaps surprisingly, this does *not* appear to be the case. At least if we are prepared to judge quality by price, it turns out that

201

UK-manufactured exports are on average of about the same quality as German ones. In fact, Britain and Germany are exporting what are (at least in a statistical sense) the same goods to the same markets. When manufactured exports are considered at a detailed level (distinguishing over 1,300 products), the average price or more precisely, unit value, of these products appears to be roughly similar, when averaged over a run of years. And for both countries, much the greater part of manufactured exports go to the same group of high-income industrial economies. The only difference is, German exports are (depending on the market) two to four times British ones.

These facts suggest that Britain and Germany have comparative advantage in the same sort of products, but that Germany's comparative advantage is stronger. But does Germany's greater comparative advantage have anything to do with skills? I argue that the answer is yes. A theoretical argument leading to this conclusion runs along the following lines. In any sector of industry, it is possible to produce more or less sophisticated products. More sophisticated products require higher skills (in some sense). A country such as the Philippines or China is constrained at its current stage of development to produce and export predominantly unsophisticated (low-quality) products. Such a choice is not open to the UK, unless wages are to fall to Third World levels. Fortunately, such a choice is not necessary, since UK skill levels are undoubtedly vastly greater than those in the Third World. But now compare two advanced industrial countries such as the UK and Germany, each of which has comparative advantage in sophisticated (high-quality) products. If one of these two countries has a higher skill level in some sector, then that country will be able to produce and export more per person employed in that sector. By contrast, the low skill country, though exporting sophisticated products, will devote a larger share of its resources to unsophisticated products consumed domestically. Looking across all industrial sectors, the larger the gap in skills in any sector, the weaker the export performance of the low skill country in that sector is likely to be, relative to its rival. This argument can be rigorously demonstrated by means of a suitably extended version of the most basic model of international trade, the Heckscher–Ohlin model.

As with all theoretical arguments, there are drawbacks. First, though the argument may be correct as far as it goes, some other factor emphasised in a different theory (such as R&D perhaps) may be the really important one. Second, even if skills are important, what sort of skills? There is no guarantee that the type of deficiencies identified in the National Institute studies are the ones which really matter for export performance. Hence the question must be examined empirically, first by measuring the skill gaps between different sectors of British and German manufacturing and second by seeing whether skill gaps so measured are indeed correlated with export performance, holding constant the influence of other factors, such as R&D.

The chapter is organised as follows. In Section 2 I discuss the evidence for skill gaps between the UK and Germany. Estimates of the proportions of the manufacturing labour force, broken down into 26 sectors, with four different levels of qualifications are presented and discussed. Section 3 discusses the trade data and considers whether UK exports are on average of lower quality than German ones, by means of an examination of unit values of exports at a detailed level. In Section 4 a many goods version of the Heckscher–Ohlin model is shown to predict a link between skills and export performance. Then in Section 5 I bring the skills data and the trade data together in order to assess the quantitative effect of skill gaps on the relative degree of success of the two countries' exports. Here five important export markets are studied: the USA, France, Italy, Belgium and The Netherlands. Section 6 concludes.

2   Relative skill levels in Britain and Germany

In this chapter, skill levels are measured by qualifications. This is not uncontroversial, but the alternatives can also be criticised. For example, wages might be used in a cross-industry study within a single country, but not in a cross-country study: how could we know whether a higher wage for 'unskilled' labour in one country reflected a higher level of education-induced productivity or some other factor? Some studies (e.g. Courakis, 1991) employ a categorisation of labour into 'skilled' and 'unskilled', but in a cross-country study this would be inappropriate since there is no reason to think that these categories are standardised across countries; in the UK we know that such categories have in the past been influenced by trade union pressure. The advantage of using qualifications is that a great deal of work has already been done in previous National Institute studies on comparing different systems of qualifications, so that we can be reasonably confident that like is being compared with like. Some would argue that qualifications simply reflect the extent to which credentialism is prevalent. If so, they should have no significant empirical effects, so the proof of the pudding will be in the eating.

Data on qualifications were obtained from the Labour Force Survey (LFS) for Britain and from the German equivalent, the Mikrozensus, for Germany. The LFS records the highest qualification held by respondents, whether purely academic or vocational in nature. The Mikrozensus, on the other hand, records both the highest academic and the highest

Table 10.1. Comparable levels of vocational qualification in the UK and Germany

Level	Typical qualification
United Kingdom	
1. High	First or higher degrees; membership of professional institutions
2. Upper intermediate	BTEC HNC/HND; teaching, nursing qualifications
3. Lower intermediate	BTEC ONC/OND; City & Guilds; trade apprenticeships
4. No vocational qualifications	
Germany	
1. High	*Hochschulabschluss; Fachhochschulabschluss*
2. Upper intermediate	*Meister/Techniker gleichwertig Fachschulabschluss*
3. Lower intermediate	*Lehr-/Anlernausbildung gleichwertig Berufs-Fachschulabschluss; berufliches Praktikum*
4. No vocational qualifications	

vocational qualification (though 'vocational' is interpreted broadly to include university degrees). In order to achieve comparability, four levels of vocational qualification were distinguished which were as shown in Table 10.1 for the two countries.

  This comparison is a little unfair to the UK, as the last category includes people who have obtained one or more A-levels or GCSEs (previously, O-levels or CSEs). There are several reasons for not distinguishing this group separately. The first and most important reason is to achieve comparability with the German data: most of those with equivalent academic qualifications in Germany will also have achieved some vocational qualification such as the *berufliches Praktikum*, so that those with *only* the equivalent of GCSEs cannot be distinguished separately in German data. Secondly, the numbers involved are fairly small. Some 3–4% of the manufacturing labour force had one or more A-level passes as their highest qualification. Some 14–19% had one or more O-level or CSE passes (now repackaged as GCSE) in our period. But this category is very coarsely defined: those with one low-grade pass are lumped in with those with eight high-grade passes.

  The proportion of the UK manufacturing labour force achieving these qualifications in 1987 is set out in Table 10.2. Here, for the sake again of comparability, manufacturing has been broken down in accordance with a common German scheme into 26 sectors (for the correspondence

Table 10.2. Skill levels of the manufacturing workforce, by sector: UK, 1987

Sector		Employment (thousands)	No quals. (%)	Skill level 3 (%)	2 (%)	1 (%)
1	Chemicals	334	55.2	23.1	5.9	15.8
2	Mineral Oil Processing	24	44.7	31.4	6.1	17.8
3/4	Rubber & Plastics	209	70.2	25.1	1.9	2.9
5	Mineral Products	101	71.0	17.9	3.4	7.7
6/7	Ceramics & Glass	101	74.1	18.1	2.6	5.2
8	Iron & Steel	130	54.6	35.3	5.8	4.4
9	Non-Ferrous Metals	96	61.3	28.7	3.1	6.9
10	Metal Products	95	47.6	43.1	2.6	6.7
11	Mechanical Engineering	566	48.4	38.6	6.5	6.5
12	Office Machinery & Computers	154	42.7	19.0	12.0	26.4
13	Vehicles	368	57.7	32.9	4.1	5.2
14	Shipbuilding	70	36.1	52.9	5.7	5.4
15	Aerospace	187	34.7	47.3	9.3	8.7
16	Electrical Engineering	543	57.0	27.3	6.9	8.8
17	Instrument Engineering	130	52.4	29.0	7.3	11.4
18	Small Metal Items & Ordnance	251	63.7	28.5	4.6	3.2
19	Toys, Sports Goods, etc.	85	72.1	20.4	1.8	5.8
20/21	Timber & Wood Furniture	277	57.9	37.6	1.1	3.4
22/23	Pulp, Paper & Board	143	71.0	21.3	3.1	4.7
24	Printing & Publishing	352	56.4	32.7	1.9	9.0
25	Leather & Footwear	73	84.1	13.8	0.0	2.1
26	Textiles & Man-Made Fibres	225	75.0	18.8	2.6	3.6
27	Clothing & Fur	260	83.0	12.1	1.2	3.8
28	Food	429	74.6	19.0	2.1	4.4
29	Drink	115	65.1	22.2	4.5	8.2
30	Tobacco	21	68.1	21.9	1.3	8.8
	Total	5,339				
	Minimum		34.7	12.1	0.0	2.1
	Maximum		84.1	52.9	12.0	26.4
	SD		13.2	10.1	2.8	5.3
	Mean		60.7	27.6	4.1	7.6

Source: 1987 LFS. Employment is employees plus self-employed; part-timers counted as half full-time.

between these sectors and the UK SIC(1980), see Oulton (1993, appendix B)). There is a wide variation across sectors in the extent to which qualified people are employed. In 1987, those with no qualifications varied from 35% to 84%, while those with high-level qualifications varied from 2% to 26%. The same data were also extracted for the years

Table 10.3. Panel regressions, 1981–87 (dependent variable is skill proportion)

		Coefficient on time trend	t-statistic
1.	High	0.2052	4.00
2.	Higher intermediate	0.1532	3.51
3.	Lower intermediate	0.6938	6.12
4.	No qualifications	−1.0523	9.50

Note: 180 observations (30 sectors[2] and 6 years).
Source: LFS for 1981, 1983–87 (the LFS was not carried out in 1982).

1981 and 1983–86 (the change to the 1980 from the 1968 SIC precluded us from using the LFS for earlier years). Casual inspection of these figures suggests that the proportions with some vocational qualifications have increased while the proportions with no qualifications have fallen. This is confirmed by statistical analysis. Panel regressions where the dependent variable is the proportion with each skill level and the independent variables are fixed effects and a time trend produced the results shown in Table 10.3.

Despite the fact that the qualifications level has been rising, in virtually all sectors there is a large proportion with no qualifications at all. In twenty sectors this proportion was still over 50% in 1987; in eight sectors it was over 70%.

How do UK qualifications compare with German ones? Table 10.4 gives the answer for 1987 for the same sectoral breakdown of manufacturing. The pattern of qualification levels is fairly similar, though far from identical across sectors in the two countries. The closest match is for no qualifications. The correlation coefficients between the two countries are as shown in Table 10.5.

Despite the similarity in pattern, the German *level* of qualifications is substantially higher, a fact which will not come as a surprise to readers of earlier National Institute studies of comparative skill levels (e.g. Prais, 1981). The employment-weighted means of the sectoral proportions, in 1987, were as shown in Table 10.6. At the higher intermediate and lower intermediate levels, Germany has proportionately about twice as many qualified people as the UK. The UK has twice the level of workers with no qualifications. Only at the highest level does the UK have a slight advantage. Although the UK level has been rising, one cannot count on the UK automatically catching up with Germany in the near future, since the average German level has also been rising in recent years. In 1978,

Table 10.4. Skill levels of the manufacturing workforce, by sector: Germany, 1987

Sector		Employment (thousands)	No quals. (%)	Skill level 3 (%)	2 (%)	1 (%)
1	Chemicals	681	24.2	56.8	8.0	11.0
2	Mineral Oil Processing	26	23.1	57.7	7.7	11.5
3/4	Rubber & Plastics	290	35.9	54.7	5.6	3.9
5	Mineral Products	133	59.3	7.6	7.6	3.8
6/7	Ceramics & Glass	170	37.7	52.3	6.5	3.6
8	Iron & Steel	256	30.9	58.1	6.3	4.7
9	Non-Ferrous Metals	197	34.5	57.2	5.2	3.1
10	Metal Products	386	28.0	62.3	5.8	3.9
11	Mechanical Engineering	1,079	21.6	60.0	10.4	8.0
12	Office Machinery & Computers	67	16.4	53.7	11.9	17.9
13	Vehicles	776	27.7	60.0	6.8	5.6
14	Shipbuilding	51	15.7	70.3	6.0	8.0
15	Aerospace	58	12.1	51.7	12.1	24.1
16	Electrical Engineering	1,028	26.8	50.8	9.8	12.6
17	Instrument Engineering	217	26.3	57.5	10.7	5.6
18	Small Metal Items & Ordnance	614	30.8	58.9	7.6	2.7
19	Toys, Sports Goods, etc.	85	31.8	58.8	5.9	3.5
20/21	Timber & Wood Furniture	439	27.6	60.0	10.6	1.8
22/23	Pulp, Paper & Board	172	37.2	55.2	4.1	3.5
24	Printing & Publishing	267	22.9	65.8	6.8	4.6
25	Leather & Footwear	87	41.4	51.6	5.9	1.2
26	Textiles & Man-Made Fibres	285	40.7	51.8	5.4	2.1
27	Clothing & Fur	260	35.4	56.9	6.6	1.2
28	Food	679	34.2	53.7	10.8	1.3
29	Drink	106	25.5	65.0	5.7	3.8
30	Tobacco[a]	21	38.1	57.1	4.8	0.0
	Total	8,430				
	Minimum		12.1	50.8	4.1	0.0
	Maximum		41.4	70.3	12.1	24.1
	SD		7.5	4.6	2.3	5.5
	Mean		29.1	57.6	7.5	5.9

Source: 1987 Mikrozensus.

[a] Because of rounding, the true size of the percentage with high-level qualifications in this industry might be as high as 2.4%

about 36% of the German manufacturing workforce had no qualifications, but this proportion had fallen to 29% by 1987 (and has fallen further since).

It is interesting to see the extent to which skill levels are correlated with

Table 10.5. Correlations between skill levels, UK and Germany (26 sectors), 1987

1.	High	0.64
2.	Higher intermediate	0.63
3.	Lower intermediate	0.51
4.	No qualifications	0.89

Source: Tables 10.2 and 10.4.

Table 10.6. Mean skill proportions in manufacturing, 1987 (percentage)

		UK	Germany
1.	High	7.20	5.98
2.	Higher intermediate	4.37	8.19
3.	Lower intermediate	28.13	57.22
4.	No qualifications	60.30	28.61

Source: Tables 10.2 and 10.4. Weighted by each country's employment

other sectoral characteristics. Here we consider the association between skill levels on the one hand and labour productivity (value added per person employed), capital intensity (capital per person employed) and R&D intensity (R&D expenditure per person employed) on the other hand. When entered in a regression, these last three variables might be considered as a measure of human capital per person employed: value added per head is high when human capital per head is high, but the former can also be high if physical capital intensity is high. Table 10.7 gives the results for each country of regressing each of the four skill levels (measured now as proportions, not percentages) on the three variables (entered in natural logs).[3] For the UK, high-level skills are positively related to labour productivity and R&D intensity and negatively related to capital intensity. For high-level skills in Germany, only R&D intensity is significant. The latter variable is also significant and positive for upper intermediate skills in both countries. On the other hand, lower intermediate skills are not significantly related to any of the right-hand side variables in either country. This may be because the variance of this variable, relative to its mean, is fairly low, particularly in Germany. By contrast, the proportion with no qualifications (which is 100 *minus* the percentages with skill levels 1–3) is significantly higher in the UK in industries with low productivity and low R&D intensity.

Table 10.7. Skill levels and sectoral characteristics: UK and Germany, 1987, 25^a manufacturing sectors

Independent variable	Dependent variable (skill level)			
	No quals.	Lower intermediate	Upper intermediate	High
United Kingdom				
ln (V/L)	−13.39*	−0.82	1.82	12.40**
	(2.32)	(0.13)	(1.06)	(4.73)
ln (K/L)	5.00	0.84	−0.83	−5.01**
	(1.30)	(0.18)	(0.84)	(3.15)
ln $(R\&D/L)$	−4.11**	1.76	1.32**	1.04**
	(2.89)	(1.18)	(6.76)	(3.03)
R^2	0.518	0.087	0.653	0.802
Germany				
ln (V/L)	−1.57	0.07	0.36	1.14
	(0.66)	(0.06)	(0.64)	(1.03)
ln (K/L)	−0.43	0.29	−0.88	1.01
	(0.16)	(0.15)	(1.30)	(0.76)
ln $(R\&D/L)$	−3.29**	−0.83**	0.91**	3.21**
	(3.11)	(1.52)	(3.82)	(4.26)
R^2	0.423	0.099	0.372	0.672

Note: Robust t-statistics in parentheses. Constant included but not reported. V: value added; K: capital stock; L: employment.
^{a} 25 (not 26) sectors, since shipbuilding is omitted, for conformity with later analysis.
* Significant at the 5% level or better.
** Significant at the 1% level or better.

3 UK and German exports

A major practical difficulty facing any study of export competitiveness is that trade data are published on a quite different basis from industry data. The approach adopted here was to obtain UK and German exports to a number of important markets at a very detailed level, namely the five-digit level of the Standard International Trade Classification (SITC), which distinguishes over 1,800 products, of which some 1,360 are in manufacturing (United Nations, 1975). The source was the OECD's magnetic tapes. These detailed export data must then be aggregated up to the sectoral level, in order that the effect (if any) of skill gaps may be assessed.

From 1978 to 1987, UK and German trade was classified under Revision 2 of the Standard International Trade Classification, SITC(R2).

Before 1978, the system used was Revision 1 of the SITC, which was close to Revision 2 but less informative in many ways (for example, spare parts are lumped in with complete machines under Revision 1 but distinguished separately in Revision 2). After 1987, trade has been recorded under the quite incompatible Revision 3 of the SITC. The ten-year period 1978–87 therefore presents a 'window of opportunity' for analysing UK competitiveness in detail, under a consistent system of classification.

Before proceeding to the analysis, a brief discussion of the background to the UK's trade is in order. In 1987, the last year studied here, the UK's merchandise exports amounted to £79.8 billion. Despite the UK's rise to prominence as an oil producer, manufactures still accounted for some four-fifths of merchandise exports in 1987, only a little less than in 1978 (though obviously changes in oil prices will affect this proportion). Four-fifths of UK merchandise exports went to OECD countries (half to the EC) and this proportion has been rising. Of the remaining 20%, a substantial part went to countries with high per capita incomes, e.g. Hong Kong, Israel, Singapore, South Africa and oil exporters such as Saudi Arabia and the Gulf States. The period 1978–87 was also one in which the UK moved into deficit on manufacturing trade (though by 1987 there had been some recovery since the low point reached in 1983). This deterioration in manufactures is quite independent of any deterioration in the overall balance of payments, most of which occurred anyway after 1987. Adjusting for any overall current account surplus or deficit, I have calculated that the UK's manufacturing deficit with the industrial market economies was £15 billion in 1987, nearly half of which (£7 billion) was with Germany; the deficit with Japan was £4 billion (Oulton, 1990, table 2).

It therefore makes sense to concentrate the Anglo-German comparison on trade with the wealthy industrialised countries and six countries have been selected initially for analysis: Belgium, France, Italy, Japan, The Netherlands and the United States. The United States was the largest single export market for the UK in 1987, while France was for Germany (Table 10.8).

3.1   Quality: the evidence of unit values

German manufacturers have an enviable reputation for quality. But is it true that they are *on average* of higher quality than corresponding UK products? One way to investigate this vexed question is to look at the relative unit values (RUVs) of UK and German exports to some important third market. RUV is defined as the value per unit of quantity

Table 10.8. Value of UK and German exports, non-manufacturing and manufacturing, by country, 1978 and 1987

	1978		1987	
	UK exports ($m)	German exports ($m)	UK exports ($m)	German exports ($m)
Non-manufacturing				
Belgium	573	1,552	1,108	2,326
France	1,150	2,264	3,812	2,800
Italy	396	2,196	1,722	3,914
Japan	178	122	304	216
The Netherlands	1,135	1,532	3,520	3,085
USA	1,080	644	3,395	631
Manufacturing				
Belgium	3,324	9,886	5,052	18,695
France	3,554	14,448	8,372	31,785
Italy	1,653	7,289	4,803	20,822
Japan	835	1,553	2,008	5,532
The Netherlands	3,059	11,916	5,779	21,666
USA	5,246	9,270	12,984	26,529

Note: Non-manufacturing comprises Divisions 0–4 and manufacturing comprises Divisions 5–8 of the SITC(R2).
Source: OECD trade tapes.

of UK exports, divided by the value per unit of quantity of the corresponding German exports. If it were to turn out that consumers in some third country were persistently willing to pay more for one country's product than they are for what is apparently the same product exported by another country, then we would have some warrant for saying that the first country's product must be of higher quality, in some sense. Of course, value per unit of quantity is very far from being a perfect measure of quality. The hope is, however, that by considering a run of years and a very large number of products, an overall picture which is not too misleading may be gained.[4] It is not possible to calculate the RUV for every five-digit product for a number of reasons: (1) export quantity may be concealed for reasons of 'commercial confidentiality' (actually, this seems mainly to be invoked when there is a military aspect) or may be recorded using incompatible units in the two countries; (2) export value may be zero in one or both countries; (3) quantities or values may be so small as to make the results unreliable. Also, not all trade in a given product is recorded at the five-digit level; again for reasons of 'commercial confidentiality', some of it is hidden under more general classification codes, e.g. 'machinery and transport equipment' rather than 'helicopters'. However, it turns out that for a high proportion of UK and German exports, relative unit values *can* be calculated, indicating that, at this level of disaggregation, both countries are exporting what are statistically the 'same' products.

The mean RUVs for manufacturing exports (sections 5–8 of the SITC(R2)) to these six markets for the period 1978–87 are shown in Table 10.9. In general the RUVs exceed 1 and show a hump-shaped pattern, rising in the early 1980s and falling thereafter. In fact, movements in mean RUVs parallel movements in the DM–£ exchange rate, which rose sharply from 1978–81 but thereafter fell steadily. If price is a good guide to quality, then this evidence would indicate that UK exports do not face a *general* quality problem.[5]

In summary, and contrary to the popular view, there is no evidence that on average UK exports are of lower quality than German ones. This does not necessarily mean that overall UK *production* is of similar quality to German production. The NIESR case studies of clothing and kitchen furniture referred to above were concerned with the comparison of overall production, not just exports, between the industries of the two countries, so their finding of lower UK quality is not necessarily in conflict with the present finding. Nevertheless there is a widespread impression that UK exports (in this period at least) were of lower quality, so how is this impression to be explained? Partly it may be due to the British penchant for self-denigration, partly to concentration on particular sectors at particular times (e.g. cars in the late 1980s). But perhaps the most likely reason is that the volume of German exports is so much larger than UK ones: probably rightly, people attribute this success to quality, and therefore infer that UK quality must be lower. But it may be that, to compete at all, UK exports must be of similar quality to that of rivals, and the British failure (if it is one) is in her inability to supply a greater *volume* of high-quality goods. The next section will be devoted to exploring this possibility theoretically, before, in Section 5, the idea is tested empirically.

4   Exports and skills: theory

It is intuitively very plausible (at least to me) that there should be a link between skills and export performance. And this may, by itself, be considered sufficient justification for investigating the matter empirically,

Table 10.9. Mean RUVs, SITC 5–8, by country and year (UK relative to Germany)

	Importing country					
Year	Belgium	France	Italy	Japan	The Netherlands	USA
1978	1.00	1.00	1.01	1.04	1.07	0.92
1979	1.01	1.06	1.06	1.03	1.12	1.00
1980	1.09	1.15	1.14	1.18	1.24	1.08
1981	1.24	1.17	1.16	1.32	1.26	1.24
1982	1.18	1.16	1.15	1.36	1.25	1.13
1983	1.13	1.11	1.07	1.20	1.28	1.16
1984	1.18	1.16	1.05	1.28	1.24	1.10
1985	1.19	1.19	1.09	1.30	1.33	1.13
1986	1.08	1.06	0.99	1.07	1.15	1.02
1987	1.14	1.01	0.99	0.97	1.15	0.93

Note: RUVs for SITC 5–8 are weighted averages of RUVs at five-digit level. Weights are, for each country and year, the average of UK and German exports in that year. Each five-digit RUV is UK unit value divided by German unit value.
Source: OECD trade tapes.

to see whether as a matter of fact intuition is correct. But it would obviously be more satisfactory if such a link could be shown to arise from theoretical considerations.

As we have seen, in manufactures Britain and Germany are largely exporting the same products, at least down to the five-digit level of the SITC, to the same markets. Furthermore, as measured by relative unit values, the quality levels of UK and German exports are roughly the same. Is it possible to capture these features of reality by means of any of the standard models of international trade with which economists are familiar? The role of skill deficiencies suggests immediately an explanation in terms of factor endowments, the focus of the Heckscher–Ohlin (H–O) model as also of the 'specific factors' or Ricardo–Viner model. The H–O model has had a somewhat mixed record in empirical tests (Leamer, 1984; Bowen *et al.*, 1987) and theoretical interest has turned away from it towards models emphasising economies of scale, imperfect competition, and R&D. Nevertheless, an explanation of trade patterns based on factor endowments retains great intuitive appeal and the considerable body of theory erected on the basis of the H–O model in particular suggests that it would be premature to discard it unless it turns out to be incapable of explaining important facts about trade such as the ones outlined above.

4.1   *A model with many goods and two factors*

Consider an economy with N sectors, each of which contains two industries, so there are $2N$ industries in all. Each industry requires two factors, skilled labour and unskilled labour. In every sector, one industry produces a 'high value added', high-quality product and the other produces a 'low value added', low-quality product. The high-quality product is intensive in the use of skilled labour, relative to the low-quality product. For concreteness, the chemical sector might be imagined to consist of two industries, each of which requires skilled and unskilled labour. One industry might be pharmaceuticals where at given factor prices the ratio of skilled to unskilled labour is high, the other industry might be sulphuric acid, where at the same factor prices the ratio of skilled to unskilled labour is low. Both types of labour are assumed to be mobile between the two industries of their sector. In addition, it would be reasonable to assume that unskilled labour is mobile between sectors. The same assumption could be made about skilled labour, which would amount to assuming that there is only one type of skill which can be employed anywhere. Alternatively, without affecting the results to follow, each skill could be assumed specific to its own sector. If the latter assumption is made, the model would be an amalgam of the Heckscher–Ohlin model and the specific factors model.

Suppose two countries, both small in relation to the trading world. For mnemonic purposes, call the first country Germany and the second Britain. Assume that both countries have comparative advantage in the *high-quality* product of each sector. That is, in each sector, both countries export the high-quality, high-skill good, and import the low-quality, low-skill good. This seems to capture the essence of the UK–Germany comparison where, as we have seen, both countries export the same sort of products which seem on average to be of roughly similar quality.[6] All $2N$ goods are produced in each country and are freely traded.

Technology is assumed the same in both countries (a proportional difference in total factor productivity which is uniform across industries could be accommodated without changing the results much). All production functions possess constant returns to scale and do not exhibit factor intensity reversals. These assumptions, together with the fact that the number of goods is at least as great as the number of factors, ensure that factor price equalisation (FPE) holds.[7]

Let Y_1^r, Y_2^r be the outputs of goods 1 and 2 in sector r, let S^r, L^r be the demands for skilled and unskilled labour in sector r, and let $a_{ij}^r > 0$ be the requirements of factor i per unit of output of good j $(i, j = 1, 2)$. Goods are numbered so that good 1 is the skill-intensive good and factor 1 is skilled labour. Output levels and factor supplies will differ between countries. The a_{ij}^r depend on relative factor prices, which in turn are functions of relative goods prices. Assuming that the conditions for factor price equalisation (FPE) are satisfied as between the two countries, then the a_{ij}^r will be the same in both countries.

Factor demands in any country are given by

$$a_{11}^r Y_1^r + a_{12}^r Y_2^r = S^r$$
$$a_{21}^r Y_1^r + a_{22}^r Y_2^r = L^r \qquad r = 1, \ldots, N$$

The assumption about factor intensities implies

$$a_{11}^r / a_{21}^r > a_{12}^r / a_{22}^r \qquad \text{for all } r$$

Let $M^r \equiv S^r + L^r$ be total (skilled and unskilled) employment in sector r. Let the overall skill ratio in sector r be $s^r \equiv S^r / M^r = 1 - L^r / M^r$. Then dividing through by M^r and defining output per unit of employment in sector r as $y_1^r = Y_1^r / M^r$ and $y_2^r = Y_2^r / M^r$, we get

$$a_{11}^r y_1^r + a_{12}^r y_2^r = s^r$$
$$a_{21}^r y_1^r + a_{22}^r y_2^r = 1 - s^r \qquad r = 1, \ldots, N$$

Taking differences across the two countries (German value minus UK value), in matrix terms,

$$\mathbf{A}^r (\Delta y_1^r \ \Delta y_2^r)' = (\Delta s^r - \Delta s^r)' \qquad r = 1, \ldots, N$$

where $\mathbf{A}^r = [a_{ij}^r]$ is the 2×2 matrix of factor requirements. By the factor intensity assumption, $| \mathbf{A}^r | > 0$. The solution for outputs per unit of employment is

$$\Delta y_1^r = | \mathbf{A}^r |^{-1} (a_{12}^r + a_{22}^r) \Delta s^r$$
$$\Delta y_2^r = - | \mathbf{A}^r |^{-1} (a_{11}^r + a_{21}^r) \Delta s^r \qquad r = 1, \ldots, N \qquad (1)$$

Hence, if $\Delta s^r > 0$, then $\Delta y_1^r > 0$ and $\Delta y_2^r < 0$. That is, in any sector, the country with the more highly skilled labour force will produce more of the high-skill good per unit of employment in that sector, and less of the low-skill good. This result is an extension of the Rybczynski Theorem.

The crucial result for the export good can be written more compactly as follows:

$$\Delta y_1^r = f^r \Delta s^r \qquad r = 1, \ldots, N \qquad (2)$$

where $f^r \equiv |\mathbf{A}^r|^{-1} (a_{12}^r + a_{22}^r) > 0$. Note that the f^r depend only on technology and factor prices and hence ultimately on internationally given commodity prices. The f^r will differ between sectors, but according to the model do not differ between countries. So there is no reason to expect the f^r to be correlated with the skill differences (Δs^r). Therefore there will be a positive correlation across sectors between differences in output of the export good per person employed (Δy_1^r) and differences in skills (Δs^r).

Alternatively, (2) can be put into relative terms, by dividing through by UK output per person:

$$\Delta y_1^r / y_1^r = (f^r / y_1^r) \Delta s^r \qquad r = 1, \ldots, N \qquad (3)$$

The level of y_1^r will differ between sectors because of differences in technology, but there is no reason to expect these differences in technology to be correlated with either internationally determined commodity prices or with skill differences between countries. Hence we would also expect there to be a positive correlation between *relative* differences in output of the export good per person employed and skill differences.

Equations (2) and (3) are concerned with output per person employed at the sectoral level (Y_1^r / M^r). Can anything be said about output levels, adjusted only for differences in the size of the two economies (Y_1^r / M, where $M \equiv \Sigma_r M^r$)? That is, after adjusting for scale, is there any reason to expect that differences in output *levels* will be correlated with skill differences? Putting $m^r \equiv M^r / M$, we easily find from (2) that

$$\Delta(Y_1^r / M) = \Delta m^r [Y_1^r / M]_{\text{GERMANY}} + [m^r]_{\text{UK}} \Delta y_1^r$$
$$= \Delta m^r [Y_1^r / M]_{\text{GERMANY}} + [m^r]_{\text{UK}} f^r \Delta s^r \qquad (4)$$

The relationship between output differences and skill differences will therefore be influenced by the factor $[m^r]_{\text{UK}}$. It is difficult to say what will determine the pattern of employment m^r, since in a Heckscher–Ohlin model with more goods than factors the pattern of output and employment is indeterminate (Ethier, 1984). But once again it seems reasonable to assume that the UK employment pattern ($[m^r]_{\text{UK}}$) will not be correlated across sectors with skill *differences* (Δs^r) and this assumption is testable. With this proviso, we may expect a positive correlation between skill differences and output levels of the export goods (adjusted for scale). A similar argument shows that skill differences will be negatively correlated with outputs of the import goods.

4.2 Exports and skills

Given these relationships between outputs and skills, what is the relationship between *exports* and skills? In any sector,

$$\Delta(X_1^r/M^r) = \Delta(Y_i^r/M^r) - \Delta(C_i^r/M^r) \tag{5}$$

and

$$\Delta x_i^r = \Delta y_i^r - \Delta c_i^r \qquad i = 1, 2; \; r = 1, \ldots, N \tag{6}$$

where X_i^r and C_i^r are exports (or, if negative, imports) and consumption of sector r's good i respectively, and y_i^r and c_i^r are exports and consumption per unit of employment in sector r. So even though output of the export good is higher in the high-skill country, it does not necessarily follow that exports are higher, since consumption could be higher too. However, assumptions typically made in trade theory about tastes enable a presumption to be established that what is true of production is also true of exports. Assume that tastes are homothetic and identical in the two countries. Then consumption of each good is proportional to national income, where the constants of proportionality are identical in the two countries and depend only on relative prices. Hence

$$\Delta(C_i^r/M) = v_i^r \Delta(V/M)/p_i^r \qquad 0 < v_i^r < 1; \sum_{r=1}^{N}(v_1^r + v_2^r) = 1 \tag{7}$$

where V is nominal national income, $M \equiv \Sigma_r M^r$ is total employment and p_i^r is the internationally determined price of good i. Combining (6) and (7),

$$\Delta(X_i^r/M^r) = \Delta(Y_i^r/M^r) - v_i^r \Delta(V/M)/p_i^r \qquad i = 1, 2; \; r = 1, \ldots, N \tag{8}$$

Now the last term varies across sectors but depends only on tastes and prices ($\Delta(V/M)$ is constant across sectors), so if output differences are correlated with skill differences, as (4) suggests, then so also will be export differences. A similar argument applies to exports per person employed in each sector (Δx_i^r).

What about the absolute size of exports? It is reasonable to suppose that if one country is better endowed with all types of skill then it will have higher income per person employed. This will certainly be true under FPE, which holds in the present model, since the equilibrium wage of skilled labour is higher than that of unskilled, if skills are costly to acquire. Hence the high-skill country will have higher consumption per person employed of all goods, and consequently higher imports (both terms on the right-hand side of (8) will be negative for an import good). Therefore, since trade is balanced, the high-skill country must have higher exports too, at least in total. So not only are export differences and skill differences positively correlated, but the average level of exports is higher in the high-skill country.

5   Exports and skills: empirical assessment

The hypothesis to be considered in this section is that the UK's export performance, relative to Germany's, is negatively related to the skills gap: the bigger the gap, the worse the performance. The previous section has suggested that such an hypothesis can be justified on the basis of an H–O type of model, but the results to follow should not be narrowly considered as tests of a specific model, since a relationship between skills and export success might arise for other reasons.

5.1   The data

To test the basic hypothesis, the skill data and the trade data must therefore be confronted with each other. However, the skill data discussed in Section 2 is on an industry classification basis, while the trade data uses the SITC(R2). In order to look at both together, exports were reclassified to an industry basis. This was done in three stages. First, UK and German exports were reclassified to the SIC (1980), using a correlator supplied by the DTI. Second, nominal exports were reclassified from the UK SIC to the German 26-sector basis. Third, RUV indexes were constructed for each sector using 1987 weights by aggregating over five-digit level RUVs. These indexes were then used to convert nominal exports of each sector to a volume basis.[8] Since an RUV for shipbuilding could not be calculated for all countries and all years, this sector was excluded. Given that there were only 25 sectors, all the data for each market was pooled, yielding 250 observations on each market. But note that the skills data are for one year only, 1987, so these variables function, in the regressions to be reported, as fixed effects.

5.2 Determinants of relative export success, 1978–87: regression results

In Tables 10.10 and 10.11, the results of regressing relative export performance on the skills gaps are displayed. Here, in the spirit of the model of the previous section, relative export performance is measured by (the log of) UK exports by each sector to some market, divided by German exports by the same sector to the same market. The skills gap is simply the UK proportion with a given skill level in each sector, minus the corresponding German proportion, yielding the four variables $RELSK1$–4, where $RELSK4 = 1 - RELSK1 - RELSK2 - RELSK3$ and $RELSK1 = SK1_{UK} - SK1_{G}$, etc.; note that these data are given in *percentage* form in Tables 10.2 and 10.4. Also included in each regression are two of the industry characteristics described above: the log of relative capital intensity (UK capital stock per employee divided by German capital stock per employee, $RELKL$) and the log of relative R&D intensity (UK R&D as a proportion of value added, divided by the same ratio for Germany, $RELRD$). These two industry characteristic variables are included as controls. If they were excluded, effects which are really due to them might be erroneously ascribed to skills.[9] In addition, the log of RUV is included to pick up the effect of any changes in competitiveness (whether price or non-price). I also tried including a set of year dummies, but these were generally insignificant, and in any case had virtually no effect on the coefficients on the skill variables, which are the focus of interest here.

I start by testing the simplest hypothesis, that absence of skills hampers export performance (Table 10.10). The variable of interest here is $RELSK4$, the UK proportion unqualified *minus* the German proportion unqualified. The coefficient on this variable is negative and highly significant for three of the five markets: the USA, Belgium, and The Netherlands. It is insignificant for Italy and France. A negative coefficient indicates that the larger the UK's skill deficiency, the worse its export performance. A coefficient of -4.33, as in the US case, indicates that closing the skills gap by 1 percentage point would *(ceteris paribus)* raise UK exports by 4.33%, relative to German ones.

Table 10.11 considers a slightly more complex case, replacing $RELSK4$ with the three skill variables $RELSK1$–3 entered separately. In three of the markets studied – the USA, Belgium and The Netherlands – the coefficient on $RELSK3$ (the UK proportion with skill level 3 *minus* the German proportion) is positive and highly significant: that is, the smaller

Table 10.10. Determinants of relative UK and German exports to five major markets (25 sectors, 1978–87)

	USA Coef. (*t* ratio)	France Coef. (*t* ratio)	Italy Coef. (*t* ratio)	Belgium Coef. (*t* ratio)	The Netherlands Coef. (*t* ratio)
Constant	1.0092* (2.23)	−1.7100** (7.62)	−1.8631** (4.90)	−0.5572** (2.85)	0.6227** (2.63)
ln (*RUV*)	−1.2545** (4.57)	−0.6087** (3.12)	−2.4241** (7.19)	0.2203 (1.57)	−0.3051* (2.19)
ln (*RELKL*)	−1.1860** (5.86)	−0.2382 (1.69)	−0.8059** (4.51)	−0.4961** (4.34)	−0.6157** (4.44)
ln (*RELRD*)	0.2025* (2.56)	0.2579** (3.85)	−0.1388 (1.31)	0.7660** (16.98)	0.7359** (17.49)
RELSK4	−4.3310** (3.23)	1.1245 (1.43)	1.4903 (1.21)	−3.0406** (4.78)	−6.3669** (8.72)
R^2	0.2190	0.1228	0.3045	0.5754	0.5837
SER	1.1686	0.7558	1.1456	0.6145	0.6582

Note: Dependent variable is ln (X_{UK}/X_G). Pooled time-series cross-section data: 250 observations for each market. Heteroscedasticity-consistent *t* ratios are in parentheses. Estimation method is OLS.
*   Significant at the 5% level or better.
** Significant at the 1% level or better.

the UK's deficiency in lower intermediate skills, the better the UK performs. The effect is economically as well as statistically significant. A closing of the gap by one percentage point is associated with a (relative) rise in UK exports of about 4% in the US case, and of about 6% in the case of The Netherlands; for Belgium the effect is somewhat smaller, about 2%. Since the average gap for this skill level is about thirty percentage points, a complete elimination of the gap would be predicted, if these results are taken literally, to lead to a massive rise in UK exports. Of course, a full evaluation of the effect of eliminating the skills gap requires a general equilibrium analysis, which is beyond the scope of the present study, but the partial result just cited certainly suggests that the effect could be large.

Table 10.11 shows too that deficiencies in skill level 2 (upper intermediate) significantly (in both senses) reduce export performance in three of the five markets: Italy, Belgium and The Netherlands. The UK advantage in high-level skills raises our export performance significantly in The Netherlands.

It is also noteworthy that the UK does significantly worse in sectors

Table 10.11. Determinants of relative UK and German exports to five major markets (25 sectors, 1978–87)

	USA Coef. (*t* ratio)	France Coef. (*t* ratio)	Italy Coef. (*t* ratio)	Belgium Coef. (*t* ratio)	The Netherlands Coef. (*t* ratio)
Constant	0.9398**	−1.7454**	−1.9562**	−0.5889**	0.6461**
	(2.93)	(7.92)	(5.69)	(3.27)	(2.94)
ln (*RUV*)	−1.1661**	−0.6543**	−1.8205**	0.3194*	−0.2109*
	(4.37)	(2.86)	(4.91)	(2.27)	(1.53)
ln (*RELKL*)	−1.3950**	−0.2144	−1.0077**	−0.5701**	−0.6839**
	(6.79)	(1.37)	(5.33)	(4.78)	(4.67)
ln (*RELRD*)	0.4479**	0.2137**	−0.1899	0.7764**	0.8008**
	(5.17)	(3.29)	(1.79)	(13.93)	(14.88)
RELSK1	−8.1351**	−0.1958	−8.862**	0.3513	3.7657*
	(3.36)	(0.13)	(3.41)	(0.26)	(2.38)
RELSK2	3.5400	1.5447	17.2980**	7.1580**	4.9930**
	(1.47)	(0.70)	(4.85)	(5.04)	(3.88)
RELSK3	3.7504**	−1.5389	−3.8984**	2.4497**	6.6049**
	(3.69)	(1.72)	(3.25)	(3.78)	(8.90)
R^2	0.3584	0.1326	0.3912	0.5919	0.5973
SER	1.0635	0.7547	1.0762	0.6049	0.6500

Note: Dependent variable is ln (X_{UK}/X_G). Pooled time-series cross-section data: 250 observations for each market. Heteroscedasticity-consistent *t* ratios are in parentheses. Estimation method is OLS.
*   Significant at the 5% level or better.
** Significant at the 1% level or better.

where its capital-intensity is relatively high and better in sectors where its R&D intensity is relatively high.[10]

However, there are also some anomalous results. First, in the equation for France none of the skill variables are significant. But this equation fits poorly $(R^2 = 0.13)$ and so this result can perhaps be disregarded. Clearly, the factors which determine relative success in the French market have not been identified.[11] More worrying at first sight are the results for Italy, where significant, negative coefficients are found for *RELSK3* and *RELSK1*. A negative coefficient is also found for *RELSK1* in the US market. Negative coefficients on the skill gap variables are far from impossible. First of all, it might be the case that there is an omitted variable which is positively correlated with both UK success and negatively correlated with the skill variables, though I have not been able to find a plausible example of what such a variable might be. Second, the underlying skill variables satisfy an adding-up property, since the skill proportions add up to one. If the choice is between having more of skill level 2 at the price of less of skill level 1, then a negative coefficient on the latter variable could be explained, if skill level 2 is in fact the one which leads to export success.[12]

In the results so far, no allowance has been made for the scale of the two economies. This is quite reasonable, since the population of the two countries was very similar in this period, and in any case was changing only slowly over time. Should we, however, make allowance for the different scale of the various sectors? This might make a difference, since as Tables 10.2 and 10.4 show, there are wide variations in the relative sizes in terms of employment of the various sectors, though the German manufacturing sector as a whole is considerably larger. It is not clear that any allowance *should* be made. The size of a sector reflects its success in resisting competition from imports as well as in exporting, so 'correcting' for size risks throwing out the baby with the bath water. However, there is some interest in seeing whether exports *per person employed* are influenced by skill deficiencies. Indeed, the H–O model of the previous section suggests that this is in fact the more basic relationship. Table 10.12 repeats the regressions of Table 10.11, but with the dependent variable redefined as the log of the ratio of UK exports per person employed to German exports per person employed. It will be seen that as far as the skill variables are concerned, the size and significance of the coefficients are very similar to those of Table 10.11.

How robust are these results? In any regression analysis one must beware of outlying observations which may distort the true picture. In the present context, results might be distorted by exceptional years or exceptional sectors. As mentioned above, when year dummies are added to the regressions, they are generally insignificant and have little or no effect on the coefficients of interest, so exceptional years do not seem to be a problem. To test for the possibility of exceptional sectors, the regressions of Tables 10.10 and 10.11 were rerun, omitting each of the 25 sectors in turn. The only sector which seemed to play an influential role in the results was Aerospace. In the model with all three skill variables (Table 10.11), the coefficient on *RELSK3* ceased to be significant for the USA and Belgium, when Aerospace was omitted. In the model with *RELSK4* only (Table 10.10), omitting Aerospace caused the coefficient on *RELSK4* to be insignificant in the US market, while it remained significantly negative for The Netherlands and Belgium. In general, the results for The Netherlands, Italy and France were little changed by the omission of any one sector.

Aerospace is clearly an exceptional sector in a number of respects. As

Table 10.12. Determinants of relative UK and German exports per employee to five major markets (25 sectors, 1978–87)

	USA Coef. (t ratio)	France Coef. (t ratio)	Italy Coef. (t ratio)	Belgium Coef. (t ratio)	The Netherlands Coef. (t ratio)
Constant	1.4372** (4.65)	−1.3151** (5.39)	−1.4615** (4.10)	−0.1181 (0.64)	1.1371** (5.14)
ln (RUV)	−1.2944** (5.02)	−0.8429** (3.43)	−1.9565** (5.16)	0.0790 (0.56)	−0.2798* (2.14)
ln $(RELKL)$	−0.6348** (3.21)	−0.5712** (3.62)	−0.2549 (1.22)	−0.2323* (2.07)	−0.0688 (0.53)
ln $(RELRD)$	0.2444** (2.81)	0.0161 (0.20)	−0.3947** (3.22)	0.5781** (12.14)	0.5989** (12.42)
$RELSK1$	−2.3768 (1.12)	5.7724** (3.50)	−1.9893 (0.85)	6.2538** (5.54)	9.6242** (7.07)
$RELSK2$	5.9788* (2.23)	3.1287 (1.25)	18.9930** (4.84)	8.6917** (5.18)	7.0001** (4.96)
$RELSK3$	3.5657** (3.35)	−1.8987 (1.95)	−3.9946** (3.10)	2.1385** (3.09)	6.4412** (8.48)
R^2	0.2725	0.1789	0.3315	0.6089	0.6355
SER	0.9703	0.8215	1.1242	0.5775	0.5901

Note: Dependent variable is ln $[(X_{UK}/L_{UK})/(X_G/L_G)]$. Pooled time-series cross-section data: 250 observations for each market. Heteroscedasticity-consistent t ratios are in parentheses. Estimation method is OLS.
* Significant at the 5% level or better.
** Significant at the 1% level or better.

Tables 10.2 and 10.4 show, it is the sector with the smallest gap in the proportions with skill level 3 (47% in the UK versus 52% in Germany). It is one of only four sectors in which UK employment exceeded German in 1987. UK exports from this sector usually exceed German ones by a large margin. Also, the nature of its markets sets it off from other industries. Nevertheless, in looking at relative exports we are looking at success in competing in third markets, not in the protected home market. So results influenced by Aerospace cannot simply be dismissed. Also, for Belgium and The Netherlands, the main results are robust to the exclusion of Aerospace.

5.3 Changes in export performance, 1978–87

At the level of total manufacturing exports, the UK's share of world markets, after falling continuously for many decades, seems to have stabilised some time in the early 1980s (Landesmann and Snell, 1989; Anderton, 1992). In a comparison restricted solely to Germany, however, there is no such evidence of improved performance. Table 10.13 shows the ratio of UK to German exports to five major markets – Belgium, France, Italy, The Netherlands and USA – in 1978 and 1987, in both 1978 and 1987 prices. In constant 1987 prices, the UK's performance has deteriorated in four out of five markets. In current prices, it has deteriorated in three out of five.

Is there any connection between skill levels and changes in export performance? A number of possibilities suggest themselves. First, changes in export performance might be related to the initial *levels* of skills (due, say, to ongoing trends in the world economy favouring innovation and product upgrading). Second, changes in performance might be related to *changes* in UK skill levels over time. And third, they might be related to changes in UK skill levels relative to German skill levels. The last hypothesis unfortunately cannot be tested because, so far, it has only been possible to obtain German skill levels on a comparable basis for a single year, 1987. But the other two possibilities can be tested. I was not able to find any evidence in favour of the second possibility. For the US market, there is some support for the first hypothesis, as the following regression indicates:

$$\ln\left[(X_{87}^{UK}/X_{87}^{G})/(X_{78}^{UK}/X_{78}^{G})\right] = \text{constant} - 4.05\, SK4_{81}^{UK}$$
$$(2.63)$$

$R^2 = 0.251$; $N = 25$; robust t statistic in parentheses. Here X is exports, superscripts indicate the exporting country, and subscripts indicate the year. $SK4_{81}^{UK}$ is the proportion in the UK with no qualifications in 1981 (the earliest year available). The above result shows that, relative to Germany, UK export performance deteriorated significantly in those sectors where there was initially a high proportion of workers with no qualifications.[13] However, in the other four markets (Belgium, France, Italy and The Netherlands) similar regressions produced insignificant results.

6   Conclusions

The main findings can be summarised as follows. The skill levels of UK workers in manufacturing were found to be substantially lower than those of German workers in 1987. At the higher intermediate and lower intermediate levels, Germany has proportionately about twice as many

10.13. Ratio of UK to German manufacturing exports, by market, 1978 and 1987

Exports to:	1978 (1978 prices)	1978 (1987 prices)	1987
Belgium	0.236	0.249	0.208
France	0.268	0.295	0.289
Italy	0.209	0.222	0.231
The Netherlands	0.287	0.310	0.284
USA	0.552	0.627	0.488

Note: Manufacturing exports are the totals over 25 sectors (i.e. excluding Shipbuilding). The 1978 ratio in 1987 prices is computed as the ratio in current prices multiplied by the ratio of average RUV in 1987 to average RUV in 1978. Average RUV is a weighted average of RUVs across the 25 sectors, where the weights are the 1987 shares of each sector in total UK exports.

qualified people as the UK. The UK has twice the level of workers with no qualifications (60% compared with 29%). Only in high-level qualifications (first degree and above) does the UK have a slight advantage. Although the UK level has been rising in recent years, one cannot count on the UK automatically catching up with Germany in the near future, since the average German level has also been rising.[14]

Evidence was found that the skills gap does influence export performance. However, contrary to a common view, it does *not* seem that skill deficiencies cause the UK to export low-quality products. If we are willing to judge quality by price, then a detailed comparison of the unit values of UK exports with those of German exports show that, on average across manufacturing and making allowance for the effects of exchange rate changes, the prices of UK and German products are substantially the same. But there is evidence that the UK's skill deficiencies influence the *volume* of her exports. The relative success of the UK and Germany in exporting to five major markets over the period 1978–87 was studied: USA, France, Italy, Belgium and The Netherlands. In regressions where the dependent variable is (the log of) the ratio of UK to German exports, and the explanatory variables are various measures of differences between the two countries, it was found that, for three of these markets (USA, Belgium and The Netherlands), the larger the proportion with no qualifications in the UK relative to in Germany, then the poorer is the UK's relative export performance. If three levels of skill are distinguished, then it turns out that, for the same three markets, the UK's export performance is better in industries where the gap in lower intermediate skills is least. Furthermore, these effects of skill gaps are not only statistically significant, but also economically significant, in the sense that closing the gaps would lead (other things equal) to a substantial rise in UK relative to German exports.[15]

Though the UK's performance in world markets for manufactures seems to have improved in the 1980s, in the sense that her share ceased to fall, this improvement was *not* found to apply to a comparison with Germany. Between 1978 and 1987, UK performance relative to Germany continued on average to deteriorate. For the US market, it was found that sectors which had low skills around the beginning of the period studied suffered a significantly greater deterioration in relative performance.

As Section 4 showed, a negative effect of low skills on export performance is predicted by a generalised form of the basic Heckscher–Ohlin model of comparative advantage. While still consistent with this model, a somewhat freer interpretation of these findings runs along the following lines. Comparative advantage in large, high-income countries lies nowadays in the production of sophisticated, high-quality goods. Insofar as there is still demand in these countries for less sophisticated products it can be often met by imports from newly industrializing countries, which are able to produce such products more cheaply. Hence in their trade with each other, the high-income countries for the most part exchange particular varieties of sophisticated products, since either demand is lacking for lower-quality goods or cheaper sources of supply of the latter are available. It may be the case also that less sophisticated products can still be produced in rich countries for sale in their own domestic markets, either by taking advantage of economies of scale or by exploiting natural or artificial barriers to trade, or by relying on goodwill built up in the past, though such strategies may well come under increasing pressure.

If this is the case, then we would not necessarily expect to see a country which is having difficulty maintaining its competitiveness actually exporting low-quality products to its more successful competitors. Instead we would observe the low-quality products being increasingly reserved for lower-income or less contested markets. Reduced competitiveness would then show up in the form of falling world market share, rising import penetration in the home market, or increasing trade deficits with the more successful countries.

NOTES

1 Financial support for this project was provided by the Leverhulme Trust. I am grateful to my colleague Mary O'Mahony for supplying me with

important UK and German data and for advising on reclassifying UK data to the German industrial classification system. I would also like to thank Karin Wagner for supplying data on German skill levels and for help in understanding the German Mikrozensus. I am grateful to a number of people who commented on earlier versions of this chapter, in particular Alison Booth and Dennis Snower, to colleagues at the National Institute for helpful suggestions, in particular Bob Anderton, Geoff Mason and Nigel Pain, and to participants at the CEPR Conference on the skills gap, in particular John Bishop. Dave Wilkinson and Nicholas Vaughan provided excellent research assistance. All errors remain my own. A more detailed version of this chapter is Oulton (1993).

2 For comparability with the German figures, Table 10.2 shows only 26 sectors. However, for the UK a complete breakdown into the German 30-sector scheme is possible so this was used for the regressions.

3 The data on value added, employment, capital stocks, and R&D expenditure, on a comparable basis for Germany and the UK, were kindly provided by my colleague Mary O'Mahony. For explanation, see O'Mahony (1992).

4 Other studies of UK trade which employ relative unit values include Stout (1977), Connell (1979), Brech and Stout (1981) and NEDC (1990). Oulton (1990) considers the unit value of UK exports relative to the unit value of UK imports.

5 However, more detailed analysis (Oulton, 1993) shows that there is considerable variation across markets and across Divisions of the SITC. It may well be the case that the UK has a quality problem in certain sectors (one example might be mechanical engineering in the US market), but there are also cases where the UK appears to have a quality advantage. The findings in the text for the RUVs of exports are paralleled by my earlier findings for the unit value of UK exports relative to the unit value of UK *imports*: these also show no general tendency for UK imports to be of higher quality than UK exports (Oulton, 1990).

6 However, this model is *not* capable of capturing another important feature of reality, namely that both countries import a great deal from each other and that the goods imported seem to be similar in quality. To capture this feature, a model of imperfect competition seems necessary.

7 FPE requires *inter alia* that the number of traded goods be at least as great as the number of factors (Ethier, 1984). If skilled labour in each sector is specific to that sector, but unskilled labour can be used in any sector, then there will be $N+1$ factors and $2N$ traded goods, so this condition for FPE will be satisfied. Alternatively, if skilled labour is non-specific, there will be two factors and $2N$ goods, so again the condition is satisfied.

8 This procedure assumes that changes in RUVs over this period reflect changes in price rather than changes in quality. The econometric results in Oulton (1993) suggest that this is indeed the case.

9 The third industry characteristic, value added per employee, was not included, since it might itself be regarded as a measure of the skills embodied in the labour force.

10 The role of R&D in UK trade has also been considered by Katrak (1982) and by Hughes (1986).

11 However, for France I found that omitting the three sectors Food, Drink and Tobacco produced a significantly positive coefficient of 1.6829 ($t=2.32$) on

RELSK3 and a negative coefficient on *RELSK4* in the simpler model which is significant at the 10% level (-1.3698, with $t = 1.76$).

12 I also tried a redefinition of the skill variables to see if it had any effect on the pattern of signs on these variables. Let the proportion with skill level 3 include not only those whose highest qualification this is, but also those who possess qualifications at levels 1 and 2, and analogously for skill level 2. So define $SK3' = SK3 + SK2 + SK1$ and $SK2' = SK2 + SK1$. When the regressions are rerun, with the skill gap variables correspondingly redefined (i.e. $RELSK1 = SK1'_{UK} - SK1'_{G}$, etc.), we find very similar results; in particular, for Italy the coefficients on the skill variables have the same sign pattern as in Table 10.11.

13 I also tried including the change in the log of *RUV*, $(\ln[RUV_{87}/RUV_{78}])$, in this regression. It was not significant, while the skill variable continued to be significant. However, $\ln[RUV_{87}/RUV_{78}]$ was significantly negative in similar regressions for other markets.

14 Exploring the reasons why German young people are willing and able to acquire more qualifications than their British counterparts is beyond the scope of this chapter. See Oulton and Steedman (1994) for a comparison of the institutions and the incentive structures of the two systems of youth training.

15 These findings are consistent with those of Webster (1993). He finds, based on an analysis of the factor content of UK net exports, that the UK has a comparative disadvantage in products which are intensive in the use of skilled manual labour. For further evidence on human capital and comparative advantage in the earlier part of the century, see Crafts and Thomas (1986).

REFERENCES

Anderton, R. (1992), 'U.K. Exports of Manufactures: Testing for the Effects of Non-price Competitiveness Using Stochastic Trends and Profitability Measures', *Manchester School* LX, 23–40.

Bowen, H. P., E. E. Leamer and L. Sveikauskas (1987), 'Multicountry, Multi-factor Tests of the Factor Abundance Theory', *American Economic Review* **77**, 791–809.

Brech, M. J. and D. K. Stout (1981), 'The Rate of Exchange and Non-price Competitiveness: A Provisional Study within UK Manufactured Exports', *Oxford Economic Papers* **33**, Supplement, 268–81.

Connell, D. (1979), *The UK's Performance in Export Markets – Some Evidence from International Trade Data*, London: National Economic Development Office.

Courakis, A. S. (1991), 'Labour Skills and Human Capital in the Explanation of Trade Patterns', *Oxford Economic Papers* **43**, 443–62.

Crafts, N. F. R. and M. Thomas (1986), 'Comparative Advantage in UK Manufacturing Trade, 1910–1935', *Economic Journal* **96**, 629–45.

Daly, A., D. M. W. N. Hitchens and K. Wagner (1985), 'Productivity, Machinery and Skills in a Sample of British and German Manufacturing Plants', *National Institute Economic Review* February, 48–61.

Ethier, W. J. (1984), 'Higher Dimensional Issues in Trade Theory', in *Handbook of International Economics*, volume 1, R. W. Jones and P. B. Kenen (eds.), Amsterdam: North-Holland.

Hughes, K. (1986), *Exports and Technology*, Cambridge: Cambridge University Press.

Jarvis, V. and S. J. Prais (1989), 'Two nations of shopkeepers: training for retailing in France and Britain', *National Institute Economic Review* May, 58–74.

Katrak, H. (1982), 'Labour Skills, R&D and Capital Requirements in the International Trade and Investment of the United Kingdom', *National Institute Economic Review* August, pp. 38–47.

Landesmann, M. and A. Snell (1989), 'The consequences of Mrs Thatcher for UK manufacturing exports', *Economic Journal* **99**, 1–27.

Leamer, E. E. (1984), *Sources of International Comparative Advantage: Theory and Evidence*, Cambridge, MA: MIT Press.

Mason, G., B. van Ark and K. Wagner (1993), 'Productivity, Product Quality and Workforce Skills: Food Processing in Four European Countries', NIESR, mimeo.

NEDC (1990), 'United Kingdom Trade Performance: Memorandum by the Director General', London: NEDC, mimeo.

O'Mahony, M. (1992), 'Productivity and Human Capital Formation in UK and German Manufacturing', NIESR Discussion Paper (New Series) No. 28, London.

Oulton, N. (1990), 'Quality and Performance in UK Trade, 1978–87'. NIESR Discussion Paper (Old Series) No. 197, London.

   (1993), 'Skills, Quality, and Export Performance: an Anglo-German comparison', London: NIESR, mimeo.

Oulton, N. and H. Steedman (1994), 'The British System of Youth Training: A Comparison with Germany', in *Training and the Private Sector: International Comparisons*, L. M. Lynch (ed.), Chicago: University of Chicago Press.

Prais, S. J. (1981), 'Vocational Qualifications of the Labour Force in Britain and Germany', *National Institute Economic Review* November, 47–59.

Prais, S. J. and H. Steedman (1986), 'Vocational Training in France and Britain: The Building Trades', *National Institute Economic Review* May, 45–55.

Prais, S. J. and K. Wagner (1988), 'Productivity and Management: The Training of Foremen in Britain and Germany', *National Institute Economic Review* February, 34–47.

Smith, S. R., G. M. White, N. C. Owen and M. R. Hill (1982), 'UK Trade in Manufacturing: The Pattern of Specialisation during the 1970s', Government Economic Service Working Paper No. 56, London.

Steedman, H. (1987), 'Vocational Training in France and Britain: Office Work', *National Institute Economic Review* May, 58–70.

   (1988), 'Vocational Training in France and Britain: Mechanical and Electrical Craftsmen', *National Institute Economic Review* November, 57–70.

Steedman, H. and K. Wagner (1987), 'A second look at productivity, machinery and skills in Britain and Germany', *National Institute Economic Review* November, 84–95.

   (1988), 'Productivity, Machinery and Skills: Clothing Manufacturing in Britain and Germany', *National Institute Economic Review* July, 40–57.

Stout, D. K. (1977), 'International Price Competitiveness, Non-price Factors and Export Performance', London: National Economic Development Office.

United Nations (1975), *Standard International Trade Classification Revision 2*, Statistical Papers Series M, No. 34/Rev. 2, New York.

Webster, A. (1993), 'The skill and higher educational content of UK net exports', *Oxford Bulletin of Economics and Statistics* **55**, 141–60.

Part III
Government failures and policy issues

11 Market failure and government failure in skills investment

The case for government support for education and training must rest not only on an assessment of how markets can fail to provide sufficient skills, but also on an evaluation of how governments can fail to rectify the deficiency. Accordingly, this chapter gives an overview of the salient market failures and government failures that must be compared before policy prescriptions can be formulated. With the British education and training system taken as an example, the chapter shows that, just as markets fail to provide adequate training, there are also good reasons why the government may be inefficient in responding to the problem.

Market failure and government failure in skills investment

DAVID FINEGOLD

1   Introduction

For more than a century, royal commissions and researchers have been pointing to the deficiencies of the British education and training (ET) system and linking it to the decline in the nation's economic competitiveness. One government after another has attempted to reform the ET system and yet concern about the skills problem has if anything intensified. And Britain is not alone. Virtually all of the main industrialized nations have attempted reforms of their ET systems in order to meet the needs of a rapidly changing global economy (Finegold, 1992b).

This chapter poses a simple question: why is it that government efforts to reform education and training so often don't work? In answering this question, I will attempt to build on the work of Wolf (1988) to think as systematically about the inadequacies of state ET policy making and the reasons which underlie government failure as economists have in analyzing the causes of market failure. Perhaps because of the highly political nature of ET debates, most work in this area has tended to personalize the analysis of ET policy, assigning blame to particular programs or even individual ministers, rather than looking for problems inherent in the public sector or the nature of ET itself.[1]

The theoretical discussion of market and government failure will be illustrated using British ET problems and policies, in particular the numerous reforms introduced during the third term of the Thatcher Government that are now being extended by Prime Minister John Major. These reforms present an ideal case for uniting the analysis of market and government failure, since they represent a radical attempt by the Conservatives to deal with government failures by creating market-like mechanisms to provide both compulsory education and post-16 training. The final section of the chapter will explore the problems which arise when a government attempts to adopt a 'market analogue' to address problems of government failure.

2   Market failure

The chapters in the first part of this volume focus on why the market, if left to itself, will not produce the level of ET investment which society as a whole desires. Since the reasons for market failure in ET are well covered, I will only review them briefly here in order to preface the discussion of why governments are compelled to intervene in the ET sphere.

2.1   Positive externalities

While most of the benefits of ET are captured by the individuals involved in the form of enhanced future earnings and/or the pleasure derived from ET as a consumption good, ET also yields benefits which extend beyond the societal actors (individuals and employers) who must decide how much, if any, ET to invest in. The positive externalities associated with ET (such as a more enlightened citizenry, knock-on effects of advanced research, improved quality of life through literature, arts, etc.) provide a primary reason for state intervention in general education.

More controversial is whether the positive externalities associated with firm-based training call for state action. Human capital theorists have shown that for purely firm-specific skills it is optimal for employers and individuals to share the costs of training, giving rise to no market failure (Becker, 1975; Lee and Chiplin, 1970). The difficulty arises because few skills are solely firm-specific, and in the real world it is impossible to separate general from specific skills training. This, combined with the uncertainties associated with payoffs to training, can cause rational managers to elect not to invest in their workers' transferable skills because they are trapped in a prisoner's dilemma – they recognize the risk that if they do train, their newly skilled workers could be 'poached' by competitors (for a fuller explanation see Finegold (1991) and Stevens, Chapter 2 of this volume).

The poaching argument was one of the justifications behind Britain's 1964 Industrial Training Act, which created Industrial Training Boards (ITBs) that imposed a payroll levy on all firms above a certain size in their sector to prevent some from free-riding on the training expenditure of their competitors (Senker, 1991). The majority of the ITBs were abolished by the Thatcher Government in 1982, with all but the Construction and Engineering ITBs closed in 1988.

2.2 Market imperfections

A variety of market imperfections (e.g., inadequate information, labor market rigidities, imperfect capital markets) can lead to state action in the ET area. The poor signals between the skills employers demand and the types of skills individuals acquire in the ET system have prompted the development of new qualifications systems and calls for more funds for careers information and guidance. The problems with information costs and risk assessment that may deter banks from lending money to individuals to invest in their own skill development has provided a justification for state finance for higher education (HE) or adults undertaking retraining. The presence of supply-side rigidities, however, has been the main driver of labor market reform in the last decade. The Conservative Government has concentrated on weakening those factors (e.g., trade unions, Wage Councils) that are perceived to be distorting the operation of labor markets and thereby resulting in poor or inadequate training investments; one of the objectives of Youth Training Schemes (YTS), for example, was to force down the pay of young people so that it would be more attractive for employers to take on trainees.[2]

2.3 A low-skill equilibrium

Even if skill shortages could be eliminated, there might still be reasons for market failure in ET investment. In earlier research (Finegold and Soskice, 1988), I have argued that this has been the case in Britain, where a variety of institutional factors (short-term financial markets, adversarial craft unions, weak employer organizations, etc.) have caused firms to adopt lower skill strategies than their rivals in other countries; this in turn has suppressed demands for training, trapping the economy in a *low-skill equilibrium*. The UK's low levels of firm-based innovation and relatively low-skill product strategies analyzed by Ulph, Snower and Mason *et al.* (Chapters 5, 6 and 9 in this volume) are types of market failure that result from the low-skill equilibrium.

2.4 Distributional inequities

Another reason why states do not leave ET solely to the market is concern over how access to education is distributed among individuals. This is not a case of market failure, being an issue of equity rather than efficiency: it is, however, a crucial societal question because of the dependence of individuals' future career prospects and earnings on access to educational opportunities. Therefore, all the industrialized countries make a certain number of years of schooling compulsory. The extent to which governments have seen education as a means to improve equity, as opposed to creating economic wealth, has varied over time and depending on the party in power (Guthrie and Koppich, 1988).

3   Government failure – supply side

The instances of market failure discussed above provide a powerful argument for state intervention in ET. And yet, as many of the chapters in this volume illustrate, there have been widespread and longstanding criticisms of British government efforts at ET policy making. This raises an interesting set of questions:

- What are the problems associated with government attempts at ET provisions and reform?
- Which of these problems are generic to any state actions and the democratic policy making process?
- Which are inherent in the ET process?
- Which are associated with the British political context? Which with a particular UK government?

The next section will analyze problems associated with public involvement in ET using examples from the Thatcher Government's radical reform agenda. These reforms provide a particularly useful case since they are explicitly designed to address the supply-side deficiencies of public sector activities. The Conservatives are attempting to address the problems of government failure by creating 'market analogues' in both education and training (Finegold, 1992b). These market analogues are designed to stimulate competition and raise skill levels through the creation of:

(1) clear indicators of performance and efficiency;
(2) sources of pressure to maximize efficiency; and
(3) flexibility of response to those pressures, especially so far as employment is concerned (Freedland, 1988, p. 5).

I will show how each element of the Thatcherite market-based strategy is trying to ameliorate a generic problem associated with government provision of ET.

3.1   Difficulty of defining and measuring outputs/'internalities'

There are longstanding difficulties with attempting to measure outputs in the service sector (Denison, 1989). While these measurement problems are to some extent generic to any service, they are magnified when it comes to public, rather than private services – such as education. In education there are multiple constituencies, rather than a single customer; often there is no price associated with the service provided, no clear definition of the outcomes which are sought and no agreement on the best way(s) to measure these outcomes. In the absence of well-defined outcome measurements, Wolf (1988, p. 66) argues that 'internalities' may arise, where the bureaucracy responsible for a given service area develops its own set of objectives and measurement criteria. An example of this in education is where providers are assessed on the basis of inputs (e.g., number of students recruited), rather than the extent to which they have added to individuals' knowledge and skills.

The Conservative Government has devised one strategy for addressing these measurement problems through the creation of new national systems of standard setting and assessment for both compulsory education and further training. The cornerstone of the 1988 Education Reform Act (ERA) is the establishment of a National Curriculum and National Assessment, stipulating for the first time that all students in the state system should study ten foundation subjects, with a concentration on three core areas (English, science and mathematics), until the end of compulsory schooling. Progress in these subjects is monitored through assessments of students at the ages of 7, 11, 14, and 16. These tests are meant to provide the consumers in the educational market place (parents and students) with the data necessary to make an informed choice between schools (Chitty, 1989, ch. 8; Whitty, 1990). Like a company's quarterly statement of sales and earnings, the publication of each school's results on national tests is designed as an indicator that can be used by those in the marketplace to assess the performance of the enterprise.

In the training field, the Conservatives have also attempted to address the problems of unclear outputs and the consequent development of internalities by establishing a comprehensive system of National Vocational Qualifications (NVQs) (De Ville, 1986). By the end of 1992, the National Council (NCVQ), which the government established to create and oversee NVQs, had a system in place covering 80% of the workforce, with competency-based qualifications and assessments for employees ranging from operator to professional level (Tysome, 1993). With this system in place, the state in theory no longer needs to set criteria for the delivery of training (e.g., where it should take place or how long it should be); instead, the attainment of NVQs could be taken as evidence that individuals had acquired the desired level of competence. As with the National Curriculum, the Conservatives decided that there should be a single currency for the whole system, mandating that all vocational qualifications should conform to the NVQ framework (DES, DE, 1991). Thus, NVQs represent a government initiative to remedy market failure that could enable the state to play a less interventionist role in industry, by reducing the monitoring of training provision.

3.2   Single-source production

A second potential source of government failure in state ET, as in any good or service, is the existence of a single source of provision for the service. As with monopolies in the private sector, a school or training institution which has no direct rivals may have less incentive to innovate and cater to the needs of its clients than one in a competitive situation. Because of the presence of private alternatives, state schools and training providers in the UK have never enjoyed a complete monopoly on provision; however, the vast majority of individuals have been restricted in their educational choices, by financial means and government regulations, to the closest state institution.

Educational vouchers, long advocated by conservative economists and right-wing think tanks (e.g., Seldon, 1986), represent the most radical solution to the problem of single-source production. Under voucher proposals, educational funding would be given directly to consumers who could then spend it at the school of their choice. This policy was rejected by then Education Secretary Keith Joseph in the early 1980s as unworkable and politically unviable for compulsory education. The 1988 ERA pursues the same objective, however, but through different means: it extends the powers of parental choice by making it easier for students to attend any school in their local area, and it reinforces this power of choice by providing financial incentives through a new funding formula which requires that at least 75% of schools' budgets be determined solely by student numbers, thus giving institutions an incentive to compete for customers.

The ERA also gave the Department of Education and Science (now the DFE) the formal powers to increase the degree of local competition among service providers by allowing schools to 'opt out' of Local Education Authority (LEA) control and receive funding directly from central government, an option which several hundred schools had exercised by 1992. The Thatcher Government sought to expand the array of choices open to parents by creating a new type of school – City Technology Colleges (CTCs) – modeled loosely on US magnet schools (Green, 1993). The CTCs were to provide 11- to 18-year-olds with intensive preparation in an area of the school's choice, as well as a strong general education. The area in which each school specialized (e.g., biotechnology, fashion and design) would be determined by their connections with one or more local employers who were to provide the funding for the schools along with the DES. The CTCs would operate outside LEA control, with the intent that this relatively small number of new institutions should serve as 'beacons of excellence' for the local community and the wider educational system (DES, 1986). The Colleges, however, never attracted the expected industrial support and the policy was abandoned after only a handful were created.

The government took the 'market model' for ET one step further in 1990 when it announced the launch of 11 local training credit pilot programs to be extended nationally by 1996. The idea, similar to the logic underlying the proposals for vouchers in compulsory education, is to make individuals more demanding consumers of training while encouraging competition among ET providers. Each 16- or 17-year-old receives a credit to cover the costs of training up to at least NVQ Level II. She can, in theory, redeem this voucher wherever she chooses in the local area – with an employer or in a further education (FE) college. 'With an individual credit', argued the credit's originator, the Confederation of British Industry (CBI) (1989), 'young people would, for the first time, have consciously to choose, not to enhance their skills'.

To encourage even greater competition among ET suppliers for this age group, the government has reformed the governance and financing of full-time FE. Using the model which proved successful in boosting higher education (HE) enrollments, the government took control of all colleges away from local authorities and placed it under a new central FE Funding Council (FEFC), which is directing resources to those institutions that are able to attract the most new students (Macleod, 1992).

3.3   Absence of bottom-line and termination mechanisms

The third general source of government failure that could give rise to inefficiencies in state-provided ET is the absence of pressures for performance, such as profit and loss statements and the risk of termination, that private sector managers and workers face. Even the worst-performing schools and teachers have traditionally been difficult to get rid of, while the majority of institutions have had little pressure to improve. Education institutions, for example, have been slow to invest in the latest technologies or to undertake the restructuring necessary to make these new technologies effective (Perelman, 1990).

In order to encourage schools to behave more like small businesses competing in the marketplace, the ERA shifts managerial power from

LEAs to headteachers and governing bodies. The provisions for Local Management of Schools (LMS) give headteachers and their governors greater control over the allocation of their schools' budgets, including the right to hire and fire teachers and to alter staff remuneration. Also included in the Act is the power of 'directed time', which gives school managers greater flexibility in the deployment of their teaching workforce.

Another way the government has attempted to make educational institutions more responsive to the market is by increasing the power of the school and college governing bodies, first in the 1986 Education Act and then again in the 1988 ERA (Whitty, 1990). At the same time, it has sought to give industry a greater role in the supervision of all levels of the educational system by encouraging managers to become governors of their local schools and colleges.

In youth and adult training policy, the government has attempted to simulate the pressure of the bottom line by turning the local delivery of its programs over to new, employer-led Training and Enterprise Councils (TECs). The network of 82 TECs and 20 Local Enterprise Companies (LECs) in Scotland, with budgets ranging from £5m–£50m, replaced the Training Agency's (TA) Area Manpower Boards (AMEs), the relatively weak tripartite organizations that had held nominal responsibility for overseeing the operation of TA programmes (King and Schnack, 1986). The TECs were presented as 'a locally based system ... a rare opportunity to restructure, from ground up, the nation's approach to job growth and human development, to enterprise and training' (Department of Employment, 1989, pp. 3, 4). Virtually all of national training budget was delegated to the Councils, although roughly 90% of their funds were specifically earmarked for YT and ET (Department of Employment, 1989).

3.4   Summary

The British government, like governments of all industrialized countries, has gradually evolved an ET bureaucracy in order to address the different types of market failure in ET investment. The Thatcher Government perceived a series of government failures associated with state ET provision and introduced 'market analogues' in education and youth training that attempt to overcome these inefficiencies. While it is still too early to assess the success of these reform efforts, it is possible to identify some of the problems which the Conservatives' market-driven strategy may face. As a hybrid policy – in which the state has attempted to create markets – it is potentially subject both to market failures and government failures, since it remains a state reform subject to the same rules and pressures as other political activity.

4   Government failure – demand side

Much of the recent work on government failure has concentrated on the ways in which demands for state action affect the policies which are adopted. This has identified factors inherent in the policy making process that can lead to excessive growth in the government bureaucracy from a societal perspective, e.g., the ability of special interests and lobbies to exert a disproportionate influence on decision makers, the tendency of public programs to create their own entrenched interests, and the decoupling of the benefits derived from state initiatives from the burden of financing them. Rather than review these general arguments for excessive state bureaucracies, I want to explore some of the more specific features of the British ET policy making process in the 1980s that may have led rational decision makers to adopt reforms that fail to result in long-term improvements in skill levels.

4.1   Structure of political rewards

There are a number of institutional features of British ET policy making which have increased the likelihood of government failure, by creating incentives for policy makers to use the state's power to pursue short- rather than long-term objectives with ET policy (Raffe and Tomes, 1987, p. 34). One formidable constraint hindering the government's capacity to address the deep-rooted problems of the British ET system – which I have previously characterized as a low-skill equilibrium (Finegold and Soskice, 1988) – is that the creation of higher-level skills has been a secondary priority in ET policy making. Historically, none of the government departments (Environment, Trade and Industry, Employment, or Education and Science) has had clear oversight for skills investment. The staff of the primary economic policy making body, the Treasury, 'had little industrial expertise or explicit responsibility for British industry', focusing instead on the control of expenditure and the strength of sterling (Hall, 1986, p. 252). Where the Treasury was willing to fund training, it was generally low-cost schemes for the unemployed, where the expenditure could be balanced against savings in benefit payments and potential tax revenues, rather than programs to increase the skills of the workforce, which, according to the Treasury's neoclassical model of the economy, are thought to lead to the substitution of one employed individual for another (Stanton, 1991). The central policy making capacity for training was further weakened by the dearth of accurate labor market statistics (Keep, 1991, pp. 30–31).

The establishment of the tripartite Manpower Services Commission (MSC) – a quango outside the normal departmental structure – was an attempt to distance ET policy from short-term pressures in a more powerful central body (Cousins, 1970). The ideal of emulating Swedish manpower planning (Mukherjee, 1972; MSC, 1974), however, was quickly subsumed by the pressures to design training and job creation programs to cope with growing levels of unemployment (Finegold and Soskice, 1988, p. 30). While European nations, such as France, Germany, and The Netherlands, were careful to separate schemes for the unemployed from vocational ET for higher-level skills (Raffe, 1991, p. 4), in Britain, training programs and unemployment were closely linked throughout the 1980s, as one of the government's own senior policy makers admitted (Main, 1990). This not only led to a concentration on the quantity of trainees, rather than the quality of ET provided, but also hindered later efforts to raise standards, as the term 'training' itself had become stigmatized, with individuals and employers associating the term with low-skill, low-wage jobs and temporary schemes (Unwin, 1992).

Another feature of the ET policy process that has contributed to government inefficiency is the lack of coordination of policy development, both within the central bureaucracy and between the national government and the groups responsible for policy delivery. Under the Thatcher Government three different departments – Employment, Education and Science, and Trade and Industry (DTI) – ran ET programs, while the MSC had two separate bureaucracies operating policies – YTS and TVEI – that were in direct competition for the same 16- to 18-year-olds (Finegold, 1992b). The effect of this departmental competition for the ET policy space was to produce 'initiative overload', as LEAs and ET practitioners struggled to implement overlapping, sometimes conflicting, policies.

4.2   High time discount of politicians

There are inherent differences in the timescales of elected officials and civil servants in the policy making process. Politicians naturally place a higher priority on short-term results, focusing on what can be achieved in time for the next election. Historically, this has led British politicians to shy away from major ET reforms, since the sheer scale of ET provision and the decentralized nature of power over the system (with much of the control resting with LEAs and individual institutions) meant that it was difficult to bring about major changes in the lifetime of a parliament.

Ironically, it was the creation of the MSC – originally intended to distance manpower policy from the political process – that enabled elected officials to play a more active role in the ET policy process. The MSC not only gave the government a flexible new mechanism for rapid ET reform, but it also spurred the DES to become more responsive to government ministers (for more details see Finegold (1992b)). As politicians assumed a more active role in ET reform, the policy process focused more on immediate results. This short-term bias was reinforced by Mrs Thatcher's approach to cabinet government –between 1981 and 1990 there were six different Secretaries of State at the DE and five at the DES. The combination of short job tenure and ministers' desire to make a distinctive mark on policy led to an unprecedented array of new initiatives (Rose and Page, 1990). Each program was typically designed with little or no consultation, implemented at a rapid pace, extended before evaluation could be completed, and, in many cases, lasted only a finite period (Keep, 1991). The system thus created incentives for ministers to pursue a rapid-fire approach to ET policy making, rather than persevering with a predecessor's policies or investing in long-term skill development that would produce few results in time for the next election.

5   Market failures in the market analogue

5.1   Externalities

The decision to abolish the ITBs and then decentralize training policy to the TECs has meant that the state no longer has a mechanism for overcoming the externalities associated with high-skill investment. While the TECs have far greater resources and a much higher profile than past British employer organizations (Leadbeater, 1988, II.I), they are in keeping with the Conservative Government's general desire to return to Britain's voluntarist training tradition. TECs have no power to raise funds through a levy on employers in their area, nor do they have any means of enforcing training quality or quantity on companies who choose to free-ride on the system.

5.2   Imperfect information/inadequate outcome measures

The success of the Conservative Government's attempts to create a market analogue in ET will depend, like all market systems, on the quality of the information available to the main decision makers. The first test of how information will be disseminated came in 1993 with the release of school 'league tables', ranking institutions based on their average scores in national exams. This use of raw test data has been heavily criticized for failing to take into account the differences in student populations which schools serve; controlling for the nature of student intake, and thereby measuring the educational value-added provided by schools, yields a very different ranking.[3]

In post-compulsory education there is a danger that, in its efforts to stimulate competition and increase enrollments, the government has created perverse incentives for institutions and individuals. Because schools are now funded almost exclusively on the basis of student numbers, rather than outcomes achieved, they are encouraged to sign-up more young people in full-time education (particularly during a time of sharp demographic decline), even if the students fail to complete the courses or obtain certificates that are poorly rewarded in the labor market. The way the government funds FE and HE creates an even more distorted set of choices for individuals: those who opt for the costliest form of provision to the state – full-time, residential degree courses – pay no tuition, while those who study part-time, through distance learning, on a sub-degree level course or in a short training course to renew their skills, receive little or no direct state support.

For training, the outcome measures (NVQs achieved, trainees placed in jobs) which are used to judge TEC performance may not be adequate or reliable. Ryan (1992) and others have pointed to concerns that the use of employer-based assessments may encourage firms to cheat on the system. Even if NVQs are recorded accurately, using them as performance indicators may create incentives for TECs to perpetuate the low-skill equilibrium. The Councils can best meet their targets by providing narrow, employer-specific training, concentrating on low-cost, low-capital intensive courses (e.g., hairdressing over engineering), and focusing on those low-skilled occupations, such as retailing, where high turnover rates make it easier to place people in jobs (Peck, 1991). Those TECs that seek to develop a strategy for investing in higher-level skills must also overcome the short-termism built into their contracts with the government, which are assessed and renegotiated each year with no guarantee of future resources.

5.3 *Accountability and distributional equity*

The attempts to create a market for the delivery of publicly funded training have also highlighted the tensions between the motives and behavior of private sector actors (the employers on TEC boards) and the requirements of state bureaucracies. Since their inception, TEC boards have complained about the amount of paperwork and micromanagement that they have been subjected to by the Department of Employment, as well as arguing the need for retargeting resources from the unemployed to workers requiring training (Finegold, 1992a). This has left the government in a quandary: if it gives TECs the greater budgetary and staffing freedom they desire, then the already serious concerns of the Treasury over accountability – entrusting public money to non-elected, non-representative private companies – would be magnified (Bailey, 1993); however, if TECs' remit is not broadened then the government faces the political embarrassment of losing the commitment of TEC boards and with it the remaining capacity to provide programs for the unemployed.

The market analogue strategy for education also raises equity concerns at both the individual and institutional level. Children whose parents do not actively participate in the educational process could suffer a double disadvantage, as they are not only less stimulated at home, but are also left in 'sink schools', which more active parents have deserted. Using Hirschman's terms, a market analogue in schools encourages parents to *exit*, rather than exercise the *voice* option to improve the existing school's performance (Hirschman, 1971; Miliband, 1991). The potential inequities this generates may be reinforced by the differences in resource allocation among schools that are generated by the government's policy of offering financial inducements for schools that elect to opt out of local authority control.

6   Problems inherent in the supply of education

There is a final set of problems, which does not sit easily in either the market or government failure categories, but which may be inherent in the nature of educational provision, given existing technological capabilities.

6.1   Inelastic supply

Schools, however much they may compete, are not businesses. One of the factors which distinguishes the two is the relative inelasticity of educational supply. Unlike a business with a profitable product, a successful school cannot simply double in size to meet increased demand; indeed, if it did, it would risk damaging the educational quality responsible for its popularity. Conversely, schools which lose students due to demographic trends or greater competition will not go bankrupt in the near term, though the breadth of their course offerings may suffer.

As a consequence of this inelasticity of supply, encouraging competition among institutions may not provide meaningful incentive for improved performance.

6.2   Is education technologically non-progressive?

Baumol (1967), in his seminal work on *Macroeconomics of Unbalanced Growth*, suggests an even more fundamental problem facing education. He argues that the perceived inefficiencies in the delivery of education may be inherent in the structure of this service, and moreover that the relative costs of education will increase over time. He makes this argument through a simple economic model, positing that all activities can be divided into technologically progressive (those with continuous productivity growth due to capital, new technology and economies of scale) and non-progressive (labour-intensive activities with limited scope for productivity improvements). In the latter category he places education as well as other services (e.g. municipal government, healthcare); indeed, in education, labor may be seen 'as an end in itself . . . where class size is often taken as a critical index of quality'.[4] If his assumptions are correct and the wages of the two sectors cannot be kept totally separate, than it follows that the costs of running such services will rise continuously relative to manufacturing and that they will consume a larger share of the labor force. While he wrote before the computer revolution, and thus may have underestimated the potential for information technology to transform some service sector jobs, the basic logic of his argument appears to hold true unless a radical change takes place in the way education is delivered. He argues that the problems facing education and other services in large cities may be intensified by the phenomenon of 'cumulative urban decay', as the groups with the greatest means to finance the service depart for private schools or the suburbs, thereby further weakening the school system and causing more parents to leave the system, *ad infinitum*.

7   Conclusion and policy recommendations

This chapter began by outlining the characteristics of ET – *positive externalities, imperfect markets* and *distributional inequities* – that give rise to market failures. These market failures provide the justification for state intervention in ET. State involvement in ET, however, is itself subject to a number of government failures. I have tried to move beyond critiques of particular ET policies or systems and specify the problems that are common to the public delivery of collective goods such as education. Britain's Conservative Government has attempted to over-come some of the supply-side sources of government failure – *difficulties of measuring outputs, single-source production* and *the absence of bottom-line or termination mechanisms* – through the creation of market analogues. These reforms in turn, however, have been subject to both demand-side government failures, generated by *the structure of political rewards* and *high discount time of politicians,* as well as the market failures discussed in the first section. In addition, they have been hampered by other problems – *inelastic supply* and *technological non-progressiveness* – which may be inherent in the delivery of education as currently constituted.

The foregoing analysis of how market and government failures have manifested themselves in British ET policy suggests some possible ways of improving the system:

- *Improve performance measures* – the outcomes used to assess and fund ET providers, whether schools or private training organizations, should reflect the value they add to the individual and not simply the gross outcome; school league tables, for example, should show student improvement (i.e. from National Assessments at 11 and 16) and not simply publish final test results which will be largely determined by the quality of their intake. Likewise, NVQs could be altered, perhaps in conjunction with the development of new GNVQs, to ensure they do not lead employers to concentrate on narrow, job-specific training.
- *Create uniform post-compulsory ET incentives* – the state should alter the funding mechanisms for FE, HE and vocational training so that individuals who choose part-time or sub-degree level routes are not discriminated against. Those who choose the most expensive and highly rewarded option – full-time degree courses – should pay part of the costs back through a graduate tax (IPPR, 1992).
- *Give TECs power to discourage free riders* – TECs should be allowed to impose a small subscription charge on local employers (say 0.3% of payroll), as German chambers of commerce are. They could then use these resources to fund high-quality training and other services (export marketing, technology transfer, cooperative R&D etc.) that are necessary to compete in high value-added global markets, but often beyond the capacity of small and medium-sized employers. Those firms who do not carry a fair share of the local training burden could be excluded from access to these services.
- *Coordinate and distance ET policy from party politics* – to reduce the different types of government failure, the state should abandon its highly political, fragmented and frequently changing approach to ET

policy and place responsibility for the system under a non-partisan agency. This body should have a semi-independent research arm capable of conducting long-term evaluations of reforms and providing data on the performance of all aspects of the system.

- *Explore alternatives to government and markets* – free markets and state provision are not the only two options in ET policy making. Comparisons with other countries (e.g. Germany, Japan, Northern Italy) suggest that between these two ends of the policy spectrum there are a variety of institutional alternatives (e.g., employer organizations, strong internal labor markets, business-government cooperatives) that can overcome some market failures without all of the accompanying difficulties associated with direct government intervention.[5] It is important to recognize, however, that the existence of these policy alternatives in other nations does not mean that they can be easily translated into the British institutional and cultural context (Finegold *et al.*, 1993). The hope of this chapter is to move the policy debate beyond the false dichotomy between benign governments and perfect markets toward a more productive, realistic assessment of the mix between imperfect markets and imperfect government that policy makers face in designing solutions to complex ET problems.

NOTES

1   The lack of this type of analysis may also be accounted for by the relative dearth of political scientists working in the ET field. Some exceptions are: Salter and Tapper (1981, 1985) and Finegold (1992b).

2   Comparative research on the German system was influential in shaping this policy, as it showed the link between lower trainee wages for German apprentices and the greater supply of training places (Jones, 1985); Marsden and Ryan (1991) have done a historical analysis of the UK which demonstrates that the success of apprentices in raising their wage rates relative to adult workers led to a reduction in the supply of places.

3   The problem of using raw test data for the later stages of education may be reduced when the National Curriculum and Assessment have been fully implemented, since it will be possible to compare students' progress from the first test at age 7.

4   In the USA, for example, it is definitionally impossible for there to be improvements in productivity, since the Bureau of Labor Statistics defines output based on the number of teacher inputs into the system.

5   I am part of an ongoing project that is attempting to analyze these different institutional mechanisms. This project is being conducted by myself, Colin Crouch, David Soskice, and Mari Sako, and will cover five European countries, the USA, and Japan.

REFERENCES

Bailey, T. (1993), 'The Mission of TECs and Private Sector Involvement in Training', in Finegold *et al.* (1993).

Baumol, W. (1967), 'Macroeconomics of Unbalanced Growth: The Anatomy of Urban Crisis', *American Economic Review* June, 415–26.

Becker, G. (1975), *Human Capital*, Chicago: University of Chicago Press.

Buchanan, J. (1969), *Cost and Choice: An Inquiry in Economic Theory*, Chicago: Markham.

CBI (1989), *Towards a Skills Revolution*, London: Confederation of British Industry.

Chitty, C. (1989), *Towards a New Education System: The Victory of the New Right?* London: Falmer.

Cousins, F. (1970), *Review of the Central Training Council*, London: HMSO, Cmnd. 4335, April.

Department of Employment (DE) (1989), 'Education and Labour Market Status of Young People in Great Britain'. *Employment Gazette* **97** (May), 262–3.

Denison, E. (1989), *Estimates of Productivity Change by Industry, an Evaluation and an Alternative*, Washington, DC, The Brookings Institution.

DES (Department of Education and Science) (1986), *City Technical Colleges – A New Choice of School*, London: HMSO.

DES, DE, Welsh Office (1991), *Education and Training for the 21st Century*, Vol. 2, Cmnd. 1536, London: HMSO.

De Ville, H. G. (1986), *Review of Vocational Qualification in England and Wales – A Report by the Working Group*, London: MSC and DES, April.

Finegold, D. (1991), 'Institutional Incentives and Skills Creation: Understanding the Skills Investment Decision', in P. Ryan (ed.), *International Comparisons of Vocational Education and Training for Intermediate Skills*, London: Falmer, pp. 93–118.

Finegold, D. (1992a), 'TECs and Education', report prepared for the National Training Task Force, University of Warwick, Centre for Education and Industry, Coventry.

Finegold, D. (1992b), 'The Low-Skill Equilibrium: An Institutional Analysis of Britain's Education and Training Failure', D.Phil. in Politics, Oxford University.

Finegold, D. and D. Soskice (1988), 'The Failure of British Training: Analysis and Prescription', *Oxford Review of Economic Policy* **4**(3), 21–53.

Finegold, D. L. McFarland and W. Richardson (1993), *Something Borrowed, Something Blue? A Study of the Thatcher Government's Appropriation of American Education and Training Policy*, 2 vols., Oxford: Triangle Books.

Freedland, M. (1988), 'The Education Reform Bill 1987', paper presented at Law/Labour Relations Seminar, Oxford University, 18 January 1988.

Green, A. (1993), 'Magnet Schools, Choice and the Politics of Policy Borrowing', in D. Finegold *et al.* (1993).

Guthrie, J. and J. Koppich (1988), 'Exploring the Political Economy of National Education Reform', in W. Boyd and C. Kerchner (eds.), *The Politics of Excellence and Choice in Education*, New York: Falmer.

Hall, P. (1986), *Governing the Economy*, Oxford: Polity Press.

Hirschman, A. (1971), *Exit, Voice and Loyalty*, Cambridge, MA: Harvard University Press.

IPPR (1992), 'Higher Education: Expansion and Reform', London: Institute for Public Policy Research.

Jones, I. (1985), 'Pay Relativities and the Provision of Workplace-Based Training', NIESR Discussion Paper No. 77.

Keep, E. (1991), 'The Grass Looked Greener', in P. Ryan (ed.), *International Comparisons of Vocational Education and Training for Intermediate Skills*, London, Falmer.

King, R. and K. Schnack (1986), 'The MSC's Area Manpower Boards', *The Political Quarterly* **57**(3), 256–66.

Leadbeater, C. (1988), 'Employer Networks Need Further Cash for Survival', *Financial Times* 5 April, p. 12.

Lee, D. and B. Chiplin (1970), 'The Economics of Industrial Training', *Lloyds Bank Review* April, 29–41.

Macleod, D. (1992), 'College Funding System Set for Radical Change', *The Independent* 11 December.

Main, D. (1990), 'TECs: An Agenda for Action', *Regional Studies* **24**, 69–71.

Marsden, D. and P. Ryan (1991), 'Initial Training, Labour Market Structure and Public Policy in Britain and the FRG', in P. Ryan (ed.), *International Comparisons of Vocational Education and Training for Intermediate Skills*, London: Falmer Press.

Miliband, D. (1991), *Markets, Politics and Education*, London, IPPR.

Minford, P. (1988), 'Mrs. Thatcher's Economic Reform Programme', in R. Skidelsky (ed.), *Thatcherism*, Oxford: Basil Blackwell, pp. 93–106.

MSC (1974), *There's Work to be Done: Unemployment and Manpower Policies*, London: HMSO.

Mukherjee, S. (1972), *Making Labour Markets Work*, London: PEP.

Peck, J. (1991), 'The Politics of Training in Britain: Contradictions in the TEC Initiative', *Capital and Class* **44** (Summer), 23–34.

Perelman, L. (1990), *The 'Acanemia' Deception*, Hudson Institute Briefing Paper No. 120, Indianapolis, IN, Hudson Institute.

Raffe, D. (1991), 'Compulsory Education and What Then? Signals, Choices, Pathways', paper presented at OECD Seminar, Phoenix, AZ, 19–22 March 1991.

Raffe, D. and N. Tomes (1987), 'The Organization and Content of Studies at the Post-Compulsory Level in Scotland', paper prepared for OECD, University of Edinburgh Centre for Educational Sociology, May.

Rose, R. and E. Page (1990), 'Acting in Adversity: Responses to Unemployment in Britain and Germany', *West European Politics* **13**(4), 66–84.

Ryan, P. (1992), 'Information Costs, Training Quality, and Trainee Exploitation', paper presented at LSE Centre for Economic Performance, July.

Seldon, A. (1986), *The Riddle of the Voucher*, Hobart Paperback 21, London: IEA.

Senker, P. (1991), *The EITB – 1964 to 1991*, Watford: Engineering Training Authority.

Stanton, D. (1991), 'Remarks on the Economics of Training', presented at Cardiff Business School Conference on 'The Economics of Training', 23–24 September 1991.

Streeck, W. (1989), 'Skills and the Limits of Neo-Liberalism: The Enterprise of the Future as a Place of Learning', *Work, Employment and Society* **3**(1), 89–104.

Tysome, T. (1993), 'Patten Quietly Makes the NVQ Mark', *Times Higher Education Supplement* 8 January, 8.

Unwin, L. (1992), 'Evaluation of a Training Credit Pilot: South and East Cheshire TEC', paper presented at the University of Warwick, ESRC Post-16 Seminar, March.

Whitty, G. (1990), 'The New Right and the National Curriculum: State Control or Market Forces?', in M. Flude and M. Hammer (eds.), *The Education Reform Act: Its Origins and Implications*, London: Falmer Press.

Wolf, C. (1988), *Markets or Governments: Choosing Between Imperfect Alternatives*, Cambridge, MA: MIT Press.

12 Training implications of regulation compliance and business cycles

This chapter argues that training may do little to improve the skills of the British workforce where it is undertaken in response to government regulations on health and safety or to occupational requirements, or as the outcome of drives to achieve quality 'kitemarks' or standards. The significance of this type of training appears to have grown in the recession. For example, off-the-job training courses have become much shorter during the recession and more qualifications are now being awarded for short courses, suggesting that they may not be of a particularly high standard and certainly not of any depth. Yet these factors have helped to maintain training volumes in economic circumstances which have hitherto seen training cut back.

It would therefore be incorrect to conclude that it was unbridled market forces that held up training activity in the early 1990s, with British employers at last realizing the importance of training for their own and Britain's long-term future. On the contrary, it is argued in this chapter that the force of regulation has served to protect training from the business cycle. While the maintenance of this sort of training should be welcomed, it may well do little to upgrade the skills of the British workforce and thereby lay the grounds for a more prosperous future.

Training implications of regulation compliance and business cycles

ALAN FELSTEAD and FRANCIS GREEN

1 Introduction

> Even where [training] provision exists, it can often be highly vulnerable when recession or restructuring make their demands. Training is costly and may not always be seen as producing a prompt return.
>
> (House of Lords, 1990, p. 208)

It has become almost conventional wisdom to assume that training volumes in Britain move pro-cyclically, and that they are particularly prone to fall in times of recession. There is agreement on this issue from both sides of industry – the Confederation of British Industry (CBI) and the Trades Union Congress (TUC) (cf. Banham, 1992, p. 9–10; Monks, 1992, p. 21). At the same time, academic theorists who characterise the British training system as a 'market model' in contrast to the 'educational model' in Germany and France (Rainbird, 1993; Campinos-Dubernet and Grando, 1988) also assert the vulnerability of the British system to short-termist retrenchment during recession. The purpose of this chapter is to assess the empirical and theoretical foundations on which the notion of 'cycles of training', so often quoted and assumed, is based.

An examination of the connections between the economic cycle and training is especially relevant at this time. It is now widely recognised that one of the reasons for the slow long-term growth of the British economy has been the relatively low levels of training received by workers at all levels (see for example, Finegold and Soskice (1988), Steedman and Wagner (1989) and Ashton et al. (1989)). In the last decade, training has become a major public policy issue, not only as a means of countering unemployment, but also as a way of redressing UK skills deficiencies. There has been a dramatic transformation in Britain's training system, both public and private. Although the traditional apprenticeship has become a relatively rare phenomenon, there is now a

257

much wider sector of the working population who are experiencing at least some form of training. This expansion has spread to industries outside traditional manufacturing, and to older age groups (especially older women) who in previous decades received very little ongoing training (Greenhalgh and Mavrotas, 1993; Green, 1993). All of this has been interpreted as part of a 'skills revolution' (Banham, 1992). Nevertheless there remains a widespread concern amongst advocates of enhanced training that the recession of the early 1990s may be hindering progress towards a more highly skilled workforce.

This chapter examines the link between training and the business cycle. We show in Section 2 that the theoretical connections between the economic cycle, training activity and the skills deficiency are complex, and that there is no necessary theoretical basis for the conventional wisdom that training declines in recessions. We then proceed to examine this issue from an empirical angle, focusing on Britain. Section 3 briefly summarises evidence from the early 1980s, on which hitherto the assumption that training in Britain falls in recession has been based. We find this evidence is less conclusive than the conventional wisdom assumes. Section 4 presents national level evidence on how training has fared during the recession of the early 1990s. Contrary to the conventional wisdom, we find that Britain's training held up quite well despite the length and severity of the recession. However, this is only part of the story. Off-the-job training courses have become shorter during the recession. More qualifications are now being awarded for short courses, suggesting that they may not be of a particularly high standard and certainly not of any great depth. And across the UK there has been a decline of over one million skilled workers' jobs during the recession.

We conducted our own survey, detailed in Section 5, to examine the factors underlying firms' training strategies during the recession. We find that those firms most affected by the recession were indeed the most likely to have cut back on their training. However, the propensity to cut training was curtailed, and training sometimes increased, where firms had clear training plans and budgets, and also where firms were operating in markets with notable technical change. Furthermore, we find that outside regulations have become important in determining firms' decision to train, and that this often overrides any specific intention of raising the skills of the workforce. It was not, it appears, simply the unbridled forces of the market that held up the level of training. On the contrary, it was the force of regulation which served to protect training from the economic cycle.

In conclusion we question whether the trend to shorter training courses, which seems to have been accentuated by the recession, implies an upskilling of the British workforce. While the regulations that have emerged as factors driving training in Britain may be desirable in their own right, they hardly serve as appropriate vehicles for stimulating the widespread acquisition of higher-level skills.

2 Theoretical links between the economic cycle and training

We shall assume here that in the 'market model' of training, the level of employee training is primarily, though not exclusively, driven by employers' decisions.[1] As has been widely recognised, there are good reasons to expect forms of market failure, especially externalities, in any training market, even within a stable macroeconomic environment. The question at issue is whether a recession is likely in theory to raise the intensity of training and thereby lessen the impact of the market failures which lead to sub-optimal training, or whether, as the conventional wisdom has it, the deficiency in training is exacerbated by macroeconomic failure.

During a mild downturn in business activity, there are some theoretical grounds for expecting that there will be an increase in training activity by rational employers who expect to survive the downturn. Owing to turnover costs, firms may choose to 'hoard' labour, especially skilled or semi-skilled labour, rather than make workers redundant, in the expectation that the workers will soon be needed in the upturn to follow. This hoarding in effect provides slack time, thereby reducing the opportunity costs (in terms of lost output) of training. Such hoarding of labour is likely to be most prevalent in a relatively short and mild downturn. In the case of youth labour, a related argument applies to the new employment of trainees and apprentices. In anticipation of the upturn, employers may continue to take on apprentices even in recession, since if they wait until demand picks up they will be faced with shortages of trained labour which it will prove costly to fill in a hurry. A counterpart of this argument applies to individual or government-sponsored training for those not in employment. For lack of any reasonable job prospects, the 16-year-old may be inclined to stay on at school, while the graduating bachelor's degree student strives harder for entrance to a graduate programme.

A further reason why recessions could increase employers' training effort is that the increased competition for sales in slack markets may induce business strategies that require more training. Recessions intensify competition which may itself increase the need for training to keep pace with, or forge ahead of, competitors. And, for training which has a relatively quick return, employers may note that, since voluntary quit rates are likely to fall in times of recession, their returns are more likely to be realised. Here the enforced restriction of mobility would be operating to internalise part of the previously external benefit of training, thereby reducing the skills gap.

However, in a prolonged recession expectations change, uncertainty increases and confidence typically dwindles, so that there remains little reason to keep employing workers for whom there is little prospect of productive work. In these circumstances the benefits of training are much more doubtful and the costs of training can only be reduced so far (they still involve the wages of the trainees net of any severance costs). The costs of training may increasingly begin to outweigh the benefits.

There are also further reasons to expect some reduction in training participation in any recession. First, employers are likely to begin to reduce their workforces in the least cost way simply by freezing or severely reducing recruitment. New recruits are more likely than the average worker to require and receive initial training, as the evidence confirms (see for example, Green, 1993). Hence, firms' training requirements will also be lowered. Second a charge of short-termism has often been levelled at British industry which, if valid, would be reflected in decisions to cut training, as well as physical investment, in order to meet short-run needs. There are two possible aspects to this charge. One is the hypothesis that, owing to financial constraints, in particular the necessity of having a healthy cash flow in the face of an imperfect capital market, firms will be forced to cut everything in their power in order to satisfy their bankers and stay in business. This we refer to as 'institutional short-termism'. The other refers to the attitudes of employers who fail to recognise the long-term value of investments in training, or who so discount the future that they in effect do not look much beyond the immediate future. These have been strong, frequently made, propositions, lying behind the generally held presumption that recessions are likely to exacerbate the degree of sub-optimality of training in Britain.[2]

Nevertheless, short-termist attitudes towards training may be a less important factor in the recession of the early 1990s. Both the widening of training incidence in the 1980s, and the ascent of training towards the top of the political agenda, with the founding of Training and Enterprise Councils (TECs) and the all-party expressed concern with training issues, may lead us to expect a greater awareness of the value and necessity of training. It is possible that this will lead employers to be less likely to regard training as an 'expense' to be jettisoned during hard times. If so, this would still leave the problem of financial constraints, the institutional short-termism.

The impact of a recession on the deficiency of training is, therefore, complex. From a macroeconomic perspective, if workers cannot obtain work then the 'second-best' activity should be to train. But, as is widely recognised, much training needs to be work-related to be effective, so a key issue is what happens to work-based training and skills. Are those who remain in jobs able to keep up with their training? The rest of this chapter is primarily devoted to an empirical analysis of this question.[3]

3   Training during the last major recession

We begin with a glance at some historical evidence. The conventional wisdom that training falls in times of recession rests primarily on perceptions of the experience of the last major British recession in 1980–82.[4] Apart from anecdotal evidence (Banham, 1992, p. 9), the assumption is based on the numbers of apprentices and other trainees in manufacturing industries following formal training programmes (see Figure 12.1). Manufacturing is only one (minority) sector of the economy, and, from the middle-1980s onwards, the figure presents a misleading picture of the national trend in overall training activities because of the declining importance of apprenticeships in relation to other forms of training. In 1979, however, apprentices constituted one in two of all males undergoing training, and one in five of the much smaller number of females undergoing training (Greenhalgh and Mavrotas, 1993, table 5). Other forms of training were much less frequent then than they later became, especially in the private sector. Figure 12.1 shows the collapse in apprenticeships from 1981 onwards, and of other formal traineeships from 1979. This probably represents a valid quantitative picture of what happened to training in that recession.

Before that time, training incidence had been on a downwards trend for at least a decade, but it was not obviously cyclical. Moreover, there was by the end of the 1970s a widely recognised need for some kind of reform of time-serving apprenticeships, and it is possible that the recession may have interacted with the sense of dissatisfaction to trigger the more precipitate fall in the number of apprentices. To some extent, also, the training collapse was helped along by deliberate and direct government policy. In June 1979 the incoming administration initiated an initial round of expenditure cuts, lopping £170 million off the Special Employment Measures (*Employment Gazette*, June 1979, p. 539). By the same token, some of the increased numbers in training in 1984 and beyond

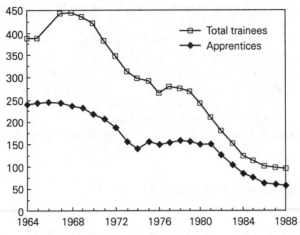

Source: *Employment Gazette*, September 1980 and
subsequent years, table 1.15.

Figure 12.1   Trainees in manufacturing industries, Great Britain (000s)

were participants in newly initiated government training schemes,
principally Youth Training Scheme.

Evidence from past decades, then, provides only limited support for the
conventional wisdom about the vulnerability of training during a
recession in Britain. Developments in training during the recession of the
early 1990s should shed some further light on the issues.

4   Training in the early 1990s recession: the national picture

Consider first the policy context of this recession. It became the source of
some political controversy as to how far the government was reducing
the funds for its own training schemes in the years following the launch
of the TECs. For example, the numbers on Youth Training (YT) fell by
23% from March 1989 to March 1992, yet funding decreased by 31%.
Much of the fall in YT numbers is related to demographic factors but,
whatever the explanation, it was always apparent that the maintenance
of existing training intensity would have to derive from employers'
strategies rather than from government.

Unlike during the early 1980s recession, there are a number of existing
series with which to track the results of employers' decisions through the
recession of the early 1990s. Many surveying organisations now monitor
employers' training activities. The CBI, for example, began to track the

training activity of its member companies by adding a training question to its quarterly industrial trends survey in October 1989.[5] It asks whether respondents 'expect to authorise more or less expenditure in the next twelve months than you authorised in the past twelve months on training and retraining?' A simple balance of opinion is constructed by subtracting the negative answers from the positive ones (see Figure 12.2). This fell to a low, though still positive, level in July 1991 and began to recover until October 1992 when it reached its lowest level ever. It has bounced back somewhat in April 1993, but remains a long way from its pre-recession level.

The Industrial Society has also begun to survey its members on their training activities. This, too, shows that corporate training budgets are under increasing pressure because of the recession. For example, in August 1991 13% of employers reported that they intended to spend less on training in the next six months compared to the last six months, whereas in April 1993 this had risen to 22% (see Table 12.1). However, a significant minority of respondents continued to remain 'bullish' about training expenditure despite the severity and length of the recession.

There is a danger that employers may be over-optimistic and talk-up their business prospects rather than offer a more accurate assessment. Subjective views may be a poor guide to how employers' training activity has changed (Employment Department, 1992b). Moreover, employers' surveys are often biased in some way. For example, both the CBI and the Industrial Society use their members as respondents and so their representativeness may be in doubt.

A better guide to how employee training has fared in the early 1990s is provided by the annual Labour Force Survey (LFS) and, since spring 1992, by the Quarterly Labour Force Survey. Since 1984 the question: 'Over the (last 4 weeks) have you taken part in any education or training connected with your job, or a job you might be able to do in the future?' has been asked as well as a number of other training-related questions. Figures derived for training incidence have been widely quoted in government circles and the media (Employment Department, 1992a; *LFS Quarterly Bulletin*, September 1992; *Financial Times*, 6 August 1992). They show a marked increase in the numbers and proportions of workers receiving job-related training throughout the 1980s; the numbers almost doubled and the proportions involved rose from 9.2% in 1984 to 15.4% in 1990 (see Table 12.2). At that point, the rising trend was broken and, in the subsequent two years, the number of employees declined by over one million and the number receiving training fell by over 300,000. Training incidence dropped to 14.5%. This fall confirms suspicions that the CBI and Industrial Society surveys, which predicted

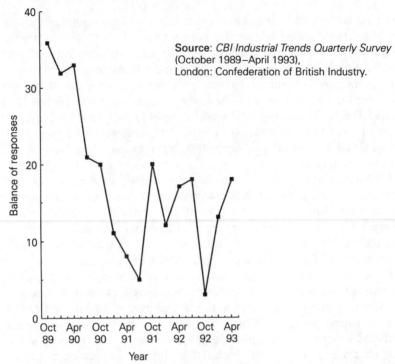

Figure 12.2   Trends in expected training expenditure during the recession of the early 1990s (all companies)

Table 12.1. Anticipated movements in training expenditures: Industrial Society evidence

Date	Training expenditure next 6 months compared to last 6 months		
	More	About the same	Less
August 1991	38	49	13
December 1991	32	40	24
April 1992	33	47	18
August 1992	30	47	20
December 1992	38	41	20
April 1993	30	47	22

Note: All respondents are asked: 'Just considering the location at which you work, do you think that much the same or less, in broad terms, will be spent on training in the next six months than in the last six months?'
Source: The Industrial Society (various) *Training Trends: The Industrial Society Training Survey* (London: Industrial Society).

rising training expenditures, present an inaccurate picture of training activity. Nevertheless, the fact that the fall has as yet not been more precipitous is the best evidence to date that, at least in the first two years of the recession, job-related training exhibited greater resilience than was expected by the conventional wisdom, and that some of the theoretical factors making for greater training in recession may be empirically important. Indeed, changes in the percentage of individuals doing an apprenticeship at the time of the survey appeared to respond little to the economic cycle – it hovered closely around 1.5% during the recession of the 1990s, as it had for much of the mid- to late-1980s. Our own research therefore set out to dig beneath these headline figures for aggregate training incidence, in order to shed further light on the nature of the, albeit small, decline recorded for the 1990–92 period.

The fall in training incidence has not been evenly distributed across the employed population. On the contrary, the biggest falls have been among those whose training incidence has been highest, and vice versa. So, those in 'intermediate occupations', for example, have seen the likelihood of their receiving job-related training in the four weeks prior to interview fall by three percentage points (see Table 12.3). At the other end of the scale, unskilled workers have seen their training incidence rise from 3.5% to 5.4%. However, despite the narrowing of the differences between the social classes in terms of training incidence, the differences remain pronounced; workers in professional occupations are almost five times as likely to receive job-related training than their unskilled counterparts in 1992 (compared to about eight times as likely in 1990).

Table 12.3 also highlights a potentially worrying aspect of the impact of recession on employment in Britain. The British economy lost over one million 'skilled employees' – falling from 10.5 million workers in 1990 to 9.4 million in 1992. In addition, even the 'partly skilled' workforce shrank over this period – 400,000 workers disappeared – thereby reducing the numbers of workers immediately available for upskilling at work. Even though such a cut in employment is unsurprising in a severe recession, its possible consequences for Britain's skills base should not be underestimated. Depending on how many regain jobs in the post-recessionary period, at least a part of their skills will be devalued or lost forever.[6] Although it will be hard to measure the extent of this loss, it fits ill with the oft-mentioned deficiency in middle-level skills in Britain.

An examination of training incidence by industry reveals a great deal of unevenness (see Table 12.4). For example, in 1992 nearly a fifth of those working in 'other services' (this mainly consists of government services such as education, health and so on) reported that they had had job-related training in the four weeks before the survey. By contrast, only

Table 12.2. Trends in job-related training received by employees[a] of working age[b] and the number on an apprenticeship[c] in the four weeks before the survey, Great Britain

Date of LFS survey	Total numbers receiving job-related training (in 000s)	Percentage receiving job-related training	Total number doing an apprentice-ship (in 000s)	Percentage doing an apprentice-ship
Spring 1984	1,832	9.2	332	1.6
Spring 1985	2,091	10.4	357	1.7
Spring 1986	2,178	10.8	318	1.5
Spring 1987	2,382	11.7	314	1.5
Spring 1988	2,776	13.3	329	1.5
Spring 1989	3,102	14.4	367	1.6
Spring 1990	3,337	15.4	352	1.5
Spring 1991	3,161	14.9	330	1.5
Spring 1992	3,025	14.5	312	1.4

Notes: [a] Employees are those in employment, excluding the self-employed and those on government-sponsored training schemes.
[b] Working age refers to men aged 16 and under 65, and women aged 16 and under 60.
[c] Apprentices include those on government-sponsored training schemes. When calculating the percentage doing an apprenticeship the numerator used is employees plus those on government employment and training programmes.
Source: Labour Force Survey Historical Supplement – April 1993 tables 1 and 8 (London: Employment Department); *Training Statistics 1992*, table A1.17 (London: HMSO), and apprentice numbers for spring 1992 calculated from Quarterly Labour Force Survey, spring 1992.

6.2% of agricultural employees, 7.2% in 'other manufacturing' and 10.6% in 'distribution' etc. received training. These are the industries which most fit the picture of a low-skills equilibrium with little training in Britain (Finegold and Soskice, 1988; Keep and Mayhew, Chapter 14 of this volume). Apprenticeships by industry are also uneven. Construction recorded the highest incidence of individuals doing an apprenticeship (5.8% in 1992) and agriculture recorded the lowest (0.4% in 1992). A comparison of the figures for 1990 with those for 1992 reveals little variation in the direction or extent of change. However, it is interesting to note that those industries most exposed to international competition (SIC codes 2–4) record training incidence below the industrial average for both years, while the industry that is least exposed to international competition ('other services', containing much of the public sector) trained the most of all.

Table 12.3. Trends in the numbers of employees[a] of working age[b] receiving job-related training[c] in the four weeks before the survey, by social class (total numbers in each social class is shown in brackets), Great Britain

Social class	Spring 1990 LFS		Spring 1992 LFS	
	Number (in 000s)	Percentage	Number (in 000s)	Percentage
Professional occupations	269 (1,017)	26.5	278 (1,143)	24.3
Intermediate occupations	1,371 (5,559)	24.7	1,282 (5,905)	21.7
Skilled non-manual occupations	879 (5,732)	15.8	687 (5,196)	13.2
Skilled manual occupations	505 (4,732)	10.7	428 (4,210)	10.2
Partly skilled occupations	241 (3,423)	7.2	233 (3,016)	7.7
Unskilled occupations	35 (1,028)	3.5	60 (1,116)	5.4

Notes: [a] Employees are those in employment, excluding the self-employed and excluding those on government-sponsored training schemes.
[b] Working age refers to men aged 16 and under 65, and women aged 16 and under 60.
[c] Percentage of all in the group receiving job-related training in the four weeks before interview. These percentages have been calculated with missing values included in the numerator (i.e. ed4wk and edlastwk $-9 = 8$) so as to replicate the published figures.
Source: Labour Force Survey, (1990), and Quarterly Labour Force Survey, spring 1992; our calculations.

Measuring training incidence against other individual characteristics such as sex, age, size of establishment, employment status and job tenure reveals few noticeable differences – the small reductions in training incidence were relatively evenly distributed.[7] In particular, it is worth noting that the training of experienced workers was reduced broadly in line with the aggregate change, and that the aggregate fall cannot be attributed to a curtailment of induction training.

However, the two-year period did see a shift towards shorter courses among those who received job-related training (see Table 12.5). For example, courses lasting less than one month now make up about 45% of all job-related training courses compared to 40% in 1990. The shift has been even greater for courses lasting less than one week – rising from 34% in 1990 to 40% in 1992. The rise in short courses has been most

Table 12.4. Trends in the numbers of employees[a] of working age[b] receiving job-related training[c] or on an apprenticeship in the four weeks before the survey, by industry

Industry division	Spring 1990 LFS		Spring 1992 LFS	
	Percentage job-related training	Percentage doing an apprentice-ship	Percentage job-related training	Percentage doing an apprentice-ship
All employees	15.4	1.4	14.7	1.4
0 Agriculture	7.5	0.6	6.2	0.4
1 Energy & water supply industries	18.2	1.3	18.3	1.3
2 Extraction of minerals & ores other than fuels; manufacture of metals, mineral products & chemicals	12.2	0.7	14.2	0.8
3 Metal goods, engineering & vehicles	13.7	2.5	12.4	2.9
4 Other manufacturing industries	8.0	1.2	7.2	1.3
5 Construction	11.2	6.2	11.7	5.8
6 Distribution, hotels & catering; repairs	11.2	1.4	10.6	1.3
7 Transport & communication	13.0	0.8	12.6	0.5
8 Banking, finance, insurance, business services & leasing	20.5	0.9	17.0	0.9
9 Other services	21.2	0.7	19.7	0.7

Notes: [a] For the purposes of calculating training incidence 'employees' are those in employment, excluding the self-employed and *excluding* those on government-sponsored training schemes. For the purposes of apprenticeship incidence 'employees' refers to those in employment excluding the self-employed and *including* those on government-sponsored training schemes.

[b] Working age refers to men aged 16 and under 65, and women aged 16 and under 60.

[c] Percentage of all in the group receiving job-related training in the four weeks before interview. These percentages have been calculated with missing values included in the numerator (i.e. ed4wk and edlastwk $-9 = 8$), so as to replicate the published figures.

Source: Labour Force Survey, 1990, and Quarterly Labour Force Survey, spring 1992; our calculations.

Table 12.5. Length of training course^a, by social class, Great Britain

Social class	Spring 1990 LFS		Spring 1992 LFS	
	%<1 week	%<1 month	%<1 week	%<1 month
All workers	34.4	40.2	39.6	44.8
Professional occupations	35.3	41.1	40.4	44.1
Intermediate occupations	39.8	45.5	45.2	50.6
Skilled non-manual occupations	31.7	37.7	36.2	41.5
Skilled manual occupations	27.5	34.6	35.6	40.3
Partly skilled occupations	23.8	31.2	30.9	36.3
Unskilled occupations	21.6	33.1	30.6	35.3

Notes: ^{a} Respondents are asked: 'What was/is the total length of the training course?'
Source: Labour Force Survey, 1990, and Quarterly Labour Force Survey, spring 1992; our calculations.

pronounced among the unskilled. These changes are consistent with the theoretical expectation (see above) that the value of training with a relatively quick payoff is especially enhanced by recession. They constitute an acceleration of a longer-run trend in the 1980s towards more people taking shorter courses (Greenhalgh and Mavrotas, 1993).

Job-related training may, or may not, lead to qualifications being awarded. The Labour Force Survey asks those who are doing job-related training whether it leads to a qualification, a credit for a qualification or neither. According to this evidence, in 1992 there were 42,445 fewer workers whose training was leading to a qualification compared to 1990 (see Table 12.6). However, there was a shift towards training for qualifications among those who still received job-related training (37.1% to 39.1%). Indications of a shift towards qualification training can also be found among even the shortest of courses. For example, the chances of getting a qualification from a course lasting less than one week rose from about one in twenty in 1990 to one in twelve in 1992 (see Table 12.7). The same goes for a credit for a qualification – rising from about one in six to around one in four. This must serve to cast some doubt on the quality of the qualifications attained, particularly as only about 10% of these short courses potentially lead to technician or higher-level qualifications.

Table 12.6. Trends in training which leads to a qualification[a], Great Britain

| | Spring 1990 LFS | | Spring 1992 LFS | |
Outcome of training	Number	Percentage	Number	Percentage
Leading to a qualification	1,219,134	37.1	1,176,689	39.1
Credit for a qualification	160,460	4.9	164,692	5.5
Neither	1,902,310	58.0	1,664,617	55.4

Note: [a] Respondents are asked: 'Does the training you have been doing lead to a qualification or a credit towards a qualification or neither?'
Source: Labour Force Survey, 1990, and Quarterly Labour Force Survey, spring 1992; our calculations.

Table 12.7. Length of training course by outcome of training, Great Britain

| | Spring 1990 LFS | | Spring 1992 LFS | |
Length of training course	Qualification	Credit	Qualification	Credit
< 1 week	5.2%	18.1%	8.4%	25.0%
< 1 month	7.9%	26.8%	11.7%	32.7%

Source: Labour Force Survey, 1990, and Quarterly Labour Force Survey, spring 1992; our calculations.

5   Determinants of employers' training decisions in the recession

While the LFS evidence has shown that training activity remained relatively resilient in the latest recession, there remain several unanswered empirical questions. What are the factors leading to a rise or fall in company training activity? Where training has increased, what strategies underlie the decision? For those companies which have reduced training, to what extent has the recession instigated short-termist decisions? These questions can only be answered by examining how and why employers' training policies and practices have changed during the recession. This section presents some detailed evidence based on a survey of 157 firms.

Our sample was a group of 202 training managers who were first interviewed on a face-to-face basis in autumn 1990. The 1990 interviews were conducted as part of a project on Work-Related Further Education (WRFE) (see Maguire (1991)). A target sample of fifty private sector employers was set for each of four localities: Bradford; Buckinghamshire; Lincolnshire; and Mid-Glamorgan. The sample was required to be broadly representative, by industrial sector, of the local distribution of industry, but was aimed predominantly at small to medium-sized firms of up to 100 employees, with 75% known users of WRFE. These factors imply that the contacted sample was not necessarily representative of all firms. Indeed, the high proportion using WRFE suggests a predominance of firms with some form of active training policy. The target samples were identified through a variety of sources, including lists obtained from the then Training Agency local offices, Careers Services and Colleges of Further Education. The target respondent in each firm was the person who was identified as having responsibility for decisions concerning training. Within larger establishments this tended to be the Training Officer or Personnel Officer.

For the current research we conducted a follow-up survey in late summer and autumn 1992, aiming to re-contact the same individuals where possible (or those who had taken their place) to ask how training had fared during the recession. Since we already had a considerable amount of data on the companies themselves, it was felt to be more cost-effective to conduct most of the interviews on the telephone. A total of 140 were successfully reinterviewed on the telephone, with an 'average' interview lasting 35 minutes. A further 17 were interviewed on a face-to-face basis; each interview lasted between 1 hour and 2 hours 10 minutes (an average of just over 1 hour 30 minutes).[8]

Our survey findings are consistent with a wide diversity of experience. One of the key questions asked of respondents was the following: 'How has the *overall* amount of training given to employees (both existing and new recruits) changed over the last two years (as measured by hours of training)?' Of the 157 responding firms, 68 (43%) claimed to have increased their training activities over the last two years, 45 (27%) reported no change in their overall training commitment and 39 (25%) report cutbacks in training. Given the nature of our sample, these figures cannot be taken as indicative of national trends. Moreover, 'training', as is well-known, is interpreted in different ways by different people – a point confirmed by our interviews. Yet, so long as respondents are each consistent in their interpretation over time, the responses given do provide a reasonable measure of changes in training within each firm.

5.1   Analysis

The change in the level of training was examined by means of a standard quantitative analysis complemented by a synthesis of the great deal of qualitative information emerging from the interviews.

We begin with a simple model. From responses to the above question, the change in the overall volume of training (TR) is categorised as 'Decreased', 'Remained the same' or 'Increased'. This being an ordinal ranking, we model the determinants of TR as an ordered probit, with exogenous variables **X** (to be discussed below) affecting the probability that individual firms will fall into each of the above categories. Let

$$TR^* = \mathbf{b}X + u$$

where $u \sim N(0,1)$ and

$$TR = 0 \text{ if } TR^* \leq 0 \text{ ('Increased')}$$
$$TR = 1 \text{ if } 0 < TR^* \leq m \text{ ('Remained the same')}$$
$$TR = 2 \text{ if } m < TR^* \text{ ('Decreased')}$$

TR^* is the latent variable, of which the observed counterpart is TR.

The main econometric drawbacks of this procedure here are, first that the sample of firms is not a random draw but is biased towards those that in 1990 were users of Work Related Further Education, and, second, that some of the exogenous variables, characteristics of the firms, might not be exogenous (e.g. the existence of a training budget could conceivably depend on the response of the firm to recession, rather than the other way round). Moreover, because of missing values on one or more variables the sample size was reduced to 120 for this analysis. Hence the precise estimates now to be discussed should be treated with caution. Where appropriate we supplement our conclusions with the qualitative analysis and with simpler tabular analyses which utilise a larger proportion of the data set.

The results are presented in Table 12.8. The first group of independent variables entered were an attempt to capture directly the influence of the recession, through changes in firms' product and labour markets. *DEMPL*, the change in employment (averaging a fall of 9%) was found to have a substantial and significant impact on training: the greater the fall in employment the greater the likelihood of a fall in training and the less chance of an increase in training. In fact, three-quarters of firms which reduced training had experienced employment cuts of over 10%.

*PR*1 and *PR*2 are dummy variables indicating whether firms operate in, respectively, an increasing or declining product market, while *T*1 and *T*2 indicate rising or falling turnover. (In each case the reference category is 'Remained the same'). The results show that both a declining product market, and a fall in turnover, increased the likelihood of cuts in training, though in the latter case the effect was insignificant. Since the product market and the turnover variables were, unsurprisingly, well correlated, we also ran probits entering these variables separately; in each case the product market and the turnover variables had significant effects, as predicted.

Even during recession, and perhaps more so, many firms struggling to compete need to keep up with new technology, and such changes tend to bring associated training needs. The next variable, *TECH*, indicates whether the level of technology had been raised over the previous five years. Its impact is significant, indicating that where the level of technology was increasing it was less likely that training volumes were decreased and more likely that they were increased.

The final set of variables entered were all designed to proxy the extent to which firms took a strategic or long-term approach to training decisions, or whether these decisions were more affected by short-term considerations. First, we entered a 0/1 variable indicating whether or not the firm was the ultimate controlling company. Its impact was insignificant.[9] Second, we also entered the size of the company (as measured by employment in 1990). The rationale here is that smaller firms might be more subject to external financial pressures to ensure cash flow, that is, more affected by institutional short-termism. The results show no significant effect, however, and this is consistent with our finding from the LFS analysis reported earlier that training fell slightly in both large and small establishments. A third variable designed to pick up strategic considerations was a 0/1 dummy indicating whether firms had a semi-formal or formal written training plan. Some 30% of the sample had no such plan, and the results show that this factor significantly raised the probability of training cuts in the recession. Finally, the absence of a training budget also raised the probability of training cuts but in this case the coefficient was not highly significant.

Formal modelling of the above kind is able only partly to explain the training decisions that firms took. For example, even though the depressing influence of recession on training was confirmed, there were 27 firms in our sample which were operating in declining product markets and which nevertheless increased their training activities. Our interviews revealed a number of factors affecting training decisions which were not initially anticipated by theory and could not readily be inserted into our quantitative model. In addition, they drew attention to ways in which training activities had been re-focused during the recession on different areas within the firm. Together these factors go a long way to explain why training held up despite the recession-induced cutbacks in employment.

We begin by building on the result, from our model, that the existence of a formal training plan and/or a training budget serve to lower the chance of training cutbacks. The interviews revealed that behind these

Table 12.8. The decline in training: ordered probit analysis

		Mean values	Coefficient estimates (*t*-statistics in parentheses)
Constant		1	−0.45 (−0.94)
DEMPL	Proportionate increase in employment, 90–92	−0.089	−1.47 (−2.43)
PR1	Expanding product market	0.19	0.15 (0.29)
PR2	Declining product market	0.61	0.79 (1.99)
T1	Rising turnover	0.36	0.20 (0.41)
T2	Falling turnover	0.49	0.63 (1.45)
TECH	Increasing level of technology	0.41	−0.78 (−2.83)
C	Ultimate controlling company	0.88	−0.55 (−1.23)
EMPL 90	Employment in 1990	297	0.00034 (1.25)
NTRP	No training plan	0.30	0.87 (2.38)
NTRBU	No training budget	0.42	0.41 (1.41)
m			1.17 (6.54)
Log likelihood			−95.027
Log likelihood ratio			0.27
χ^2			69.9
n			120

Notes: With the exception of *EMPL*90 and *DEMPL* all independent variables are 0/1 dummies.

The categories of the dependent variable are: 2 = training declined; 1 = training stayed the same; 0 = training increased.

factors there typically lay a competitive strategy based on the production of quality products and/or the delivery of a quality service.[10] Many of those who increased their training activities were also those who had registered or had already qualified for British Standard 5750 (or its international equivalents ISO 9000 in the USA and Japan, and EN 29000 in Europe). Often this connection was explicitly made by respondents.

The aim of BS 5750 is to ensure that quality standards are met for each accredited firm's product.[11] Central to accreditation is evidence that training manuals exist for each job, enabling workers new to the job to learn the required skills without recourse to trial and error. Maintaining registration also requires at least two annual quality audits. The result is that training for this purpose is a routine, complementary characteristic for BS 5750-accredited firms. A few quotations serve to illustrate the point:

> the increase in our training has gone hand in glove with our BS 5750 accreditation in 1991.

> BS 5750 prompted us to give more detailed job instruction on-the-job – this was associated with the Quality Manual we had to produce for accreditation.

> Training was not a priority before. Historically this was a jobbing shop with autocratic management. BS 5750 gave increased emphasis to training.

> Once you achieve BS 5750, the regular audits make training budgets that much 'harder' – they become difficult to cut.

The significance of this complementarity for present purposes is not just that there are now some 17,000 BS 5750-accredited firms in Britain. In addition, our respondents reported that in the intensified competitive climate of the recession, many firms were able to choose from a wider list of potential suppliers and were using the BS 5750 kitemark as a criterion for making their choice. Many large companies were even refusing to do business with those who did not hold BS 5750 accreditation. Several respondents were accordingly under strong pressure to seek accreditation. Meanwhile, parallel to this official process of regulation, certain large companies – including Marks and Spencer, Ford, Boots and Rover – enforce their own quality standards (which require training) on their suppliers. Many Japanese companies in the UK place particular emphasis on suppliers' training systems. None of these forms of regulation are statutory, but taken together with the intensification of competition they have acquired their own force.[12]

Competition also induced more training and a reforming of training effort in other ways. In some companies we found that training effort had been concentrated on management, since it was deemed that this had the most impact on company performance. Elsewhere, where technology was changing, the focus was on new technology training. A further significant new focus for training, induced by the recession, was in customer care. A good deal of management advice for companies under pressure is to concentrate effort more on retaining existing customers than on winning new ones. Consistent with this advice, several of our respondents had introduced customer care programmes, entailing an increase in training activity in order to diffuse knowledge of what the company is selling, and of its customers' needs.

Apart from these recession-induced pressures for training, our interviews also uncovered certain basic training needs that could not be set aside even under the axe of a severe cost-cutting management. We refer to these as 'training floors'. First, some production processes dictate that without some minimal training even for the unskilled workforce considerable costs can ensue from accidents and mistakes. Second, a number of regulations, some new, are in force to minimise dangers to workers and customers, such as the Food Safety Act 1990 (HMSO, 1990) and the Control of Substances Hazardous to Health Regulations (HMSO, 1988). Compliance with all such regulations generally necessitates training. Thus, an increasing number of food workers now hold hygiene certificates showing they have been on the necessary courses. Such courses tend to be short and basic, a finding consistent with the national picture revealed in the Labour Force Surveys.

An example of an industry-specific regulation cited by our respondents is the set of requirements imposed by the Financial Services Act 1988. Similarly, to spray pesticides training is needed to obtain the relevant certification; to work in radioactive areas requires going through a training programme by the National Radiological Protection Board; or to maintain a franchise agreement often confers an obligation for certain forms of training.[13] Despite the overall deregulatory approach taken by the government in the 1980s, there are many more such government- or industry-imposed training requirements.

In addition, further externally imposed obligations arise from occupational labour markets. Respondents cited professional bodies such as the Royal Institution of Chartered Surveyors, the Law Society, the Royal Institute of British Architects, the Institute of Chartered Accountants, the Institution of Civil Engineers and the Institute of Structural Engineers as acting in such a role. To remain members of their respective professional bodies, qualified individuals are required to keep their qualifications up to date by accumulating a set number of training points during the year. Non-professionals, too, may have to demonstrate their continued occupational competence. For example, the International Air Transport Association insists that travel agents hold valid Certificates of Travel Agency Competence. These certificates have a finite life and have to be renewed if the travel agency wishes to issue air tickets, giving a need for ongoing training.

To sum up so far, from our qualitative analysis of the interview data we found that the explanation for training holding up through the recession where it did is largely a combination of intensified competition and externally imposed standards together with the presence of 'training floors' in many areas governed by various types of external regulation. It is worth noting at this stage that we did not find in any of our conversations with employers any direct or even indirect evidence of training being induced by labour-hoarding – that is, in no case did it appear that employees were putting in more training because there was insufficient work to be done.

From our quantitative analysis we found that those firms which had been hit worst by recession were more likely to be cutting their training. The principal reason for the fall in training was simply the cutback in employment and in recruitment, but in addition most companies which cut training also reduced the average amount of training they gave to their existing workers. One reason cited by some respondents was the reduction in labour turnover: less mobility within internal labour markets requires less associated training. Another was the pressure for a more flexible workforce. For example, one respondent explained how the company she worked for offered part-time, insecure work to the bulk of the workforce, offering little career development and training for all but a very small minority.

Beyond these relatively straightforward rationales for training cutbacks, is there any evidence for the kind of short-termism we referred to in Section 2? A number of our findings are relevant. First, we found no evidence that the type of company – small or large, British or foreign ownership and so on – made any difference. Insofar as it might be thought that small companies might be more short-termist, we found no evidence for this. Second, however, it was clear that a large minority of companies had no training plan, and that this impinged upon many companies' training decision. Third, amongst the 39 firms which cut training we asked whether the 'need to cut cost' was a significant factor in deciding to reduce training volumes. Of the 39 decreasing firms that cut overall training, 16 declared cost-cutting to be important or fairly important. Meanwhile, 16 other firms declared it to be fairly unimportant or totally irrelevant, but it should be noted that, of these, 10 had had no new recruits. There was, thus, a good proportion of firms whose training expenditures were targeted at a time of financial stringency. Fourth, this evidence of short-termism was confirmed by unsolicited comments from some of our respondents who feared that training cutbacks in their companies would lead to a later re-emergence of skill shortages but who felt powerless to resist the obligation to cut costs:

> When we cast our minds back to the mid 1980s/early 1990s there were cries that there were not enough skilled people out there. If that was the case then, then later on in the 1990s things are going to get really desperate. This will hold back business. Businesses are operating for today – they are short-termist. The work isn't there, the costs of training are high and the business isn't turning over anywhere near the volume it was before the recession. ... There are short-term reasons for hemming in training today, but in the longer term the price will be high.

> The company has a short-termist approach – we'll lose out in terms of motivated employees. Lack of interest in doing things correctly, we'll lose our sharp edge – this will be very difficult to recoup in a couple of years, it is difficult to fit in something you should have done earlier ... To my great regret all that good work is 'on ice' for lack of money.

6   Conclusions

We began by asking the question: how closely do training volumes mirror the economic cycle? Our answers to this question are based on theory and on different pieces of empirical evidence. A clear message emerges – recessions do not necessarily cause a disastrous cutback in training. Indeed, the cutbacks in the previous recession at the start of the 1980s were not so sharp as is commonly perceived. At that time, certain types of training were indeed reduced in manufacturing industry, but this was largely an acceleration of a longer-run trend. We are in the dark as to what happened to other types of training, especially non-formal training, during that recession. The evidence for the latest deep recession is that, while the trend towards expansion of training has been brought to a halt, at least in its first two years there has only been a small overall dip in the proportions of employees receiving some form of training. In this respect the conventional wisdom that existed before the recession has so far been proved wrong.

Nevertheless, our further analysis has shown that it is equally incorrect to conclude that market forces have been keeping training up to an optimal level, a sentiment recently expressed by those taking an optimistic interpretation of the CBI data (CBI, 1993, p. 32). The truth is a good deal more complex. Examination of our sample of employers has revealed a variety of changes in training practices over the recession period, with many reducing their training and many others maintaining or increasing it. The reasons for the cuts in training have been those commonly expected: they have arisen in those firms severely affected by the recession, which have made substantial cutbacks in employment. We have also found some limited evidence of 'short-termism' in these firms, in that a fair proportion admitted to reducing their training as an exercise in cost-cutting, and many had no plan for training.

Why has training held up or expanded in other firms? In our theoretical analysis we have noted that, insofar as firms are hoarding labour, which they are liable to do in a mild recession, the opportunity cost of training in terms of lost output is likely to be smaller. We did not, however, detect much of an impact from this direction in the latest recession. This could be a reflection of the fact that the recession has been far from mild, and hence that firms have laid off labour rather than hoarded it (we have no independent evidence for this). Rather, the forces holding up training turned out to be a combination of the intensification of competition and a whole series of regulations, which together served to 'harden up' otherwise soft budgets and prevent training expenditures being cut even with the intensified pressures of the recession. The external intervention that appeared to have most impact on the ability to compete was the British Standard 5750. Other more diverse government and professional regulations served to provide floors to training intensity in a number of industries and occupations. Ironically, then, the 'training market' had been prevented from experiencing a more substantial implosion as much by the forces of regulation as by those of competition. The notion that Britain has a 'market model' of a training system should therefore be qualified. Moreover, while such regulations continue, it would seem likely that training of this kind would also be less vulnerable than hitherto supposed in any future recessions.

Yet the conclusions are not especially propitious for those who hope that expanded training will solve Britain's skills deficiencies. There has been a notable tendency towards having relatively more short courses of training, and although there is a continued expansion in training for qualifications, the fact that many of these qualifications are being achieved for very short courses of training suggests that they are not to a particularly high standard. Only a small proportion of those employees in training are working towards qualifications that would seem to equip them for the sorts of high-skill/technological frontier jobs upon which it is regularly said that future prosperity depends.

The findings must serve also to raise some questions about the longer-term trend in training in Britain and its relation to the skills gap. In examining the growth of training incidence indicated by successive Labour Force Surveys, Greenhalgh and Mavrotas (1993) cast doubt on the simple notion that growing international competition is driving the training increase, in that they note that by far the greatest amount of training takes place in the non-tradeables sector. They hypothesise that there emerged in the 1980s a need for more general training and that, with the more uncertain economic environment management opted more for shorter courses with early payoffs that were more likely to be realised. To these explanations we can now add the hypothesis that the widening scope of certain regulations was gradually imposing more training requirements. It is difficult to say just how important such factors were during the 1980s, but our survey data would suggest they cannot be ignored. Thus, the BS 5750 kitemark, introduced in 1979, expanded its scope over the decade to reach some 17,000 firms by 1992.

Nevertheless, it remains the case that, in contrast to our knowledge about the cross-sectional determinants of training incidence,[14] relatively little is known about the reasons for and impact of the observed growth in training incidence over the last 10 years, and further research is called for. Relatedly, it will help to clarify further the meaning and purpose of 'training' as it is understood by survey respondents. At present, an act of training can be interpreted in many different ways by different respondents. Particular differences have been found between employers and employees – for example over the definition (hence numbers) of apprenticeships.[15] Cross-country comparisons are all but impossible owing to the different cultural attachments to the idea of training. Even within the domain of individual-based surveys in Britain, different measures of training intensity appear.[16] And it is also possible that the same activity might one year be seen as simply being told what to do and in a later year come to be regarded as a form of job-related training.

Individual-based surveys are also limited in what they reveal about the purpose of training since in most cases it is the employer who has arranged and sponsored the training. They therefore cannot distinguish between training that is there simply to fulfil a government regulation and training that is aimed at upskilling a company's workforce. Both types of training constitute an augmentation of human capital, considered in its widest sense, but the sort of training likely to be relevant to addressing Britain's skills gap will have a longer-term payoff than that of satisfying immediate regulatory needs. It will be necessary to make more effective use of employer-based surveys to tease out such distinctions in the future. For the present, however, it is impossible to take much reassurance from the Labour Force Survey's upward trend in the 1980s as indicating a move away from a 'low-skills equilibrium': given our lack of knowledge about the purpose of training it could be that much of the training is precisely to support those low-level skills to which many researchers have referred.

NOTES

The research for this paper was funded by the Leverhulme Trust, Grant No. F. 212K. Material from the Labour Force Survey made available through the OPCS and the ESRC Data Archive has been used by permission of the Controller of HM Stationery Office. We should like to thank Malcolm Maguire for his helpful comments and assistance with the sample of employers, and John Goodwin for computing assistance.

1 Two stylised facts support this assumption: first, almost three-quarters of adult workers getting trained are employer-funded; second, there is considerable unmet demand for access to training by employees (Rigg, 1989, tables 11.4 and 7.4a).

2 The point may be highlighted by means of a contrast with normal business practices in Japan, where there is evidence that many manufacturing firms raised their training during the period of slower growth from 1973 to 1983, specifically in order to prepare for the later period of improvement in the economy (Ishikawa, 1991, p. 21).

3 To consider the overall impact of recession on the extent of the sub-optimality of training would require a wider remit, beyond the bounds of this chapter, to include the question: do those who lose their jobs lose part or all of their skills, and can they be re-acquired through training for the unemployed or, later, through re-employment?

4 For example, according to the Industrial Society in 'the recession of the early 1980s ... training was one of the first priorities for cutback' (Industrial Society, 1991, p. 8).

5 Some localised surveys of employers also carry similar questions. For example, Leicester City Council carries out a survey of local employers three times a year. The question on training is much the same as that asked of the CBI's national sample.

6 This process is one cause of unemployment hysteresis (Cross, 1988).

7 See Felstead and Green (1993, tables B1, B2, B3, B6 and B7).

8 Forty-five respondents did not participate in the follow-up, because either they were unwilling to cooperate for a second time (35) or they could not be contacted (10) presumably because they had gone out of business. Analysis of the non-respondents revealed no consistent picture: they were neither 'good' nor 'poor' trainers so far as the previous survey could detect. For further details and results of the survey see Felstead and Green (1993).

9 Not shown, another analysis also indicated no impact according to whether the firm was foreign-owned.

10 The Employers' Manpower and Skills Practices Survey (EMSPS) has also found quality considerations to be a strong motivating factor behind employers' training policies and practices (Dench, 1992).

11 BS 5750 is not itself a guarantee of high-quality products or services. Rather it is a guarantee of the consistency of product quality, so that only where separate high-quality standards exist does it necessarily lead to high standards.
12 Some companies had also registered on the government's Investors in People initiative. However, other than kudos there was no incentive so to register, and there was no evidence that this initiative had, at the time of interview, induced any more training, as opposed to merely confirming training that already existed.
13 See Felstead (1993).
14 For a survey, see Green (1993).
15 Felstead and Green (1993).
16 The 1987 General Household Survey asked about training incidence over a four-week period but, because it utilises a slightly wider definition of training and because its interviewers prompt respondents with cards, it gets a measure of training intensity different from that of the Labour Force Survey of 1987 (Green, 1993).

REFERENCES

Ashton, D., F. Green and M. Hoskins (1989), 'The Training System of British Capitalism: Changes and Prospects' in F. Green (ed.), *The Restructuring of the British Economy*, Brighton: Harvester Wheatsheaf.
Banham, J. (1992), 'Taking Forward the Skills Revolution', *Policy Studies* **13**(1), 5–12.
Campinos-Dubernet, M. and J.-M. Grando (1988), 'Formation Professionelle Ouvriére: Ivois Modèles Européennes', *Formation/Emploi* no. 22, 5–29.
CBI (1993), *Routes for Success: Careership – A Strategy for All 16–19 Year Old Learning*, London: Confederation of British Industry.
    (various), *CBI Industrial Trends Quarterly Survey*, London: Confederation of British Industry.
Cross, R. (ed.), (1988), *Unemployment, Hysteresis and the Natural Rate of Unemployment*, Oxford: Blackwell.
Dench, S. (1992), 'EMSPS – Some Research Findings on Employers' Training Activities in Britain', paper presented at the Vocational Training in Britain and Europe post-1992, Oxford, 7–8 September 1992.
Employment Department (1992a), *Labour Market and Skills Trends 1993–1994* London: Employment Department.
    (1992b), 'Skills Needs in Britain – 1992: What Training are Employers Doing?', *Skills and Enterprise Network*, issue 30/92, November.
Felstead, A. (1993), *The Corporate Paradox: Power and Control in the Business Franchise*, London: Routledge.
Felstead, A. and Green, F. (1993), *Cycles of Training: Evidence from the British Recession of the Early 1990s*, University of Leicester, Department of Economics, Discussion Papers in Economics, 93/3.
Finegold. D. and Soskice, D. (1988), 'The Failure of British Training: Analysis and Prescription', *Oxford Review of Economic Policy* **4**(3), 21–53.
Green. F. (1993), 'The Determinants of Training of Male and Female Employees in Great Britain', *Oxford Bulletin of Economics and Statistics* **55**(1), 103–22.

Greenhalgh, C. A. and G. Mavrotas (1993), 'Workforce Training in the Thatcher Era – Market Forces and Market Failures', *International Journal of Manpower*, **14**(2–3), 17–32.

HMSO (1988), *The Control of Substances Hazardous to Health Regulations*, no. 1657, (Statutory Instrument), London: HMSO.

(1990), *Food Safety Act 1990*, HMSO: London.

House of Lords (1990), 'Vocational Training and Re-training', *Select Committee on the European Communities 21st Report, Session 1989/90*, HL Paper 78–1, London: HMSO.

Industrial Society (various), *Industrial Society Training Trends*, London: Industrial Society.

Ishikawa, T. (1991), *Vocational Training*, revised edition, Tokyo: The Japan Institute of Labour.

Maguire, M. (1991), *Employers' Views of Work Related Further Education*, Leicester: University of Leicester, Centre for Labour Market Studies.

Monks, J. (1992), 'The Trade Union View', *Policy Studies* **13**(1), 13–21.

OPCS (1982), *Labour Force Survey 1981*, London: HMSO.

OPCS (1986), *Labour Force Survey 1983 and 1984*, London: HMSO.

Rainbird, H. (1993), 'Comparative Perspectives on Training: Britain, France and Germany', in M. Gold (ed.), *Europe: the Social Dimension*, London: Macmillan.

Rigg, M. (1989), *Training in Britain: Individuals' Perspectives*, Sheffield: Training Agency.

Steedman, H. and Wagner, K. (1989), 'Productivity, Machinery and Skills: Clothing Manufacture in Britain and Germany', *National Institute Economic Review* May, 40–57.

Training Agency (1989), *Training in Britain: A Study of Funding, Activity and Attitudes, Main Report*, Sheffield: Training Agency.

13 On apprenticeship qualifications and labour mobility

This chapter points out that the apprenticeship system may function as an institution to overcome the poaching externality analysed in Chapter 2. The British apprenticeship system of the 1970s is used as an example. The form of training provided by an apprenticeship is typically general; thus in the absence of mobility restrictions, the benefits of training may accrue not only to the provider of training and to the trained worker, but also to other firms. The apprenticeship, with its 'indenture' period acts as an institutional device to assist firms providing the training to appropriate the benefits in the immediate post-training period.

The chapter analyses the effect of apprenticeships on employment duration, as exemplified by the available British evidence from the 1970s, from Sweep 4 of the National Child Development Study. The statistical analysis indicates that young men completing apprenticeships were less likely to leave employment in their first jobs than were individuals with no training. Some commentators have argued that accreditation of training is an important means of overcoming market failure where there is asymmetry of information about the value of firm-provided training (for example, where a firm providing training knows its worth, but other firms do not). The formal qualification associated with some apprenticeships is a means of conveying to non-training firms the value of firm-provided general training. The chapter shows that whether or not the apprenticeship was formally accredited had no significant influence on the effect of young male apprenticeships on employment duration. For British apprenticeships in the 1970s, accreditation appears not to have had a significant effect on early labour mobility.

On apprenticeship qualifications and labour mobility

ALISON L. BOOTH and STEPHEN SATCHELL

1   Introduction

What impact does vocational training have on the labour market experience of young school leavers? How does early training affect employment duration and labour mobility? Much recent research has been directed at modelling training incidence and its impact on earnings as a proxy for productivity.[1] However, with the exception of Lynch (1991) and Booth and Satchell (1994), there has been little empirical work estimating the impact of early training on employment duration. In this chapter, we examine the impact of a particular form of training that has been attracting the interest of British and US policy makers recently – the apprenticeship – on the duration of employment in the first 'permanent' job a youth has on entering the labour market. Our particular goal is to test the hypothesis that apprenticeships resulting in nationally recognised vocational qualifications have a different impact to apprenticeships without qualifications. The chapter also examines the determinants of apprenticeship receipt, conditional on entering the labour market at age 16.

As in Germany, apprenticeships in Britain date from the guild system. While apprenticeships were originally found only in the artisan trades, following industrialisation they spread rapidly to engineering, ship-building, plumbing and electrical trades. By the late nineteenth century, apprenticeships were increasingly supported by the development of multi-employer collective bargaining, allowing trade union intervention. Apprenticeships at that time were characterised by a low starting wage, and formal or informal agreements as to the length of service, an arrangement that acted as an incentive for workers to complete their training. Since the skills acquired were largely general to a particular trade or industry, apprenticeships have been viewed as an institutional response to the poaching problem, allowing firms to bear at least some of the costs of training provision.[2] Apprenticeships thereby encouraged investment in workers with generally recognised skills. It has been argued that apprenticeships were an efficient response to the poaching problem, since they made three parties better off: trainee workers, because the apprenticeship gave them skills portable across firms; firms, because firms with apprenticeships could recoup their training costs over the period of the 'indenture'; and finally, trade unions, because the apprenticeship offered a means of controlling entry to skilled trades (Gospel, 1993). Indeed, it might be argued that it is the increasing power of the last party that has contributed to some of the negative aspects of apprenticeships emphasised by later commentators.

During the twentieth century, apprenticeships increasingly provided trainees with formal qualifications, and the 'indenture' period was reduced from 7 years to 3–5 years. But by the mid-1960s the apprenticeship system was widely seen as being in need of reform. The Donovan Report (1968) criticised apprenticeships because they were time-serving, perpetuated trade demarcations, and were restricted to young men. The 1964 Industrial Training Act established Industrial Training Boards coupled with a levy system to finance approved training, and generally supported apprenticeships while also aiming to encourage their reform and extend their coverage. But by the mid-1970s, in the face of rising unemployment, governments increasingly conflated unemployment and training schemes. The Thatcher Government introduced in the early 1980s the Youth Training Scheme, and abolished mandatory Industrial Training Boards with their training levy schemes, thereby effectively reducing trade union involvement and monitoring of training. These reforms of the Thatcher Government are documented in Gospel (1993), Finegold (Chapter 11 of this volume) and Keep and Mayew (Chapter 14 of this volume), and have had the net effect of undermining apprenticeship training.

The numbers of apprenticeships have declined dramatically (see Felstead and Green, Chapter 12 of this volume). Yet this appears to have occurred as an unplanned result of a number of piecemeal and ad hoc government reforms, with little public discussion as to the advantages and disadvantages of the British apprenticeship system. It is clear that there have been problems with the apprenticeship system, in particular with respect to the fact that they are narrow in scope and have been largely restricted to young men. But the apprenticeship system also has some good features. The institution of apprenticeships can be viewed as an efficient institutional response to the problem of providing employer-based general training, facilitating investment by one or both parties in workers. Apprenticeships also offer a means of screening workers and signalling their value (Maw, 1992; Soskice, 1993).[3] There is considerable interest in vocational training in the form of apprenticeships both in the USA and in Britain. The US government is considering the further development of apprenticeship training as a means of increasing the level of skills for non-college youth.[4] In Britain there is a body of opinion favouring the development of 'traineeships' or apprenticeships, with nationally recognised qualifications, as a means of increasing vocational training for young people leaving school at age 16 (see, for example, Layard (1992)).

Until very recently, there have been no statistical analyses using large-scale data sets to examine British apprenticeships.[5] So what discussion there has been on apprenticeships has not been based on systematic survey evidence. In this context, the aim of our chapter is to take a data set of young men who left school at age 16 and began an apprenticeship *prior to* the labour market reforms of the Thatcher and subsequent governments, and to use these data to inform the debate about pre-reform apprenticeships. How restrictive were these apprenticeships? Did they offer nationally recognised qualifications? Who got them? Were individuals gaining qualifications from their apprenticeship more mobile than those who did not?

To answer some of these questions, we examine in the chapter apprenticeships and apprenticeship qualifications for a cohort of young men in their first 'permanent' job after entering the labour market at age 16. The data set used is the British National Child Development Study Sweep 4 (NCDS4), conducted in 1981. The NCDS has comprehensive information about the first job experienced by school leavers at age 16 and any training received within this job. An advantage of the survey is that it contains valuable benchmark information about the incidence and timing of apprenticeship schemes before the Thatcher Government reforms. This benchmark information should inform the current debate about the impact of apprenticeship schemes on employment duration, mobility and unemployment.

The remainder of the chapter is set out as follows. In Section 2, we describe the data source and the explanatory variables. Section 3 presents conditional logit estimates of the probability of undertaking an apprenticeship with and without qualifications. In Section 4 we present a statistical model of job tenure with multiple destinations and time varying covariates, in order to examine the impact of apprenticeships on tenure in the first job. The final section summarises our findings.

2   The data source and the explanatory variables

The National Child Development Study is a longitudinal survey of all children born in Britain in the week of 3–9 March 1958.[6] For the statistical analysis in this paper, we use a subset of these data. The subsample comprises 2,105 young men who left school at the minimum school-leaving age of 16, who obtained employment in their first job within a year of entering the labour market, and who did not return to further education.[7]

The principal source of training for young men who began employment within a year of leaving school at age 16 in 1974 was the apprenticeship. Of our estimating subsample, 43% began an apprenticeship in their first job. These apprenticeships provided a mix of on-the-job experience and day- or block-release courses at local colleges. There were so few young men receiving other forms of training in their first jobs that we omitted these from our analysis, both because of the small cell sizes and because we wished to focus on apprenticeships and job tenure.[8] We focus on men only in our study, because the NCDS4 data show that relatively few women undertook apprenticeship training, and female apprenticeships were predominately in hairdressing. (See Cook (1983) for a gender breakdown of completed apprenticeships.) Of young men starting an apprenticeship in their first job, 72% completed. The average duration of a completed apprenticeship was 46 months, while the average length of a terminated apprenticeship was 15 months. On average, youths who began an apprenticeship in their first job started the apprenticeship just under a month after beginning employment. Of those completing an apprenticeship, 90% gained a formal nationally recognised qualification.[9] Of young men completing an apprenticeship in their first job, 32% gained the City and Guilds Craft qualification, 35% achieved the City and Guilds Advanced qualification (a prerequisite for which is the City and Guilds Craft qualification), while 23% gained a miscellany of other qualifications. Of those youths who did not complete, only 28% did so because the employer terminated the arrangement, by sacking the worker or making him redundant, or through firm closure. Individuals beginning an apprenticeship were also asked if their apprenticeship had affected their long-term job prospects; 77% of those starting an apprenticeship thought it had improved their long-term job prospects 'a lot'.

The NCDS contains information about a number of variables which are potential determinants of the probability of undergoing an apprenticeship and which may affect tenure in the first job. Information on *individual attributes* includes the type of secondary school the respondent attended (independent, grammar, or other), ethnic origin, months spent unemployed between leaving school and starting the first job, information about the father's social class, and finally, the individual's ability. We use as an academic ability measure the sum of age 16 maths and comprehension test scores (*ABILITY*). This is a continuous variable, with a maximum of 66. This ability measure is used in preference to the O-level and CSE public examination results of the summer of 1974 because these are likely to be endogenous to the school-leaving decision. Once a youth has decided to leave school as soon as legally possible, or if a job has been found before leaving school, he may not work for the public examinations or even sit them. However, we did experiment with inclusion of O-level and CSE results instead of the ability measure. In all cases, the coefficient to this variable took the same sign as the *ABILITY* score, and was significant.[10]

Firm characteristics used in the estimating equations include the size of the establishment employing the youth, whether the establishment is in the private sector or not, and sometimes industry dummy variables.[11] Full definitions of the variables used and their means are given in the Appendix.

3   Who starts an apprenticeship in their first job?

The reduced form logit estimates of the probability of embarking on an apprenticeship, conditional on having left school at age 16 without returning to full-time education, are presented in Table 13.1. What do the estimates reveal about the conditional apprenticeship probability? First consider the impact of individual attributes. The estimates show that the probability of a young man beginning an apprenticeship is significantly increased by his measured ability, *ABILITY*, and if his father is a skilled manual worker. The positive impact of *SKILLPA* suggests either nepotism in the obtaining of apprenticeships or a paternal role model effect.[12] The conditional apprenticeship probability is reduced significantly with months spent in unemployment before beginning the first job, with the variable *DISABLED*, if the youth attended a grammar school, and if his father is a semi-skilled manual worker.

Now consider the impact of firm or industry characteristics. Relative to the base of all omitted industrial groups, apprenticeships are significantly more likely to be found in 'metal manufacturing', and 'construction'. Apprenticeships are significantly less likely to be found in 'agriculture, forestry and fishing', 'banking and financial services', and 'other services'. Apprenticeships are significantly less likely to be found in the private sector; it will be interesting to see in time series work if privatisation has had a negative impact on apprenticeship training in Britain. Finally, note

Table 13.1. Conditional logit estimates of the probability of entering an apprenticeship

Parameter	Estimate
Constant	−2.188
	(−8.2)
Individual characteristics	
ABILITY	0.046
	(9.0)
DISABLED	−0.380
	(−1.4)
GRAMMAR	−1.270
	(−4.4)
ETHNIC	0.384
	(0.9)
UNEMP	−0.157
	(−2.9)
SKILLPA	0.241
	(2.3)
SEMISKILLPA	−0.504
	(−3.1)
Firm characteristics	
ESTSIZE	0.203
	(5.4)
PRIVATE SECTOR	−0.453
	(−3.0)
Industry dummy variables	
AGRICULTURE	−1.525
	(−3.5)
METAL MANUFACTURING	1.021
	(7.3)
OTHER MANUFACTURING	−0.317
	(−2.0)
CONSTRUCTION	1.243
	(8.7)
BANKING, FINANCE, PUBLIC ADMIN. ETC.	−1.135
	(−5.5)
MISIND	0.660
	(1.4)
Log-likelihood	−1,221.4
Log-likelihood with constant only	−1,443.6
$\chi^2(7)$	444.4
Number of cases	2,105

Asymptotic t-statistics given in parentheses.

Table 13.2. Predicted apprenticeship probabilities conditional on leaving school at age 16 (percentages)

Variable	
Base[a]	48.48
Base + ability score of 45 points	62.03
Base + *SKILLPA*	54.49
Base + 12 months' unemployment prior to first job	12.51
Base + *SEMISKILLPA*	36.24
Base + largest size establishment	58.54
Base + private sector establishment	37.43

[a] The base individual represents a youth with average ability (33 points), employed in an establishment of average size in the public sector, with no history of unemployment before starting the first job, and with other dummy variables set to zero.

from Table 13.1 that larger firms also provide more apprenticeships. Note that the specification in Table 13.1 passes the log-likelihood ratio test.

The picture of apprenticeships sketched by the NCDS4 data is that, in the late 1970s, apprenticeships were offered to young men of higher ability than the bulk of school leavers at age 16 who did not enter further education; they were more likely to be undertaken by youths whose fathers were skilled manual workers but less likely if the father was a semi-skilled manual worker; they were prevalent in larger firms and in the public sector; and they were found in a narrow range of industries. The predicted apprenticeship probabilities for some of the significant variables are shown in Table 13.2

We now consider the impact of apprenticeships, with and without various possible qualifications, on the tenure and mobility decisions of young men.

4   The impact of apprenticeship qualifications on mobility

What is the impact of apprenticeships and apprenticeship qualifications on the tenure and mobility decisions of young men? Employment in the first job may end in a number of mutually exclusive ways; because of the nature of the data, we consider three destinations for men leaving their first job – *voluntary* quits to another job, *voluntary* quits into unemployment, and *involuntary* termination of employment (which may result in unemployment or employment).[13] Employment in the first job may not have ended by the survey date of 1981, in which case the observation is *right*-censored. An advantage of our duration data is that they begin with entry into the labour market, so problems of *left*-censoring of employment spells are avoided.[14] This section reports the results of estimation of a competing risks duration model explicitly taking into account the timing of apprenticeships with and without qualifications, their duration, and the impact of apprenticeships on the hazards of departure to the various destinations. The model with two competing risks is derived in Booth and Satchell (1994). We recognise that the apprenticeship is typically of a fixed duration, and therefore our job duration modelling does not really capture the structure of the problem, since a man completing an apprenticeship has to be employed for nearly 4 years on average by definition.[15] Therefore we regard the results in this section as at best suggestive. We hope in the future to model the impact of apprenticeships on job tenure using the Fifth Sweep of the NCDS, with longer durations after apprenticeship completion. This would allow us to follow the modelling strategy outlined in the previous footnote.

In Table 13.3, we present the results of estimation of the competing risk model with the three destinations.[16] Estimation of the model was carried out using LIMDEP Version 6.0, employing the Weibull specification. The Weibull was chosen as it nests the exponential as a special case, and has a closed form expression for the hazard rate (unlike the Gamma distribution which nests the Weibull as a special case). The impact of apprenticeships and apprenticeship qualifications has been captured by the inclusion of five dummy variables – *APPNOQUAL* (which takes the value one where the youth completed an apprenticeship in first job, with no qualifications, and zero otherwise), *APPCRAFT* (completed apprenticeship in first job with City and Guild craft qualifications), *APPADV* (completed apprenticeship in first job with City and Guild advanced qualifications), *APPOTHQUAL* (completed apprenticeship in first job with other qualifications), and finally *APPTERM* (terminated apprenticeship in first job). There has been some speculation in the literature that training with nationally recognised qualifications makes labour more mobile and poaching by other firms easier. If this is the case, it might be expected that apprenticeships with qualifications have a relatively larger impact on mobility than apprenticeships without.

From Table 13.3, it can be seen that all the apprenticeship variables are significant. Completed apprenticeships, with and without qualifications, significantly *reduce* the exit rate to each of the three destinations, while terminated apprenticeships *increase* each exit rate, relative to the base of no training. The finding that completed apprenticeships significantly reduce the exit rate to each of the three destinations suggests that both employers and youths with completed apprenticeships wish to continue

Table 13.3. Competing risks estimates with time-varying covariates

Parameter	Voluntary job-to-job	Voluntary job-to-unemployment	Involuntary job termination
Constant	−4.233	−6.185	−5.220
	(−20.28)	(−10.35)	(−17.37)
ABILITY	0.005	−0.019	−0.014
	(1.35)	(−1.98)	(−2.90)
DISABLED	−0.234	0.427	0.139
	(−1.00)	(1.00)	(0.58)
UNEMP	−0.087	0.192	0.152
	(−1.84)	(2.77)	(4.52)
GRAMMAR	−0.451		0.096
	(−1.92)		(0.30)
ESTSIZE	−0.105	−0.012	−0.056
	(−3.46)	(−0.16)	(−1.34)
PRIVATE	0.484	0.458	1.000
	(3.83)	(1.21)	(4.94)
Apprenticeship variables			
APPNOQUAL	−3.124	−2.251	−1.909
	(−4.91)	(−1.91)	(−4.11)
APPCRAFT	−2.663	−2.561	−2.289
	(−8.46)	(−2.98)	(−6.35)
APPADV	−2.466	−2.264	−2.439
	(−9.17)	(−3.23)	(−6.79)
APPOTHQUAL	−2.607	−3.002	−2.694
	(−7.30)	(−2.54)	(−5.26)
APPTERM	0.419	1.048	0.797
	(2.90)	(3.46)	(5.04)
Weibull exponent	0.836	0.882	0.849
	(SE 0.027)	(SE 0.080)	(SE 0.039)
Log-likelihood	−4,667.45	−964.21	−3,004.25
Log-likelihood constant only	−4,969.14	−1,025.98	−3,235.37
No. of cases	902	139	538

1. Other variables included in the estimation but not reported in the table are industry dummies, with base of industries 60–69 SIC.
2. Asymptotic t-ratios are given in parentheses.
3. Number of cases in the censored category is 526.
4. GRAMMAR omitted from second category, owing to small cell size.

the employment relationship. Employers are relatively more likely to retain trained workers, since involuntary layoffs are reduced by the four completed apprenticeship dummy variables. Moreover, trained workers are relatively more likely to want to stay, since voluntary quits are reduced by these completed training variables. It is interesting to note that the negative impact of a completed apprenticeship varies according to the type of qualification received. Those men completing with no qualification are relatively less likely to move voluntarily to another job than men with some form of general qualification. Men with no qualifications after an apprenticeship are also relatively more likely to be involuntarily terminated.

It is likely that financial inducements are provided by employers to workers who have revealed their skill and perseverance through the long period of a completed apprenticeship. Unfortunately, the NCDS does not contain wages data at the point of exit from the first job or at the starting date of the second job.[17]

What is the impact of the other explanatory variables on tenure in the first job? Voluntary quits to another job are significantly increased if the young man is employed in the private sector, and significantly reduced if he has attended a grammar school for his secondary education, or is employed in a larger establishment, or with months unemployed before his first job. For the second risk category (voluntary mobility into unemployment), the quit rate is significantly increased if the youth has already experienced unemployment before his first job, but significantly reduced by *ABILITY*. For the third risk category (involuntary exit), the exit rate is significantly reduced by *ABILITY*, and significantly increased by previous unemployment or if the youth is employed in the private sector. None of the parental socio-demographic variables had any impact on mobility, and were therefore omitted from the reported specification.

The log-likelihood ratio test statistic (minus twice the difference between the model log-likelihood and the log-likelihood for constants and Weibull exponents only) is 1,189.2, which is asymptotically $\chi^2(59)$. The critical value at the 99.99% confidence level is 95.969. Thus the model easily passes this test. The second test of the model is to test if $\alpha = 1$, (where α is the Weibull exponent). The t-statistics for $\alpha = 1$ from Table 13.3 are, for each risk category, given by -6.07, -1.48, and -3.87 respectively. This indicates that it would be appropriate to estimate only the job-to-unemployment category as a negative exponential.[18]

It is apparent from inspection of Table 13.3 that the coefficients for all the *completed* apprenticeship dummy variables are of the same sign and similar in magnitude. We therefore test the hypothesis that the coefficients to the completed apprenticeship variables are the same – in other words, that the qualification achieved does not matter. The apprenticeship estimates from the model where all the *completed* apprenticeship variables are combined into the single variable *APPQUAL* are presented in Table 13.4 (the other variables are omitted

Table 13.4. Competing risks estimates with completed apprenticeship variables combined

Parameter	Voluntary job-to-job	Voluntary job-to-unemployment	Involuntary job termination
Apprenticeship variables			
APPCOMPLETE	−2.607	−2.484	−2.354
	(−14.4)	(−5.2)	(−10.5)
APPTERM	0.419	1.048	0.796
	(2.9)	(3.5)	(5.0)
Weibull exponent	0.836	0.883	0.849
	(SE 0.028)	(SE 0.080)	(SE 0.039)
Log-likelihood	−4,668.1	−964.5	−3,005.0
Log likelihood constant only	−4,969.1	−1,026.0	−3,235.4
No. of cases	2,105		

from the table for brevity – the signs and magnitude are virtually unaltered).

The total model log-likelihood is −8,637.6. The likelihood ratio test statistic (minus twice the difference between the model log-likelihood and the log-likelihood for constants and Weibull exponents only) is 1,185.84, which is asymptotically $\chi^2(50)$; this model thus easily passes the test. Now consider the difference in log-likelihoods between the model in Table 13.3 with the completed apprenticeship variables combined, and the model of Table 13.2; the log-likelihood ratio test statistic is asymptotically $\chi^2(9)$, and is given by 3.4. Therefore we cannot reject the hypothesis that the coefficients of the completed apprenticeship variables are the same. This is an interesting finding, for it suggests that it is the completion *per se* of an apprenticeship that affects the exit rates, and not the type of qualification obtained nor how advanced it was. While it may be the case that the type and level of qualification received while undergoing an apprenticeship has a significant influence on subsequent labour market experience, our results suggest that the exit rates from the first job are unaffected. It is the completion or termination of apprenticeships that appear to have significant and opposite effects on early job tenure and mobility of young men in our sample. However, since the 'excess duration' – the period in months between apprenticeship completion and the survey date – is typically small for men in the censored category, we hope to investigate this issue further when the NCDS5 data become available.

5   Conclusion

The apprenticeship was the principal form of training received by male school leavers at age 16 in the 1970s. The picture of apprenticeships sketched by the NCDS4 data is that, in the late 1970s, apprenticeships were offered to young men of higher ability than the bulk of school leavers at age 16 who did not enter further education; they were more likely to be undertaken by youths whose fathers were skilled manual workers but less likely if the father was a semi-skilled manual worker; they were prevalent in larger firms and in the public sector; and they were found in a narrow range of industries. Very few women received apprenticeship training in Britain over the period, and therefore we did not examine female apprenticeships in this chapter.

We also estimated a competing risks model of the hazards of exit from the first job into several competing destinations, in order to examine the impact of apprenticeship qualifications on tenure and job mobility. Our estimates produce the following results, which are tentative owing to the limited data in NCDS4 on employment duration after apprenticeship completion. It appears that it is the completion or termination of apprenticeships that have significant and opposite effects on early job tenure and mobility of young men in our sample. However, it is interesting to note that the negative impact of a completed apprenticeship varies according to the type of qualification received. Men completing with no qualification are relatively less likely to move voluntarily to another job than men with some form of general qualification. Men with no qualifications after an apprenticeship are also relatively more likely to be involuntarily terminated.

Appendix: Variable definitions

Variable name	Definition	Mean
Individual attributes		
ABILITY	Sum of age 16 maths (0–31) and comprehension (0–35) test scores	32.738
ETHNIC	Non-white ethnic origin	0.0114
DISABLED	Handicapped or disabled	0.0380
GRAMMAR	Educated at grammar school (state-run for children of higher measured ability at age 11)	0.0352
UNEMPL	Months spent unemployed before starting first job (maximum 12)	2.5548
SKILLPA	Skilled manual father or male head of household	0.3553

Variable name	Definition	Mean
SEMISKILLPA	Semi-skilled manual father or male head of household	0.1192
TENURE	Months in first job	39.664
Firm characteristics		
ESTSIZE	Banded variable indicating numbers employed at establishment 1 denotes ≤ 10 2 denotes 11–24 3 denotes 25–99 4 denotes 100–499 5 denotes ≥ 500	2.9397
PRIVATE	First job in a private firm or limited company	0.8366
Apprenticeship variables		
APPNOQUAL	Completed apprenticeship in first job with no qualifications	0.0271
APPCRAFT	Completed apprenticeship in first job with craft qualifications	0.0813
APPADV	Completed apprenticeship in first job with advanced qualifications	0.0884
APPOTHQUAL	Completed apprenticeship in first job with other qualifications	0.0580
APPTERM	Abandoned apprenticeship in first job	0.1083
APPCOMPLETE	Completed apprenticeship in first job	0.3311
Industry dummy variables		
AGRICULTURE	Agriculture, forestry, fishing SIC 1–3	0.0337
ENERGY	Energy and water supply SIC 11–17	0.0266
MINING	Extraction minerals/ores other than fuels SIC 21–26	0.0565
METAL MANUFACTURE	Metal manufacturing SIC 31–38	0.2000
OTHER MANUFACTURE	Manufacture of food, leather goods; wood, paper, rubber etc. SIC 41–49	0.1558
CONSTRUCTION	Construction SIC 50	0.1696
DISTRIBUTION	Distribution etc.; hotels, catering SIC 61–68	0.2119
TRCOM	Transport; post and telecommunications SIC 71–79	0.0451
BANKING-FINANCE	Banking, financial services etc. SIC 81–86	0.0228
OTHER SERVICES	Public administration, education, other services SIC 91–99	0.0675

NOTES

We would like to thank the Leverhulme Trust for financial support, and Peter Shepherd of the Social Statistics Unit at the City University for facilitating access to the National Child Development Study, and for advice with the data. We would also like to thank Raj Badiani for careful research assistance and Nigel Foster for computing assistance. Any errors are our responsibility.

1 Recent studies of training and its earnings impact include Barron *et al.* (1989), Blanchflower and Lynch (1995), Booth (1991, 1993), Lillard and Tan (1992), Lynch (1992), and Tan *et al.* (1992).

2 According to general human capital theory, training that is general should be financed by the individual (assuming perfect capital markets). If the firm were to bear all the costs of general training provision, the worker might quit as soon as training is completed, and the firm would lose its training investment to the poaching firm. The poaching problem arises through the fact that labour is ex post mobile, and can use the training in another firm. Firms are therefore unwilling to pay the costs of general training. But if the worker pays for the training costs in this situation through very low wages while training, neither the firm nor the worker will lose.

   The apprenticeship represents an alternative institutional response to this problem: the firm can pay the training costs but create an indenture scheme of a sufficiently long period to amortise its training investment. Such a scheme is particularly attractive if either imperfect capital markets prevent workers from borrowing to finance themselves during their training period, or if unions prevent a low youth wage.

3 In the German system of apprenticeship, for example, prospective trainees compete for places with firms offering apprenticeships, and are selected on the basis of their performance in interviews and examinations. The training firms then retain the cream of the apprentices once their training period has finished (Soskice, 1993).

4 See for example US Department of Labor Reports such as *Work-Based Learning: Training America's Workers* (1989), and initiatives funded by the US Department of Education, such as the *Consortium on Youth Apprenticeship*. US Congress is currently considering a bill to provide grants to states and local areas for the development of youth apprenticeship programmes. For evidence of British government interest, see Her Majesty's Inspectorate (1991).

5 Blanchflower and Lynch (1995) examine the impact of apprenticeships on the earnings of British youth using the National Child Development Study Sweep 4 (NCDS4).

6 See the National Children's Bureau (1984) for further discussion.

7 Cases with missing information were eliminated. Our estimating subsample is comparable to that of Micklewright (1989), although we have slightly fewer cases because of missing information on the timing of employment in the first job and of apprenticeships.

8 There were just 164 men in our initial subsample who received company training in their first job; 72 of these men received training outside the company. We chose to delete these cases from our estimating subsample for two reasons. First, the cell sizes for each risk category or destination were extremely small and hence the results would not be robust. Secondly, we wished to focus attention on apprenticeships.

9 Individuals completing an apprenticeship in Britain typically gain a certificate indicating completion. In addition, they may gain nationally recognised qualifications giving separate certification.

10 NCDS4 has a large number of missing cases for ability at age 16. In another paper (Booth and Satchell, 1994), we experiment with alternative methods of using these missing data, and our results suggest that our specifications are not sensitive to their omission.

11 NCDS4 also asks if individuals were promoted while they were with their first employer. However, the timing of this variable was not requested. Since promotion is likely to be endogenous in a model of job tenure and training, we do not include it as an explanatory variable.

12 We also experimented with the inclusion of a number of other variables measuring parental attributes, such as the educational history of mother and father, whether the father was in work or not, whether both parents were present at all sweeps, and other measures of social class apart from those reported in Table 13.1. None of these variables had any impact, apart from the reported skilled and semi-skilled categories for the father.

13 The NCDS4 contains information about the reason *employment* in the first job was terminated. We group the responses to this question into two classifications: those who left involuntarily, and those who left of their own accord. The involuntary classification includes the following reasons for job termination: firm closed down, redundancy, sacking, and 'other'. The voluntary classification comprises all men who stated they left of their own accord.

14 Averaged over *all* youths with completed apprenticeships, the mean number of months from completion to exit from the first job was 10 months. For youths with terminated apprenticeships, the mean number of months from termination to the end of the first job was just over one month.

15 An attractive alternative approach is to model the *excess duration* of job tenure after completion of a man's apprenticeship, and then to model separately the durations of men whose apprenticeships were terminated and of non-apprenticed men. The expected durations for a typical man with and without an apprenticeship can then be compared. We experimented with estimation of this model, but do not present the results, as the excess duration period was too short to allow for estimation of this model.

16 As noted in Booth and Satchell (1994), the model can be estimated by considering one exit at a time, and treating *all* other observations as censored with respect to that exit. See Cox and Oakes (1984) for a discussion of this in the competing risks model without time-dependent covariates.

17 It was not possible to include a wages variable in the duration model, although we would like to have done so, since an individual considering a job change may move if the offered alternative wage exceeds his current wage. However, the NCDS data preclude this. First, wages data for the first job are starting wages, but final wages are relevant at the job termination point. The difference between these may be large for individuals with tilted wage schedules. Secondly, some youths gave net wages and others gross wages for their starting wage; however, since the deduction was not recorded it is impossible to make all wages data comparable.

18 We did not test for either a more general specification, or for omitted heterogeneity. There are considerable problems with dealing with omitted heterogeneity (see Heckman and Singer (1984)).

REFERENCES

Barron, J. M., D. A. Black and M. A. Loewenstein (1989), 'Job Matching and On-the-job Training', *Journal of Labor Economics* **71**(1), 1–19.

Blanchflower, D. G. and L. M. Lynch (1995), 'Training at Work: A Comparison of US and British Youths', in L. M. Lynch (ed.), *Training and the Private Sector*, Chicago: Chicago University Press.

Booth, A. L. (1991), 'Job-related Formal Training: Who Receives it and What is it Worth?', *Oxford Bulletin of Economics and Statistics* **53**(3), 281–94.

(1993), 'Private Sector Training and Graduate Earnings', *Review of Economics and Statistics* **76**(1), 164–70.

Booth, A. L. and S. E. Satchell (1994), 'Apprenticeships and Job Tenure: A Competing Risks Model with Time-varying Covariates', *Oxford Economic Papers*, Vol. 46(4), pp. 676–95.

Cook, L. (1983), 'Completed Apprenticeships', Working paper No. 15, National Children's Bureau, November.

Cox, D. R. and D. Oakes (1984), *Analysis of Survival Data*, London: Chapman & Hall.

Finegold, D. and D. Soskice (1988), 'The Failure of Training in Britain: Analysis and Prescription', *Oxford Review of Economic Policy* **4**(3), 21–53.

Gospel, H. (1993), 'Whatever Happened to Apprenticeship Training? and What Has Replaced it?', University of Kent, mimeo.

Heckman, J. and B. Singer (1984), 'A Method for Minimising Distribution Assumptions in Econometric Models for Duration Data', *Econometrica* **52**(2), 279–320.

Her Majesty's Inspectorate (1991), *Aspects of Vocational Education and Training in the Federal Republic of Germany*, London: Department of Education and Science, HMSO.

Layard, R. (1992), 'The Training Reform Act of 1994', ESRC Annual Lecture.

Lillard, L. and H. Tan (1992), 'Private Sector Training: Who Gets it and What Are its Effects?', *Research in Labor Economics* **13**, 1–62.

Lynch, L. M. (1991), 'The Role of Off-the-job vs. On-the-job Training for the Mobility of Women Workers', *American Economic Review Papers and Proceedings* **81**(2), 151–5.

(1992), 'Private Sector Training and the Earnings of Young Workers', *American Economic Review* **82**(1), 299–312.

Maw, J. W. (1992), 'Time-serving Apprenticeships', University College Swansea, mimeo.

Meyer, B. (1990), 'Unemployment Insurance and Unemployment Spells', *Econometrica* **58**(4), 757–82.

Micklewright, J. (1989), 'Choice at Sixteen', *Economica* **56**, 25–39.

National Children's Bureau (1984), *National Child Development Study (1958 Cohort) Fourth Follow-up: Final Report to Sponsors*, London: NCB.

Soskice, D. (1993), 'How the German Apprenticeship System Works', WZB Berlin, mimeo.

Tan, H., B. Chapman, C. Peterson and A. Booth (1992), 'Youth Training in the US, Britain and Australia', *Research in Labor Economics* **13**, Fall.

US Department of Labor (1989), *Work-based Learning: Training America's Workers*, Report prepared under the direction of J. Van Erden, Bureau of Apprenticeship and Training, Employment and Training Administration.

14 Evaluating the assumptions that underlie training policy

This chapter discusses the assumptions underlying official training policy in the UK. It is argued that UK training policy ignores the fact that Britain's vocational education and training problem is one of lack of employer demand for skills rather than one of lack of supply.

Particular attention is focused on the presumption that employers will require ever more highly trained workers at all levels, that training is crucial to their economic success, and that any government support for training must make use of the price system and must place primary responsibility for training decisions in the hands of the employers. It is argued that, in important respects, these views are out of touch with reality.

Keep and Mayhew acknowledge the potential importance of market failures associated with training. But they argue that there is an additional problem of what might be termed 'managerial failure', a problem that is particularly prevalent in Britain. Here managers opt for a low-skill employment strategy relying on cost-competitiveness, which limits their demand for skilled labour. The reasons advanced for 'managerial failure' are as follows. Managers in Britain have been brought up in a confrontational system of industrial relations, where workers are not required to think, and where initiative and talent are required of a minority. Training is a positional good, more of which may threaten existing power relationships. Moreover, the volatility of the British economy relative to other OECD economies makes returns to training harder to quantify than easily comprehended costs. This chapter also argues that short-termism has become institutionalized in Britain through a variety of mechanisms.

Evaluating the assumptions that underlie training policy

EWART KEEP and KEN MAYHEW

The aim of this chapter is to examine the assumptions underlying British training policy in recent years. It argues that many of these assumptions are questionable, and explores the policy implications of this clash between official perceptions and reality. In particular, Britain's skill problem is at least as much one of low demand for skills as one of inadequate supply. Policy concentrates on enhancing supply in a system which is employer-led and which to a large extent ignores deep-seated reasons for lack of employer demand. Thus its effectiveness is likely to be limited.

1   The assumptions that lie behind policy

Analysis of official policy statements reveals a series of interlinked beliefs underpinning initiatives in the 1980s and early 1990s. The main ones have been:

- that training and development act as key determinants of economic success, at the levels of both national economy and individual firm;
- that the UK increasingly will require a labour force consisting of highly educated, skilled, flexible and autonomous workers;
- following on from this, a belief that UK employers will require a highly educated and trained workforce at all levels;
- that a market-based approach, with little place for direct legislative backing for training, is best;
- that this approach will work because the payoff from training, whether for the employer or the employee, will generally be positive;
- that employment and promotion opportunities ought to be strongly influenced by formal skills and qualifications;
- that control of the new training system should be vested with employers, upon whom falls primary responsibility for deciding the nature and volume of training that is required.

We consider each of these assumptions.

2   The link between VET and economic success

What evidence is there to support the notion that levels of training affect economic performance? Beyond a commonsense belief of long standing that this must be so, the evidence is patchy. At the level of the national economy, there is no lack of comparative studies which indicate that other developed countries have more highly qualified workforces (NEDO/MSC/IMS, 1984; Worswick, 1985; Daly, 1986). It is also true that most of these countries have achieved higher rates of long-term growth than Britain, and there is a general presumption that there is a direct link between national economic efficiency and high levels of vocational education and training. Though not everyone accepts this linkage (see, for example, Pratten (1990) and Shackleton (1992)), comparative studies of VET mapping the scale of the UK's relative deficiencies have been used to define the terms on which debate about the need for improvements in national training effort has been conducted (Keep, 1991, p. 25–6).

However, problems occur when we come to look for proof at the level of the individual firm of links between training and good performance. The evidence here indicates that the linkages are complex and indirect. The difficulty stems in part from the fact that it is not always certain to which aspects of company performance training is being linked. If high levels of productivity, or the production of high-quality goods and services is the measure of success, then the evidence available from the studies conducted by NIESR in, for example, clothing (Steedman and Wagner, 1989), furniture manufacturing (Steedman and Wagner, 1987), and retailing (Jarvis and Prais, 1989) suggests a link. However, if profitability, share value or return on investment are the measures of success, the story is much less clear. For example, a large-scale study of management training in the UK found that 'there is no clear evidence on which to conclude that an association exists between return on capital and the proportion of managers trained' (Mangham and Silvers, 1986, p. 20).

Moreover, as the NIESR matched plant comparison studies and other evidence suggests, significant sectors of the UK economy have survived and probably in their own terms viewed themselves as successful, at least to date, despite low levels of productivity, high scrap and wastage rates, and the adoption of product market strategies that require only very low levels of skill. There are also examples of large companies that have been highly profitable without laying much overt stress on having a highly qualified workforce. Equally, investment in training has not guaranteed corporate success.

Disentangling the beneficial results that derive exclusively from training, as opposed to other variables, is a complicated task and there is a danger of confusing cause and effect, not least because of the complex 'virtuous circle' relationships that often exist between skill levels and choice of product market strategies. Many companies recognise this. As *A Challenge to Complacency* noted, 'we found few firms which were prepared to state that they believed in a direct causal relationship from training to profits' (Coopers and Lybrand, 1985, p. 10), though many companies were willing to acknowledge a linkage between training and quality.

The fact that many firms are often apparently less than convinced of a link between training and profits has important consequences for the success of an employer-led training strategy and for reliance on a market-based approach to investment in human capital. This is an issue to which we will be returning later in the chapter.

3   The nature of the UK's future work and occupational structure

The next two assumptions are interlinked: firstly, that the future of work in the UK will increasingly require highly educated and skilled, flexible, autonomous workers; and, following on from this, a belief that UK employers will require a highly educated and trained workforce at all levels. These assumptions are reflected in the work of popularisers of a vision of 'post-industrial' society, such as Toffler, Handy, and Drucker, and in macroeconomic models of labour market developments, such as those undertaken by the Institute of Manpower Studies (IMS) and the Institute of Employment Research (IER).

It has been a commonplace assertion during the last decade that Britain is faced with a fundamental choice about the basis on which the economy faces international competition. One major strand of the official prescription for economic development in the UK has tended to embrace a particular conception of a competitive strategy based upon high-quality, technologically advanced, flexible production. Coupled with this have been frequent references to the changing structure of employment. The decline of manual occupations, craft apprenticeships and craft-based occupations, the reduction of manufacturing jobs, the rise in demand for technicians, and the growth in white collar and professional employment are constant themes in official policy statements (see, for example, MSC (1981, 1983a, 1983b), ED (1988) and CBI (1989)). Increasing competition and demand for quality, coupled with these shifts in occupational structure, are seen as pointing to a future where an independent, self-reliant, flexible and highly skilled workforce will be a necessity (IoD, 1991).

It is undoubtedly true that there have been very significant changes in the composition of the workforce, with a considerable growth in 'higher level' occupations, particularly the professions. This has coincided with an increase in the number of people within the workforce holding qualifications. Projections of future skill demand appear to show a continued rise in employment in white-collar higher-level occupations and a continued decline in manual, semi-skilled and craft occupations (see for example, ED (1992)). However, there have also been developments that may point to a rather different view of skill requirements within the national economy.

3.1   The growth of small firms

Government policy since 1979 has placed great importance on an 'enterprise culture', a standard bearer of which was to be a revitalised small business sector. Small businesses accounted for a disproportionately large share of total job creation. In the services sector, between 1987 and 1989, firms with fewer than ten employees accounted for half of net job creation. In the production sector over the same period firms with fewer than ten employees accounted for 40% of net job generation (Daly et al., 1992). By 1989 firms employing between one and five people accounted for 87.7% of all the businesses in the UK, and 22.4% of all employment; and firms with fewer than fifty workers accounted for 98.8% of the total number of businesses, and 42.3% of employment (Daly and McCann, 1992, p. 48).

Significant sections of the revitalised small firms sector do not chime well with the vision of those who embrace hopes of a high-skill, high-tech UK economy competing successfully in world markets. For instance, Storey's studies of small firm formation in Cleveland in the 1970s and 1980s showed that in the 1980s small firms were often being established in non-tradeable areas, with only 1% of sales being made outside the UK (Storey, 1982; Storey and Strange, 1992). Moreover, no less than 26% of all new firms in Cleveland in the 1980s were engaged in hairdressing, car breaking and garage activities – not sectors whose growth suggests a massive increase in demands for higher-level skills and formal qualifications.

Moreover, a variety of econometric studies (Booth, 1991; Green, 1991) have indicated that small firms are significantly less likely to train their employees than are larger ones, even allowing for the nature of the goods and services they produce. As Finegold (1992) notes, *Training in Britain*

(TA, 1989) suggested that the majority of all training days were accounted for by enterprises with more than 1,000 employees. Yet the number of enterprises of this size was only about a thousand and they employed no more than 27.5% of the workforce (Daly and McCann, 1992).

Data from a 1992 ED survey of small firms' training needs conducted by IFF (IFF, 1992) and from the survey of individuals' perspectives on training, undertaken as part of the *Training in Britain* study (Rigg, 1989) tend to confirm that training provision is relatively weak in very small firms. The IFF survey showed that less than 20% of establishments with between one and four employees were providing off-the-job training, as compared with more than 40% of establishments with between ten and twenty-four employees. The *Training in Britain* survey of adults suggested that workers in establishments with fewer than five people were half as likely to have been trained in the last three years as other employees (Rigg, 1989).

3.2 The growth in self-employment

Between 1981 and 1991 self-employment increased by 1.1 million (a rise of 52%), to a total of 3.3 million (Campbell and Daly, 1992). The incidence of training among the self-employed is far lower than for the employed workforce. The 1992 Labour Force Survey indicated that whereas 14.9% of the sample as a whole had received job-related training in the preceding four weeks, the figure for the self-employed was only 6% (ED, 1992, p. 57).

3.3 The growth in part-time work

There has been a significant increase in part-time employment in the UK, with the result that by 1988 there were more than five million part-time workers, representing almost a quarter of all employees. The vast bulk of part-time jobs are concentrated in relatively low-level occupations such as clerical work, selling, catering, cleaning, hairdressing and other personal services. Such is the clustering in lower-status, lower-skill occupations that Dex remarks, 'part-time work appears to be being defined as inherently low skilled' (1988, p. 290). An Employment Department analysis of the 1992 LFS data commented that, 'a large proportion (14 per cent) of women full timers received training, more than men or women working part time ... Nearly as many women work part time as full time and very few of the former received training' (Labour Market Quarterly Report, February 1992, p. 6). If the proportion of part-time jobs is growing, then it is at least possible that the proportion of jobs regarded by employers as unskilled is also growing. As in the case of small firms, econometric evidence suggests that, even controlling for other variables, part-time employment involves relatively little training.

Finally, forecasts of future employment growth suggest that, while the largest expansion of job opportunities will be concentrated in the managerial, professional and technical levels (ED, 1992, p. 19), 'personal and protective services represent the main growth area for employment outside the managerial and professional occupations with an additional 300,000 (16 per cent) by the end of the century' (ED, 1992, p. 20). The only other area showing above average rates of growth will be sales-based occupations. Thus the skill requirements of managerial, technical and professional occupations may justify the forecast decline in skilled craft employment in manufacturing, and the continued growth of employment in the relatively low-skilled parts of the service sector, such as personal and protective services, where part-time employment is also prevalent.

The foregoing comments about small firms, self-employment, part-time work and shifts in occupational structure are not meant to suggest that the trends towards a higher global requirement for skill within the British economy reported by bodies such as the IER and IMS are wrong. They simply point to countervailing developments in the structure of employment that mean that there are large areas of employment where skill requirements and training effort are and will remain limited and where there may be active de-skilling of segments of the workforce.

4   The need for a highly trained workforce

This brings us to the belief that UK employers will require a highly educated and trained workforce at all levels. In general the high-skills route is probably the only one that advanced, high-wage economies can sustain in the long term (Streeck, 1989); and indeed it is this realisation which, at least in part, motivates the training debate. Nevertheless, in the shorter term it is perfectly possible for high-skill, high-wage sectors to co-exist with low-wage, low-skill sectors (Ashton *et al.*, 1987; King, 1990, pp. 150–1; McNabb and Ryan, 1990). At the same time, while the changes in organisational structure and workforce utilisation that are being advocated by the evangelists of a high-skill, high-tech future may be the best strategic direction in which to proceed, they are not the only options available to many UK enterprises, at least in the short- to medium-term. These alternatives include increasing use of crude work-intensification practices, low pay, insecure and casualised employment, and the subcontracting of more complex parts of production.

There is some ambiguity in the government's stance towards the choice of competitive strategy. On the one hand, ministers and civil servants have painted the vision of a high-wage, high-tech, high-skill future outlined above. On the other, the utilisation by companies of strategies centred on price-based competition would not be inconsistent with those strands of government policy which have sought to emphasise low wage costs as a source of competitive advantage, and which have laid considerable stress on the benefits to be reaped from possessing the most deregulated labour markets in Europe (Emerson, 1988).

Utilisation of competitive strategies based on price rather than quality plays an important role in determining managements' perceptions of the levels of skill they require. The case for up-skilling and high-value-added strategies may also be undermined by the structure of demand in the UK economy. Producing high-tech, high-quality goods and services that require high levels of skill is not, in itself, intrinsically important to a company. The issue of overriding concern is whether or not its product market strategy allows it to survive and to make adequate (however defined) levels of profit. If companies can achieve these ends through the production of low-cost, low-quality, high-volume goods and services that require minimal skill levels, then there is little reason for them to alter their strategies.

For example, much has been made in recent years of the improvement in profit that retailers can realise by abandoning a pile-it-high-and-sell-it-cheap approach, and moving upmarket, thereby achieving higher value added per unit of goods or service sold. The examples of retailers like Marks and Spencer and J. Sainsbury are held out as proof of the value of adopting such a strategy, and others, for example Tesco, have followed in their footsteps. However, the pursuit of a price-based competition strategy may be highly rational if the goods and services which companies are producing are aimed largely at certain segments of the UK home market. Put simply, Britain contains a large number of people of modest disposable income, who are not in a position to purchase expensive, high-quality goods and services. There is likely to be a significant market for goods and services that have low cost as their main selling point.

Given the influences outlined above, it is hardly surprising that the product market strategies of sections and skill requirements of the British economy exhibit considerable diversity. There is little doubt that there are companies, such as British Steel (Morris *et al.*, 1991), Rover Group (Muller, 1991), and ICI, where competitive strategies based on high-quality production and high value added mean that a more flexible, autonomous and highly skilled workforce is regarded as an essential prerequisite for success. There are a great many other employers (Keep, 1990) pursuing product market strategies based on the production of low-quality, low-cost goods and services using Taylorist methods of work organisation, who are more likely to want a cheap, relatively low-skilled workforce of people who do what they are told.

4.1   Low-skill jobs

Of the existence of a significant number of these types of jobs there can be little doubt. As Sir Bryan Nicholson, chair of the National Council for Vocational Qualifications (NCVQ) has commented, 'there are jobs in the British economy that can be achieved with only modules of NVQ Level 1' (Nicholson, 1991). A report on skills in the plastics industry, commissioned by the Training Agency, the EITB, and the Plastics Processing Industry Training Board (Rigg *et al.*, 1989), demonstrated that not only was training provision in the sector weak, but that many employers viewed training for process operators as a waste of time because the skill requirements of the job were so limited. One employer commented that the requirements for being a process operator were 'two arms and two legs' (1989, p. 52).

Perhaps some of the clearest indications that many employers believe in the necessity of only a very limited span of training for many employees came when the move from one-year to two-year YTS was announced (Chapman and Tooze, 1987, p. 60). Jim Foulds, the personnel director of DRG Group, commented:

> Given the nature of many of the jobs available, it is already hard to provide sufficient content for the one-year scheme and still be credible in the eyes of those concerned. Youngsters are quick to see the difference between the training being given and the tasks which they will be required to do ... The crux of the issue on the move from one-year to two-year YTS is that we are moving from building a bridge between education and business, something most businesses can cope with, to real vocational education and training, something many of the schemes may have difficulty in coping with. (Milton, 1986, p. 29)

The presence of a substantial residual of jobs where low skills are likely to remain the norm for the foreseeable future, casts serious doubt on the ability of the new market-based training system to function as intended. The existence of a large number of such employment opportunities will help to undermine the training strategy being advocated by government and bodies such as the CBI. For example, the planned reform of the youth labour market, via the introduction of Training Credits, is crucially dependent upon the removal of the significant number of dead-end jobs without training which are currently on offer to young people. In the absence of any statutory obligation to provide training for young employees, there are good reasons for doubting that employers in low-skill sectors will cooperate (Cassels, 1990, pp. 32–7; Lee *et al.*, 1990).

4.2   Discrimination and equality of access to training

Official training policy in the 1980s had relatively little to say about issues of equality of access to training for disadvantaged groups. Failure to address these issues is an important omission given the volume of econometric and survey evidence suggesting that, holding other variables constant, gender, race and age can play a crucial role in determining access to training opportunities.

Even worse, these other variables are not in fact constant. For example, the distribution of women across occupational groupings is heavily skewed. They are under-represented in skilled manufacturing employment. Indeed women's share of skilled work in manufacturing in Britain has shrunk throughout this century (Purcell, 1988, p. 168). This skewed distribution, as Cockburn (1987) demonstrates, tends to exhibit a capacity to be self-sustaining. The young are channelled by the existing structure of employment and gender segregation into making 'realistic' choices about training and career opportunities, i.e. choices that reflect existing patterns of segregation. The result is the danger of a vicious circle that ensures that the employment pattern of the past remains more or less unchanged in the future.

What is the impact of this on training? The most obvious is that many people may be being misdirected into occupations where their talents cannot be made best use of. Attempts by individuals to challenge these divisions indicate that the ability of a trainee to exercise choice of future occupation is currently heavily circumscribed by gender barriers, as, for example, Cockburn's (1987) work on YTS underlines.

Gender also plays a major part in defining what is skilled work. As Dex comments, 'there is a sense in which "unskilled" comes to be defined as anything which women do' (1988, p. 289). In some sectors access to skilled status, and the pay that goes with it, is largely a factor of gender. Thus, 'for a woman to become skilled in the clothing industry, she would have to change her sex' (Dex, 1988, p. 290). One consequence of gender-based definitions of skill, and of poorer pay and promotion opportunities, is to make investment by women in their own training highly problematic. Given the record of employers in investing more heavily in training men than women, current public policy of leaving training decision making in the hands of employers does not augur well for women (Payne, 1990).

In the mid-1980s, the major force that had been expected to provide the impetus for a market-based challenge to discrimination was enlightened self-interest on the part of companies, in the light of demographic change (specifically falling numbers of young people entering the labour market) and associated shifts in the structure of the UK labour market. The subsequent sharp and prolonged recession has created very different labour market conditions, including a significant increase in youth unemployment. The tight labour market that was supposed to drive employers towards enlightened self-interest has vanished, and it is uncertain when, and indeed if, it will return.

There is a more deep-seated reason to doubt that a market-based approach reliant on voluntarism, exhortation and a willingness on the part of employers to change themselves, would be able to deliver significant shifts in the divisions that structure occupational choice and opportunity. Discrimination and segregation of career and training opportunities start early on in life, well before people reach the labour market. Attempts at fundamental change therefore have to address broader questions than simply the training opportunities that are being offered. Certainly the evidence of YTS and YT suggests that the largest attempt to provide structured vocational preparation for young people in the UK has had little more than marginal effects upon traditional gender divisions within training provision and occupational choice (Cockburn, 1987; TA *Youth Training News*, No. 55, June/July 1989, p. 24; Lee *et al.*, 1990).

Gender is but one example of discrimination within the training and labour markets. Much the same sorts of difficulties arise with regard to race and age. Current policies have tended to passively reflect rather than actively challenge the status quo. Efforts to promote change have been largely limited to exhortation.

5   Market-based approaches to training

As there is insufficient space here to probe every aspect of reliance on market mechanisms, what follows concentrates on the key question of the payoffs that result from investment in training. An individual worker or an employer will make an investment in training only if the net payoff is perceived to be positive. First the payoffs to the individual are examined, and then the company's perspective.

5.1   The growing emphasis on the individual

Of late, perhaps because of some of the difficulties with achieving greater employer investment, the individual 'has taken centre stage in government policy on training in Britain' (Payne, 1992, p. 1). Government policy asserts that, 'for individuals, investment in training is the best way to ensure both greater job security and enhanced earnings over the course of their working lives' (ED, 1988, p. 59). Investment by an individual is likely to take the form of time, effort, and income forgone while under training. Unless the subsequent payoffs are positive, in terms of higher subsequent lifetime earnings, a training market is unlikely to produce significant increases in the supply of skills. Thus reliance on a training market supported by individual investment carries with it a conviction that a strong link exists between qualifications and skill, and employment and promotion opportunities.

5.2   Skill and reward structures

The evidence to support such assumptions is in many instances weak. Indeed, with the possible exception of degree-level education, there is very scant evidence that British pay and reward structures are able to provide substantial incentives to the individual to acquire skills. To begin with, the financial returns available to young people who invest in obtaining post-16 vocational and academic qualifications are often extremely poor. Research by Bennett et al. (1992) showed that the returns to post-compulsory education and training are mixed, with degrees and higher-level vocational qualifications generally enhancing lifetime earnings, but with low-level vocational qualifications, and for many males even A-levels, producing only very modest and in some cases negative returns. They conclude that low demand for skills from employers produces inadequate returns to young people who invest in skills and qualifications, and that this situation in turn reduces the demand of young people for post-compulsory education and training. Thus, 'many young people are quite rational in not pursuing training – it does not give them great enough reward' (1992, p. 2).

These findings reflect broader problems with the links between skill and reward in the workplace. As the survey of employers' training activities reported in *Training in Britain* (TA, 1989) demonstrated, more than a quarter of those establishments that train regarded it 'as a serious drawback that newly trained employees might want more money' (Mayhew, 1991). Training poses this problem because, in many UK enterprises, 'pay and status are rarely linked to the attainment of qualifications or to attendance at training courses, so they provide little incentive to British employees to seek further training' (Coopers and Lybrand Associates, 1985, p. 13). Differentials in the UK between the skilled and unskilled are often low by international standards (Layard *et al.*, 1992).

While the overall picture on differentials is gloomy, there are signs that some British employers are beginning to shift payments systems and reward structures towards a greater recognition of skills (*Employee Development Bulletin*, **31**, July 1992, pp. 2–7). The development of skills-based pay is so far limited, but the fact that some major employers are making moves in this direction may be an indication that UK employers are at last beginning to realise the significance of links between investment in skill and pay.

5.3   The influence of past deficiencies on perceived payoffs

Another problem with relying on individual investment in a training market is the fact that the likelihood of obtaining training is heavily correlated with the individual's position within occupational and management hierarchies. Research suggests that an individual's capacity to perceive the benefits of training is structured by levels of prior educational qualification and the degree to which the receipt of training has already figured in their working lives. Hence those most in need of training, because they have to date received very little, are often the least likely to perceive it as being of value (Rigg, 1989; Fuller and Saunders, 1990). In the absence of access to well-developed internal labour markets (ILMs) for many manual and semi-skilled employees (Millward and Stevens, 1986), such beliefs may be well-founded.

5.4   Job structures, ILMs and internal progression

The idea that the individual can be expected to foot the bill for his or her own training presupposes certain features of the labour market in which the individual is working, or seeking work. A recent White Paper on training proposes that:

> Skills and qualifications will be crucial factors shaping the prospects of individual people at work. For many they may make the difference between success and failure. They have the potential to enable individuals to take control of their working lives and shape them – far more than was possible in the past – into careers that reflect their personal ambitions and preferences. The aim must be to enable them to

obtain the skills and qualifications they need and want ... It is central to the White Paper as whole. (*People, Jobs and Opportunity*, 1992, p. 23)

The authors of this statement appear to assume the job structures that pertain in professional jobs are also found in other forms of employment. Yet to talk about careers, in any meaningful sense, for many employees is simply to ignore reality. For the majority of process and non-craft skilled workers in many sections of manufacturing industry well-formed ILMs and job security are often lacking, whilst opportunities for progression are minimal with the current employer and limited within the sector as a whole. In the clothing industry, for example, the current situation is that, 'a typical female machinist enters the industry in her early twenties and retires from the industry maybe forty years later – as a machinist' (Bosworth *et al.*, 1990, p. 45).

Retailing, cleaning, distribution, hotels, food and tobacco, clothing and textiles, catering, and leisure and tourism would be examples of sectors where well-developed ILMs and career structures frequently do not exist. These sectors employ a significant proportion of the national workforce. In order to progress, workers employed in such sectors must take the risk of changing jobs and employer.

5.5   The role of skills and qualifications in recruitment

Even where job ladders and ILMs do exist, research suggests that initial access to employment, and promotion thereafter may not be closely linked to the possession of formal skills and qualifications (Jenkins and Troyna, 1983).

Research such as that undertaken by Collinson for the EOC (1988) suggests that problems of informality in recruitment and promotion procedures means that, even in large, sophisticated organisations, 'formal' skills and qualifications may count for relatively little in securing employment or a better job within the organisation, since other criteria dominate the selection process. These criteria include the possession of 'informal' or tacit skills, as well as social and behavioural characteristics – personality, attitude, motivation, health and fitness, appearance, age, marital status, stable work record. In recruiting young workers, research certainly suggests that qualifications may come a long way down the list of desired characteristics. An Employment Department study undertaken in 1990 (ED, 1991) showed that vocational qualifications figured eighth out of nine in the ranking of things employers desired of school-leaver candidates. There are strong indications that social criteria often play a dominant role in the selection of adult workers, in particular the acceptability of candidates in terms of their potential ability to 'fit in' in the workplace (Oliver and Turton, 1982).

As Wood points out (1988), social characteristics and skills may be valid criteria to take into account when seeking to recruit, as the productive process, particularly in the case of the delivery of services, is about social processes and skills as well as technical ones. Nevertheless, insofar as recruitment is dependent upon a range of characteristics and attributes, of which formal skills and qualifications are but one part, and not always the most important, then the case for the individual worker to invest in the acquisition of skill may be weakened.

5.6   *Training and qualification as positional goods*

Training aims to raise the capacity of individuals, or groups of individuals, to deal with problems, undertake new tasks, and assume greater responsibilities. As such, sooner or later, it is likely to disturb existing hierarchies and power relationships within the workplace.

Much of the research on British attitudes towards training has tended to explore the proposition that its benefits have not been fully appreciated. Perhaps one element of the problem is quite the reverse. Perhaps the lack of greater investment in training stems, at least in part, from a very real appreciation by some managers, and other sections of the workforce, of the disadvantages that can accrue from having better educated and trained employees and co-workers. Training may be seen as a threat of erosion of managerial power relationships, traditional pay relativities and status divides.

5.7   *The company's perspective on investment in training*

Many companies see training not as an investment, but as a cost (Coopers and Lybrand Associates, 1985; Hyman, 1992). However, to the extent that training is treated as an investment, research within companies indicates that it is but one of a range of possible solutions to skill shortages – others include recruitment, changes in payment systems, or investing in technology to downgrade skill requirements (Pettigrew *et al.*, 1989, pp. 18–20). It would seem logical to assume that attempts are made, however informally, to weigh the relative costs and advantages of each option.

One of the factors that is likely to complicate this process is the difficulty posed by the 'poaching' of skilled labour. The essence of the problem is easily stated. If a shot of training is transferable rather than specific, then the skills acquired are capable of being used by other employers in addition to the one who pays for the training. In other words there is an externality problem – other chapters in this volume by Stevens and Acemoglu discuss such problems in more detail. In order to recoup his costs, at some point the employer will have to pay the worker less than what other employers who have not borne the initial cost can afford to pay. Companies may rationally choose not to train and to rely on poaching skilled labour from those firms that do. The problem comes in the fact that the more companies that adopt this stance, the fewer remain to undertake training, and the greater the risk they bear of losing those they have trained. Thus, the aggregated result of individually rational self-interested actions may be a self-defeating collective under-supply of training (Streeck, 1989).

Both practitioner and academic opinion is sharply divided as to the importance of the problem that poaching poses. Many employers believe it is a major obstacle. The CBI's Vocational Education and Training Task Force cited poaching of skilled labour as one of the 'four basic weaknesses that will need to be tackled if the skills gap is to be bridged successfully' (1989, p. 33), and a case study from the steel industry (Morris *et al.*, 1991) reveals the degree to which British Steel regarded investment in multi-skilled craft workers as a risk because of the danger of poaching. By contrast, the authors of *A Challenge to Complacency* were 'not convinced that poaching is a major deterrent to the total volume of training undertaken – even if it is for some individual (usually small) firms' (Coopers and Lybrand Associates, 1985, p. 11).

Even if the potential difficulties posed by externalities are left to one side, the process of evaluating the return on a company's investment in training remains problematic. The fundamental difficulty is the weakness of the information on both the costs and benefits of training (Pettigrew *et al.*, 1989; Coopers and Lybrand Associates, 1985). As *Training in Britain* (TA, 1989) indicated, only 19% of training establishments attempted to assess the benefits arising from training, and just 3% tried to measure cost against benefit. If the return on training is relatively uncertain or difficult to forecast, the case for spending on training may be harder to sustain. Indeed, the inability to calculate returns on investment in training might help breed a culture which reinforces the tendency to think of training not as an investment, but rather as a cost (Mayhew, 1991).

Firms may be further encouraged in this view by financial institutions. What is known about the basis upon which many UK takeover bids are made contrasts sharply with the rhetoric about the importance to competitive advantage of investment in training and development. A study by London Business School and Egon Zehnder International (LBS/EZI, 1987) suggested that in only 37% of takeovers had any attempt been made by bidders to evaluate or audit the human resources of the bid target. Even in those cases where efforts were made, they appeared chiefly to be limited to obtaining very basic information about the pensions and salaries of the target's senior managerial employees. Nor has training figured to any great extent in the factors that City analysts choose to use in assessing the future prospects of companies (Coopers and Lybrand Associates, 1985, pp. 13–14).

5.8   The volatility of the UK economy

A further factor which affects the ability of both individuals and their employers to be assured of a reasonable payback on investment in human capital is the volatility of the UK economy. CBI analysis of OECD figures (CBI, 1991, pp. 26–9) shows that the UK has 'experienced a more volatile economic cycle than Germany and Japan, particularly in the 1970s and 1980s' (CBI, 1991, p. 26). The volatility of the UK economy renders problematic investment in anything that has long lead-times and a relatively slow pay back, like training. *A Challenge to Complacency* tends to confirm this problem. It noted that 'overall, uncertainty was the reason most commonly cited by the companies we interviewed for not doing more training' (Coopers and Lybrand Associates, 1985, p. 10). This uncertainty, and the misgivings it promotes about sustained investment in training, may be well placed. The recessions of the early 1980s and 1990s have witnessed the scrapping of significant investments, both in terms of physical capital (plant and equipment), and human capital through the redundancy of skilled workers.

To summarise, major difficulties confront a market-based approach to training in the UK. The failure of reward systems to link skill adequately with pay, the lack of ILMs and job structures that offer opportunity for advancement, the insecurity of employment in many sectors, the weak connection between qualifications and recruitment, the difficulties posed by the role of skills as positional goods and the threat effect of a more meritocratic approach to hiring and promotion, the uncertainty of the payoff from training *vis-à-vis* other forms of investment, the volatility of the UK economy, and the product market strategies being pursued by firms in many sectors, all pose questions for the viability of a system geared solely to responding to market forces.

6   The primacy of the employer in the new system

The final assumption underpinning the new training system is that the views of employers should be afforded primacy within it. The institutional structure that the government has erected to facilitate and oversee the new training market thus hinges upon the actions and abilities of employers. The creation of TECs, Industry Lead Bodies, NCVQ, and the National Training Task Force all reflect beliefs that managers, particularly private sector managers, have access to a set of techniques, knowledge and skills that are not available to other sections of the population, and that possession of these attributes make them uniquely qualified to 'solve' a series of deep-seated structural problems in the country's education and training system.

6.1   The prospects for an employer-led system

After a period in the 1980s when employers did increase their spending and give training to more of their employees, it might seem churlish to doubt this strategy, but there are reasons for concern. There is some suggestion that much of the increased activity involved the relatively narrow fields of developing personal skills and IT competencies (Gallie and White, 1993). More generally the evidence that is available tends to cast doubt on the idea that British management, taken as a whole, constitutes an elite capable on its own of fundamental transformation of VET provision. The general training record of UK private sector companies is, by European standards, relatively poor. Indeed, British managers' perceptions of the value of training are part of the problem which they are now being expected to single-handedly solve.

We do not suggest that all British employers are incompetent or are poor trainers. There are within the UK economy companies, such as ICI and British Steel, which are world leaders in their field, and whose training matches best practice abroad. The problem comes in the fact that the variation in performance between the best and the worst UK manufacturing employers is extremely wide and too few UK companies are world-class players (CBI, 1991).

We would also argue that this situation is caused by a series of deeply rooted and interrelated forces within the UK's industrial structure – forces which constrain the choices open to management.

6.2   The weakness of personnel management

One set of structural factors comes in the shape of the distinctive historical legacy of the UK's industrial relations system and the attitudes it has spawned towards the management of the employment relationship. Many companies lack the types of sophisticated personnel management systems necessary to make effective training and utilisation of workers' abilities a reality. Moreover, a significant proportion of firms offer their employees extremely limited opportunity for progression. This situation reflects a continuing belief on the part of many managements that their staff are 'incapable of thought' (James (1991, p. 4); see also Plowman (1990)).

The reasons for this belief are various. An important one is the legacy of low-trust industrial relations, where passive consent rather than active commitment was the norm, and where knowledge and skill were the contested terrain over which managers and workers (particularly craft workers) fought for control of the work process. The overall effect has been to encourage a reliance by many UK firms on a narrow managerial elite leading a mass of ill-trained workers. It is noticeable that those companies that have invested heavily in training (BS, Rover Group, Norsk Hydro) have normally done so as simply one part of a broader shift to very different models of industrial relations and personnel management, which stress commitment, trust, good communication between management and employees, and the breakdown of status divides (Fox, 1988; Muller, 1991; Williams, 1990).

Unfortunately, as Whipp (1992) indicates, the creation and implementation of human resource management (HRM) policies even within large, relatively sophisticated British companies has often proved halting. Furthermore, there is some evidence which suggests that sophisticated personnel management policies of the type espoused by HRM textbooks may only be appropriate to those product market strategies and production technologies and processes that demand workers with skills that are difficult to replace, and 'to workers who have jobs that are or could be redesigned to engender commitment, individual initiative' (Lloyd and Rawlinson, 1992, p. 189). As the NIESR studies suggested, there are sectors of the British economy where such conditions may not pertain. Lloyd and Rawlinson (1992), for example, demonstrate the irrelevance of HRM techniques to firms in the clothing industry, who see low-cost labour, piecework wage systems, and de-skilling as more accessible routes to competitive advantage. Furthermore, insofar as some government policies, such as the abolition of wages councils, encourage reliance on low wages as a source of competitive advantage, they arguably reduce the pressure on companies to contemplate more radical redesign of jobs and production systems that might enhance opportunities for skill acquisition and utilisation.

It might be argued that this situation is being improved by the 'demonstration effect' of inward investors. However, the evidence for a positive effect on training and skill usage is not encouraging. For example, Peck and Stone's (1991) study of 105 inward investors in north-east England indicated that they employed a higher proportion of unskilled and semi-skilled operatives than native companies, and that over half of the foreign-owned companies relied upon poaching to meet their skill needs. Furthermore Knell's (1992) examination of two large inward investors in West Yorkshire concluded that 'the existing stock of skills in a locality exerts a powerful influence on the ongoing nature of indigenous and inward investment, which as a consequence adapts to, rather than attempts to transform, inherited weaknesses in the local labour force' (1992, p. 18).

Overall, the evidence for a widespread and thoroughgoing transformation of British personnel management and IR along the lines of the sophisticated HRM model is limited (Edwards *et al.*, 1992; Sisson, 1992). Some organisations have attempted to introduce isolated aspects of human resource management (HRM), with greater or lesser degrees of effectiveness, but a coherent, consistent approach has often been lacking (Edwards *et al.*, 1992; Storey, 1992). This incoherence may in turn reflect the low priority that has been afforded to IR and human resource issues in strategic decision making within many British businesses. Sir John Cassels' comment, made apropos of the 'demographic timebomb' is apposite, 'the unfortunate truth is that ... in personnel matters (because labour is so cheap?), most employers live hand-to-mouth and the idea of taking a strategic view and of doing so at board level is quite alien' (Cassels, 1989, p. 6).

6.3   Short-termism in the British economy

Many commentators have suggested that the failure of senior British managers to deal with personnel issues strategically, and their weak performance in making long-term investments in research and development and training, has stemmed in part from the short-term pressures generated by the structure of UK finance capital and the City's preoccupation with the maximisation of short-term profit. Others, such as Marsh (1990) and the CBI Task Force on relations between the City and industry (CBI, 1987) have sought to refute these allegations.

Perhaps the point to be emphasised is that even those who dismiss arguments about structural short-termism within capital markets in the UK are often inclined to criticise the tendency for the management systems of large UK organisations to produce an internal dynamic that encourages a short-term perspective on decision-making (Marsh, 1990). Whatever the reality of external pressures on companies to take a short-term view, many corporate headquarters have developed internal financial control mechanisms that 'peer at the business through numbers'

(Goold and Campbell, 1986). These mechanisms create internal markets within companies, whereby subsidiaries focus on short-term performance as a means of winning investment from the corporate HQ, which acts as a banker. Companies managed on this basis are unlikely to be committed to developing sophisticated human resource strategies, or to make substantial long-term investments in training and developing their workforce.

In more general terms, the distinctive dominance of the finance and accounting function within British management (Armstrong, 1987) has encouraged a situation where management accountancy provides the 'core organisational technology of modern management'. The result has been to concentrate a disproportionate degree of managerial attention on labour cost containment, rather than on increasing the 'performance capacity of labour' (Hyman, 1992, p. 17). In some instances, concentration on labour costs has led to the curtailment of training expenditure, which by accounting convention figures as a cost that is incurred, not as an investment that will produce productivity benefits (CBI, 1985).

The pressures created by financial control systems can be reinforced by their linkage to the reward structure. To the extent that reward systems such as performance-related pay are geared to the achievement of short-term goals, particularly short-term profit maximisation, they may discourage long-term thinking and encourage managers to avoid or defer investment that will only pay back in the long-term, such as training and R&D (Murlis, 1990; Marsh, 1990). By contrast with British and American practice, Japanese companies reward their executives very differently, using systems that place considerable emphasis upon long-term performance within the organisation (Marsh, 1990).

One reason underlying the rise in financial control systems and portfolio planning techniques has been the growth of conglomerates and diversified companies within the UK economy since the Second World War. By 1980, no less than 67% of the top 200 manufacturing and services businesses in the UK could be regarded as being diversified, while only 9% remained in the single business category. The results have been the use of internal control structures that make predominant use of financial criteria of performance, and which place heavy reliance on portfolio management techniques. Portfolio management means that the centre has little long-term commitment to any particular business. If it starts to fail, the preferred option may be to sell it and use the money raised to buy something more profitable. This situation has obvious implications for long-term planning and investment in human resources (Purcell, 1989).

It is probably no accident that those firms normally held up as examples of good training practice in Britain in the 1980s, e.g. British Steel, ICI,

ICL and motor vehicle builders such as Ford, have tended to be single business or related business firms, rather than diversified conglomerates.

6.4   British employers' commitment to the UK economy

Some of the problems of limited demand for skills may be rooted in other developments within the industrial structure of the UK. Large companies dominate output (in 1983 those employing 500 plus represented about 75% of manufacturing value added), and have generally dominated formalised training provision. However, there is a problem in assuming that large UK companies are quite what they seem to be any more. The growth of global competition and the removal of exchange control regulations meant that the 1980s witnessed a very significant shift overseas. Many companies that we tend to think of as 'British' no longer employ the majority of their workforce in this country.

To take just one example, Pilkingtons is usually seen as a major British glass manufacturer, but by 1990 only about 21.6% of the company's workforce was actually employed in the UK, and the company has recently announced the decision to transfer the corporate HQ for its flat glass making businesses to Brussels. Policy makers tend to continue to refer to many of the household names of the British economy as 'big British companies', when in fact they have become multinational enterprises within which the British component of the company's operations, whether measured in terms of employment, or sales, or turnover, has become a dwindling proportion of the whole. For instance, evidence suggests that no more than 40% of the turnover of the top 20 UK-owned engineering companies is now generated within the UK (Williams et al., 1990).

Since the end of exchange control regulations many British-owned companies have been directing an increasing proportion of their investments overseas. In 1987, for example, UK firms spent $31.7 billion on acquisitions in the USA alone (Rodgers and Tran, 1988). Between 1980 and 1988 outward investment by UK companies was in total $133.2 billion. Of course an obvious response is that it is all a matter of swings and roundabouts – the arrival of foreign-owned firms in the UK balances the picture. Against this it is important to note that, over the same period, inward investment into the UK by foreign-owned firms did not balance this outflow, running at slightly less than half ($64.7 billion) the outward figure (CBI, 1991, p. 34). In 1990 inward investment did exceed outward investment, but this year is the exception rather than the rule.

A survey of the annual report of The Times Top 100 Companies for the year 1989/90 indicates the extent of these developments. Annual reports were trawled for data on the distribution of employment between UK and overseas operations. In some cases the details were not available. In others, figures for the UK were aggregated with those for Europe. Moreover, of the 100, several are foreign-owned subsidiaries of overseas multinationals, such as IBM and Esso. Nevertheless, from the data available it was apparent that of the British-owned firms, at least seventeen now employ the majority of their workforce outside the UK. These were, BP (73.9% of employees overseas), Shell Transport and Trading, ICI, BAT (93% overseas), Unilever, Glaxo (65.5% overseas), GKN (56.8% overseas), Redland (69% overseas), Cable and Wireless (75.1% outside Europe), BTR, RTZ (71.2% overseas), Lonhro (89.6% overseas), Beecham Group (68.5% overseas), Cadbury Schweppes (55.1% overseas), Pilkingtons, BOC, and Tate & Lyle.

Other large companies show signs of moving in this direction. These include GEC (with more than a quarter of its workforce overseas), Trust Houses Forte (with 20% overseas), Reed International (41% overseas), Coats Viyella (46.3% overseas), Dixon Group (26.4% overseas), Racal (44.7% outside Europe), Allied Lyons (30% of full-time employees outside the UK), P & O (42.6% outside the UK), and Courtaulds (44% overseas).

While growing internationalisation is a common phenomenon among the developed countries, the British economy is distinctive. Whereas 40% of the total employment of British-owned companies was located abroad, the proportion for American and German-owned companies was 25%, and only 20% for French and Japanese-owned companies (Marginson, 1992). These structural features of ownership, investment and employment have implications for UK training policy. At least some major firms now find themselves with domestic operations that are a dwindling and increasingly marginal proportion of the company's overall activities, and investment in them and the people they employ may no longer be regarded as crucial to the long-term well-being of the firm.

At the very least, the increasing globalisation of economic activity and the UK's tendency to be in the vanguard of overseas investment, raise questions for policies that implicitly link the success of individual major companies to the overall health of the UK economy and its skills supply system, and which explicitly see major UK firms as the engine that drives changes in that skill system. Companies have a choice about where they locate production and where they find skills. If skill supply and a well-educated and trained workforce is a problem in the UK, why not shift that section of production that demands those skills overseas?

6.5 Employer leadership and the low skills equilibrium

Outlined above has been a series of structural factors that, it can be argued, weaken the ability and willingness of many British employers to make major adjustments to their current skill requirements. Perhaps most importantly of all, as Finegold and Soskice (1988) have argued, much of the British economy is arguably trapped in a 'low-skills equilibrium'. Many UK employers find themselves caught in a vicious circle of self-reinforcing factors that perpetuate limited demand for training and skills. Amongst these factors is the possibility that, in the past, firms were forced into a low-skill, low-quality strategy because of their inability to acquire skilled workers. The resort by some sectors of the British economy to product market strategies based on a concentration on simple, standardised products and services and upon low-cost, low-skill competition (see Saunders, 1978; Carter, 1981; Reich, 1983; New and Myers, 1986; Sharp et al., 1987; Steedman and Wagner, 1987; Greenhalgh, 1988; Fonda, 1989; Steedman and Wagner, 1989; Jarvis and Prais, 1989; Mason et al., Chapter 9 in this volume), creates a weak demand for skill. This weak demand for skill within the economy reduces the incentives to training, which in turn produces a poorly skilled workforce. Lack of skill then inhibits moves towards competitive strategies that stress quality as opposed to cost. As evidenced above, the job structures found in many sectors of the economy reflect the broad effects of this problem.

The possible existence of a low skills equilibrium, within at least some parts of the UK economy, in the context of a national training system where employers are the sole determinants of what constitutes an adequate level of training, could be a system that meets the short-term perceived private demands of companies, while failing to supply sufficient training to satisfy the social and strategic needs of the national economy.

7 Conclusions

7.1 The concentration on supply at the expense of demand

Many of the assumptions that have formed the basis of policy have been founded on the underlying prior belief that it is weakness in the supply of skills, rather than weakness in demand, that is the root of Britain's difficulties. During the 1980s vocational education and training (VET) policy was dominated by attempts to adjust the institutional mechanisms of VET supply, in the belief that if only supply could be boosted, demand would take care of itself. History suggests that the opposite may be true.

The example of YTS is a useful one. Moves from a one-year to a two-year scheme revealed that simply offering employers a new supply mechanism through which to upgrade skills failed to produce any fundamental change, because the underlying attitudes towards skill and the demand for it did not change (Chapman and Tooze, 1987). Indeed, British employers may often be providing their workforce with levels of VET which are more or less appropriate to the product market strategies which they are following, and which reflect the levels of service which they currently aim to provide. Case studies conducted in twenty companies as part of the *Training in Britain* exercise, reached the conclusion that 'training decisions are not strongly influenced by the VET infrastructure' (Pettigrew *et al.*, 1989, p. 107).

It follows that attempts to boost the supply of VET without simultaneously tackling those structural characteristics within firms that limit demand for higher levels of education and skill run the risk of creating a situation where the returns from investment in VET will be inadequate – to the individual, to their employer, and to society as a whole. Does this mean that current VET policies are doomed to failure? The answer to this question depends on how one chooses to define the overall thrust of Britain's current education and training strategy. If the aim is to provide a training system that meets, more or less adequately, the current needs of British employers, then success may be possible. If, on the other hand, the policy objectives are more ambitious, and encompass goals such as much greater equality of access to training opportunities, and the provision of levels of training equal to those in other developed economies, levels which could support the general transformation of the British economy towards a high-skill, high-productivity, high-wage equilibrium, then the prospects for success are much less rosy.

7.2   Policy and the internal workings of the firm

Although in the early 1980s the MSC and the Central Policy Review Staff (CPRS) pointed to the problems for training policy created by various rigidities in the deployment of skilled labour within firms, such as demarcation issues, there has been relatively limited interest from policy makers in addressing the internal workings of the firm, in particular the crucial questions of job design and work organisation. This despite the fact that a growing volume of research indicates that the demand for skill and its effective utilisation within the productive process are inextricably bound up with the ways in which work is organised and the employment relationship is managed (see, for example, Lam and Marsden (1992) and Campbell and Warner (1991)). In view of the importance of the ways in which companies deal with skill in the workplace, and the relationship of this with business strategy, Hendry (1990) concludes that, 'it makes more sense to try to influence a company's business and technology strategy than its training activity alone' (1990, p. 6).

The difficulty for policy makers has been that while a convincing case can be made to suggest that questions of training and skill supply are inextricably linked with other issues such as work organisation, job design, product market strategies, employee participation and involvement, and reward systems, these issues have been defined, by the parameters within which training policy has normally been discussed, as falling within the confines of managerial prerogative. For the state, or other outside parties, to intervene in these crucial areas has generally been regarded as fruitless or as anathema. Where interventions have occurred, they have done so either as part of government's attempts to promote, in the face of threatened EC legislation, a distinctive, British voluntarist approach to employee participation, or, in the case of reward structures, as elements within policies designed to weaken trade unions and collectivism.

These examples aside, intervention has been deemed to represent an industrial policy of the sort that the government has refused to countenance. While many other developed countries, such as Germany and Japan have favoured the use of broad industrial policies that establish a contextual framework within which companies can direct their efforts, the UK in the 1980s firmly rejected such notions. In the place of such corporatist devices, market forces and the 'enterprise' or individual entrepreneurs and company managements have been regarded as sufficient to maximise economic efficiency. The result has been that many of the key variables that determine the demand for skill and its efficient utilisation have remained firmly 'off limits' to any form of outside influence. One of the few admissions that the internal workings of the firm have to be addressed if training policy is to succeed, comes in the Investors in People (IIP) initiative.

The current inability of policy to confront head-on the question of skill utilisation in the workplace, and its relationship with other aspects of the management of work organisation and of the employment relationship, raises questions about the ability of those policies, and the institutions they have spawned, to tackle the underlying problems. For so long as the employing organisation, and the use to which it puts skills, remains more or less a 'black box', it seems improbable that lasting progress towards a fundamental transformation of Britain's skill supply and utilisation can be made.

For a long time economists have stressed the importance of externalities in causing the amount of training and consequently the supply of skills to be less than is socially optimal. This paper argues that leaving aside such externality problems, employers as whole exhibit a low demand for skilled labour. This may well represent a rational short-term strategy, but for many firms carries substantial longer-term dangers. Meanwhile for the economy as whole this strategy imposes a rather different type of externality. We have described a 'systems flaw', to which there is no easy policy response; but recognition that it exists would be an important first step.

REFERENCES

Armstrong, P. (1987), 'The Rise of Accounting Controls in British Capitalist Enterprises', *Accounting Organizations and Society* **12**(5), 415–36.

Ashton, D., M. Maguire and M. Spilsbury (1987), 'Labour Market Segmentation and the Structure of the Youth Labour Market', in P. Brown and D. Ashton (eds.), *Education, Unemployment and Labour Markets*, Lewes: Falmer.

Bennett, R., H. Glennerster and D. Nevison (1992), *Learning Should Pay*, Poole, British Petroleum.

Booth, A. L. (1991), 'Job-Related Formal Training: Who Receives it and What is it Worth?', *Oxford Bulletin of Economics and Statistics* **53**(3), 281–94.

Bosworth, D., C. Jacobs and J. Lewis (1990), *New Technologies, Shared Facilities and the Innovatory Firm*, Aldershot: Avebury/Gower.

Campbell, A. and M. Warner (1991), 'Training Strategies and Microelectronics in the Engineering Industries in the UK and Germany', in P. Ryan (ed.), *International Comparisons of Vocational Education and Training for Intermediate Skills*, London: Falmer.

Campbell, M. and M. Daly (1992), 'Self-employment into the 1990s', *Employment Gazette*, June.

Carter, C. (ed.) (1981), *Industrial Policy and Innovation*, London: Heinemann.

Cassels, J. (1989), 'Facing the Demographic Challenge', *Personnel Management* November, 6.

(1990), *Britain's Real Skill Shortage and What to Do about it*, London: Policy Studies Institute.

CBI (1985), *Change to Succeed – The Nationwide Findings*, London: Confederation of British Industry.

(1987), *Investing for Britain's Future: Report of the City/Industry Task Force*, London: Confederation of British Industry.

(1989), *Towards a Skills Revolution*, London, Confederation of British Industry.

(1991), *Competing with the World's Best – The Report of the CBI Manufacturing Advisory Group*, London: Confederation of British Industry.

Centre for Economic Performance (1991), 'Corporate Governance Meeting, June 1991', Working Paper No. 151, London School of Economics, CEP, mimeo.

Chapman, P. G. and M. J. Tooze (1987), *The Youth Training Scheme in the United Kingdom*, Aldershot: Avebury.

Cockburn, C. (1987), *Two-Track Training*, Basingstoke, Macmillan.

Collinson, D. (1988), *Barriers to Fair Selection: A Multi-sector Study of Recruitment Practices*, London, HMSO.

Coopers and Lybrand Associates (1985), *A Challenge to Complacency: Changing Attitudes to Training*, Sheffield: Manpower Services Commission/National Economic Development Office.

Daly, A. (1986), 'Education and Productivity: A Comparison of Great Britain and the United States', *British Journal of Industrial Relations* 24(2), 251–67.

Daly, M. and A. McCann (1992), 'How Many Small Firms?', *Employment Gazette* February, 47–51.

Daly, M., M. Campbell, G. Robson and C. Gallagher (1992), 'Job Creation 1987–89: preliminary analysis by sector', *Employment Gazette* August, 387–92.

Dex, S. (1988), 'Gender and the Labour Market', in D. Gallie (ed.), *Employment in Britain*, Oxford: Blackwell, pp. 281–309.

ED (Employment Department) (1988), Employment for the 1990s, Cmnd 540, London: HMSO.

(1991), 'Into Work', *Skills and Enterprise Briefing*, Issue 15/91 October, Sheffield: ED.

(1992), *Labour Market and Skills Trends 1993/94*, Sheffield: ED.

Edwards, P., M. Hall, R. Hyman, P. Marginson, K. Sisson, J. Waddington and D. Winchester (1992), 'Great Britain: Still Muddling Through?', in A. Ferner and R. Hyman (eds.), *Industrial Relations in the New Europe*, Oxford: Blackwell.

Emerson, M. (1988), 'Regulation or de-regulation of the labour market?', *European Economic Review* 32, 775–817.

Finegold, D. (1992), 'The Implications of "Training in Britain" for the Analysis of Britain's Skill Problem: A Comment on Paul Ryan's "How Much Do Employers Spend on Training"', *Human Resource Management Journal* 2(1), 110–15.

Finegold, D. and D. Soskice (1988), 'The Failure of Training in Britain: Analysis and Prescription', *Oxford Review of Economic Policy* 4(3), 21–53.

Fonda, N. (1989), 'In Search of a Training Strategy', *Personnel Management* April, 6–7.

Fox, J. (1988), 'Norsk Hydro's New Approach Takes Root', *Personnel Management* January.

Fuller, A. and M. Saunders (1990), 'The Paradox in Open Learning at Work', University of Lancaster, Institute for Post-Compulsory Education, mimeo.

Gallie, D. and M. White (1993), *Employee Commitment and the Skills Revolution*, London: Policy Studies Institute.

Goold, M. and A. Campbell (1986), *Strategies and Styles: The Role of the Centre in managing Diversified Corporations*, Oxford: Blackwell.

Green, F. (1991), 'Sex Discrimination in Job-related Training', *British Journal of Industrial Relations* 29(2), 295–304.

Greenhalgh, C. (1988), *Employment and Structural Change: Trends and Policy Options*, Oxford University, mimeo.

Hendry, C. (1990), 'Corporate Strategy and Training', paper presented to the National Economic Development Office 'Training Policy Seminar', Coventry, University of Warwick, Centre for Corporate Strategy and Change.

Hirsch, F. (1977), *The Social Limits to Growth*, London: Routledge & Kegan Paul.

Hyman, J. (1992), *Training at Work: a Critical Analysis of Policy and Practice*, London: Routledge.

IFF (Industrial Facts and Forecasting) (1992), *Small Firms' Skill Needs and Training Survey*, London, IFF.

IOD (Institute of Directors) (1991), *Performance and Potential – Education and Training for a Market Economy*, London: IoD.

James, G. (1991), *Quality of Working Life and Total Quality Management*, Work Research Unit Occasional Paper No. 50, London: ACAS, WRU.

Jarvis, V. and S. Prais (1989), 'Two Nations of Shopkeepers: Training for Retailing in Britain and France', *National Institute Economic Review* **128**, 58–74.

Jenkins, R. and B. Troyna (1983), 'Educational Myths, Labour Market Realities', in B. Troyna and D. I. Smith (eds.), *Racism, School and the Youth Labour Market*, Leicester: National Youth Bureau.

Keep, E. (1990), 'Training for the Low-Paid', in A. Bowen and K. Mayhew (eds.), *Improving Incentives for the Low-Paid*, London: Macmillan/NEDO.

(1991), 'The Grass Looked Greener – Some Thoughts on the Influence of Comparative Vocational Training Research on the UK Policy Debate', in P. Ryan (ed.), *International Comparisons of Vocational Education and Training for Intermediate Skills*, London: Falmer, pp. 23–46.

King, J. (1990), *Labour Economics*, London: Macmillan.

Knell, J. (1992), 'TNCs and the Dynamics of Human Capital Formation: Evidence from West Yorkshire', Leeds University, School of Business and Economic Studies, mimeo.

Lam, A. and D. Marsden (1992), 'Shortages of Qualified Labour in Britain: A Problem of Training or of Skill Utilisation?', paper presented to CEDEFOP conference on vocational training, Berlin.

Layard, R., K. Mayhew and G. Owen (1992), *The Training Reform Act of 1994*, Swindon: ESRC and the Centre for Economic Performance.

LBS/EZI (1987), *Acquisitions, The Human Factor*, London: London Business School.

Lee, D., D. Marsden, P. Rickman and J. Duncombe (1990), *Scheming For Youth. A Study of YTS in the Enterprise Culture*, Buckingham: Open University Press.

Lillard, L. A. and H. W. Tan (1992), 'Private Sector Training: Who Gets it and What Are its Effects?', in R. G. Ehrenberg (ed.), *Research in Labor Economics*, Greenwich, CT: JAI Press, pp. 1–62.

Lloyd, C. and M. Rawlinson (1992), 'New Technology and Human Resource Management', in P. Blyton and P. Turnbull (eds.), *Reassessing Human Resource Management*, London: Sage, pp. 185–99.

Mangham, I. L. and M. S. Silvers (1986), *Management Training: Context and Practice*, University of Bath, School of Management, ESRC/DTI report.

Marginson, P. (1992), 'Multinational Britain: Employment and Work in an Internationalised Economy', paper for the Warwick VET Forum Conference 'Multinational Companies and Human Resources: a Moveable Feast?', Warwick University, 22–24 June 1992.

Marsh, P. (1990), *Short-termism on Trial*, London: Institutional Fund Managers' Association.

Mayhew, K. (1991), 'Training – The Problem for Employers', *Employment Institute Economic Report* **5**(10), March/April.

McNabb, R. and P. Ryan (1990), 'Segmented Labour Markets', in D. Sapsford and Z. Tzannatos (eds.), *Current Issues in Labour Economics*, Basingstoke: Macmillan.

Millward, N. and M. Stevens (1986), *British Workplace Industrial Relations, 1980–84*, Aldershot: Gower.

Milton, R. (1986), 'Double, Double, Toil and Trouble: YTS in the Melting Pot', *Personnel Management* April, 26–31.

Morris, J., N. Bacon, P. Blyton and H. W. Franz (1991), 'Beyond Survival: The Influence of New Forms of Work Organisation in the UK and German Steel Industries', paper prepared for Employment Research Unit conference on 'The Future of Employment Relations: International Comparisons in an Age of Uncertainty', Cardiff.

MSC (1981), *A New Training Initiative: An Agenda for Action*, London, Manpower Services Commission.

(1983a), *Towards an Adult Training Strategy – A Discussion Paper*, Sheffield, Manpower Services Commission.

(1983b), *Adult Training Strategy: Proposals for Action*, London, Manpower Services Commission, mimeo.

Muller, F. (1991), 'A New Engine of Change in Employee Relations', *Personnel Management* July, 30–3.

Murlis, H. (1990), 'A Long-term View of Reward Systems', *Personnel Management* August, 10.

NEDO/MSC/IMS (National Economic Development Office/Manpower Services Commission/Institute of Manpower Studies) (1984), *Competence and Competition*, London: National Economic Development Office.

New, C. C. and A. Myers (1986), *Managing Manufacturing Operations in the UK 1975–1985*, London: British Institute of Management.

Nicholson, B. (1991), Response given at LSE Centre for Economic Performance/ Anglo-German Foundation Seminar on the UK and German training systems, 8 October 1991.

Oliver, J. and J. Turton (1982), 'Is There a Shortage of Skilled Labour?', *British Journal of Industrial Relations* 20(2), 195–217.

Payne, J. (1990), *Women, Training and the Skills Shortage. The Case for Public Investment*, London: Policy Studies Institute.

(1992), 'Motivating Training', paper presented to the CEP project on VET, January, mimeo.

Peck, F. and J. Stone (1991), *New Inward Investment in the Northern Region Labour Market*, Newcastle Economic Research Unit, Newcastle upon Tyne Polytechnic.

People, Jobs and Opportunity (1992), Cm 1810, London: HMSO.

Pettigrew, A., C. Hendry and P. Sparrow (1989), *Training in Britain: Employers' Perspectives on Human Resources*, London, HMSO.

Plowman, B. (1990), 'Management Behaviour', *TQM Magazine* 2(4), 217–19.

Pratten, C. (1990), 'The Limits to Training', *Financial Times*, 3 April.

Purcell, J. (1989), 'The impact of corporate strategy on human resource management', in J. Storey (ed.), *New Perspectives on Human Resource Management*, London: Routledge, pp. 67–91.

Purcell, K. (1988), 'Gender and the Experience of Employment', in D. Gallie (ed.), *Employment in Britain*, Oxford: Blackwell, pp. 157–86.

Reich, R. (1983), *The Next American Frontier*, Harmondsworth: Penguin.

Rigg, M. (1989), *The Impact of Vocational Education and Training on Individual Adults*, London: HMSO.

Rigg, M., I. Christie and M. White (1989), *Advanced Polymers and Composites: Creating the Key Skills*, Sheffield: Training Agency.

Rodgers, P. and M. Tran (1988), 'US Feathers Ruffled at British Invasion', *Guardian*, 26 April.

Saunders, C. T. (1978), 'Engineering in Britain, West Germany and France: Some Statistical Comparisons of Structure and Competitiveness', Sussex European Papers, No. 3, Falmer: University of Sussex.

Shackleton, J. R. (1992), *Training Too Much?*, London: Institute of Economic Affairs.

Sharp, M., M. Shepherd and D. Marsden (1987), *Managing Change in British Industry*, Geneva: International Labour Office.

Sisson, K. (1992), 'Change and Continuity in UK Industrial Relations: "Strategic Choice" or "Muddling Through"?', paper for the meeting of the International IR/HR Project, Warwick University, Industrial Relations Research Unit, mimeo.

Steedman, H. and K. Wagner (1987), 'A Second Look at Productivity, Machinery and Skills in Britain and Germany', *National Institute Economic Review* November, 84–95.

(1989), 'Productivity, Machinery and Skills: Clothing Manufacture in Britain and Germany', *National Institute Economic Review* **128**, 40–57.

Storey, D. J. (1982), *Entrepreneurship and the New Firm*, London: Croom Helm.

Storey, D. J. and A. Strange (1992), *Entrepreneurship in Cleveland 1979–1989: A Study of the Effects of the Enterprise Culture*, Employment Department Research Series No. 3, Sheffield: Employment Department.

Storey, J. (1992), *Developments in the Management of Human Resources: An Analytical Review*, Oxford: Blackwell.

Streeck, W. (1989), 'Skills and the Limits of Neo-Liberalism: The Enterprise of the Future as a Place of Learning', *Work, Employment and Society* **3**(1), 89–104.

TA (1989), *Training in Britain: Employers' Activities*, Sheffield, Training Agency.

Whipp, R. (1992), 'Human Resource Management, Competition and Strategy: Some Productive Tensions', in P. Blyton and P. Turnbull (eds.), *Reassessing Human Resource Management*, London: Sage, pp. 33–55.

Williams, K., J. Williams and C. Haslam (1990), 'The Hollowing Out of British Manufacturing and its Implications for Policy', *Economy and Society* **19**(4), November, 456–90.

Wood, S. (1988), 'Personnel Management and Recruitment', in P. Windolf and S. Wood (eds.), *Recruitment and Selection in the Labour Market*, Cambridge: Gower.

Worswick, G. D. N. (ed.) (1985), *Education and Economic Performance*, London: Gower.

15 Conclusions: government policy to promote the acquisition of skills

This chapter concludes the book by providing an overview of a wide variety of training policies. These policies are viewed against the backdrop of the major market failures in skill acquisition, government failures in training policy, and the available evidence on the economic consequences of these failures. The chapter discusses the efficiency and equity implications of alternative policy strategies, identifies the circumstances under which various proposed measures are likely to be effective, and explores the implications for employment, production, and economic growth. Finally, it highlights a limited number of policies that deserve closer attention, and outlines areas for future research that could clarify how the appropriate choices among these policies are to be made.

Conclusions: government policy to promote the acquisition of skills

DENNIS J. SNOWER and ALISON L. BOOTH

In many advanced industrial countries there is a growing concern that people are not acquiring sufficient skills. In the comparatively flexible labour markets of the USA and the UK, wage differentials between skilled and unskilled workers have grown dramatically over the past decade and a half, suggesting that the rising demand for skilled labour has not been met by an equally rising supply.[1] In the less flexible labour markets of Denmark, France, Spain and other European countries, this widening wage gap is far less pronounced, but everywhere the problem of unemployment is concentrated among the unskilled people, once again indicating that it is the unskilled rather than the skilled jobs that are in short supply.

The fact that the unemployed are predominantly unskilled has made the problem of skill acquisition particularly acute. The high unemployment sustained in Europe since the mid-1970s has been a human tragedy and a colossal waste of resources. The unemployed also impose large costs on the rest of society, ranging from unemployment benefits to crime prevention. So workers who fail to acquire skills are not merely fated to have comparatively low productivity; they run the risk of being completely unproductive by being out of work.

And not only that. It is the unskilled workers who tend to be poor, uneducated and unhealthy. They thus make far greater demands on a country's welfare system, requiring far greater state support than the rest of the population on average. They thereby become an important source of the growing government budget deficits.

All these problems have become increasingly acute in many advanced industrial countries since the 1970s. One reason has been the revolution in information technology that has raised the demand for skilled people, while putting the unskilled ones out of their jobs in growing numbers. Another reason has been the expansion of international trade, where the advanced industrial countries tend to have a comparative advantage in

337

skill-intensive goods and a comparative disadvantage in goods that make heavy use of unskilled labour. As the unskilled workers of Europe and the USA have increasingly come into competition with the low-wage labour of the Far East, they have inevitably seen their living standards decline.

The forces of technological change and international trade have transformed the labour market, continually changing the nature of jobs and raising the rate at which skills become obsolescent. Increasingly, employers are demanding more than a well-defined, stable set of skills; they are demanding adaptability, the ability to adapt one's skills to ever-changing circumstances. And there is no easy way for workers to become adaptable in this sense, other than going through a continual process of training and retraining.

These developments have also changed the nature of unemployment. In the 1950s and 60s there was a widespread presumption that when people became unemployed in Europe and the USA, they could expect to return to their old jobs, or to jobs very much like them, after a limited period of time. Unemployment insurance systems were built on this presumption: they were to provide people with temporary assistance before they returned to their accustomed jobs. But this presumption is no longer valid. Many of the jobs that disappear nowadays are gone for good. What many workers require now is not income support that sustains them while they are finding jobs appropriate to their skills; rather, what they appear to need is training support that helps them make their skills appropriate to the changing jobs.

For all these reasons, increasing public attention has been devoted to the danger of remaining unskilled and the challenge of providing institutional and governmental support for training. But much of the public debate in this area is not based on any clear guidelines on when government intervention is required, when labour market institutions need revision, and when the free market mechanism can be left to its own devices. Politicians and journalists would have a lot to learn from economic principles about the conditions under which free enterprise does its jobs well.

As noted in Chapter 1, free enterprise generates an efficient amount of training when people get paid for all the advantages and pay for all the disadvantages this training confers on others. It is clear why this must be so. When people are compensated for all the benefits from training, then their own self-interested objectives will necessarily coincide with those of society at large.

So there is no efficiency case for government intervention in the market for training unless there are uncompensated benefits and costs from training under free enterprise. Unfortunately, government training policies are rarely designed on this basis. Politicians do not tend to spend their days puzzling over whether particular benefits and costs of training are uncompensated before drafting legislation providing government support. Furthermore, they frequently interfere with the free market where it could be working well.

There are countless examples. Consider, for instance, the disparity in UK policy on education versus training. The UK government pays the tuition and provides partial maintenance grants for most British students receiving academic education, but little support is given for non-degree level vocational education and training (VET). It would be absurd to believe that students are not compensated for any of the benefits from academic education (so that this needs to be substantially subsidized), whereas they are compensated for most of the benefits from vocational training.

Of course efficiency is not the only goal of government's training policy. Besides correcting for any waste of resources under free enterprise, government also use their provision and finance of training to achieve equity goals. Government training support could, under certain conditions, be a particularly powerful way of equalizing the distribution of income, since it aims to give people the skills that will enable them to earn higher incomes on their own. It is the unskilled who tend to be poor; training support may give them the opportunity to work their way out of poverty. This could be a cheaper way of reducing inequality than straight redistribution.

But it is of course impossible to argue that UK support for academic education is a much more effective or less costly way of redistributing income than VET.

Yet regardless of what relative importance the government attaches to efficiency versus equity considerations with regard to training, let us begin with efficiency. After all, there are few good excuses for wasting resources – either by interfering with the free market where agents are compensated for most of the benefits and costs of training, or by laissez faire when large uncompensated benefits are evident (particularly when the costs of implementing corrective policies are low). Such efficiency considerations in training policy are most unlikely to go at the expense of equity in practice. Besides, even when training policy is driven by equity objectives alone, it is still desirable to redistribute income with as little waste of resources as possible.

It is for this reason that this book takes the uncompensated benefits and costs from training, and the resulting externalities and other market failures, as the critical starting point in thinking about training policy.

We have seen that when a particular set of skills is useful to a limited number of firms in the economy – more than one and less than all – it may be impossible for the suppliers and demanders of training to capture more than a fraction of the benefits of that training and pay the relevant costs. As a prelude to our discussion of training policy, it is well to summarize what the major sources of market failures are. Many of these sources have received detailed analysis in Part I of this book, while the rest have already been given attention in the existing public policy literature. But our object here is to go beyond an overview of what has been done, to capture the broader spectrum of salient market failures that may well require policy treatment.

One important reason for the existence of uncompensated benefits and costs from training is **imperfect competition**. When certain skills are useful to a limited number of firms, these firms exert some market power, enabling them to drive workers' wages beneath their marginal products. If firms are too powerful, they will off-load too much of the cost of training onto their employees, and then they will fail to internalize the full cost of dismissing trained workers. If workers are too powerful, they will fail to internalize the full cost of quitting to their employers. In either case, there will be too little training.

Another reason is **poaching**. If trained workers can be poached, some of the benefits from training fall on the poachers. These benefits are not captured by the trainee or the training firm, who bear the cost of the investment, and who consequently have deficient training incentives.

Yet another reason is **imperfect information**. When firms are poorly informed about the attributes of the training provided by their competitors, workers' skills that are potentially applicable in many alternative jobs become poorly transferable. In the process, workers lose some of their incentive to bear the cost of on-the-job training by accepting lower wages during their training period, since they have difficulty capturing the reward for this training when they switch firms.

In addition, the free market may provide insufficient incentives for skill acquisition on account of **credit constraints**. Since human capital cannot be used as collateral against loan default, these credit constraints may prevent workers from acquiring sufficient training.

Moreover, training generates uncompensated benefits and costs through the **job matching process**, by affecting the speed with which skilled jobs are filled, the speed with which skilled workers are employed, and the fall-back positions of workers and firms in wage negotiations. As the number of skilled workers in an economy rises, firms face improved fall-back positions and therefore are able to capture more rent in the wage bargaining process. This reduces employees' returns from training and leads to under-investment in skills.

The '**low-skill, bad-job trap**' can also occur in this context: if few workers are skilled, firms have little incentive to create skilled vacancies, which in turn reduces the workers' incentives to acquire skills.

An analogous trap could also emerge with regard to the **interaction between innovation and skills**. When successful innovation requires highly trained workers, economies can get stuck in a vicious cycle in which firms do not innovate sufficiently because the workforce is insufficiently skilled and workers do not train sufficiently because there is insufficient demand for them from the innovating firms.

A related problem is that of **R&D imitation market failures**. Firms may have insufficient incentives to train their workforces in the production and use of new products because of the danger that these products will be imitated and that the ensuing competition would compete away the resulting profits. The existing patent laws may not provide the innovating firms with sufficient opportunities to appropriate the gains from training their employees to reap the fruits of research and development activities.

Furthermore, the social return from vocational training, particularly in areas associated with R&D, may well exceed the private returns due to **market failures in risk management**. Private risk premia are frequently higher than the corresponding social risk premia, since individuals are generally unable to insure themselves against the risk that their training costs are not covered by the resulting rise in earnings,[2] whereas the government can pool risks across many different training initiatives and can spread the burden of failed projects widely across the population (via the tax system).

Under **external production economies**, each firm's output depends not only on the labour and capital it employs, but also on the average skill level in the economy. Since firms do not take this uncompensated benefit into account when making their training decisions, they under-invest in skills.

When firms provide little training, young workers may be unwilling to accept relatively low wages, because they recognize that they have poor chances of acquiring the skills necessary to generate significantly higher wages in the later years. And when young workers receive high wages, firms are unable to pass on the costs of training to them, and that is why they provide little training. There is some evidence that this problem has plagued Great Britain over the 1980s.[3] It may be termed the '**high-wage, low-skill trap**'.

Furthermore, since unskilled workers are prone to low earnings and comparatively long spells of unemployment, they tend to impose significant uncompensated costs on others via the **unemployment benefit system** and various **welfare programmes**. Since these measures off-load some of the costs of remaining unskilled onto the rest of society, the unskilled workers are left with a reduced incentive to acquire skills.

A closely related problem is that of market failures arising from **tax and regulatory distortions**. Taxes obviously often lead to uncompensated benefits from training. When income taxes, for example, appropriate a slice of workers' and firms' returns from training, they inevitably make these agents less willing to bear the costs of training. Taxes on profits, capital gains, and wealth, as well as tax deductions for capital formation, affect the returns to education and training by influencing the returns to investment in physical capital The magnitude and direction of these effects clearly depends on the degree of complementarity or substitutability between labour and capital. Regulations restricting the entry of new firms to the economy will also affect the returns to skill acquisition.

Then there are market failures arising from the **interaction between education and vocational training**. Education and vocational training are generally complements. Thus public support for education will influence employers' and employees' returns from vocational training. If the support is inappropriate or the education is insufficiently relevant to the available jobs, the free market may generate insufficient vocational training.

Most of the problems above are exacerbated by **complementarities between labour and capital**. When workers acquire insufficient skills – for any of the reasons above – the machines with which they work are insufficiently productive. Consequently firms have too little incentive to invest in physical capital, which reduces the productivity of the workers even more. When firms fail to acquire sophisticated capital equipment because they do not expect to find enough skilled labour to operate it, the result may be called a '**low-skill, low-tech trap**'.[4]

The literature on the 'new growth theory' shows how under-investment in skills leads to deficient economic growth. In this way, each generation exerts an influence on the living standards of the next generation. But since unborn generations cannot make their needs felt, the current generation has insufficient incentives to acquire skills. These **intergenerational effects** are also augmented through complementarities between labour and capital, since the level of skills affects the productivity of capital and the latter, in turn, affects the incentives to invest; thus the size of the capital stock available to future generations depends on the skills of the current generations.

Identifying the sources of the uncompensated benefits and costs associated with training is a matter of prime policy importance. As noted, a salient message of this book has been that the government has no efficiency reason to intervene in the free market for training unless individuals are not fully compensated for the benefits and costs of such training. And that is not all, for the nature of the intervention should match the nature of the uncompensated benefits and costs.

Put simply, it should be the business of training policy to identify the uncompensated costs and benefits and then to devise measures that make up for the missing compensation. Then the government should in fact only implement those measures for which the costs of implementation and the costs associated with government failure are likely to be lower than the costs of the underlying market failure. All this might sound self-evident to the impartial observer, but it is generally ignored in the making of training policy.

So the uncompensated benefits and costs of training described above provide a crucial key for policy design. It is simple to see how this works.

A number of the market failures above – and particularly those arising from the low-skill, bad-job trap, market failures in risk management, external production economies, and the low-skill, low-tech trap – can be addressed through **training vouchers**, financed out of general government revenues. This policy aims to compensate firms more fully for providing training by giving them an explicit subsidy for this purpose; it seeks to compensate workers more fully for acquiring skills, since they permit higher take-home pay to be negotiated over the training period.

Market failures arising from firms' imperfect information about the training attributes of their competitors can be addressed by **accreditation programmes**, whereby employer-initiated training leads to generally recognized credentials. Such programmes require a system of national (and, if possible, international) qualifications, involving substantial external assessment. Accreditation programmes also address other problems of imperfect information; for instance, they prevent firms from attempting to retain their employees by making their training excessively firm-specific, and the presence of external assessors keeps firms from diverting funds from their training budgets to other purposes.

The high-wage, low-skill trap may be tackled through **apprenticeship contracts**. Here young people are put on programmes that provide on-the-job training on some days of the week and off-the-job vocational training on the other days. Such contracts encourage emphasis on the complementarities between work and education, and thereby help make the acquired skills particularly relevant to the available jobs. The German and Danish training systems rely heavily on apprenticeship contracts. The contract period is often specified by law and is meant to ensure that trainees receive enough training to bring their skills into the vicinity of the incumbent employees' skill levels. Trainees accept low wages during the training period in return for the prospect of much higher wages as remuneration for their skills once the period is over. Firms are willing to release their new employees for part-time vocational education on account of the low apprenticeship wages.[5]

Clearly, another way of dealing with the high-wage, low-skill trap is to **remove institutional obstacles to widening wage differentials** between skilled and unskilled workers. Dismantling certain aspects of job security legislation, reducing the monopoly power of labour unions, encouraging decentralized collective bargaining may all contribute to widening these differentials and thereby give unskilled people a greater incentive to become trained.

In creating incentives for firms to train young people, apprenticeship systems and measures to allow widening wage differentials obviously also have a number of indirect effects that help alleviate a number of other market failures. For example, by increasing the amount of youth training for any given stock of capital, these policies help overcome intergenerational externalities and job matching externalities, as well as market failures associated with poaching and the low-skill, bad-job trap.

Investment tax credits and **depreciation allowances** help overcome the problems arising from external production economies and complementarities between labour and capital. **Establishing property rights on innovation** and enforcing patent laws addresses R&D market failures and uncompensated benefits and costs generated by the interaction between innovation and skills and the low-skill, low-tech trap.

Public support for education is required to make up for uncompensated benefits and costs arising from the interaction between education and vocational training.

Reducing barriers to the entry of new firms – by relaxing government regulations on the creation of new firms, implementing tax reforms that make it easier to start new firms, giving financial institutions incentives to treat new firms on less unfavourable terms, reducing barriers to international trade, and so on – may all help to reduce market failure from imperfect competition and from tax and regulatory distortions.

Market failures arising from credit constraints and training risk can be addressed through **government provision of loans** for training and education. These loans could be financed through taxes on the earnings that follow. By letting the tax payments rise with earnings, the government in effect spreads the training risk across the relevant cohort of trainees.

Alternatively the government could provide **conditional loan guarantees**[6] for training and education, thereby giving banks an incentive to lend on the basis of human capital (see, for example, Snower (1993)). This policy helps deal with the problem of credit constraints, but not that of individual training risk, since the banks will require each individual borrower to repay his or her loan. The reason why banks generally do not lend on the basis of human capital is that they have difficulty tracing people who change jobs and geographic locations, and thus such loans would encourage risk of default. Default is an uncompensated cost imposed by borrowers on lenders. The government, however, has a comparative advantage in this area, since it is able to trace people through the tax system. Thereby loan guarantees could help mitigate capital market imperfections.

Market failures resulting from poaching and the low-skill, bad-job trap could be mitigated through a **levy system**, whereby firms in each selected industry are required to pay levies into a central fund that is then used to finance training programmes in that industry. But this system is a mixed blessing: it not only encourages training, it also discourages employment, since it reduces employers' freedom to dispose of their revenue in any way they see fit. In the presence of market failures that depress employment – such as those arising from efficiency wage, insider–outsider, or labour union pressures – it may therefore be preferable for the government simply to subsidize training, for example by paying a fixed proportion of firms' training expenditures on nationally accredited programmes, and to finance this through consumption or energy taxes. Besides, the levy system aims to correct for uncompensated benefits from training that fall on firms, but not explicitly for those falling on workers. Apart from raising workers' chances of finding skilled jobs,[7] this policy gives workers no further incentive to bear the costs of training.

In countries such as Austria, Germany, and Sweden, market failures arising from imperfect competition and risk may be mitigated through a 'social partnership', whereby representatives of employers, employees, and the government jointly determine the structure, provision, and finance of training programmes. Such a consensual negotiating framework is meant to help the parties internalize the benefits and costs of training that would otherwise remain uncompensated in the prevailing structures of wage bargaining and risk management.

This decision making process is not the same thing as mere **centralization in collective bargaining over training**, since the latter can be thoroughly confrontational, but even centralized bargaining is generally able to dispose of some of the market failures from imperfect competition and risk, though to a lesser degree. Regarding the imperfect competition market failures, it could be argued (analogously to the argument about wage moderation in Calmfors and Driffill (1988)) that extreme centralization and extreme decentralization are both preferable to intermediate bargaining structures, the former because it makes employers and employees take account of the feedback effects of their training decisions, and the latter because it reduces the degree of imperfect competition in the market for training.

Market failures generated through the unemployment benefit system and welfare programmes can be tackled by **linking training subsidies to unemployment benefits and other welfare payments**. In particular, the unemployed could be given the opportunity to use a fraction of their unemployment benefits (and associated welfare state payments) to provide training vouchers for firms that hire them. The government would then effectively be paying an employment and training subsidy to firms hiring the unemployed, of an amount equal to a fraction of the unemployment benefits and associated welfare payments. The wage would be negotiated by the formerly unemployed workers and the firms. In this way firms would be given an extra incentive – over and above the more general ones discussed above – to take on workers who may otherwise have been unemployed and whose unemployment benefits would impose uncompensated costs on their tax-paying counterparts. The unemployed workers would moreover gain an incentive to find jobs and acquire skills: whereas unemployment benefits discourage these activities (for when an unemployed person finds a job, the benefits are withdrawn and a tax bill is imposed), the training vouchers encourage them, since they permit workers to receive wage offers in excess of their previous unemployment benefits.

This policy is an ingredient in the Benefit Transfer Programme (described by Snower (1994)). It is also effective with regard to the market failures from credit constraints, since the unemployed are comparatively prone to be credit constrained. The low-skill, bad-job trap may also be circumventable through this policy, since it raises firms' intensity of search for skilled workers and unemployed workers' intensity of search for skilled jobs. By reducing firms' training costs, the policy also helps make up for some benefits from training that are not compensated owing to poaching.

There is a strong case for directing this policy at the long-term unemployed (i.e. allowing the long-term unemployed to use a relatively large fraction of their unemployment benefits as training vouchers), since these people are particularly likely to be credit-constrained, particularly susceptible to the poaching externality,[8] and particularly reliant on unemployment benefits.[9] By letting workers give training vouchers to their new employers, who would cash these vouchers when they send their new recruits on nationally accredited training programmes, the policy gives people the incentive to target the training that is most appropriate to the available jobs. In the process, the policy could also help overcome regional unemployment problems, since regions of high unemployment would become ones containing a relatively high proportion of workers with training subsidies, thereby giving firms an incentive to relocate there and retrain the local workforce.

Moreover, the policy could be extended beyond the unemployed to include all unskilled workers (see, for example, Phelps (1996)). After all, the unskilled are relatively heavy users of welfare state services, and they could be given the opportunity to use a fraction of the cost of these extra services to finance training vouchers as well.

Since there may be reason to believe that various market failures associated with unskilled youths are significantly more severe than those associated with unskilled adults, there does not appear to be a good case for the common policy of giving young people favourable treatment in support for their training and education. It is true that young people have a relatively long pay-back period for their training and this may give the abovementioned market failures more leverage. But this tendency is mitigated by the forces of technological change, that continuously make skills obsolete and make it necessary for people of all ages to retrain in order to remain in demand.

Similarly, there is no compelling reason to favour full-time training over part-time training. The common practice of discriminating against those who choose to educate themselves part-time, while granting subsidies to full-time education, has little to recommend it. Equal training support, in pro rata terms, would usually be in the public interest here.

Government failures in the finance and provision of training can be mitigated in a variety of ways. For example, integrating the design of training and education in the hands of a single non-partisan agency could help ensure that training and education receive equitable support in relation to one another and that governments do not use training budgets to achieve short-term political goals (such as reducing the number of registered unemployed by 'hiding' them on government training programmes). It could also help avoid the government failure of excessive reorganization, as each successive reshuffle of political posts creates a host of new training schemes and abolishes a host of old ones. Since training is a longer-term investment for both employers and employees, continual restructuring of training programmes is not conducive to the acquisition of skills and consequently is likely to make these programmes less effective than they would otherwise be. Finally, linking government support for training to unemployment benefits, in the Benefit Transfer Programme, would prevent governments from cutting their training expenditures in times of high unemployment, when governments' budget deficits tend to be high as well.[10] It would also encourage firms to train people in slack times, so as to be able to draw on the fruits of this training when economic activity is brisk.

George Bernard Shaw said, 'Reformers have the idea that change can be achieved by brute sanity'. The policy approach outlined above – to identify the uncompensated benefits and costs associated with training under free enterprise and then to design policies that make up for the missing compensation, making allowance for implementation costs and government failures – is inevitably vulnerable to this pitfall. If policy makers genuinely wish to avoid the consequences of national skill deficiencies or of wasteful, inappropriate government training programmes, they have little alternative but to adopt this approach. Even if brute sanity is not sufficient to get there, it surely cannot hurt to have sanity on our side.

NOTES

1 Chapter 7, on 'Changes in the Relative Demand for Skills', has documented this phenomenon in the UK.
2 The inability to insure is due to the standard adverse selection and moral hazard reasons.
3 See, for example, Bennett *et al.* (1991).
4 See, for example, Prais (1989).
5 Government support for trainee loans can make it easier for the trainees to accept the low wages that firms require to keep apprentices profitable. An alternative is for firms to offer a flatter wage profile and a longer indenture period, so that the firms' initial training investment can be recovered after training has finished.
6 Clearly, the guarantees would have to be conditional on the fulfilment of requirements making it likely that the borrowers would be able to repay the loans.
7 This effect may well be weak in practice since, as noted, the levy system not only stimulates the number of skilled jobs, but it also reduces the total number of jobs offered.
8 If long-term unemployed people were given training, a relatively large share of the benefits from that training would fall on poaching firms, since the long-term unemployed have had comparatively little opportunity to acquire firm-specific skills. Training programmes that provide basic skills such as literacy and numeracy and develop work habits such as reliability and punctuality, are especially prone to the poaching problem.
9 The reason is that the probability of employment tends to fall as the duration of unemployment rises.
10 Chapter 12, on 'Training implication of regulation compliance and policy cycles', provides some evidence of this tendency in the UK.

REFERENCES

Bennett, Robert, Howard Glennerster and Douglas Nevison (1991), *Learning Should Pay*, LSE, London: BP Educational Service.

Calmfors, Lars, and John Driffill (1988), 'Centralisation of Wage Bargaining and Macroeconomic Performance', *Economic Policy* **11**, 397–448.

Prais, Sigmund (ed.), *Productivity, Education, and Training*, London: National Institute of Economic and Social Research.

Phelps, Edmund S. (1996), 'Wage Subsidy Programs: Alternative Designs', in Guillermo de la Dehesa and Dennis J. Snower (eds), *Unemployment Policy*, Cambridge: Cambridge University Press.

Snower, Dennis J. (1993), 'The Future of the Welfare State', *Economic Journal* **103**, 700–717.

Snower, Dennis J. (1994), 'Converting Unemployment Benefits into Employment Subsidies', *American Economic Review, Papers and Proceedings*, May.

Index